THEORY OF AUTOMATA, FORMAL LANGUAGES AND COMPUTATION

SECOND EDITION

S P EUGENE XAVIER
Education and Research Department
Infosys Technologies Limited
Chennai (Tamil Nadu)

Committed to Educate the Nation

NEW AGE

Publishing Globally

IN INDIA

NEW AGE INTERNATIONAL (P) LIMITED, PUBLISHERS

LONDON • NEW DELHI

Bangalore • Chennai • Cochin • Guwahati • Hyderabad • Kolkata • Mumbai

Visit us at **www.newagepublishers.com**

Published by New Age International (P) Ltd., Publishers
First Edition: 2004
Second Edition: 2026

GLOBAL OFFICES

• **New Delhi** **NEW AGE INTERNATIONAL (P) LIMITED, PUBLISHERS**
7/30 A, Daryaganj, New Delhi-110002, (INDIA), **Tel.:** (011) 23253472, 23253771, **Mob.:** 9315905300
E-mail: contactus@newagepublishers.com • Visit us at www.newagepublishers.com

• **London** **NEW AGE INTERNATIONAL (UK) LTD.**
27 Old Gloucester Street, London, WC1N 3AX, UK
E-mail: info@newacademicscience.co.uk • Visit us at www.newacademicscience.co.uk

BRANCHES

• **Bangalore** 37/10, 8th Cross (Near Hanuman Temple), Azad Nagar, Chamarajpet, Bangalore- 560 018
Tel.: (080) 26756823, **Mob.:** 9315905288, **E-mail: bangalore@newagepublishers.com**

• **Chennai** 26, Damodaran Street, T. Nagar, Chennai-600 017, **Tel.:** (044) 24353401, **Mob.:** 9315905309
E-mail: chennai@newagepublishers.com

• **Cochin** CC-39/1016, Carrier Station Road, Ernakulam South, Cochin-682 016
Tel.: (0484) 4051304, **Mob.:** 9315905289, **E-mail: cochin@newagepublishers.com**

• **Guwahati** Hemsen Complex, Mohd. Shah Road, Paltan Bazar, Near Starline Hotel
Guwahati-781 008, **Tel.:** (0361) 2513881, **Mob.:** 9315905296
E-mail: guwahati@newagepublishers.com

• **Hyderabad** 105, 1st Floor, Madhiray Kaveri Tower, 3-2-19, Azam Jahi Road, Near Kumar Theater
Nimboliadda Kachiguda, Hyderabad-500 027, **Tel.:** (040) 24652456, **Mob.:** 9315905326
E-mail: hyderabad@newagepublishers.com

• **Kolkata** RDB Chambers (Formerly Lotus Cinema) 106A, 1st Floor, S N Banerjee Road
Kolkata-700 014, **Tel.:** (033) 22273773, **Mob.:** 9315905319
E-mail: kolkata@newagepublishers.com

• **Mumbai** 142C, Victor House, Ground Floor, N.M. Joshi Marg, Lower Parel, Mumbai-400 013
Tel.: (022) 24927869, 24915415, **Mob.:** 9315905282, **E-mail: mumbai@newagepublishers.com**

• **New Delhi** 22, Golden House, Daryaganj, New Delhi-110 002, **Tel.:** (011) 23262368, 23262370
Mob.: 9315905300, **E-mail: sales@newagepublishers.com**

C-25-09-15049

Printed in India at Ajit Printing Press, Delhi.
Typeset at In-house, Delhi.

NEW AGE INTERNATIONAL (P) LIMITED, PUBLISHERS
7/30 A, Daryaganj, New Delhi - 110002
Visit us at **www.newagepublishers.com**
(CIN: U74899DL1966PTC004618)

Preface to the Second Edition

After the good response of the earlier edition it is a great honour for us to present the second edition of the book. The earlier edition was well accepted by the readers as well as the teachers. In this edition we have added an appendix A(*Undecidability*).

This book has been thoroughly read by our subject experts and efforts have been made to present an error free edition. Though the overall format is not disturbed but the presentation and the rubric has been amplified. More clarity is incorporated wherever necessary and the figures are redrawn for better understanding. Suggestions for further improvement shall be received with appreciation.

We are thankful to those who have given us suggestions and criticism for the improvement of the book and we hope that this edition will be more useful than the earlier one.

Publisher

Preface to the First Edition

This book deals with a fascinating and important subject which has the fundamentals of computer hardware, software and some of their applications. This book is intended as an introductory graduate text in computer science theory. I have taken care to present the material very clearly and interestingly.

As an introductory subject to computer science, this book has been written with major stress on worked examples. **Chapter 0** covers the basics required for this subject *viz.*, sets, relations, functions, graphs, trees, languages, and fundamental proof techniques.

Chapter 1 deals with the different aspects of Deterministic Finite Automata (DFA) and Non-Deterministic Finite Automata (NFA). A brief introduction to pumping lemma and some theorems relating to Regular Sets have also been given.

Chapter 2 covers the concepts relating to context free grammar *viz.*, derivation trees, parsing, ambiguity, and normal forms.

Chapter 3 deals with Pushdown Automata and their relation to Context-Free Grammar with some introduction to decision algorithms.

Chapter 4 deals with the Turing Machine model and the variations of Turing Machines with introduction to Church-Turing Thesis and the concept of undecidability.

Chapter 5 explains the concepts *viz.*, regular grammars, unrestricted grammars and Chomsky hierarchy of languages.

Chapter 6 deals with the different aspects of computability with an introduction to formal systems, recursive functions, primitive recursive functions, and recursion.

Chapter 7 covers the various aspect of complexity theory such as polynomial time algorithms, non-polynomial time algorithm class P and NP problems.

Chapter 8 covers propositions and predicates with lot of illustrative examples.

I wish to thank my teachers who helped me to get a good grasp of the subject and for having motivated me to write this book.

I want to place on record my sincere thanks to my family—Shri. Papu Antony, my father; Mrs. Maria Daisy, my mother; Mrs. Assumpta Eugene, my wife; and Ms. E. Catherine Praveena, my only daughter, for their great patience and prayers while I was writing this book.

My heartfelt thanks to my friends—Rajeevan Lal, Mohana Sundar, Gayathri Suresh, Lakshmi Menon, Rajagopal Raman, Dr. A. Kannan and Ilamadhi for their prayers and great encouragement.

I wish to thank M/s. New Age International (P) Ltd., Publishers, for publishing this book in a very short span of time.

Suggestions are most welcome from the readers of this book.

Happy Learning!

S.P. EUGENE XAVIER

Notations

Symbol	Meaning
$\varnothing$	Empty set
$\lvert S \rvert$	Cardinality of set S.
$\cup$	Set Union
$\cap$	Set Intersection
$a \in A$	a belongs to the set A
$A \subseteq B$	A is a subset of B
—	Set Difference
A^c	Complement of A
2^A	Powerset of A
$A \times B$	Cartesian products of A and B
$\bigcup_{i=1}^{n} A_i$	Union of sets $A_1, A_2, \ldots\ldots A_n$
$\overline{L}$	Complement of L
L^R	Language Reversal
L^*	Kleene Star
L^+	Kleene Plus
Σ^*	All finite strings over the alphabet Σ
Σ^n	All strings over the alphabet Σ of length exactly n.
λ	Empty string
$\lvert x \rvert$	Length of string x.
$\vee$	The OR function
$\wedge$	The AND function
$x \,\Re\, y$	x is related to y under relation $\Re$
R^+	Transitive closure of R
$R_1 \circ R_2$	Composite of relations R_1 and R_2
$f : x \rightarrow y$	Function from x to y.
$f(x)$	Image of x under f.

Symbol	*Meaning*
$\lceil x \rceil$	Ceiling function of x (least integer not less than x)
$\lfloor x \rfloor$	Floor function of x (greatest integer not exceeding x)
$\Rightarrow$	Logical connective — If … … then … …
$\forall$	For every
$\exists$	There exists
$\equiv$	Equivalence of predicate formulae
χ_A	Characteristic function of set A
$Z(x)$	Zero function
$S(x)$	Successor function
$p_i^n(x)$	Projector Function
$(Q, \Sigma, \delta, q_0, F)$	Finite automaton
$(Q, \Sigma, \Delta, \delta, \lambda, q_0)$	Moore-Mealey Machine
(V_N, Σ, P, S)	Grammar
$(Q, \Sigma, \Gamma, \delta, q_0, b, F)$	Turing machine
$O(f(n))$	Set of functions whose growth r is order $f(n)$.
N	Set of Natural numbers
Z	Set of Integers
Q	Set of Rational Numbers
R	Set of Real Numbers

Contents

Chapter 0

Introduction

0.1 BASICS

0.1.1 Sets

A "set" is a collection of objects. For example, the collection of four letters a, b, c and d is a set, which is written as

$$L = \{ a, b, c, d \}$$

The objects comprising a set are called its "elements" or "members".

A set having only one element is called a "singleton". A set with no element at all is called the "empty set", which is denoted by $\varnothing$.

It is essential to have a criterion for determining, for any given thing, whether it is or is not a member of the given set. This criterion is called the "Membership criterion" of the set.

There are two common ways to indicate the members of a set:

(i) List all the elements, e.g, $\{a, e, i, o, u\}$.
(ii) Provide some kind of an algorithm or a rule, such as a grammar.

Let us now take a look at the notation that is being used to denote sets.

(a) To indicate that x is a member of the set S, we write $x \in S$.
(b) If every element of set A is also an element of set B, we say that A is a "subset" of B, and write $A \subseteq B$.
(c) If every element of set A is also an element of set B, but B also has some elements not contained in A, we say that A is a "proper subset" of B and write $A \subset B$.
(d) We denote the "empty set" as { } or $\varnothing$.

The set operations are as described below.

(a) Union

The "union" of two sets is the set that has objects that are elements of at least one of the two given sets, and possibly both.

That is, the union of sets A and B, written $A \cup B$, is a set that contains everything in A, or in B, or in both.

$$A \cup B = \{x : x \in A \text{ or } x \in B\}$$

Example: $A = \{1, 3, 9\}$ $B = \{3, 5\}$

Therefore, $A \cup B = \{1, 3, 5, 9\}$

(b) Intersection

The "intersection" of sets A and B, written $A \cap B$, is a set that contains exactly those elements that are in both A and B.

$$A \cap B = \{x : x \in A \quad \text{and} \quad x \in B\}$$

Example: Given $A = \{1, 3, 9\}$, $B = \{3, 5\}$, $C = \{a, b, c\}$

$$A \cap B = \{3\}$$
$$A \cap C = \{\ \}$$

(c) Set Difference

The "set difference" of set A and set B, written as $A–B$, is the set that contains everything that is in A but not in B.

$$A - B = \{x : x \in A \quad \text{and} \quad x \notin B\}$$

Given $A = \{1,3,9\}$, $B = \{3,5\}$

$$A - B = \{1, 9\}$$

(d) Complement

The "complement" of set A, written as $\bar{A}$ is the set containing everything that is not in A.

Properties of set operations

Some of the properties of the set operations follow from their definitions. The following laws hold for the three given sets A, B and C.

Idempotency : $A \cup A = A$
$A \cap A = A$

Commutativity : $A \cup B = B \cup A$
$A \cap B = B \cap A$

Associativity : $(A \cup B) \cup C = A \cup (B \cup C)$
$(A \cap B) \cap C = A \cap (B \cap C)$

Distributivity	:	$(A \cup B) \cap C = (A \cap C) \cup (B \cap C)$ $(A \cap B) \cup C = (A \cup C) \cap (B \cup C)$
Absorption	:	$(A \cup B) \cap A = A$ $(A \cap B) \cup A = A$
DeMorgan's Laws	:	$A - (B \cup C) = (A - B) \cap (A - C)$ $A - (B \cap C) = (A - B) \cup (A - C)$

Example 0.1.1: Show that $A - (B \cup C) = (A - B) \cap (A - C)$.

Solution

$$\begin{aligned} x \in A - (B \cup C) &\Rightarrow x \in A \text{ and } x \notin B \cup C \\ &\Rightarrow x \in A \text{ and } x \notin B \text{ and } x \notin C \\ &\Rightarrow (x \in A \text{ and } x \notin B) \text{ and } (x \in A \text{ and } x \notin C) \\ &\Rightarrow x \in A - B \text{ and } x \in A - C \\ &\Rightarrow x \in (A - B) \cap (A - C) \end{aligned}$$

Therefore $\quad A - (B \cup C) \subseteq (A - B) \cap (A - C) \quad$ (1)

Conversely,

$$\begin{aligned} x \in (A - B) \cap (A - C) &\Rightarrow x \in A - B \text{ and } x \in A - C \\ &\Rightarrow (x \in A \text{ and } x \notin B) \text{ and } (x \in A \text{ and } x \notin C) \\ &\Rightarrow x \in A \text{ and } (x \notin B \text{ and } x \notin C) \\ &\Rightarrow x \in A \text{ and } x \notin B \cup C \\ &\Rightarrow x \in A - (B \cup C) \end{aligned}$$

Therefore, $(A - B) \cap (A - C) \subseteq A - (B \cup C)$.

Hence $A - (B \cup C) = (A - B) \cap (A - C)$.

Example 0.1.2: Given sets A and B are the subsets of a universal set U, prove that

(a) $A - B = A \cap B'$
(b) $A - B = A$, if and only if $A \cap B = \varnothing$
(c) $A - B = \varnothing$, if and only if $A \subseteq B$.

Solution

(a) Let $x \in A - B$. Then

$$\begin{aligned} x \in A - B &\Rightarrow x \in A \text{ and } x \notin B \\ &\Rightarrow x \in A \text{ and } x \in B \\ &\Rightarrow x \in A \cap B' \end{aligned}$$

$$A - B \subseteq A \cap B' \quad (1)$$

Conversely, Let $x \in A \cap B'$. Then

$$\begin{aligned} x \in A \cap B' &\Rightarrow x \in A \text{ and } x \in B \\ &\Rightarrow x \in A \text{ and } x \notin B \\ &\Rightarrow x \in A - B \end{aligned} \tag{2}$$

Hence from (1) and (2)

$$A - B = A \cap B'$$

(b) We have $A \cap B = \varnothing$. Then

$$\begin{aligned} & A = (A - B) \cup (A \cap B) \\ \Rightarrow\ & A = A - B \cup \varnothing \text{ since } A \cap B = \varnothing \\ \Rightarrow\ & A = A - B. \end{aligned}$$

Again we have $A - B = A$. Then

$$\begin{aligned} & A = (A - B) \cup (A \cap B) \\ \Rightarrow\ & A \cap B = A - A \text{ Since } A - B = A \\ \Rightarrow\ & A \cap B = \varnothing. \end{aligned}$$

(c) We have $A \subseteq B$. Then

$$\begin{aligned} & A \cap B = A \\ & A - B = A - (A \cap B) \\ \Rightarrow\ & A - B = A - A \text{ Since } A \cap B = A \\ \Rightarrow\ & A - B = \varnothing. \end{aligned}$$

If $A - B = \varnothing$, then

$$\begin{aligned} & A \cap B = A - (A - B) \\ \Rightarrow\ & A \cap B = A - \varnothing \\ \Rightarrow\ & A \cap B = A \\ \Rightarrow\ & A \subseteq B. \end{aligned}$$

Example 0.1.3: Given three sets A, B and C, prove that

$$A \cup (B \cup C) = (A \cup B) \cup C.$$

Solution

(i) Let us show that

$$A \cup (B \cup C) \subset (A \cup B) \cup C$$

$$\begin{aligned} & x \in A \cup (B \cup C) \\ \Rightarrow\ & x \in A \text{ or } x \in (B \cup C), \text{ by definition of union} \\ \Rightarrow\ & x \in A \text{ or } (x \in B \text{ or } x \in C) \\ \Rightarrow\ & (x \in A \text{ or } x \in B) \text{ or } x \in C \end{aligned}$$

$$\Rightarrow x \in (A \cup B) \text{ or } x \in C$$
$$\Rightarrow x \in (A \cup B) \cup C.$$

Therefore we have

$$A \cup (B \cup C) \subset (A \cup B) \cup C \quad (1)$$

(ii) Let us now show that

$$(A \cup B) \cup C \subset A \cup (B \cup C).$$

Assume that y is any element of the set $(A \cup B) \cup C$

$$y \in (A \cup B) \cup C$$
$$\Rightarrow y \in (A \cup B) \text{ or } y \in C$$
$$\Rightarrow (y \in A \text{ or } y \in B) \text{ or } y \in C$$
$$\Rightarrow y \in A \text{ or } (y \in B \text{ or } y \in C)$$
$$\Rightarrow y \in A \cup (B \cup C)$$

Therefore we have

$$(A \cup B) \cup C \subset A \cup (B \cup C) \quad (2)$$

From (1) and (2), we have

$$A \cup (B \cup C) = (A \cup B) \cup C$$

Example 0.1.4: Prove that the intersection of sets is associative i.e., if *A, B* and *C* are three sets, then

$$A \cap (B \cap C) = (A \cap B) \cap C.$$

Solution

Let us prove that $A \cap (B \cap C) \subset (A \cap B) \cap C$

Let x be an element such that

$$x \in A \cap (B \cap C)$$
$$\Rightarrow x \in A \text{ and } x \in (B \cap C)$$
$$\Rightarrow x \in A \text{ and } (x \in B \text{ and } x \in C)$$
$$\Rightarrow (x \in A \text{ and } x \in B) \text{ and } x \in C$$
$$\Rightarrow x \in (A \cap B) \text{ and } x \in C$$
$$\Rightarrow x \in (A \cap B) \cap C$$

Therefore $A \cap (B \cap C) \subset (A \cap B) \cap C$ (1)

Let us prove that $(A \cap B) \cap C \subset A \cap (B \cap C)$.

Let us assume the element $y \in (A \cap B) \cap C$

$$\Rightarrow y \in (A \cap B) \text{ and } y \in C$$

$$\Rightarrow (y \in A \text{ and } y \in B) \text{ and } y \in C$$
$$\Rightarrow y \in A \text{ and } y \in B \text{ and } y \in C$$
$$\Rightarrow y \in A \text{ and } y \in (B \cap C)$$
$$\Rightarrow y \in A \cap (B \cap C)$$

Therefore we have $(A \cap B) \cap C \subset A \cap (B \cap C)$ (2)

From (1) and (2), we have

$$A \cap (B \cap C) = (A \cap B) \cap C$$

Example 0.1.5: For any two sets A and B, prove the DeMorgan's Laws

(a) $(A \cup B)' = A' \cap B'$
(b) $(A \cap B)' = A' \cup B'$

Solution

(a) $x \in (A \cup B)' \Leftrightarrow x \notin A \cup B$
$\Leftrightarrow x \notin A$ and $x \notin B$
$\Leftrightarrow x \in A'$ and $x \in B'$
$\Leftrightarrow x \in A' \cap B'$

(b) $y \in (A \cap B)' \Leftrightarrow y \notin A \cap B$
$\Leftrightarrow$ either $y \notin A$ or $y \notin B$
$\Leftrightarrow$ either $y \in A'$ or $y \in B'$
$\Leftrightarrow y \in A' \cup B'$

Hence we have $(A \cap B)' = A' \cup B'$.

Example 0.1.6: If the symmetric difference of the two sets A and B is refined as $(A - B) \cup (B - A)$ and denoted by $A \Delta B$, prove that

(a) $A \Delta B = B \Delta A$
(b) $(A \cup B) - (A \cap B) = A \Delta B$.

Solution

(a) $A \Delta B = (A - B) \cup (B - A)$
$= (B - A) \cup (A - B)$
$= B \Delta A$

(b) $(A \cup B) - (A \cap B) = (A \cup B) \cap (A \cap B)'$
$(\because x - y = x \cap y')$
$= (A \cup B) \cap (A' \cup B')$
$= ((A \cup B) \cap A') \cup ((A \cup B) \cap B')$
$= (A \cap A') \cup (B \cap A') \cup (A \cap B')$
$\cup (B \cap B')$

$$= (A \cap B') \cup (B \cap A')$$
$$(\because (A \cap A') = (B \cap B') = \varnothing)$$
$$= (A - B) \cup (B - A)$$
$$= A \Delta B.$$

Additional Terminology

(a) Disjoint Sets. If A and B have no common element, that is, $A \cap B = \varnothing$, then the sets A and B are said to be disjoint.

(b) Cardinality. The "Cardinality" of a set A, written $|A|$, is the number of elements in set A.

(c) Powerset. The "powerset" of a set A, written 2^A, is the set of all subsets of A; i.e., a set containing 'n' elements has a powerset containing 2^n elements.

(d) Cartesian Product. Let A and B be two sets. Then the set of all ordered pairs (x, y) where $x \in A$ and $y \in B$ is called the "Cartesian Product" of the sets A and B and is denoted by $A \times B$, i.e.

$$A \times B = \{(x, y) : x \in A \text{ and } y \in B\}$$

Example 0.1.7: Given $A = \{1, 2, 3\}$ determine $P(A)$ (powerset of A).

Solution

As the set $A = \{1, 2, 3\}$ has 3 elements the powerset $P(A)$ will have $2^3 = 8$ elements.

$$P(A) = \{\varnothing, \{1\}, \{2\}, \{3\}, \{1,2\}, \{2,3\}, \{3,1\}, \{1,2,3\}\}$$

Example 0.1.8: Given $A = [\{a, b\}, \{c\}, \{d, e, f\}]$ determine the powerset $P(A)$.

Solution

Since A has 3 elements, $P(A)$ has $2^3 = 8$ elements.

$$P(A) = \left\{\begin{matrix} A, [\{a, b\}, \{c\}], [\{a, b\}, \{d, e, f\}], [\{c\}, \{d, e, f\}], \\ [\{a, b\}], [\{c\}], [\{d, e, f\}], \varnothing \end{matrix}\right\}$$

Example 0.1.9: Prove that $(A \times B) \cup (A \times C) = A \times (B \cup C)$

Proof:
$$\begin{aligned}(A \times B) \cup (A \times C) &= \{(x, y) : (x, y) \in A \times B \text{ or } (x, y) \in A \times C\} \\ &= \{(x, y) : x \in A,\ y \in B \text{ or } x \in A,\ y \in C\} \\ &= \{(x, y) : x \in A, \text{ and } y \in B \text{ or } y \in C\} \\ &= \{(x, y) : x \in A,\ y \in B \cup C\} \\ &= A \times (B \cup C)\end{aligned}$$
□

Example 0.1.10: Given $A = \{1,2\}$, $B = \{x, y, z\}$ and $C = \{3, 4\}$, find $A \times B \times C$ and $n(A \times B \times C)$.

Solution

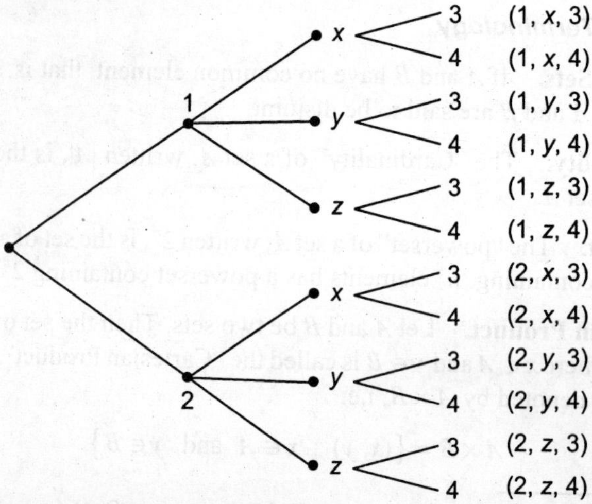

$$n(A \times B \times C) = n(A) \cdot n(B) \cdot n(C) = (2)\,(3)\,(2) = 12.$$

0.1.2 Relations and Functions

Definition of Relation: A relation on sets S and T is a set of ordered pairs (s, t), where

(a) $s \in S$ (s is a member of S)
(b) $t \in T$
(c) S and T need not be different
(d) The set of all first elements in the "domain" of the relation, and
(e) The set of all second elements is the "range" of the relation.

Example:

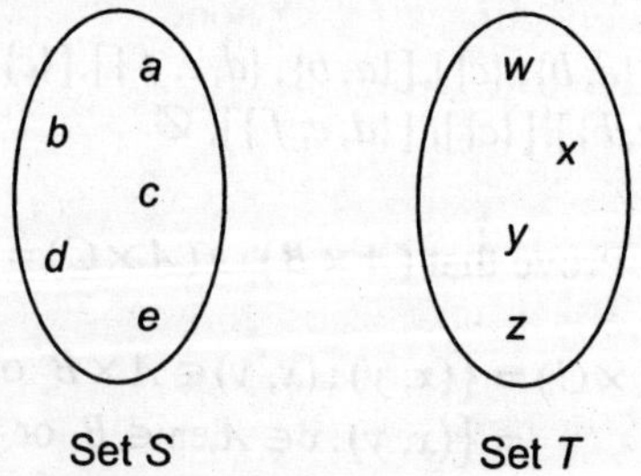

Fig. 1 Sets S and T are disjoint

Suppose S is the set $\{a, b, c, d, e\}$ and set T is $\{w, x, y, z\}$.

Then a relation on S and T is

$$R = \{(a, y), (c, w), (c, z), (d, y)\}$$

The four ordered pairs in the relation is represented as shown in Fig. 2.

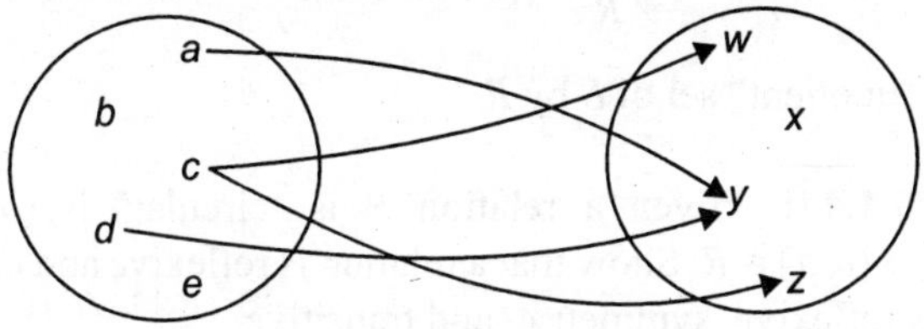

Fig. 2 Relation $R = \{(a, y), (c, w), (c, w), (c, z), (d, y)\}$

Equivalence Relation

A subset R of $A \times A$ is called an equivalence relation on A if R satisfies the following conditions:

(i) $(a, a) \in R$ for all $a \in A$ (R is reflexive)
(ii) If $(a, b) \in R$, then $(b, a) \in R$, then $(a, b) \in R$ (R is symmetric)
(iii) If $(a, b) \in R$ and $(b, c) \in R$, then $(a, c) \in R$ (R is transitive)

Partial Ordering Relations

A relation R on a set S is called a "Partial ordering" or a "Partial order", if R is reflexive, antisymmetric and transitive.

A set S together with a partial ordering R is called a "Partially ordered set" or "Poset".

Example: The relation $\leq$ on the set R of real numbers is reflexive, antisymmetric and transitive. Therefore $\leq$ is a "Partial ordering".

Partition

A Partition P of S is a collection $\{A_i\}$ of nonempty subsets of S with the properties:

(i) Each $a \in S$ belongs to some A_i,
(ii) If $A_i \neq A_j$, then $A_i \cap A_j = \varnothing$.

Thus a partition P of S is a subdivision of S into disjoint nonempty sets.

If R is an equivalence relation on a set S, for each 'a' in S, let $[a]$ denote the set of elements of S to which 'a' is related under R, i.e.

$$[a] = \{x : (a, x) \in R\}$$

Here $[a]$ is the Equivalence class" of 'a' in S.

The collection of all equivalence classes of elements of S under an equivalence relation R is denoted by $S/_R$, i.e.,

$$S/_R = \{[a] : a \in S\}.$$

It is known as "quotient" set of S by R.

Example 0.1.11: Given a relation R is 'circular' if $(a, b) \in R$ and $(b, c) \in R \Rightarrow (c, a) \in R$. Show that a relation is reflexive and circular if and only if it is reflexive, symmetric, and transitive.

Solution

Let the relation R be reflexive and circular. We shall prove that R is reflexive, symmetric and transitive.

$$(a, b) \in R,\ (b, c) \in R \Rightarrow (c, a) \in R, \text{ since } R \text{ is circular and}$$

$$(a, a) \in R \text{ since } R \text{ is reflexive.}$$

We have $(c, a) \in R$, $(a, a) \in R \Rightarrow (a, c) \in R$, since R is circular.
Thus shows $(a, c) \in R$ and $(c, a) \in R$. Hence R is symmetric

$$\begin{aligned}(a, b) \in R, (b, c) \in R &\Rightarrow (c, a) \in R, \text{ since } R \text{ is circular}\\ &\Rightarrow (a, c) \in R, \text{ since } R \text{ is symmetric}\\ &\Rightarrow R \text{ is transitive}\end{aligned}$$

It is given that R is reflexive.

Conversely, if R is reflexive, symmetric, and transitive then we show that R is reflexive and circular.

$$\begin{aligned}(a, b) \in R, (b, c) \in R &\Rightarrow (a, c) \in R, \text{ since } R \text{ is transitive}\\ &\Rightarrow (c, a) \in R, \text{ since } R \text{ is symmetric}\\ &\Rightarrow R \text{ is circular}\end{aligned}$$

$$\begin{aligned}(a, c) \in R, (c, a) \in R &\Rightarrow (a, a) \in R, \text{ since } R \text{ is transitive}\\ &\Rightarrow R \text{ is reflexive}\end{aligned}$$

Example 0.1.12: Show that the relation "congruence modulo m" over the set of positive integers is an equivalence relation.

Solution

Assume that N = Set of all positive integers
and m = given positive integer.

For $x, y \in N, x \equiv y \pmod m$ if and only if $x - y$ is divisible by m, i.e.

$$x - y = km, \text{ for } k \in z.$$

Let $x, y, z \in N$. Then

(a) As $x - x = 0\ m.$, $x \equiv x \pmod{m}$, for all $x \in N$. Therefore this relation is reflexive

(b) $x \equiv y \pmod{m} \Rightarrow x - y = km$, for integer k

$$\Rightarrow y - x = (-k)m$$
$$\Rightarrow y \equiv x \pmod{m}$$

Therefore the relation is symmetric.

(c) $x \equiv y \pmod{m}$ and $y \equiv z \pmod{m}$

$$\Rightarrow x - y = km \ \ and \ \ y - z = lm \text{ for integers } k, l.$$
$$\Rightarrow (x - y) + (y - z) = (k + l)m$$
$$\Rightarrow (x - z) = (k + l)m$$
$$\Rightarrow x \equiv z \pmod{m} \text{ since } k + l \text{ is also an integer}$$

Therefore the relation is transitive.

Since the relation is reflexive, symmetric and transitive, the relation "congruence modulo m" is an equivalence relation.

Example 0.1.13: Give examples of relations R on $A = \{1, 2, 3\}$ with

(a) R being both symmetric and antisymmetric
(b) R being neither symmetric nor antisymmetric

Solution

A possible set of examples are:

(a) $R = \{(1,1),\ (2,2)\}$
(b) $R = \{(1,2),\ (2,1),\ (2,3)\}$

Example 0.1.14: Given the relation R in A as

$$R = \{(1,1), (2,2), (2,3), (3,2), (4,2), (4,4)\}$$

(a) Is R (i) reflexive (ii) symmetric (iii) transitive?
(b) Is R antisymmetric?
(c) Determine R^2.

Solution

(a) (i) R is not reflexive because
$3 \in A$ but $3 \not R 3$, i.e. $(3,3) \notin R$

(ii) R is not symmetric because
$4R2$ but $2 \not R 4$, i.e.,$(4,2) \in R$ but $(2,4) \notin R$

(iii) R is not transitive because
$4R2$ and $2R3$ but $4 \not R 3$, i.e.,
$(4,2) \in R$, $(2,3) \in R$ but $(4,3) \notin R$

(b) R is not antisymmetric because $2R3$ and $3R2$ but $2 \neq 3$

(c) For each pair $(a, b) \in R$, determine all $(b, c) \in R$. As $(a, c) \in R^2$,
$R^2 = \{(1,1), (2,2), (2,3), (3,2), (3,3), (4,2), (4,3), (4,4)\}$.

Functions

Suppose every element of S occurs exactly once as the first element of an ordered pair. In Fig shown, every element of S has exactly one arrow arising from it. This kind of relation is called a "function".

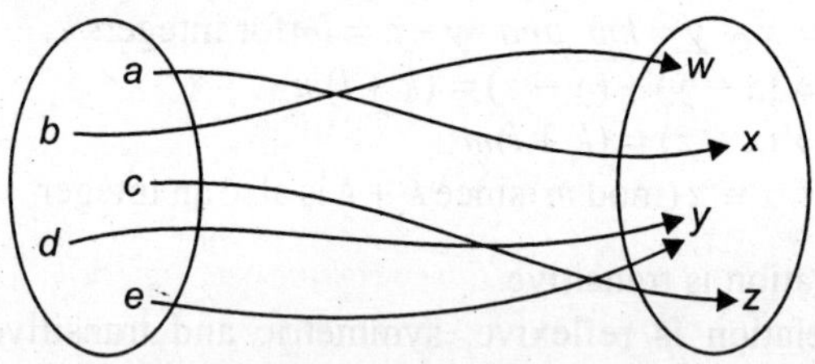

Fig. A Function

A function is otherwise known as "Mapping". A function is said to map an element in its domain to an element in its range.

Every element in S in the domain, i.e., every element of S is mapped to some elemet in the range. No element in the domain maps to more than one element in the range.

Functions as relations

A function $f : A \rightarrow B$ is a relation from A to B i.e., a subset of $A \times B$, such that each $a \in A$ belongs to a unique ordered pair (a, b) in f.

Kinds of Functions

(a) *One-to-One Function* (*Injection*): A function $f : A \rightarrow B$ is said to be one-to-one if different elements in the domain A have distinct images in the range.

A function f is one-to-one if $f(a) = f(a')$ implies $a = a'$.

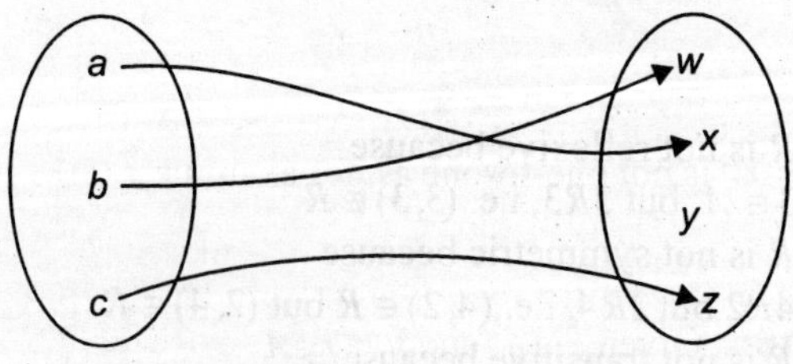

Fig. An Injection (one to one function)

(b) *Onto function (Surjection): A function $f: A \to B$ is said to be an onto function if each element of B* is the image of some element of *A*.

i.e., $f: A \to B$ is onto if the image of *f* is the entire codomain, i.e. if $f(A) = B$. i.e., *f* maps *A* onto *B*.

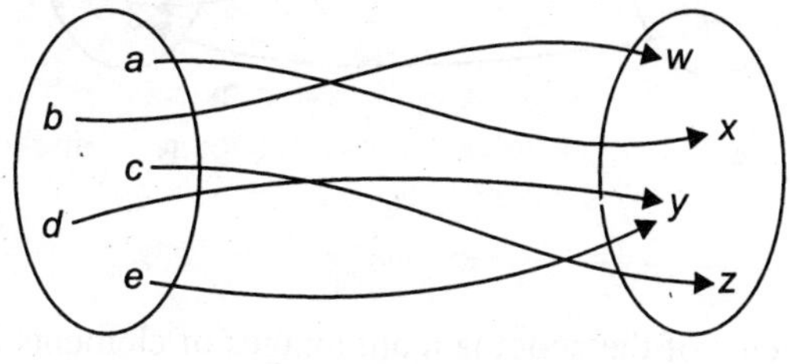

Fig. A Surjection

(c) *One-to-one onto Function (Bijection): A function that is both one-to-one and onto is called a "Bijection". Such a function maps each and every element of A* to exactly one element of *B*, with no elements left over. Fig. below shows bijection.

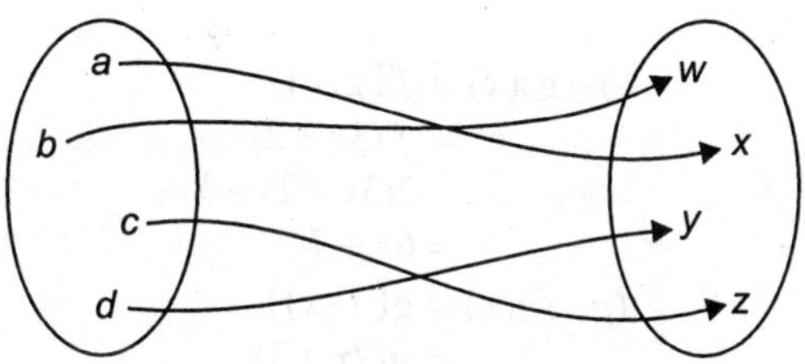

Fig. A Bijection

(d) *Invertible function*: A function $f: A \to B$ is invertible if its inverse relation f^{-1} is a function from *B* to *A*.

A function $f: A \to B$ is invertible if and only it is both one-to-one and onto.

Example 0.1.15: Find whether the function $f(x) = x^2$ from the set of integers to the set of integers is one-to-one.

Solution

The function $f(x) = x^2$ is not one-to-one as, for example $f(1) = f(-1) = 1$, but $1 \neq -1$.

Example 0.1.16: Given *f* is a function $f: A \to B$ where $A = \{a, b, c, d\}$ and $B = \{1, 2, 3\}$ with $f(a) = 3, f(b) = 2, f(c) = 1$, and $f(d) = 3$. Is the function *f* an onto function?

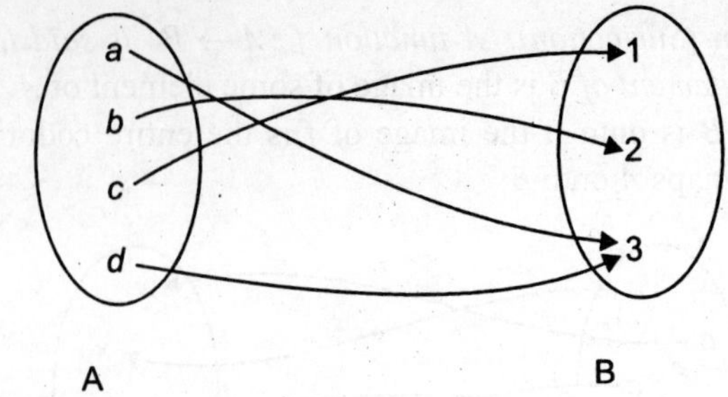

Solution

As all three elements of the codomain are images of elements in the domain, we have *f* as an "onto function".

Example 0.1.17: Given $f(x) = 2x + 3$ and $g(x) = 3x + 2$

Check if commutative law holds good for composition of functions.

Solution

$$\begin{aligned}(f \cdot g)(x) &= f(g(x)) \\ &= f(3x+2) \\ &= 2(3x+2)+3 \\ &= 6x+7 \\ (g \cdot f)(x) &= g(f(x)) \\ &= g(2x+3) \\ &= 3(2x+3)+2 \\ &= 6x+11\end{aligned}$$

Since $(f \cdot g)(x) \neq (g \cdot f)(x)$, commutative law does not hold for composition of functions.

Example 0.1.18: Check whether the mapping $f: X \to X$ where $X = \{x \in R, x \neq 0\}$ defined by $f(x) = \frac{1}{x}$ is one to one and onto.

Solution

x = set of all non-zero real numbers. Let $x_1, x_2 \in X$.

Then $$f(x_1) = f(x_2) \Rightarrow \frac{1}{x_1} = \frac{1}{x_2}$$
$$\Rightarrow x_1 = x_2$$

Hence *f* is one-to-one.

For every non-zero real number $x \in X$ there exists a non-zero real number $\frac{1}{x} \in X$ such that

$$f\left(\frac{1}{x}\right) = \frac{1}{\left(\frac{1}{x}\right)} = x.$$

Hence every element $x \in X$ is an image of $\frac{1}{x}$. Therefore f is onto.

Therefore f is one-to-one and onto.

0.1.3 Graphs and Trees

Graphs

A graph G consists of a finite set V of objects called "Vertices", a finite set E of objects called "Edges", and a function γ that assigns to each edge a subset $\{v, w\}$, where v and w are vertices (and may be the same).

Therefore we write $$G = (V, E, \gamma).$$

Example: Given $V = \{1, 2, 3, 4\}$ and $E = \{e_1, e_2, e_3, e_4, e_5\}$

γ is defined by

$$\gamma(e_1) = \gamma(e_5) = \{1, 2\}$$
$$\gamma(e_2) = \{4, 3\}$$
$$\gamma(e_3) = \{1, 3\}$$
$$\gamma(e_4) = \{2, 4\}$$

Then $G = (V, E, \gamma)$ is a graph shown below.

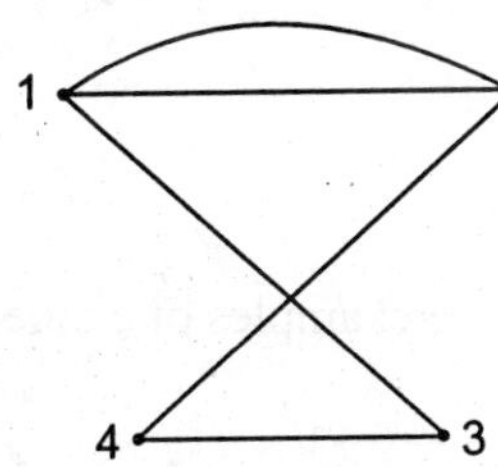

Degree of a vertex: It is defined as the number of edges having that vertex as an end point.

Loop: A graph may have an edge from a vertex to itself, such an edge is called a "loop".

Degree of a vertex is 2, for a loop since that vertex serves as both endpoints of the loop.

Isolated vertex: A vertex with "zero" as degree is called an "Isolated vertex."

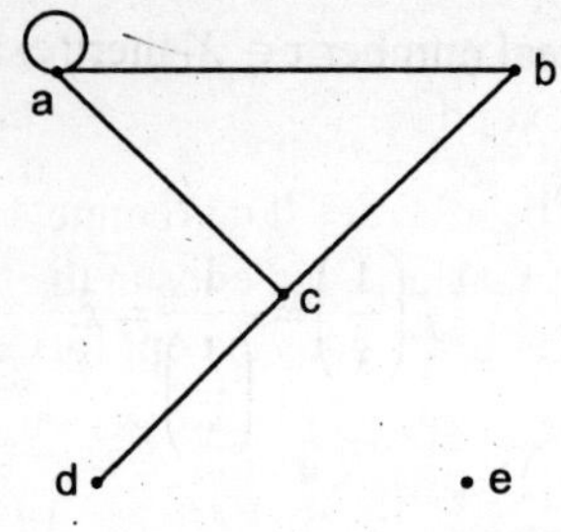

Adjacent vertices: A pair of vertices that determine an edge are "adjacent" vertices.

In the graph shown above, vertex '*e*' is an "Isolated vertex", '*a*' and '*b*' are adjacent vertices, vertices '*a*' and '*d*' are not adjacent.

Path: A path in a graph *G* consists of a pair (*V*, *E*) of sequences.

Circuit: A circuit is a path that begins and ends at the same vertex.

Simple Path: A path is called "simple" if no vertex appears more than once in the vertex sequence.

Connected Graph: A graph is called "connected" if there is a path from any vertex to any other vertex in the graph, otherwise, the graph is "disconnected".

Components: If the graph is disconnected, the various connected pieces are called the "components" of the graph.

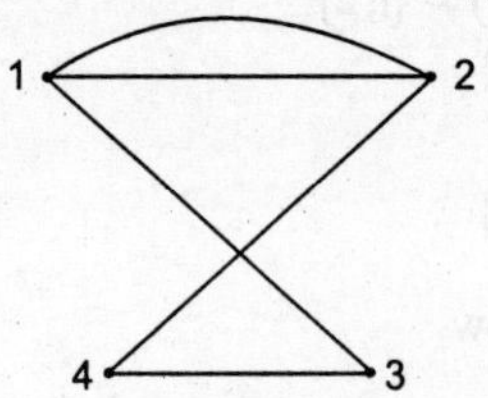

(a)

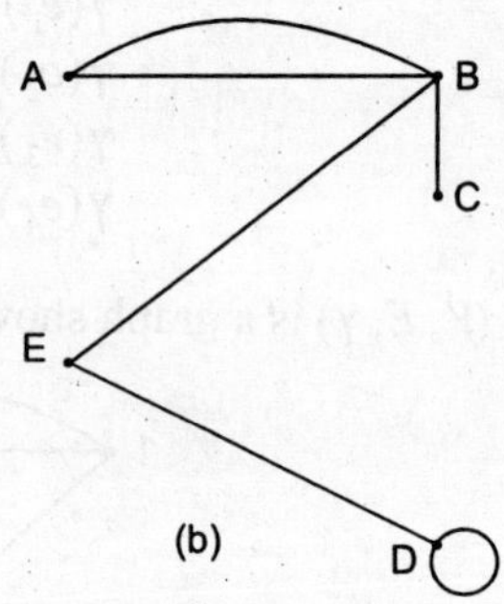

(b)

The above two graphs are examples of connected graphs.

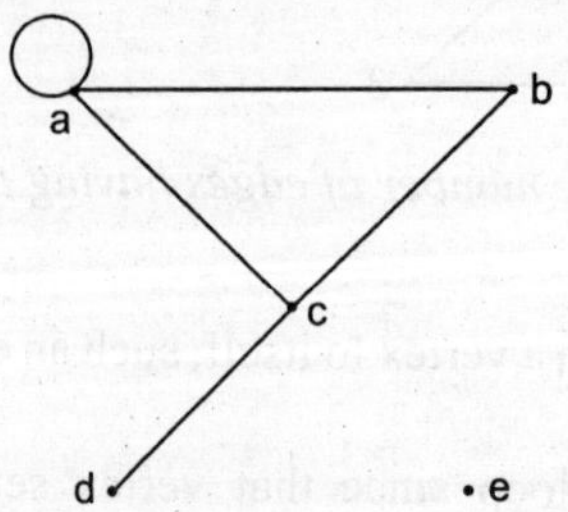

(c)

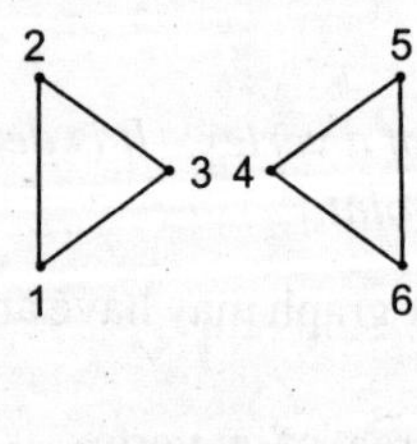

(d)

The above two graphs are examples of disconnected graphs.

(A "walk" is a sequence of edges, where the finish vertex of each edge is the start vertex of the next edge).

Tree: A graph is said to be a "Tree" if it is connected and has no simple cycles.

(A "path" is a cycle if it starts and ends in the same node. A "*simple cycle*" is one that does not repeat any nodes except for the first and last).

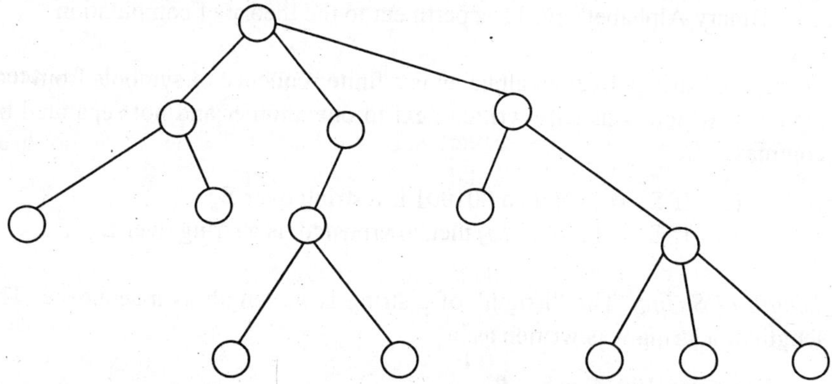

Fig. A Tree

Directed Graph: The graph is said to be a "directed graph" if it has arrows in stead of lines.

Outdegree: The number of arrows pointing from a particular node is the "outdegree" of that node.

Indegree: The number of arrows pointing to a particular node is the "indegree".

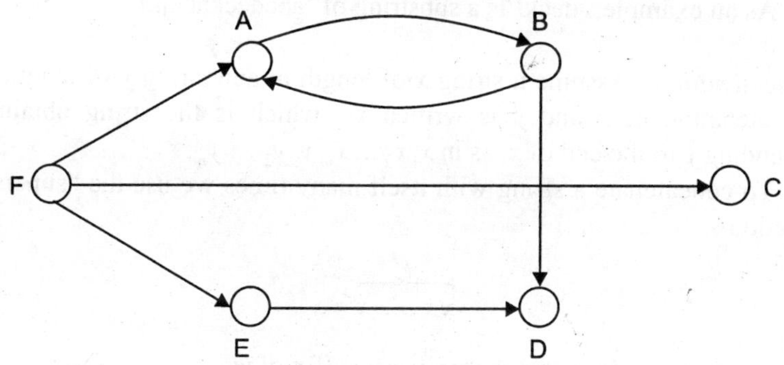

Fig. Directed Graph

Directed graphs (as shown in fig.) are an easy way of depicting binary relations.

0.1.4 Strings and Languages

The mathematical study of the "Theory of Computation" begins by understanding the Mathematics of strings of symbols.

Alphabet: It is defined as a finite set of symbols.

Example: Roman alphabet $\{a, b, ... z\}$.

"Binary Alphabet" $\{0, 1\}$ is pertinent to the theory of computation.

String: A "string" over an alphabet is a finite sequence of symbols from that alphabet, which is usually written next to one another and not separated by commas.

(i) If $\Sigma_a = \{0,1\}$ then 001001 is a string over Σ_a.

(ii) If $\Sigma_b = \{a, b, \ldots, z)$ then axyrpqstcd is a string over Σ_b.

Length of String: The "length" of a string is its length as a sequence. The length of a string w is written as $|w|$.

Example: $|10011| = 5$

Empty String: The string of zero length is called the "empty string". This is denoted by $\in$.

The empty string plays the role of 0 in a number system.

Reverse String: If $w = w_1 w_2 \ldots w_n$ where each $w_i \in \Sigma$, the reverse of w is $w_n w_{n-1} \cdots w_1$.

Substring: z is a substring of w if z appears consecutively within w.

As an example, 'deck' is a substring of 'abcdeckabcjkl'.

Concatenation: Assume a string x of length m and string y of length n, the concatenation of x and y is written xy, which is the string obtained by appending y to the end of x, as in $x_1 x_2 \ldots x_m y_1 y_2 \ldots y_n$.

To concatenate a string with itself many times we use the "superscript" notation:

$$\overbrace{x x \ldots x}^{k} = x^k$$

Suffix: If $w = xv$ for some x, then v is a suffix of w.

Prefix: If $w = vy$ for some y, then v is a prefix of w.

Lexicographic ordering: The Lexicographic ordering of strings is the same as the dictionary ordering, except that shorter strings precede longer strings.

The lexicographic ordering of all strings over the alphabet {0, 1} is (∈, 0, 1, 00, 01, 10, 11, 000, ...).

Language: Any set of strings over an alphabet Σ is called a language.

The set of all strings, including the empty string over an alphabet Σ is denoted as Σ^*.

Infinite languages L are denoted as

$$L = \{w \in \Sigma^* : w \text{ has property } P\}$$

Examples:

(a) $L_1 = \{w \in \{0,1\}^* : w \text{ has an equal number of 0's and 1's}\}$

(b) $L_2 = \{w \in \Sigma^* : w = w^R\}$ where w^R is the reverse string of w.

Concatenation of Languages: If L_1 and L_2 are languages over Σ, their concatenation is $L = L_1 \bullet L_2$, or simply $L = L_1 L_2$, where

$$L = \{w \in \Sigma^* : w = x \bullet y \text{ for some } x \in L_1, \text{ and } y \in L_2\}$$

Example: Given $\Sigma = \{0,1\}$

$$L_1 = \{w \in \Sigma^* : w \text{ has an even number of 0's}\}$$

$$L_2 = \{w : w \text{ starts with a 0 and the rest of the symbols are 1's}\}$$

then

$$L_1 L_2 = \{w : w \text{ has an odd number of 0's}\}$$

Kleene Star: Another language operation is the "Kleene Star" of a language L, which is denoted by L^*.

L^* is the set of all strings obtained by concatenating zero or more strings from L.

$$L^* = \left\{ \begin{array}{l} w \in \Sigma^* : w = w_1 \bullet \dots \bullet w_k \text{ for some } k \geq 0 \text{ and} \\ \qquad\qquad\qquad\qquad \text{some } w_1, w_2, \dots, w_k \in L \end{array} \right\}$$

Example: If $L = \{01, 1, 100\}$ then $110001110011 \in L^*$, since $110001110011 = 1 \bullet 100 \bullet 01 \bullet 1 \bullet 100 \bullet 1 \bullet 1$, each of these strings is in L.

Example 0.1.19: Prove that $|uv| = |u| + |v|$, for any two given strings u and v.

Solution

For all $a \in \Sigma'$ and w any string on Σ, we make a recursive definition as

$$|a| = 1, |wa| = |w| + 1$$

With this formal definition, we can prove

$$|uv| = |u| + |v|.$$

By this definition made, $|uv| = |u| + |v|$ holds for all u of any length and v of length 1, which is the basis.

Let us assume v of length $n + 1$ and we write it as

$$v = wa.$$

Therefore we have, $|v| = |w| + 1$,

$$|uv| = |uwa| = |uw| + 1$$

But by inductive hypothesis,

$$|uw| = |u| + |w|$$

so that

$$|uv| = |u| + |w| + 1 = |u| + |v|$$

Hence for all u and all v of length upto $n + 1$, we have

$$|uv| = |u| + |v|$$

which is the inductive step.

Example 0.1.20: Use induction on to show that $|u^n| = n|u|$ for all strings u and all n.

Solution

Basis: For $n = 1$, $|u^1| = |u| = 1$ (assume)

$$n|u| = 1|u| = |u| = 1$$

Inductive Hypothesis: Let us assume that it is true for n.

$$|u^n| = n|u|.$$

Inductive Step:
$$\begin{aligned} |u^{n+1}| &= |u^n \bullet u^1| = |u^n| + |u| \\ &= n|u| + |u| \\ &= (n+1)|u| \end{aligned}$$

which is the required Inductive step to be proved.

Hence we have $|u^n| = n|u|$.

Example 0.1.21: The reverse of a string is defined by the recusive rules

$$a^R = a,$$
$$(wa)^R = aw^R$$

for all $a \in \Sigma, w \in \Sigma^*$. Using this prove that

$$(uv)^R = v^R u^R$$

for all $u, v \in \Sigma^+$.

Solution

Given that $a^R = a$,

$$(wa)^R = aw^R.$$

Now we have to prove $(uv)^R = v^R u^R$.
Let us assume that $u = wb$ and $v = wa$.

$$\begin{aligned} LHS = (uv)^R = (wbwa)^R &= bw^R \cdot aw^R \\ &= (bw^R)(aw^R) \\ &= (bw)^R (aw)^R \\ &= v^R \cdot u^R = RHS \end{aligned}$$

Hence proved.

Example 0.1.22: Given $\Sigma = \{a, b\}$ obtain Σ^*.

(a) Give an example of a finite language in Σ.
(b) Given $L = \left\{a^n b^n : n \geq 0\right\}$, check if the strings *aabb*, *aaaabbbb*, *abb* are in the language *L*.

Solution

$$\Sigma = \{a, b\}$$

Therefore we have $\Sigma^* = \{\lambda, a, b, aa, ab, ba, bb, aaa,\}$

(a) $\{a, aa, aab\}$ is an example of a finite language in Σ.

(i) $\underline{aa}\ \underline{bb} \rightarrow$ a string in L. ($n = 2$)
(ii) $\underline{aaaa}\ \underline{bbbb} \rightarrow$ a string in L. ($n = 4$)
(iii) $abb \rightarrow$ not a string in L (since there is no n satisfying this).

Example 0.1.23: Given $L = \{a^n b^n : n \geq 0\}$ obtain (a) L^2 (b) L^R.

Solution

Given $L = \{a^n b^n : n \geq 0\}$

(a) $L^2 = \{a^n b^n a^m b^m : n \geq 0, m \geq 0\}$

where n and m are unrelated.

For example, the string aabbaaabbb is in L^2.

(b) Reverse of L is given by

$$L^R = \{b^n a^n : n \geq 0\}$$

Example 0.1.24: Let $L = \{ab, aa, baa\}$. Which of the following strings are in L^*.

(a) *abaabaaabaa*
(b) *aaaabaaaa*
(c) *baaaaabaaaab*
(d) *baaaabaa*

Solution

Please note that L^* is the "star-closure" of a language L, given by

$$L^* = L^0 \cup L^1 \cup L^2 \ldots\ldots$$

and L^+ is the "positive closure" defined by

$$L^+ = L^1 \cup L^2 \ldots\ldots$$

(a) $\underline{ab}\ \underline{aa}\ \underline{baa}\ \underline{ab}\ \underline{aa} \rightarrow$ This string is in L^*

(b) $\underline{aa}\ \underline{aa}\ \underline{baa}\ \underline{aa} \rightarrow$ This string is in L^*

(c) $\underline{baa}\ \underline{aa}\ \underline{ab}\ \underline{aa}\ \underline{aa}\ b$ or $\underline{baa}\ \underline{aa}\ \underline{ab}\ \underline{aa}\ a\ \underline{ab}$

$\uparrow$ (*undefined*) $\uparrow$ (*undefined*)

This string is not in L^*.

(d) $\underline{baa}\ \underline{aa}\ \underline{ab}\ \underline{aa} \rightarrow$ This string is in L^*.

Example 0.1.25: Given $L = \{a^n b^{n+1} : n \geq 0\}$. It is true that $L = L^*$ for the given language L?

Solution

We know $L^* = L^0 \cup L^1 \cup L^2 \ldots\ldots$

and $L^+ = L^1 \cup L^2 \cup L^3 \ldots\ldots$

Now for given $L = \{a^n b^{n+1} : n \geq 0\}$, we have

$$L^0 = a^0 b^{0+1} = b$$
$$L^1 = a^1 b^{1+1} = ab^2$$
$$L^2 = a^2 b^{2+1} = a^2 b^3.$$
$$\ldots\ldots\ldots$$
$$\ldots\ldots\ldots$$

Therefore, we have $\quad L^* = L^0 \cup L^1 \cup L^2 \ldots\ldots$

$$= b \cup ab^2 \cup a^2 b^3 \ldots\ldots$$

Hence it is true that $L = L^*$.

Example 0.1.26: Given $u = a^2 ba^3 b^2$ and $u = bab^2$, obtain

(a) uv (b) vu (c) v^2 (d) u^2 (e) $||u||$ (f) $||v||$ (g) $||uv||$ (h) $||vu||$ (i) $||v^2||$ (j) $||u^2||$

Solution

(a) $uv = (a^2 ba^3 b^2)(bab^2) = a^2 ba^3 b^3 ab^2$

(b) $vu = (bab^2)(a^2 ba^3 b^2) = bab^2 a^2 ba^3 b^2$

(c) $v^2 = vv = (bab^2)(bab^2) = bab^3 ab^2$

(d) $u^2 = uu = (a^2 ba^3 b)(bab^2) = a^2 ba^3 b^2 ab^2$

(e) $||u|| = 8$ (as there are 8 letters in the word u)

(f) $||v|| = 4$

(g) $||uv|| = 12$

(h) $||vu|| = 12$

(i) $||v^2|| = 8$

(j) $||u^2|| = 11$

Example 0.1.27: For any word u and v, prove that

(a) $||uv|| = ||u|| + ||v||$

(b) $||uv|| = ||vu||$.

Proof: (a) Let us assume $||u|| = m$ and $||v|| = n$. Therefore uv will have 'm' letters of u followed by 'n' letters of v.

Therefore we have

$$||uv|| = m + n = ||u|| + ||v||.$$

(b) Now, $||uv|| = |u|| + ||v||$ (from (a))

$\Rightarrow \quad = ||v|| + ||u||$

$\Rightarrow ||uv|| = ||vu||.$

□

Example 0.1.28: Given $A = \{a, b, c\}$, find L^* where

(i) $L = \{b^2\}$ (ii) $L = \{a, b\}$ (iii) $L = \{a, b, c^3\}$

Solution

(i) For $L = \{b^2\}$, L^* has all words b^n, where n is even (including the empty word λ).

(ii) For $L = \{a, b\}$, L^* has words in a and b.

(iii) For $L = \{a, b, c^3\}$

L^* has all words from $A = \{a, b, c\}$ with the length of each maximal subword composed entirely of C's is divisible by 3.

Example 0.1.29: For the language $L = \{ab, c\}$ over the set $A = \{a, b, c\}$. Find (a) L^3 (b) L^{-2} (c) L^0.

Solution

(a) For $L = \{ab, c\}$, we have

$$L^3 = \text{All 3-word sequences from } L$$

$$= \{ababab, ababc, abcab, abc^2, cabab, cabc, c^2ab, c^3\}$$

(b) L^{-2} is "Not defined" as negative power of a language is not defined.

(c) $L^0 = \{\lambda\}$, where λ is empty word.

Example 0.1.30: Given $L_1 = \{a, ab, a^2\}$ and $L_2 = \{b^2, aba\}$ are the languages over $A = \{a, b\}$, determine {a} L_1L_2 (b) L_2L_2.

Solution:

(a) To find L_1L_2, we concatenate words in L_1 with words in L_2 so that

$$L_1L_2 = \{ab^2, a^2ba, ab^3, ababa, a^2b^2, a^3ba\}$$

(b) To find L_2L_2, we concatenate words in L_2 with words in L_2 so that

$$L_2L_2' = \{b^4, b^2aba, abab^2, aba^2ba\}$$

Example 0.1.31: Find (i) uvu (ii) λu, $u\lambda$, $u\lambda v$ given $u = a^2b$ and $v = b^3ab$.

Solution

(i) $uvu = (a^2b)(b^3ab)(a^2b)$
$= a^2b^4aba^2b$

(ii) We know that λ is an empty word. Therefore we have

$$\lambda u = u\lambda = u = a^2b$$
$$u\lambda v = uv = (a^2b)(b^3ab)$$
$$= a^2b^4ab$$

Example 0.1.32: Given $A = \{a, b, c\}$ check if L_1, L_2, L_3 and L_4 are all languages over the alphabet A., where

$$L_1 = \{a, aa, ab, ac, abc, cab\}$$
$$L_2 = \{aba, aabaa\}$$
$$L_3 = \{\ \}$$
$$L_4 = \{a^icb^i \geq 1\}$$

Solution

All the languages L_1, L_2, L_3 and L_4 are defined over the alphabet A.

Example 0.1.33:

(a) Given $L_1 = \{a^ib^j \mid i > j \geq 1\}$ and
$L_2 = \{a^ib^j \mid 1 \leq i < j\}$ find $L_1 \cup L_2$.

(b) Given $L_3 = \{a^ib^ic^j \mid i, j \geq 1\}$ and
$L_4 = \{a^ib^jc^j \mid i, j \geq 1\}$ find $L_3 \cap L_4$.

Solution

(a) $L_1 \cup L_2 = \{a^ib^j \mid i > j \geq 1\} \cup \{a^ib^j \mid 1 \leq i < j\}$
$= \{a^ib^j \mid i \neq j,\ i, j \geq 1\}$

(b) $L_3 \cap L_4 = \{a^i b^i c^j \mid i, j \geq 1\} \cap \{a^i b^j c^j \mid i, j \geq 1\}$
$= \{a^i b^i c^i \mid i \neq 1\}$

Example 0.1.34: Given L_1 is English language and L_2 is French language, what do you mean by (a) $L_1 \cup L_2$ and $L_1 \cap L_2$.

Solution

(a) $L_1 \cup L_2$ = Set of all sentences someone who speaks both English and French can recognize.

(b) $L_1 \cap L_2$ = Language that contains all the sentences that are in both L_1 and L_2.

Example 0.1.35: Given $A = \{a, b, c\}$, $B = \{b, c, d\}$ and

$$L_1 = \{a^i b^j \mid i \geq 1, j \geq 1\}, \qquad L_2 = \{b^i c^j \mid i \geq j \geq 1\}$$
$$L_3 = \{a^i b^j c^i d^j \mid i \geq 1, j \geq 1\}, \quad L_4 = \{(ad)^i a^j d^j \mid i \geq 2, j \geq 1\}$$

Determine whether each of the following statements is true or false.

(a) L_1 is a language over A.
(b) L_1 is a language over B.
(c) L_2 is a language over $A \cup B$.
(d) L_2 is a language over $A \cap B$.
(e) L_3 is a language over $A \cup B$.
(f) L_3 is a language over $A \cap B$.
(g) L_4 is a language over $A \oplus B$.
(h) L_1 is a language over $A - B$.
(i) L_1 is a language over $B - A$.
(j) $L_1 \cup L_2$ is a language over A.
(k) $L_1 \cup L_2$ is a language over $A \cup B$.
(l) $L_1 \cup L_2$ is a language over $A \cap B$.
(m) $L_1 \cap L_2$ is a language over B.
(n) $L_1 \cap L_2$ is a language over $A \cup B$.
(o) $L_1 \cap L_2$ is a language over $A \cap B$.

Solution

From the given sets A and B, we have

$$A \cup B = \{a, b, c, d\}$$
$$A \cap B = \{b, c\}$$
$$A - B = \{a\}$$
$$B - A = \{d\}.$$

Hence we conclude the following

(a) True (b) False (c) True (d) True (e) True (f) False
(g) True (h) False (i) False (j) True (k) True (l) False
(m) True (n) True (o) True.

0.1.5 Boolean Logic

"Boolean logic" is a system built with two values TRUE and FALSE. "Boolean values" are represented by values 0 and 1. There are many Boolean operations.

(a) *Negation:* It means the NOT operation, represents by $\neg$.

Example: $\neg 0 = 1$ and $\neg 1 = 0$.

(b) *Conjunction:* It means the AND operation, represented by $\wedge$.

(c) *Disjunction:* It means the OR operation, represented by $\vee$

The truth tables of the above Boolean operations are shown as below:

A	B	$C = A \wedge B$
0	0	0
0	1	0
1	0	0
1	1	1

AND

A	B	$C = A \vee B$
0	0	0
0	1	1
1	0	1
1	1	1

OR

(d) *Exclusive-OR operation:* 1 if either but not both of its operands are 1. Exclusive-OR is denoted by $\oplus$.

A	B	$C = A \oplus B$
0	0	0
0	1	1
1	0	1
1	1	0

Exclusive-OR

(e) *Equality:* The equality operation, written with the symbol $\leftrightarrow$, is 1 if both its operands have the same value.

(f) *Implication:* This operation is designated by the symbol → and is 0 if its first operand is 1 and its second operand is 0; otherwise → is 1.

0.1.6 Fundamental Proof Techniques

(a) Principle of Mathematical Induction

Proof of induction is used to show that all elements of an infinite set have a specified property. The proof by induction has two parts, (i) Induction step (ii) Basis.

The induction step proves that for each $i \geq 1$, if $P(i)$ is true, then so is $P(i+1)$. The basis proves that $P(1)$ is true. When both these parts are proved, then for each i, $P(i)$ is proved.

Let us illustrate the method of writing a proof by induction.

Basis: To prove that $P(1)$ is true.

Induction Step: For each $i \geq 1$, assume that $P(i)$ is true and use this assumption to show that $P(i + 1)$ is true.

(b) Pigeon-hole Principle

If A and B are finite sets and $|A| > |B|$, then there is no one-to-one function from A to B. i.e., If an attempt is made to pair off the elements of A (the "pigeons") with elements of B (the "pigeonholes"), sooner or later we will have to put more than one pigeon in a pigeonhole.

By induction, the pigeonhole principle can be proved.

Example 0.1.36: A sack has 50 marbles of 4 different colours. Show that there are at least 13 marbles of the same colour.

Solution

Since we need to partition the set of 50 elements (marbles) into 4 sets (colours), according to the Pigeon-hole principle at least one of the sets (same colour) has $\lceil 50/4 \rceil = 13$ elements (marbles). That is to say that at least 13 marbles have the same colour.

Example 0.1.37: Show that $2^n > n^3$ for $n \geq 10$ by Mathematical Induction.

Proof: (i) Basis: For $n = 10, 2^{10} = 1024 > 10^3$

(ii) Inductive Step: Assume $2^k > k^3$

Now,

$$\begin{aligned} 2^{k+1} = 2\cdot 2^k &> \left(1+\frac{1}{10}\right)^3 \cdot 2^k \\ &\geq \left(1+\frac{1}{k}\right)^3 \cdot 2^k \\ &\geq \left(1+\frac{1}{k}\right)^3 \cdot k^3 \\ &\geq k^3 \frac{(k+1)^3}{k^3} \\ 2^{k+1} &\geq (k+1)^3. \end{aligned}$$

Hence $2^n > n^3$ for $n \geq 10$. □

Example 0.1.38: Prove that for every integer $n \geq 0$, the number $4^{2n+1} + 3^{n+2}$ is a multiple of 13.

Proof: We use induction on n, starting with $n = 0$.

$$P(0) = 4^{2(0)+1} + 3^{(0)+2} = 4 + 3^2 = 13(1) \quad (1)$$

Assume $\quad P(k) = 4^{2k+1} + 3^{k+2} = 13t$, for some integer t. (2)

We need to prove that

$$P(k+1): 4^{2(k+1)+1} + 3^{(k+1)+2} \text{ is a multiple of 13.}$$

Now,

$$\begin{aligned} 4^{2(k+1)+1} + 3^{(k+1)+2} &= 4^{(2k+1)+2} + 3^{(k+2)+1} \\ &= 4^2(4^{2k+1}) + 4^2(3^{k+2} - 3^{k+2}) + 3\cdot 3^{k+2} \\ &= 4^2(4^{2k+1} + 3^{k+2}) + 3^{k+2}(-4^2 + 3) \\ &= 16(13t) + 3^{k+2}(-13) \quad \text{[from (2)]} \\ &= 13[16t - 3^{k+2}] \end{aligned} \quad (3)$$

From (3) it follows that $P(k+1)$ is a multiple of 13. Hence we have, $4^{2n+1} + 3^{n+2}$ is a multiple of 13. □

Example 0.1.39: Show that for any integer $n \geq 0$, $(11)^{n+2} + (12)^{2n+1}$ is divisible by 133.

Proof: Basis: When $n = 0$, $11^2 + 12^1 = 133$ is divisible by 133.

Inductive Hypothesis: When $n = k$.

$$11^{k+2} + 12^{2k+1} = 133p$$

Inductive Step: When $n = k + 1$

$$\begin{aligned} 11^{k+3} + 12^{2k+3} &= 11 \cdot 11^{k+2} + 12^{2k+3} \\ &= 11(133p - 12^{2k+1}) + 12^{2k+3} \\ &= 133(11p) - 12^{2k+1}\ (11 - 12^2) \\ &= 133(11p + 12^{2k+1}) \end{aligned}$$

Hence it is true for $n \geq 0$. □

Example 0.1.40: It is known that for any positive integer $n \geq 2$,

$$\frac{1}{n+1} + \frac{1}{n+2} + \cdots \frac{1}{2n} - A > 0$$

where A is a constant. How large can A be?

Solution

Let the value of A be x.

$$n = 2, \frac{1}{3} + \frac{1}{4} - x > 0 \qquad \left(\text{Assume} \quad x < \frac{7}{12}\right)$$

Inductive Hypothesis:

$$\text{For } n = k, \frac{1}{k+1} + \frac{1}{k+2} + \cdots + \frac{1}{2k} - x > 0$$

Inductive Step:

$$\text{For } n = k+1, \frac{1}{k+2} + \frac{1}{k+3} + \cdots + \frac{1}{2(k+1)} - x$$

$$= \left[\frac{1}{k+1} + \frac{1}{k+2} + \cdots + \frac{1}{2k}\right] + \frac{1}{2k+1} + \frac{1}{2k+2} - \frac{1}{k+1} - x$$

$$\left(\text{Adding and substracting } \frac{1}{k+1}\right) \qquad (1)$$

$$= 0$$

But $$\left[\frac{1}{k+1} + \frac{1}{k+2} + \cdots \frac{1}{2k}\right] = x + p \quad (p \text{ - positive})$$

From (1), we have

$$\left[\frac{1}{k+2}+\frac{1}{k+3}+\cdots\frac{1}{2k+2}-x\right]=(x+p)+\frac{1}{2k+1}+\frac{1}{2k+2}-\frac{1}{k+1}-x$$

$$=p+\frac{1}{2k+1}-\frac{1}{2k+2}$$

$$=p+\frac{1}{(2k+1)(2k+2)}$$

Hence the value of x is increasing for increase in n.

$$\Rightarrow \text{Maximum value of } A<\frac{7}{12}.$$

Example 0.1.41: For the sequence of integers $\langle F_n\rangle_{n\geq 1}$ defined by $F_1 = 1$, $F_2 = 1$ and $F_n = F_{n-1} + F_{n-2}, n\geq 3$ prove by Mathematical Induction that

$$F_1=\frac{1}{\sqrt{5}}\left[\left(\frac{1+\sqrt{5}}{2}\right)^n-\left(\frac{1-\sqrt{5}}{2}\right)^n\right]$$

Proof: Basis: $n = 1$,

$$F_1=\frac{1}{\sqrt{5}}\left[\left(\frac{1+\sqrt{5}}{2}\right)-\left(\frac{1-\sqrt{5}}{2}\right)\right]$$

$$=\frac{1}{\sqrt{5}}\left[\frac{1}{2}+\frac{\sqrt{5}}{2}-\frac{1}{2}+\frac{\sqrt{5}}{2}\right]$$

$$=1$$

Inductive Hypothesis: $n = k$,

$$F_k=\frac{1}{\sqrt{5}}\left[\left(\frac{1+\sqrt{5}}{2}\right)^n-\left(\frac{1-\sqrt{5}}{2}\right)^k\right]$$

Inductive Step: $n = k + 1$,

$$F_{k+1}=F_k+F_{k-1}$$

$$=\frac{1}{\sqrt{5}}\left[\left(\frac{1+\sqrt{5}}{2}\right)^k-\left(\frac{1-\sqrt{5}}{2}\right)^k\right]+\frac{1}{\sqrt{5}}\left[\left(\frac{1+\sqrt{5}}{2}\right)^{k-1}-\left(\frac{1-\sqrt{5}}{2}\right)^{k-1}\right]_\square$$

Example 0.1.42: Show that any positive integer, $n \geq 2$ is either a prime or a product of primes.

Proof: Basis: $n = 2$ is a prime.

Inductive Hypothesis: For $n = k$, k is either a prime or a product of primes.

Inductive Step: For $n = k + 1$, if $k + 1$ is prime the given statement is true else,

$$k + 1 = pq, \quad p, q < k$$

$\Rightarrow$ k + 1 is a product of primes.

□

Example 0.1.43: Prove by Mathematical Induction, for $n \geq 1$,

$$\sum_{k=1}^{n} k^2 = \frac{n(n+1)(n+2)}{6}$$

Proof: Let $P(n) = 1^2 + 2^2 + \cdots n^2 = \dfrac{n(n+1)(2n+1)}{6}$

Basis: For $n = 1$, $P(1) = 1^2 = 1$ (on calculating LHS)

$$RHS = P(1) = \frac{1(1+1)(2+1)}{6} = \frac{(1)(2)(3)}{6} = 1$$

Therefore $P(1)$ is true.

Inductive Hypothesis:

$$P(K) = 1^2 + 2^2 + \cdots k^2 = \frac{k(k+1)(2k+1)}{6} \text{ is true.}$$

Inductive Step: We claim that

$$P(K+1) = 1^2 + 2^2 + \cdots + (k+1)^2 = \frac{(k+1)(k+2)(2k+3)}{6} \text{ is true.}$$

Now,

$$\begin{aligned} 1^1 + 2^2 + \cdots + k^2 + (k+1)^2 &= (1^1 + 2^2 + \cdots + k^2) + (k+1)^2 \\ &= \frac{k(k+1)(2k+1)}{6} + (k+1)^2 \\ &\qquad (\because P(k) \text{ is true}) \\ &= \frac{k(k+1)(2k+1) + 6(k+1)^2}{6} \\ &= \frac{(k+1)[2k^2 + 7k + 6]}{6} \end{aligned}$$

$$= \frac{(k+1)(k+2)(2k+3)}{6}$$

$\Rightarrow P(k+1)$ is true.

Thus we have, if $P(k)$ is true, $P(k+1)$ is also true. By principle of Mathematical Induction, we have

$$\sum_{k=1}^{n} k^2 = \frac{n(n+1)(2n+1)}{6}, \ n \geq 1$$ □

Example 0.1.44: Prove that $2^n > n$, for all $n \in N$, by using Mathematical Induction.

Proof: Let $P(n) = 2^n - n > 0$.

Basis: For $n = 1$, $P(1) = 2^1 - 1 = 2 - 1 = 1 > 0$.
Therefore $P(1)$ is true.

Inductive Hypothesis: Let us assume that $P(k)$ is true. Here we have k as a positive integer.

$$\Rightarrow 2^k - k \text{ is positive integer}$$

$$\Rightarrow 2^k - k = m \quad (1)$$

Inductive Step: To prove that $P(k + 1)$ is also positive. Let us consider $2^{k+1} - (k+1)$.

We have

$$\begin{aligned} 2^{k+1} - (k+1) &= 2(2)^k - k - 1 \\ &= 2(k+m) - k - 1 \\ &= k + 2m - 1 \\ &= \text{positive } (\because\ m \text{ is positive}) \end{aligned}$$

$\Rightarrow$ If $P(k)$ is true, $P(k + 1)$ is also true.

Hence by Mathematical Induction, $P(n)$ is true, i.e.,

$$2^n - n > 0 \Rightarrow 2^n > n, \forall\, n \in N$$ □

Example 0.1.45: A wheel of fortune has the numbers from 1 to 36 painted on it in at random. Prove that irrespective of how the numbers are situated, three consecutive numbers total 55 or more.

Solution

Let n_1 be any number on the wheel.

Counting clockwise from n_1, label the other numbers $n_2, n_3, \ldots\ldots, n_{36}$. For the result to be false, we should have

$$\begin{aligned} &n_1 + n_2 + n_3 < 55, \\ &n_2 + n_3 + n_4 < 55, \\ &\ldots\ldots\ldots \\ &\ldots\ldots\ldots \\ &n_{34} + n_{35} + n_{36} < 55, \\ &n_{35} + n_{36} + n_1 < 55, \\ &n_{36} + n_1 + n_2 < 55. \end{aligned}$$

In all the inequalities above, the terms n_1, n_2, n_3, ... appear exactly three times.

Therefore adding the 36 inequalities we get

$$3\sum_{j=1}^{36} n_j = 3\sum_{j=1}^{36} j < 36(35) = 1980.$$

But $$\sum_{j=1}^{36} j = (36)(37) = 666.$$

But this gives the contradiction that

$$1998 = 3\,(666) < 1980.$$

Example 0.1.46: Prove by induction,

$$1.3 + 2.4 + 3.5 + \cdots n\,(n+2) = \frac{n(n+1)(2n+1)}{6}$$

Proof:

Basis: $$1.3 = \frac{(1)(2)(9)}{6} = 3$$

This result is true for $n = 1$.

Inductive Hypothesis: Assume that the result is true for $n = k (\geq 1)$.

i.e.,

$$1.3 + 2.4 + 3.5 + \cdots k(k+2) = \frac{k(k+1)(2k+7)}{6}$$

Inductive Step: For $n = k + 1$,

$$\begin{aligned} &[1.3 + 2.4 + \cdots k(k+2)] + (k+1)(k+3) \\ &= \left[\frac{k(k+1)(2k+7)}{6}\right] + (k+1)(k+3) \end{aligned}$$

$$= \frac{(k+1)}{6}[k(2k+7)+6(k+3)]$$
$$= \frac{(k+1)(2k^2+13k+18)}{6}$$
$$= \frac{(k+1)(k+2)(2k+9)}{6}$$

Hence the result follows for all $n \in Z^+$, by the principle of Mathematical induction. □

Example 0.1.47: Prove by induction

$$\sum_{i=1}^{n} \frac{1}{i(i+1)} = \frac{n}{n+1}$$

Proof: Assume $S(n): \sum_{i=1}^{n} \frac{1}{i(i+1)} = \frac{n}{n+1}$.

For $n = 1$,

$$S(1) = \sum_{i=1}^{1} \frac{1}{i(i+1)} = \frac{1}{1(2)} = \frac{1}{1+1}$$
$$\Rightarrow S(1) \text{ is true.}$$

Assume $S(k): \sum_{i=1}^{k} \frac{1}{i(i+1)} = \frac{k}{k+1}$ is true.

Now consider $S(k+1)$.

$$\sum_{i=1}^{k+1} \frac{1}{i(i+1)} = \sum_{i=1}^{k} \frac{1}{i(i+1)} + \frac{1}{(k+1)(k+2)}$$
$$= \frac{k}{(k+1)} + \frac{1}{(k+1)(k+2)}$$
$$= \frac{[k(k+2)+1]}{(k+1)(k+2)}$$
$$= \frac{k+1}{k+2}$$

Therefore, $S(k) \Rightarrow S(k+1)$. Hence the result follows by Mathematical Induction.

Example 0.1.48: Prove by induction for $n \in z^+$,

$$n > 4 \Rightarrow n^2 < 2^n$$

Proof: For $n = 5$, $2^5 = 32 > 25 = 5^2$.

Assume the result for $n = k(\geq 5)$:

$$2^k > k^2.$$

For $k > 3$, we have

$$\begin{aligned} & k(k-2) > 1 \\ \Rightarrow\ & k^2 > 2k+1 \\ \Rightarrow\ & 2^k > k^2 \\ \Rightarrow\ & 2^k + 2^k > k^2 + k^2 \\ \Rightarrow\ & 2^{k+1} > k^2 + k^2 > k^2(2k+1) \\ \Rightarrow\ & 2^{k+1} > (k+1)^2 \end{aligned}$$

Hence the result is true for $n \geq 5$ by the principle of Mathematical Induction.

□

Example 0.1.49: Given $S(n)$ as the statement

$$\sum_{i=1}^{n} i = \frac{\left[n + \left(\frac{1}{2}\right)\right]^2}{2}$$

Prove that the truth of $S(k)$ implies the truth of $S(k+1)$ by Mathematical induction.

Proof: Assume $S(k)$. For $S(k+1)$, we have

$$\begin{aligned} \sum_{i=1}^{k+1} i &= \left(\left[k + \left(\frac{1}{2}\right)\right]^2 \Big/ 2\right) + (k+1) \\ &= \left[k^2 + k + \left(\frac{1}{4}\right) + 2k + 2\right] \Big/ 2 \\ &= \left[(k+1)^2 + (k+1) + \left(\frac{1}{4}\right)\right] \Big/ 2 \\ &= \left[(k+1) + \left(\frac{1}{2}\right)^2\right] \Big/ 2 \end{aligned}$$

Therefore $S(k) \Rightarrow s(k+1)$.

□

Example 0.1.50: Show that if we select 151 distinct computer engineering courses numbered between 1 and 300 inclusive, at least two are consecutively numbered (using Pigeonhole Principle).

Solution

Let the selected course numbers be

$$k_1, k_2, \ldots\ldots k_{151} \tag{1}$$

The 302 numbers consisting of (1) together with

$$k_1 + 1, k_2 + 1, \ldots\ldots k_{151} + 1 \tag{2}$$

range in value between 1 and 301. By Pigeonhole principle, at least two of those values coincide. The numbers (1) are all distinct and so the numbers (2) are also distinct.

It must be then that one of (1) and one of (2) are equal. Therefore we have

$$k_i = k_j + 1$$

and course k_i follows course k_j.

Example 0.1.51: Suppose there are 50 marbles of four different colours in a sack, if exactly 8 marbles are red, show that there are at least 14 of the same colour.

Solution

If we know that 8 of the marbles are red, then no other marbles could be red, and we need to partition the rest (50 – 8) = 42 marbles into the rest (4 – 1) = 3 colours.

According to the Pigeon-hole principle, there are at least $\lceil 42/3 \rceil = 14$ marbles, which must have the same colour.

0.1.7 Introduction to Grammar

Grammar is a mechanism to describe the languages.

A grammar (G) is defined as a quadruple

$$G = (V, T, S, P)$$

where

V	=	Finite set of objects called VARIABLES
T	=	Finite set of objects called TERMINAL SYMBOLS
$S \in V$	=	Start variables
P	=	Finite set of Productions.

A production rule P is of the form

$$x \rightarrow y$$

Given a string w, of the form $w = uxv$, we can use the production rule $x \rightarrow y$ and obtain a new string $z = uyv$.

The set of all strings obtained by using Production rules is the "Language" generated by the Grammar.

If the grammar $G = (V, T, S, P)$ then

$$L(G) = \{w \in T^* : S \overset{*}{\Rightarrow} w\}$$

If $W \in L(G)$, then the sequence

$$S \Rightarrow w_1 \Rightarrow w_2 \Rightarrow w_3 \;\ldots\ldots\; \Rightarrow w_n \Rightarrow w$$

is a "derivation" of the sentence w.

The string $S, w_1, w_2, \ldots\ldots\; w_n,$ which contain variables as well as terminals, are called "SENTENTIAL FORMS" of the derivation.

Example 0.1.52: Given a Grammar $G = (\{S\}, \{a, b\}, S, P)$

with P defined as

$$S \to aSb,$$
$$S \to \lambda$$

(i) Obtain a sentence in language generated by G and the sentential form
(ii) Obtain the language $L(G)$.

Solution

$$S \Rightarrow aSb$$
$$\Rightarrow aaSbb$$
$$\Rightarrow aabb$$

Therefore we have $S \overset{*}{\Rightarrow} aabb$.

(i) Sentence in the language generated by $G = aabb$.
Sentential form $= aaSbb$.
(ii) The rule $S \to aSb$ is recursive.

All sentential forms will have the forms

$$w_i = a^i S\, b^i$$

Applying the production rule $S \to aSb$, we get

$$a^i S\, b^i \Rightarrow a^{i+1} S\, b^{i+1}$$

This is true for all i.

In order to get a sentence we apply $S \to \lambda$.

Therefore we get

$$S \overset{*}{\Rightarrow} a^n S\, b^n \Rightarrow a^n b^n$$

Therefore $$L(G) = \{a^n b^n;\ n \geq 0\}.$$

Example 0.1.53: Obtain a Grammar which generates the language
$$L = \{a^n b^{n+1} : n \geq 0\}$$

Solution

With $L = \{a^n b^n : n \geq 0\}$, the grammar

$$G = (\{S\}, \{a, b\}, S, P)$$

with production rules $S \to aSb, S \to \lambda$.

Therefore $L = \{a^n b^{n+1} : n \geq 0\}$ is obtained by generating an extra b.

This is done with a production rule

$$S \to Ab.$$

Hence the grammar G is given by

$G = (\{S, A\} \{a, b\}, S, P)$ with production rules given by

$$S \to Ab,$$
$$A \to aAb$$
$$A \to \lambda$$

Example 0.1.54: Obtain the language L produced by G with production rules

$$S \to SS,$$
$$S \to \lambda$$
$$S \to aSb$$
$$S \to bSa$$

Solution

It is known from the given production rules that G has equal number of a's and b's.

If w starts with an 'a' and ends with a 'b', then $w \in L$ has the form

$$w = a\, w_1\, b$$

where $w_1 \in L$.

If w starts with a 'b' and ends with an 'a' then $w \in L$ has the form

$$w = b\, w_1\, a$$

where $w_1 \in L$.

As a string in L can begin and end with the same symbol, the string shoud be of the form

$$w = w_1\ w_2$$

where w_1 and w_2 are in L, produced by $S \to SS$.

This generates the language

$$L = \{w : n_a\ (w) = n_b\ (w)\}$$

where $n_a(w)$ and $n_b(w)$ denotes the number of a's and number of b's in the string w, respectively.

Example 0.1.55: Given $G_1 = (\{A, S\}, \{a, b\}, S, P_1)$ with P_1 defined by the production rules

$$S \to aAb \mid \lambda$$
$$A \to aAb \mid \lambda$$

show that $L(G_1) = \{a^n b^n : n \geq 0\}$.

Also show that G_1 is equivalent to G where $G = (\{S\}, \{a, b\}, S, P)$ where P is given by

$$S \to aSb$$
$$S \to \lambda.$$

Solution

Given P_1 as

$$S \to aAb$$
$$S \to \lambda$$
$$S \to aAb$$
$$A \to \lambda.$$

$S \to \lambda$ produces a string with zero length. $(n = 0)$

$S \Rightarrow aAb$	$S \Rightarrow aAb$
$\Rightarrow a\lambda b$	$\Rightarrow aaAbb$
$\Rightarrow ab$	$\Rightarrow aabb$
	$\Rightarrow a^2b^2$ and so on

Therefore $L(G_1) = \{a^n\ b^n : n \geq 0\}$.

Given $G = (\{S\}, \{a, b\}, S, P)$ where P is $S \to aSb$, $S \to \lambda$.

The rule $S \to aSb$ is recursive.

All sentential forms will have the forms

$$w_i = a^i S\ b^i$$

Applying the production rule $S \to aSb$, we get

$$a^i S b^i \Rightarrow a^{i+1} S b^{i+1}$$

This is true for all i.

In order to get a sentence we apply $S \to \lambda$.

Therefore we get

$$S \overset{*}{\Rightarrow} a^n S b^n \Rightarrow a^n b^n$$

Hence $$L(G) = \{a^n b^n : n \geq 0\}$$

Hence G_1 is equivalent to G as both the grammars are given by $\{a^n b^n : n \geq 0\}$.

Example 0.1.56: Given a grammar G defined by the production rules

$$\begin{aligned} S &\to AB \\ A &\to Aa \\ B &\to Bb \\ A &\to a \\ B &\to b. \end{aligned}$$

Show that the word $$w = a^2 b^4 \in L(G),$$

where L is a language determined by G.

Solution

$$\begin{aligned} S &\Rightarrow AB \\ &\Rightarrow AaB \\ &\Rightarrow aaB \\ &\Rightarrow aaBb \\ &\Rightarrow aaBbb \\ &\Rightarrow aaBbbb \\ &\Rightarrow aabbbb \\ &\Rightarrow a^2 b^4 \end{aligned}$$

Hence the word $w = a^2 b^4 \in L(G)$.

Example 0.1.57: Find grammars for $\Sigma = \{a, b\}$ that generate the sets of

(a) all strings with exactly one 'a'
(b) all strings with at least one 'a'
(c) all strings with no more than three a's.

Solution

(a) Given $\Sigma = \{a, b\}$
We are able to write the grammar G which produces all strings with exactly one 'a' whose production rules are

$$A \to aSb$$
$$S \to Sb$$
$$S \to \in$$

(b) For all strings with at least one 'a': Production rules of Grammar C are

$$A \to aSb$$
$$S \to bSa$$
$$S \to \in$$

(c) For all strings with no more than three a's

$$L = \left\{ a^n b^m \middle| n \le 3, m \ge 0 \right\}$$

with production rules

$$A \to aSb$$
$$S \to aBb$$
$$B \to aCb$$
$$C \to bC$$
$$C \to b \mid \in$$

Example 0.1.58: Give a simple description of the language generated by the grammar with productions

$$(a)\ S \to aA,\quad A \to bS,\quad S \to \lambda \qquad (b)\ S \to Aa,\quad A \to B,\quad B \to Aa.$$

Soution

(a) For the given production rules

$$S \to aA$$
$$A \to bS$$
$$S \to \lambda$$

we have the language L given by

$$L = \left\{ a^n b^n \,\middle|\, n \ge 1 \right\}$$

(b) For the given production rules

$$S \to Aa$$

$$A \rightarrow B$$
$$B \rightarrow Aa$$

There is no language L produced as there is no proper termination.

GLOSSARY

Set: Collection of objects

Singleton: Set having only one element.

Empty set: Set with no element

Complement: Set containing everything not contained in the base set.

Cardinality: Number of elements in a set.

Powerset: Set having 'n' elements have a powerset having 2^n elements.

Relation: A relation on two sets is a set of ordered pair.

Poset: Partially ordered set.

Mapping: A function is otherwise called Mapping.

Injection (one-to-one function): Function is one-to-one if different elements in domain of one set have distinct images in the range.

Surjection (onto function): A function is onto function if each element of a set is the image of some element of the other set.

Bijection (one-to-one onto function): Function that is both one-to-one and onto

Invertible function: Function is invertible if and only if it is both one-to-one and onto.

Degree of vertex: Number of edges having that vertex as an end point.

Loop: Graph having an edge from a vertex to itself.

Isolated vertex: Vertex with zero as degree.

Directed graph: Graph having arrows instead of lines.

Outdegree: Number of arrows pointing from a particular node.

Indegree: Number of arrows pointing to a particular node.

Alphabet: Finite set of symbols.

String: Finite sequence of symbols from an alphabet.

Lexicographic ordering: Dictionary ordering, except that shorter strings precede longer strings.

Language: Any set of strings over an alphabet.

Kleene star: Set of all strings obtained by concatenating zero or more strings from a language.

Boolean logic: System built with two values True and False.

Negation: Means NOT operation

Conjunction: Means AND operation

Disjunction: Means OR operation.

Exclusive-OR: 1 if either but not both of its operands are 1.
Mathematical Induction: Has two parts (a) Induction step (b) Basis.
Pigen-hole principle: If an attempt is made to pair off the elements of A ("the pigeons") with elements of B (the "pigeon holes"), sooner or later we will have to put more than one pigeon in a pigeon hole.

REVIEW QUESTIONS

1. Define the following terms:
   (a) Set (b) Union (c) Intersection
2. Define the following terms:
   (a) set difference (b) Complement
   Explain with examples.
3. What have you understood by the following:
   (a) Idempotency
   (b) Commutativity
   (c) Associativity in respect of sets.
4. Define the following w.r.t. sets:
   (a) Distributivity (b) Absorption (c) DeMorgan's laws
5. Stand prove DeMorgan's Laws.
6. Define the following terms w.r.t. sets:
   (a) Disjoint sets
   (b) Cardinality
   (c) Powerset
   (d) Cartesian product.
7. Define a relation. Explain with an example.
8. What is an equivalence relation? Give an example.
9. Explain the terms:
   (a) Partial ordered set/Poset (b) Partition of a relation
10. What do you mean by equivalence class?
11. Define function as a relation.
12. What are the kinds of functions?
13. Explain the following with an example for each:
    (a) one-to-one function
    (b) onto function
    (c) one-to-one onto function
    (d) invertible function.
14. Differentiate between Injection, Surjection and bijection with examples.
15. Define a graph with an example.

16. Define the following terms:
    (a) Degree of a vertex
    (b) Loop
    (c) Isolated vertex
    (d) Adjacent vertices.
17. Define the following terms w.r.t a graph
    (a) path (b) circuit (c) simple path
18. Define the following terms w.r.t. of graph
    (a) Connected graph
    (b) Components of a graph
    (c) Walk of a graph
    (d) Directed graph.
19. Define the following terms w.r.t. a graph
    (a) out degree (b) in degree
20. How will you define the following:
    (a) string (b) alphabet in languages.
21. How do you define the length of a string?
22. Define the following in respect of languages.
    (a) Empty string
    (b) Reverse string
    (c) Substring
    (d) Concatenation
22. What do you mean by lexicographic ordering of strings?
23. What do you mean by prefix and suffix of a string?
24. Define a language with an example.
25. Define concatenation of strings with an example.
26. Define "kleene star", with an example.
27. What are the kinds of fundamental proof techniques?
28. Explain the following with an example (in Boolean logic)
    (a) Negation
    (b) Conjunction
    (c) Disjunction
    (d) Exclusive-OR
    (e) Equality
    (f) Implication
29. State and explain the principle of Mathematical Induction with an example.
30. State and explain Pigeon-hole principle with an example.
31. What do you mean by Grammar?
32. What are the types of Grammars?

EXERCISES

1. Determine whether each of the following pairs of sets is equal
   (a) $\phi, \{\phi\}$
   (b) $\{\{2\}, \{2, \{2\}\}\}$
   (c) $\{1, 3, 3, 5, 5, 5\}, \{5, 3, 1\}$
2. For each of the following sets, determine whether 5 is an element of that set.
   (a) $\{x \in R \mid x \text{ is an integer greather than } 1\}$
   (b) $\{x \in R \mid x \text{ is the square of an integer}\}$
   (c) $\{5, \{5\}\}$
3. Determine whether each of the following statements is True or False.
   (a) $x \in \{x\}$ (b) $\phi \subseteq \{x\}$ (c) $\phi \in \{x\}$
4. If A, B and C are sets such that $A \subseteq B$ and $B \subseteq C$, show that $A \subseteq C$.
5. Find the Cardinality of each of the following sets.
   (a) $\{1\}$ (b) $\{\{1\}\}$ (c) $\{1, \{1\}\}$ (d) $\{1, \{1\}, \{1, \{1\}\}\}$
6. Determine the powerset of the following sets.
   (a) $\{a\}$ (b) $\{a, b\}$ (c) $\{\phi, \{\phi\}\}$
7. Determine the number of elements in each of the following sets.
   (a) $P(P(\phi))$ (b) $P(\{\phi, a, \{a\}, \{\{a\}\}\})$
8. Given $A = \{a, b, c, d\}$ and $B = \{y, z\}$, find {a} $A \times B$ (b) $B \times A$.
9. Find out the cartesian product $A \times B \times C$, where A is the set of all airlines and B and C are both the set of all cities in Australia.
10. If A is a set, show that $\phi \times A = A \times \phi = A$.
11. Determine how many elements will $A \times B$ have if A has in elements and B has n elements.
12. Show that the ordered pair (a, b) can be defined in terms of sets as $\{\{a\}, \{a, b\}\}$, (Hint: First show that $\{\{a\}, \{a, b\} = \{c\}, \{c, d\}\}$ if and only if $a = c$ and $b = d$).
13. Let $A = \{1, 2, 3, 4, 5\}$ and $B = \{0, 3, 6\}$. Find (a) $A \cup B$ (b) $A \cap B$ (c) $A - B$ (d) $B - A$.
14. Show that $\overline{\overline{A}} = A$, for a given set A.
15. Show that (a) $A \cup B = B \cup A$ (b) $A \cap B = B \cap A$.
16. Show that if A and B are sets, $A - B = A \cap \overline{B}$.
17. Show that if A and B are sets, then $(A \cap B) \cup (A \cap \overline{B}) = A$.
18. What can you say about the sets A and B if the following are true?
    (a) $A \cup B = A$
    (b) $A \cap B = A$
    (c) $A - B = A$
    (d) $A \cap B = B \cap A$

(e) $A - B = B - A$.

19. Let $A_i = \{1, 2, 3, \ldots\ldots i\}$ for $i = 1, 2, 3, \ldots\ldots$. Find (a) $\bigcup_{i=1}^{n} A_i$, (b) $\bigcap_{i=1}^{n} A_i$

20. Using Membership table show that

$$A \cap (B \cup C) = (A \cap B) \cup (A \cap C).$$

21. Using Venn diagram show that

$$A \cup (B \cap C) = (A \cup B) \cap (A \cup C)$$

22. Using set builder notation and logical equivalences show that

$$\overline{A \cap B} = \overline{A} \cup \overline{B}$$

23. State and prove De Morgan's laws.
24. Prove by (a) Venn Diagram (b) Membership table:
(i) Commutative law (ii) Distoibutive law.
25. Given $A = \{\in, a\}$, $B = \{ab\}$, find A^2, B^3 and AB.
26. Given $A = \{\in, a\}$, $B = \{ab\}$ determine A^*, B^* and B^+
27. Given A and B are subsets of Σ^* and $\in \notin A$, show that the equation $X = AX \cup B$ has a unique solution $X = A^*B$.
28. Define Σ^+ in terms of Σ^*.
29. Given $L_1 = \{ab, bc, ca\}$, $L_2 = \{aa, ac, cb\}$ determine
(a) $L_1 \cup L_2$ (b) $L_1 \cap L_2$ (c) $L_1 \cdot L_2$ (d) $L_1 L_2$.
30. What do you mean by the Kleene closure of set A?
31. What do you mean by $\in$-free closure of set A?
32. Given $A = \{a, aa\}$, $B = \{a\}$, $C = \{aa\}$ show that

$$A(B \cap C) \subset AB \cap AC.$$

33. A survey was conducted among 1000 people. Of these 595 are democrats. 595 wear glasses and 550 like icecream. 395 of them are democrats who wear glasses, 350 of them are democrats who like icecream and 400 of them wear glasses and like icecreams; 250 of them are democrats who wear glasses and like icecream.
    (a) How many of them are not Democrats, who do not wear glasses, and do not like icecreams?
    (b) How many of them are Democrats, who do not wear glasses and do not like icecreams?
34. It is known that at the "Catherine Assumption University", 60 percent of them play bridge, 70 percent jog, 20 percent play tennis and bridge, 30 percent play Tennis and jog, and 40 percent play bridge and jog. If someone claimed that 20 percent of the Professors jog and play bridge and Tennis, would you believe in this claim? Why?

35. Prove:
    (a) $A \cup (A \cap B) = A$
    (b) $A \cap (A \cup B) = A$
    (c) $A - B = A \cap \overline{B}$
    (d) $A \cup (\overline{A} \cap B) = A \cup B$
    (e) $A \cap (\overline{A} \cup B) = A \cap B$.
36. Check if the following are functions defined in R to R:
    (a) $f(x) = \frac{1}{x}$
    (b) $f(x) = \sqrt{x}$
    (c) $f(x) = \pm\sqrt{x^2 + 1}$
37. Determine the domain and range of the following functions.
    (a) The function that assigns to each positive integer the largest perfect square not exceeding this integer
    (b) The function that assigns to each bit string twice the number of zeros in that string.
38. Which of the following functions are onto from the set $\{a, b, c, d\}$.
    (a) $f(a) = b, f(b) = a, f(c) = c, f(d) = d$
    (b) $f(a) = d,\ f(b) = b,\ f(c) = c,\ f(d) = d$
39. Determine which of the following functions from Z to Z is one-to-one
    (a) $f(n) = n - 1$
    (b) $f(n) = n^2 + 1$
    (c) $f(n) = n^3$
    (d) $f(n) = \lceil n/2 \rceil$
40. Determine which of the following functions is a bijection from R to R.
    (a) $f(x) = 3x + 1$
    (b) $f(x) = 2x^2 + 1$
    (c) $f(x) = 3x^3$
    (d) $f(x) = (x^2 + 1)/(x^2 + 4)$
42. If g is a function from A to B and f is a function from B to C.
    (a) Show that if both f and g one onto functions, then $f \circ g$ is also onto.
    (b) Show that if both f and g are one-to-one functions, then $f \circ g$ is also one-to-one.
43. If f and $f \circ g$ are one-to-one, does it follow that g is one-to-one? Justify your answer.
44. Find $f \circ g$ and g of where $f(x) = 2x^2 + 1$ and $g(x) = x + 5$ are functions from R to R.

45. Show that the mapping $f : X \to X$ when $X = \{x \in R,\ x \neq 0\}$ defined by $f(x) = \frac{1}{x}$ is one-to-one and onto.
46. State which of the following are injections, surjections or bijections from R to R, where R is the set of all real numbers.
    (a) $f(x) = -2x$
    (b) $f(x) = x^2 - 1$
47. Given $X = \{1, 2, 3, 4\}$ and a function $f : X \to X$ given by $f = \{(1,2), (2,3), (3,4), (4,1)\}$. Find the composite function f^4.
48. Given $f : R \to R$ and $g : R \to R$, where R is the set of real numbers, where $f(x) = x^2 - 2$ and $g(x) = x + 4$. Determine $f \circ g$ and $g \circ f$. State whether these functions are injective, surjective and bijective.
49. Given R is the relation on the set N of all natural numbers given by the expression $x + 3y = 12$.
    (a) Express R as a set of ordered pairs
    (b) Determine the domain and range of R.
50. Given R as the relation from $A = \{2, 3, 4, 5\}$ to $B = \{3, 6, 7, 10\}$, which is defined by the expression "x divides y".
    (a) Express R as a set of ordered pairs.
    (b) Determine the domain and range.
51. For each of the following relations on the set $\{1, 2, 3, 4\}$, determine whether it is reflexive, or symmetric or antisymmetric or it is transitive.
    (a) $\{(2,2), (2,3), (2,4), (3,2), (3,3), (3,4)\}$
    (b) $\{(1,1), (1,2), (2,1), (2,2), (3,3), (4,4)\}$
    (c) $\{(2,4), (4,2)\}$
    (d) $\{(1,2), (2,3), (3,4)\}$
52. How many relations are there on a set with 'n' elements that are
    (a) symmetric
    (b) antisymmetric
    (c) asymmetric
    (d) irreflexive
    (e) reflexive & symmetric
    (f) neither reflexive nor irreflexive
53. Show that the relation R on a set A is symmetric if and only if $R = R^{-1}$ where R^{-1} is the inverse relation.
54. Assume that the relation R is irreflexive. Is R^2 necessarily irreflexive? Give reasons.
55. Given R is a reflexive relation on a set A, show that R^n is reflexive for all positive integers n.

56. Given R is a relation $R = \{(a, b) \mid a \text{ divides } b\}$ on the set of positive integers. Determine
(a) R^{-1} (b) $\overline{R}$
57. Determine whether the relation R on the set of all integers is reflexive, symmetric, antisymmetric, and/or transitive, where $(x, y) \in R$ if and only if
(a) $xy \geq 1$ (b) $x \equiv y(\text{mod } b)$ (c) $x = y^2$
58. Determine the language of grammar G given by $V = \{S, A, a, b\}$, $T = \{a, b\}$ and production $P = \{S \to aA, S \to b, A \to aa\}$.
59. Determine the grammar that generates the set $\{0^n1^n \mid n = 0, 1, 2, \ldots\ldots\}$.
60. Determine at least two grammars that generate the set $\{0^m1^n \mid m \text{ and } n$ are nonnegative integers$\}$.
61. Determine the grammar that generates the set $\{0^n1^n2^n \mid n = 0, 1, 2, \ldots\ldots\}$
62. Determine the grammar for each of the following languages.
(a) set of all bit strings containing an even number of 0^s and no 1^s.
(b) set of all strings containing more 0^s than 1^s.
(c) set of all strings containing an equal number of 0^s and 1^s.
(d) set of all strings containing an unequal number of 0^s and 1^s.
63. Determine the grammars for the following languages on $\Sigma = \{a\}$.
(a) $L = \{w : |w| \bmod 3 = 0\}$
(b) $L = \{w : |w| \bmod 3 \geq |w| \bmod 2\}$
64. Assuming $\Sigma = \{a, b\}$ with $n_a(w)$ and $n_b(w)$ as the number of a's and b's respectively in string w, find grammars for
(a) $L = \{w : n_a(w) = 2n_b(w)\}$
(b) $L = \{w : n_a(w) > n_b(w)\}$
65. Are the two grammars with respective productions

$$S \to aSb \mid ab \mid \lambda$$

and

$$S \to aAb \mid ab$$
$$A \to aAb \mid \lambda$$

equivalent?
66. Are there languages for which $\overline{L^*} = \overline{L}^*$?
67. Prove that $(L_1L_2)^R = L_2^R L_1^R$ for all languages L_1 and L_2.
68. Show that any $2^n \times 2^n$ chessboard with one square removed can be tiled

using *L*-shaped pieces, where these pieces cover three squares at a time as shown in fig. (*n*-positive integer).

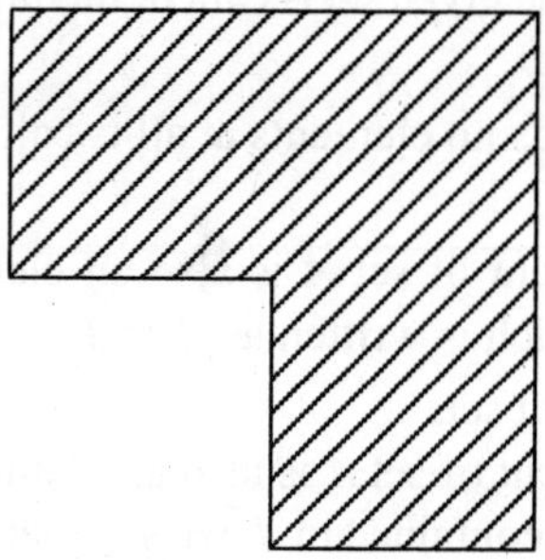

69. Using Mathematical Induction prove that $3 + 3.5 + 3.5^2 + \cdots + 3.5^n = 3(5^{n+1} - 1)/4$, where n is a nonnegative integer.
70. Using Mathematical induction prove that $n! < n^n$, where $n > 1$.
71. Show that $1^2 - 2^2 + 3^2 - \cdots + (-1)^{n-1}n^2 = (-1)^{n-1}n(n+1)/2$ where $n > 0$.
72. Determine which amounts of postage can be formed using 5-cent and 6-cent postage stamps. Prove your solution using mathematical induction.
73. Show that n lines separate the plane into $(n^2 + n + 2) / 2$ regions if no two of these lines are parallel and no three pass through a common point.
74. A computer network has 6 computers. Each computer is directly connected to at least one of the other computers. Show that there are at least 2 computers in the network that are directly connected to the same number of other computers (using Pigeonhole principle).
75. Show that in a group of 5 people where any two people are either friends/enemies, there are not necessarily three mutual friends or three mutual enemies, using Pigeon-hole principle.
76. Use induction to prove that any integer composed of 3^n identical digits is divisible by 3^n.

SHORT QUESTIONS AND ANSWERS

1. Define a set.

   A set is a collection of objects.
2. Define "elements" of a set.

   The objects comprising a set are called its elements or members.
3. Define a singleton.

   A set having only one element is called a Singleton.
4. Define an empty set.

   A set with no element at all is called the empty set.

5. What do you mean by 'membership criterion' of a set?

   The criterion for determining for any given thing, whether it is or is not a member of the given set is called 'membership criterion' of the set.

6. What is a null set?

   A set which has no elements at all is called Null set.

7. Define a subset.

   If every element of set A is also an element of set B, then A is a "subset" of B, which is written as $A \subseteq B$.

8. Define a proper subset.

   If every element of set A is also an element of set B, but B also has some element not contained in A, we say that A is a "proper subset" of B, and write $A \subset B$.

9. What is a Null set?

   A set having no element is called a Null set.

10. Define Union of two sets.

    The Union of two sets is the set that has objects that are elements of at least one of the two given sets, and possibly both.
    Union of two sets A and B is given by

$$A \cup B = \{x : x \in A \text{ or } x \in B\}$$

11. Define intersection of sets.

    The intersection of sets A and B, written $A \cap B$, is a set that contains exactly those elements that are in both A and B.

$$A \cap B = \{x : x \in A \text{ or } x \in B\}$$

12. Define set difference.

    The set difference of set A and set B, written as $A - B$, is the set that contains everything that is in A but not in B.

$$A - B = \{x : x \in A \text{ and } x \notin B\}$$

13. Define Complement of a set.

    The Complement of a set A, written as $\bar{A}$, is the set containing everything that is not in A.

14. Define the set operations

    (a) Idempotency (b) Commutativity

    (a) Idempotency: $A \cup A = A$

    $A \cap A = A$.

    (b) Commutativity: $A \cup B = B \cup A$

    $A \cap B = B \cap A$.

15. Define the set operations

    (a) Associativity (b) Distributivity

(a) Associativity: $(A \cup B) \cup C = A \cup (B \cup C)$
$(A \cap B) \cap C = A \cap (B \cap C)$

(b) Distributivity: $(A \cup B) \cap C = (A \cap C) \cup (B \cap C)$
$(A \cap B) \cup C = (A \cup C) \cap (B \cup C)$

16. Define the set operation viz., Absorption.
$(A \cup B) \cap A = A$
$(A \cap B) \cup A = A$

17. State DeMorgan's Laws.
$A - (B \cup C) = (A - B) \cap (A - C)$
$A - (B \cap C) = (A - B) \cup (A - C)$

18. What are disjoint sets?
If A and B have no common elements i.e., $A \cap B = \phi$, then the sets A and B are said to be disjoint.

19. Define cardinality of a set.
The Cardinality of a set A, written $|A|$, is the number of elements in set A.

20. Define powerset.
The set of all subsets of A, written 2^A, is called The power set of set A.

21. If a set has 'n' elements, how many elements does the powerset have?
The Powerset has 2^n elements.

22. Define Cartesian Product.
The set of all ordered pairs (x, y) where $x \in A$ and $y \in B$ is called Cartesian product of the sets A and B, denoted by $A \times B$, i.e.,

$$A \times B = \{(x, y) : x \in A \text{ and } y \in B\}$$

23. Define a relation.
A relation on sets S and T is a set of ordered pairs (s, t), whose
(a) $s \in S$ (s is a member of S)
(b) $t \in T$
(c) S and T need not be different
(d) The set of all first elements is the "domain" of the relation, and
(e) The set of all the second elements is the "range" of the relation.

24. What is an equivalence relation?
A subset R of $A \times A$ is called an equivalence relation on A if R satisfies the following conditions:
(i) $(a, a) \in R$ for all $a \in A$ (R is reflexive)
(ii) If $(a, b) \in R$, then $(b, a) \in R$, then $(a, b) \in R$
(R is symmetric)
(iii) If $(a, b) \in R$ and $(b, c) \in R$, then $(a, c) \in R$ (R is transitive)

25. What do you mean by a partial ordering relation?

A relation R on a set S is called a "partial ordering" or a "partial order" if R is reflexive, antisymmetric and transitive.

26. What do you mean by a Poset?

A set S together with a partial ordering R is called a "Partially ordered set" or "Poset".

27. What do you mean by Partition?

A Partition P of S is a collection $\{A_i\}$ of nonempty subsets of S with the properties:

(i) Each $a \in S$ belongs to some A_i,

(ii) If $A_i \neq A_j$, then $A_i \cap A_j = \varnothing$.

28. What is a function?

Suppose every element of S occurs exactly once as the first element of an ordered pair. In fig. shown, every element of S has exactly one arrow arising from it. This kind of relation is called a "function".

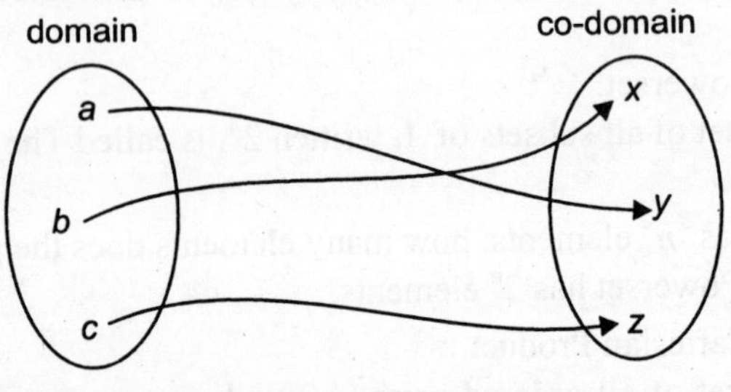

A function maps an element in its domain to an element in its co-domain.

29. What do you mean by injection?

A one-to-one function is called an Injection. A function $f : A \rightarrow B$ is said to be one-to-one if different elements in the domain A has distinct images in the range.

A function of is one-to-one if $f(a) = f(a')$ implies $a = a'$.

30. Define Surjection.

An onto function is called a Surjection.

A function $f : A \rightarrow B$ is said to be an onto function if each element of B is the image of some element of A.

31. What do you mean by bijection?

A one-to-one onto function is called a bijection. A function that maps each and every element of A to exactly one element of B, with no elements left over is a one-to-one onto function.

32. What is an invertible function?

A function $f : A \rightarrow B$ is invertible if its inverse relation f^{-1} is a function from B to A.

A function $f: A \to B$ is invertible if and only if it is both one-to-one and onto.

33. Define a Graph.

A graph a consists of a finite set V of object called "Vertices", a finite set E of objects called "Edges" and a function γ that assigns to each edge a subset $\{v, w\}$, where v and w are vertices. Here we have $G = (V, E, \gamma)$.

34. Define degree of a vertex.

Degree of a vertex is defined as the number of edges having that vertex as an end point.

35. What is an isolated vertex?

A vertex with zero as degree is called an Isolated vertex.

36. What is a circuit?

A circuit is a path that begins and ends at the same vertex.

37. What is a connected graph?

A graph is called "connected" if there is a path from any vertex to any other vertex in the graph.

38. When is a graph said to be a tree?

A graph is said to be a tree if it is connected and has no simple cycles.

39. When is a path called a cycle?

A path is a cycle if it starts and ends in the same node.

40. What is a directed graph?

A graph is said to be directed if it has arrows in stead of lines.

41. Define outdegree of a node.

The number of arrows pointing from a particular node is the outdegree of that node.

42. Define Indegree of a node.

The number of arrows pointing to a particle node is the indegree.

43. Define Alphabet with an example.

Alphabet is defined as a finite set of symbols

Example: Roman Alphabet $\{a, b, ... z\}$

44. Define a string.

A string over an alphabet is a finite sequence of symbols from that alphabet, which is usually written next to one another and not separated by commas.

45. Give examples for strings.

(a) If $\Sigma_a = \{0,1\}$ then 001001 is a string over Σ_a

(b) If $\Sigma_b = \{a, b, \ldots\ldots z\}$ then *axyrpqstcd* is a string over Σ_b.

46. Define length of a string.

The length of a string is its length as a sequence. The length of a string w is written as $|w|$.

Example: $|10011| = 5$.

47. Define an Empty string.
    The string of zero length is called the empty string, denoted by $\in$.
48. Define prefix and suffix of a string.
    Prefix: If $w = vy$ for some y, then v is a prefix of w.
    Suffix: If $w = xv$ for some x, then v is a suffix of w.
49. What do you mean by Lexicographics ordering?
    The Lexicographic ordering of strings is the same as dictionary ordering, except that shorter strings precede longer strings.
    The Lexicograhic ordering of all strings over the alphabet $\{0,1\}$ is $(\in, 0, 1, 00, 01, 10, 11, 000, \ldots\}$
50. What is a Language?
    Any set of strings over an alphabet Σ is called a Language.
51. Define Σ^*.
    The set of all strings, including the empty string over an alphabet Σ is denoted by Σ^*.
52. Define concatenation of languages L_1 and L_2.
    $L = L_1 \cdot L_2 = \{w \in \Sigma^*;\ w = x \cdot y \text{ for some } x \in L_1 \text{ and } y \in L_2\}$
53. Define Kleene star.
    Kleene star of a language L is denoted by L^* which is the set of all strings obtained by concatenating zero or more strings from L.
    $L^* = \{w \in \Sigma^* : w = w_1 \ldots w_k \text{ for some } k \geq 0 \text{ and some } w_1', w_2, \ldots w_k \in L\}$
54. What is Boolean logic?
    It is a system built with two values — True and False., represented by 1 and 0.
55. What do you mean by Negation?
    It meańs NOT operation, represented by $\neg$.
    Example: $\neg 0 = 1$ and $\neg 1 = 0$.
56. What do you mean by conjunction?
    It means the AND operation, represented by $\wedge$.
57. What do you mean by Disjunction?
    It means the OR operation, represented by $\vee$.
58. Sketch the truth table for Conjunction & Disjunction

A	B	$C = A \wedge B$
0	0	0
0	1	0
1	0	0
1	1	1

Conjunction

A	B	$C = A \vee B$
0	0	0
0	1	1
1	0	1
1	1	1

Disconjunction

59. Sketch the Ex-OR truth table.

A	B	$C = A \oplus B$
0	0	0
0	1	1
1	0	1
1	1	0

Conjunction

60. What is the principle of Mathematical Induction?

There are two parts to the method of proof by induction (used to show that all elements of an infinite set have a specified property): (i) Induction step (ii) Basis.

The Induction step proves that for each $i \geq 1$, if P(i) is true, then so is $P(i+1)$.
The basis proves that $P(1)$ is true.
When both these parts are proved, then for each i, $P(i)$ is proved.

61. State Pigeon-hole Principle.

If an attempt is made to pair off the elements of A (the "pigeons") with elements of B (the "pigeonholes"), sooner or later we will have to put more than one pigeon in a pigeonhole.

62. Define a Grammar of a Language.

A Grammar (G) is defined as a quadruple

$$G = (V, T, S, P)$$

where

V = finite set of objects called Variables
T = finite set of objects called Terminal symbols.
$S \in V$ = start symbol
P = finite set of productions.

Chapter 1

DFA and NFA

1.1 DETERMINISTIC FINITE AUTOMATA (DFA)

1.1.1 Automata—What is it?

An automaton is an abstract model of a digital computer. An automaton has a mechanism to read input, which is a string over a given alphabet. This input is actually written on an "input file", which can be read by the automaton but cannot change it.

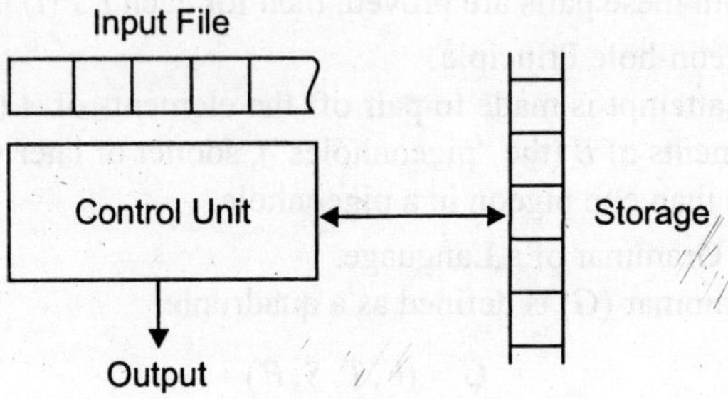

Fig. Automaton

Input file is divided into cells, each of which can hold one symbol. The automaton has a temporary "storage" device, which has unlimited number of cells, the contents of which can be altered by the automaton. Automaton has a control unit, which is said to be in one of a finite number of "internal states". The automaton can change state in a defined way.

1.1.2 Types of Automaton

(a) Deterministic Automata
(b) Non-deterministic Automata

A deterministic automata is one in which each move (transition from one state to another) is unequally determined by the current configuration.

If the internal state, input and contents of the storage are known, it is possible to predict the future behaviour of the automaton. This is said to be deterministic automata otherwise it is nondeterminist automata.

An automaton whose output response is "yes" or "No" is called an "Acceptor".

1.1.3 Definition of Deterministic Finite Automaton

A Deterministic Finite Automator (DFA) is a 5-tuple.

$$M = (Q, \Sigma, \delta, q_0, F)$$

where

Q	=	Finite state of "internal states"
Σ	=	Finite set of symbols called "Input alphabet"
$\delta : Q \times \Sigma \rightarrow Q$	=	Transition Function
$q_0 \in Q$	=	Initial state
$F \subseteq Q$	=	Set of Final states

The input mechanism can move only from left to right and reads exactly one symbol on each step.

The transition from one internal state to another are governed by the transition function δ.

If $\delta(q_0, a) = q_1$, then if the DFA is in state q_0 and the current input symbol is a, the DFA will go into state q_1.

Example 1.1.1: Design a DFA, M which accepts the language $L(M) = \{w \in (a, b)^* : w$ does not contain three consecutive b's).

Let $M = (Q, \Sigma, \delta, q_0, F)$

where

$Q = \{q_0, q_1, q_2, q_3\}$

$\Sigma = \{a, b\}$

q_0 is the initial state

$F = \{q_0, q_1, q_2,\}$ are initial states

and δ is defined as follows:

Initial state q	Symbol σ	Final state $\delta(q, \sigma)$
q_0	a	q_0
q_0	b	q_1
q_1	a	q_0
q_1	b	q_2
q_2	a	q_0
q_2	b	q_3
q_3	a	q_3
q_3	b	q_3

Solution

M does not accept specified language, as long as three consecutive *b*'s have not been read.

It should be noted that

(i) *M* is in state q_i (where $i = 0,1$, or 2) immediately after reading a run of *i* consecutive *b*'s that either began the input string or was preceded by an '*a*'.

(ii) If an '*a*' is read and *M* is in state, q_0, q_1, or *M* returns to its initial state q_0.

q_0, q_1 and q_2 are "Final states" (as given in the problem). Therefore any input string not containing three consecutive *b*'s will be accepted.

In case we get three consecutive *b*'s then the q_3 state is reached (which is not final state), hence *M* will remain in this state, irrespective of any other symbol in the rest of the string. This state q_3 is said to be "dead state" or *M* is said to be "trapped" at q_3.

The DFA schematic is shown below based on the discussion above.

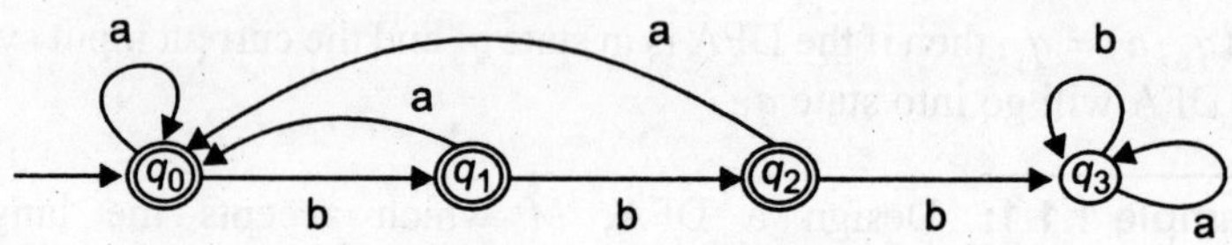

Fig. Finite Automaton with four states

Example 1.1.2: Determine the DFA schematic for $M = (Q, \Sigma, \delta, q, F)$ where $Q = \{q_1, q_2, q_3\}$, $\Sigma = \{0,1\}$, q_1 is the start state, $F = \{q_2\}$ and δ is given by the table below.

Initial state q	Symbol σ	Final state $\delta(q,\sigma)$
q_1	0	q_1
q_1	1	q_2
q_2	0	q_3
q_2	1	q_2
q_3	0	q_2
q_3	1	q_2

Also determine a Language *L* recognized by the DFA.

Solution

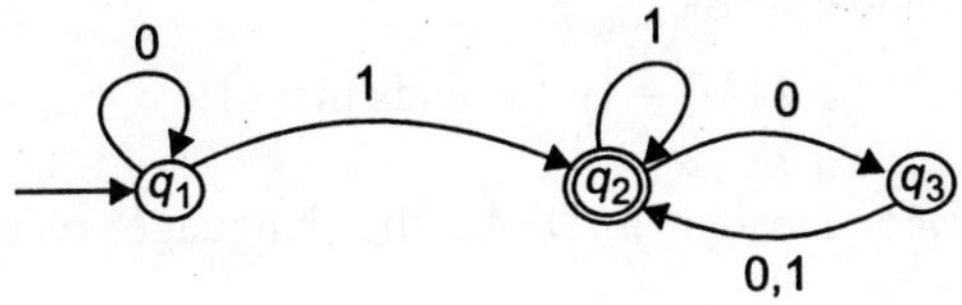

Fig. Finite Automaton having three states.

From the given table for δ, the DFA is drawn, where q_2 is the only final state.

(It is to be noted that a DFA can "accept" a string and it can "recognize" a language. Catch here is that "accept" is used for strings and "recognize" for that of a language).

It could be seen that the DFA accepts strings that has at least one 1 and an even number of 0s following the last 1.

Hence the language L is given by

$$L = \{w \mid w \text{ contains at least one 1 and an even number of 0s follow the last 1}\}$$

where $L = L(M)$ and M recognized the RHS of the equation above.

Example 1.1.3: Sketch the DFA given

$$M = (\{q_1, q_2\}, \{0,1\}, \delta, q_1, \{q_2\})$$

and δ is given by

$$\delta(q_1, 0) = q_1 \text{ and } \delta(q_2, 0) = q_1$$
$$\delta(q_1, 1) = q_2 \qquad \delta(q_2, 1) = q_2$$

Determine a Language $L(M)$, that the DFA recognizes.

Solution

From the given data, it is easy to predict the schematic of DFA as follows.

Internal states = q_1, q_2.

Symbols = 0, 1.

Transition function = δ (as defined above in the given problem)

q_1 = Initial state

q_2 = Final state.

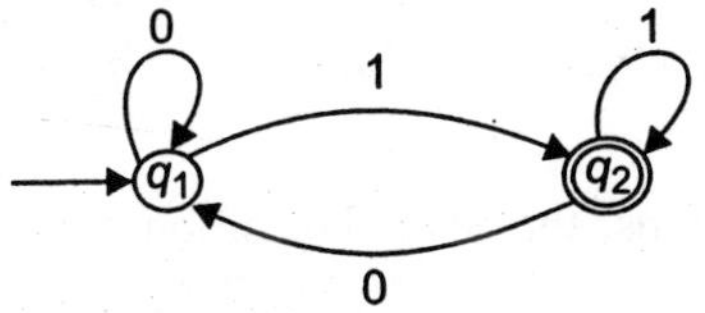

Fig. State diagram of DFA

If a string ends in a 0, it is "rejected" and "accepted" only if the string ends in a 1. Therefore the language

$$L(M) = \{w \mid w \text{ ends in a } 1\}.$$

Example 1.1.4: Design a DFA, the language recognized by the Automaton being

$$L = \{a^n b : n \geq 0\}$$

Solution

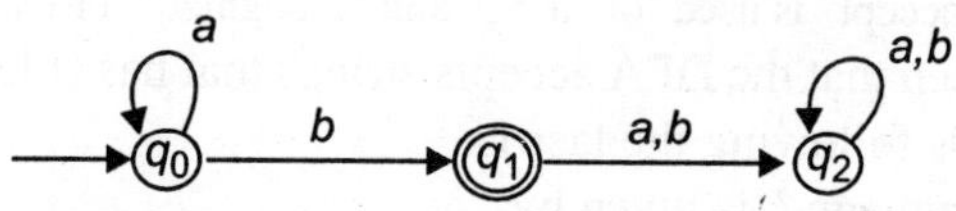

For the given language $L = \{a^n b : n \geq 0\}$, the strings could be $b, ab, a^2b, a^3b, \ldots$.

Therefore the DFA accepts all strings consisting of an arbitrary number of a's, followed by a single *b*. All other input strings are rejected.

Example 1.1.5: Obtain the state table diagram and state transistion diagram (DFA Schematic) of the finite state Automaton $M = (Q, \Sigma, \delta, q_0, F)$, where $Q = \{q_0, q_1, q_2, q_3\}$, $\Sigma = \{a, b\}$, q_0 is the initial state, F is the final state with the transistion defined by

$$\delta(q_0, a) = q_2 \quad \delta(q_3, a) = q_1 \quad \delta(q_2, b) = q_3$$
$$\delta(q_1, a) = q_3 \quad \delta(q_0, b) = q_1 \quad \delta(q_3, b) = q_2$$
$$\delta(q_2, a) = q_0 \quad \delta(q_1, b) = q_0$$

Solution

The State Table diagram is as shown below

δ	a	b
q_0	q_2	q_1
q_1	q_3	q_0
q_2	q_0	q_3
q_3	q_1	q_2

With the given definitions, the State Transition diagram/DFA Schematic is shown on next page.

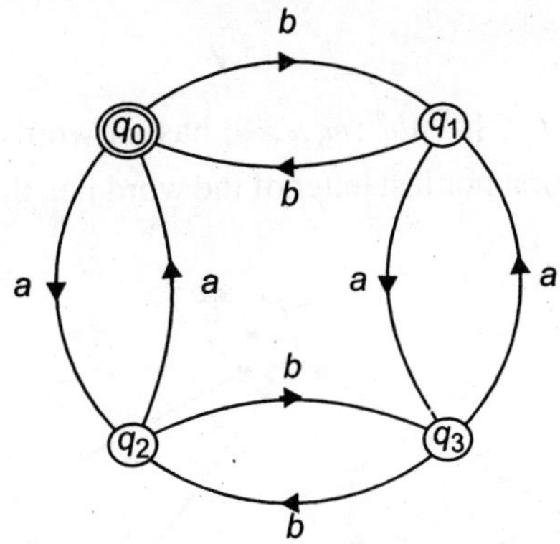

Example 1.1.6: Obtain the DFA that accepts/recognizes the language

$$L(M) = \{w \mid w \in \{a, b, c\}^* \text{ and } w \text{ contains the pattern } abac\}$$

(*Note:* This is an application of DFA's involving searching a text for a specified pattern)

Solution

Let us begin by "hard coding" the pattern into the machines states as shown in fig. (a) below.

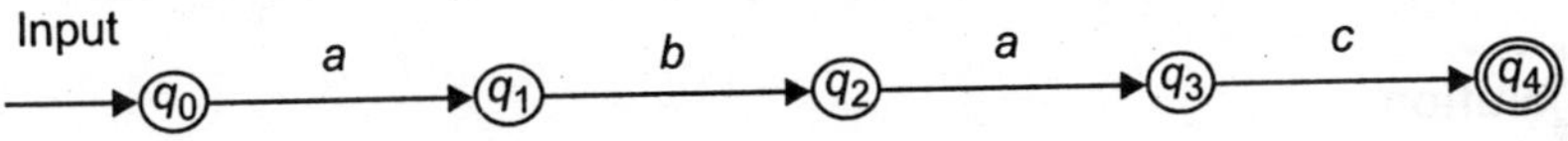

Fig. (a)

As the pattern '*abac*' has length four, there are four states required in addition to one intial state q_0, to remember the pattern. q_4 is the only accepting state required and this state q_4 can be reached only after reading '*abac*'.

The complete DFA is as shown below in Fig. (b).

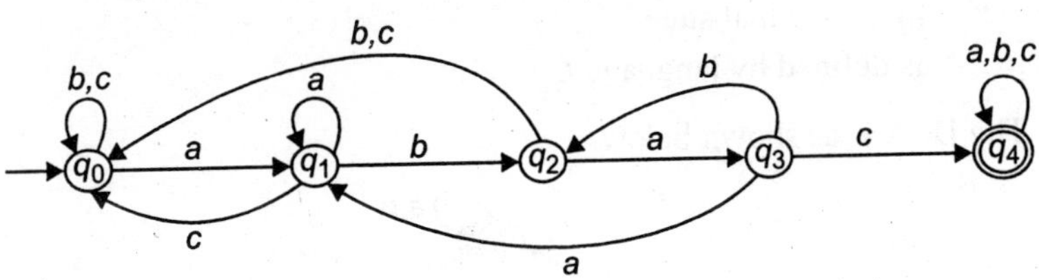

Fig. (b)

Example 1.1.7: Given $\Sigma = \{a, b\}$, construct a DFA that shall recognize the language $L = \{b^m ab^n : m, n > 0\}$.

Solution

The given language $L = \{b^m ab^n : m, n > 0\}$ has all words with exactly one 'a' which is neither the first nor last letter of the word i.e., there is one or more b's before or after 'a'.

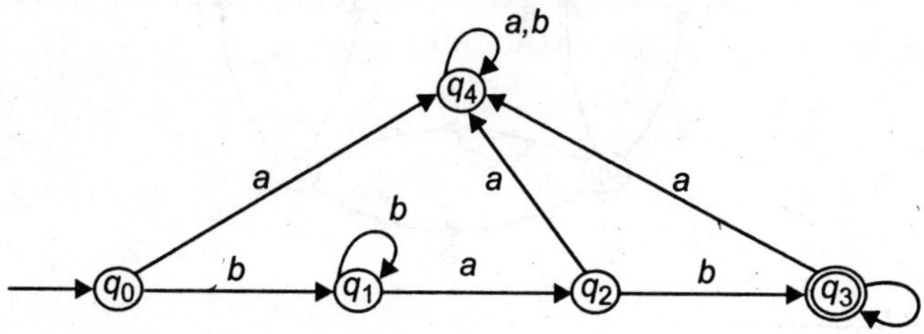

DFA is drawn above for the automaton M,

where $M = (Q, \Sigma, \delta, q_0, F)$ with
$Q = \{q_0, q_1, q_2, q_3, q_4\}$
$\Sigma = \{a, b\}$; q_0 = Initial state,
$F = \{q_3\}$ = Final state.

and δ is defined as per the language L. (q_4 is "dead" state)

Example 1.1.8: Given $\Sigma = \{a, b\}$, construct a DFA which recognize the language $L = \{a^m b^n : m, n > 0\}$.

Solution

The given language $L = \{a^m b^n : m, n > 0\}$ has all words which begin with one or more a's followed by one or more b's.

The finite automaton $M(Q, \Sigma, \delta, q_0, F)$ is with

$Q = \{q_0, q_1, q_2, q_3\}$
$\Sigma = \{a, b\}$
q_0 = Initial state
$F = \{q_2\}$ = Final state

and δ as defined by language L.

The DFA is as shown below.

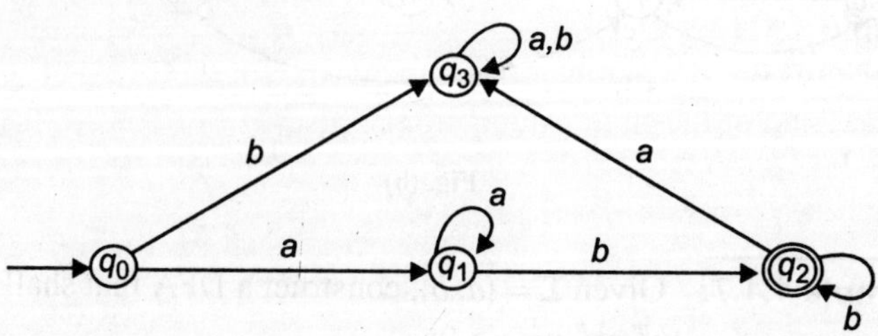

Here q_3 is a "dead" state.

Example 1.1.9: Construct a DFA which recognizes the set of all strings on $\Sigma = \{a, b\}$ starting with the prefix '*ab*'.

Solution

Only two states (q_1, q_2) are required to recognize *ab*, in addition to the input state. One additional state called the "trap" state is also required.

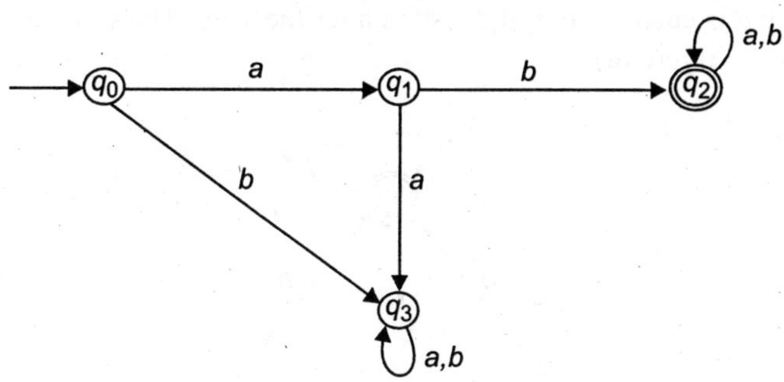

Fig. (a) DFA

Hence the DFA that recognizes the set of all strings on $\Sigma = \{a, b\}$ starting with the prefix '*ab*' is drawn above, where the automaton *M* is

$$M(\{q_0, q_1, q_2, q_3\}, \{0,1\}, \delta, \{q_2\})$$

with the state table diagram for δ as shown below.

δ	a	b
q_0	q_1	q_3
q_1	q_3	q_2
q_2	q_2	q_2
q_3	q_3	q_3

Fig. (b) State table diagram

Example 1.1.10: Determine the DFA that will accept those words from $\Sigma = \{a, b\}$ where the number of *b*'s is divisible by three. Sketch the state table diagram of the finite Automaton *M* also.

Solution

The Finite Automaton *M* is $M(Q, \Sigma, \delta, q_0, F)$ with

$$Q = \{q_0, q_1, q_2\}$$

$\Sigma = \{a, b\}$

q_0 = Initial state

F = Final state

We choose three states q_0, q_1, q_2. The states count the number of b's modulo 3, with q_0 as the input as well as accepting state where q_1 and q_2 are not accepting states. Run arrows from q_0 to q_1, q_1 to q_2 and q_2 to q_0 with label 'b'.

If any a is encountered, it does not alter the state. The suitable DFA is as shown in the figure (a).

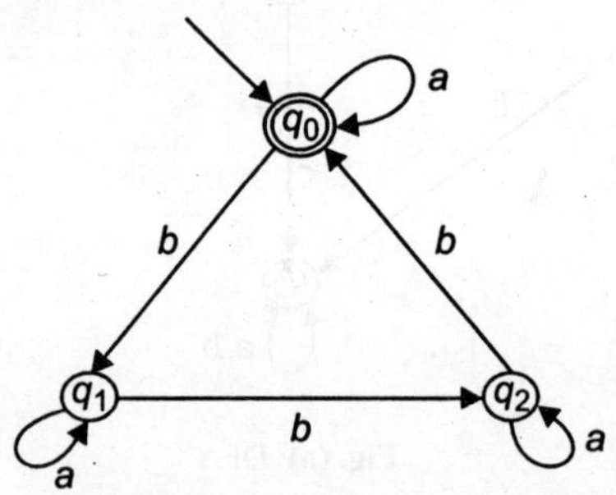

Fig. (a) DFA

The state table diagram is shown in Fig. (b).

δ	a	b
q_0	q_0	q_1
q_1	q_1	q_2
q_2	q_2	q_0

Fig. (b) State table diagram

Example 1.1.11: Construct an FA accepting all strings in $\{0,1\}^*$ having even number of 0's.

Solution

The Finite Automaton M is given by

$$M(\{q_0, q_1, q_2\}, \{0,1\}, \delta, q_0, \{q_2\}).$$

The Finite Automaton is as shown.

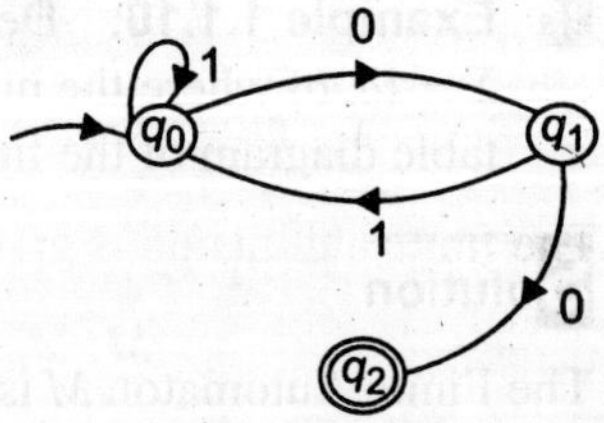

Example 1.1.12: Construct a finite automaton accpting all strings over {0, 1}

(a) having odd number of 0's
(b) having even number of 0's and even number of 1's.

Solution

(a) $M(\{q_0, q_1, q_2\}, \{0,1\}, \delta, q_0, \{q_1\})$. (*See* Fig. (a))
(b) $M(\{q_0, q_1, q_2, q_3\}, \{0,1\}, \delta, q_0, \{q_0\})$. (*See* Fig. (b))

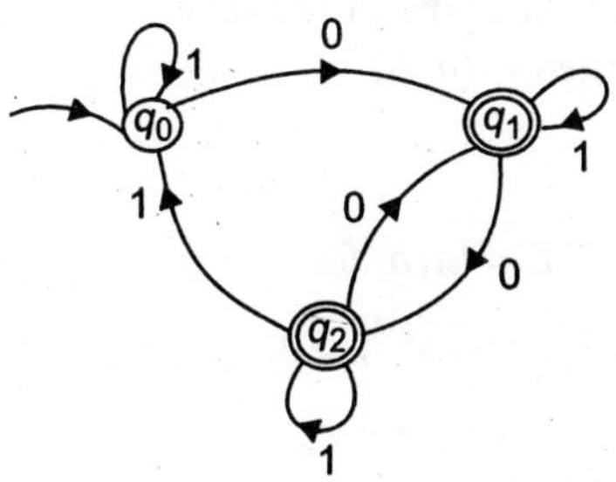

Fig. (a)

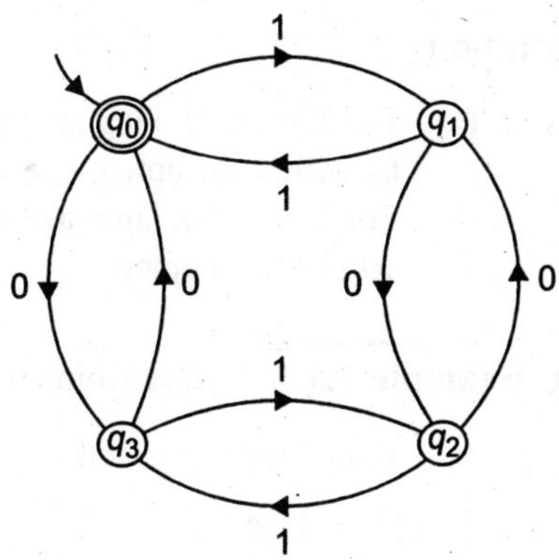

Fig. (b)

Example 1.1.13: Determine an FA, M accepting L, where $L = \{w \in \{0,1\}^* :$ Every 0 in w has a 1 immediately to its right$\}$.

Solution

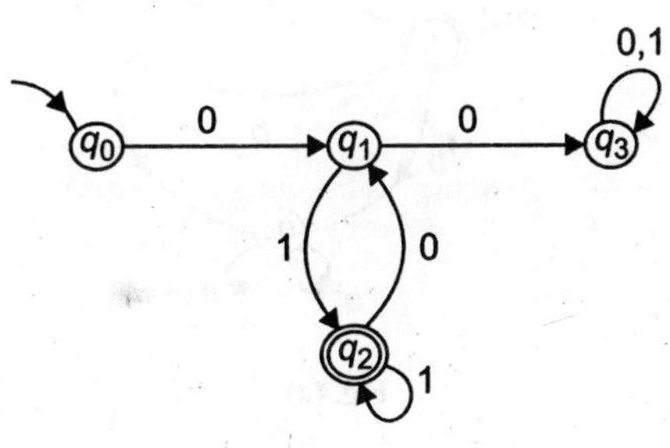

The finite automaton is given by

$$M(\{q_0, q_1, q_2, q_3\}, \{0,1\}, \delta, q_0, \{q_2\}).$$

Example 1.1.14: Determine the languages produced by the FA shown in Figs. (a) and (b).

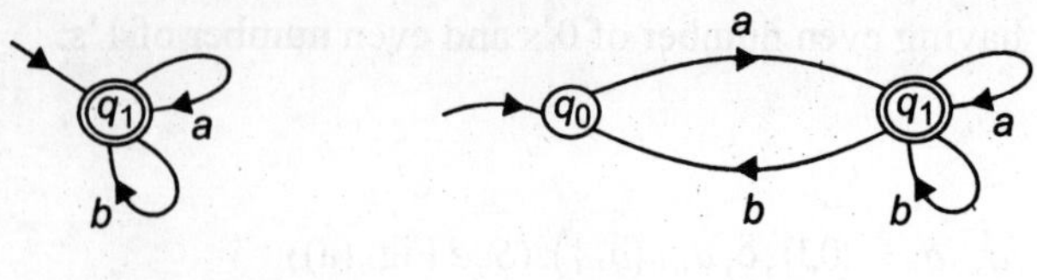

Solution

(a) For $\Sigma = \{a, b\}$, language generated $= \{a,b\}^*$
($\in$ will be accepted when initial state equal final state).

(b) For $\Sigma = \{a, b\}$, language generated $= \{a, b\}^+$
{$\in$ is not accepted).

Example 1.1.15: Determine the FA if $\Sigma = \{a, b\}$ for

(a) Language generated $L_A = (ab)^* = \{(ab)^n \mid n \geq 0\}$
($\in$-not accepted)

(b) Language generated $L_B = \{(ab)^n \mid n \geq 1\}$
($\in$-not accepted)

Solution

(a) Given $L_A = \{(ab)^n \mid n \geq 0\}$.

The FA is shown below in Fig. (a).

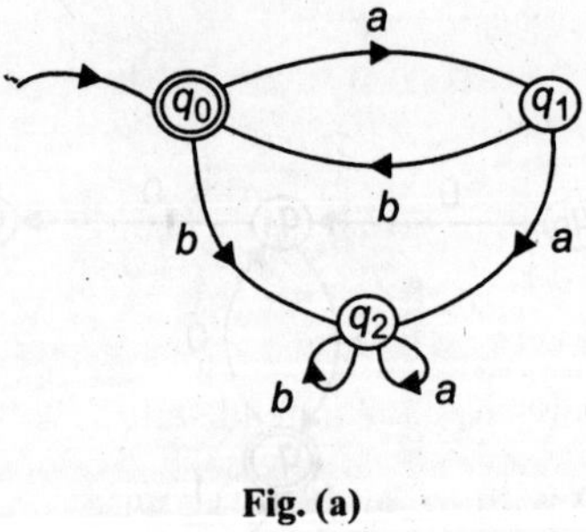

Fig. (a)

The FA is given by

$$M(\{q_0, q_1, q_2\}, \{a, b\}, \delta, q_0, q_0)$$

where q_2 is a "dead state".

(b) Given $L_B = \{(ab)^n \mid n \geq 1\}$ ($\in$-not accepted) i.e., initial state $\neq$ final state).
The FA for this language L_B is shown in Fig. (b).

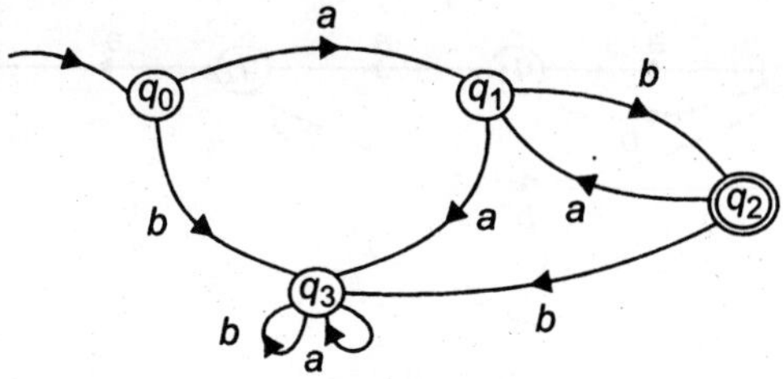

Fig.(b)

The FA is given by

$$M(\{q_0, q_1, q_2, q_3\}, \{a, b\}, \delta, q_0, q_2)$$

where q_3 is a "dead state".

Example 1.1.16: Determine the FA with the

(a) Set of strings beginning with an '*a*'.
(b) Set of strings beginning with '*a*' and ending with '*b*'.
(c) Set of strings having '*aaa*' as a subword.
(d) Set of integers
(e) Set of signed integers.

Solution

(a) Set of strings beginning with an '*a*'.

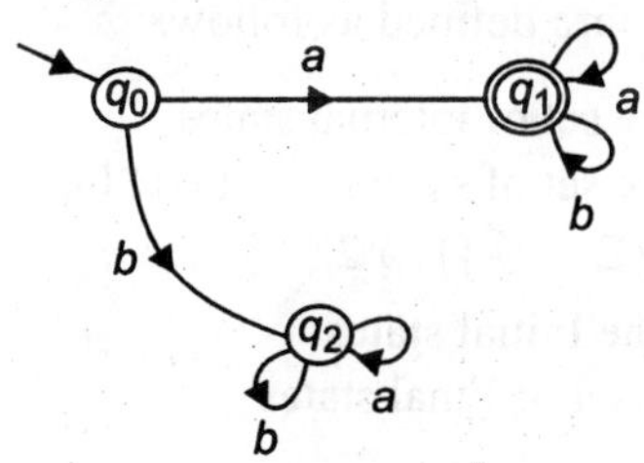

[It is not necessary always to have a dead state]

(b) Set of strings beginning with '*a*' and ending with '*b*'.

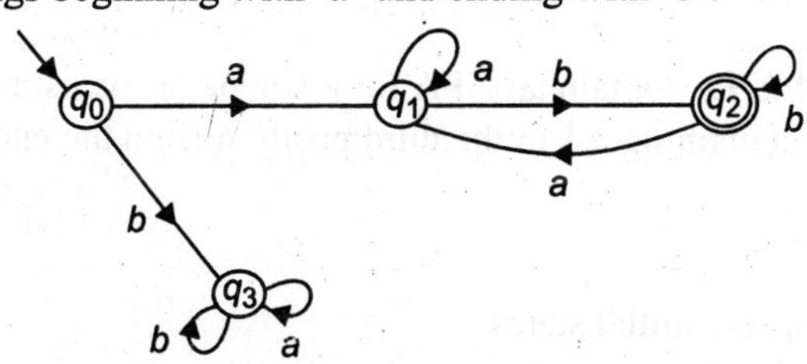

(c) Set of strings having '*aaa*' as a subword.

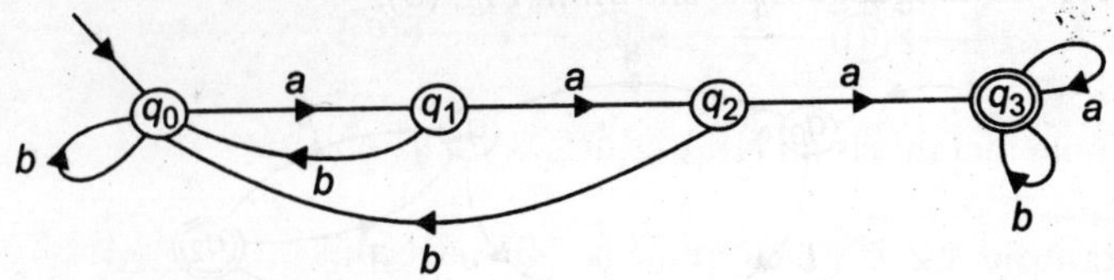

(d) Set of integers.

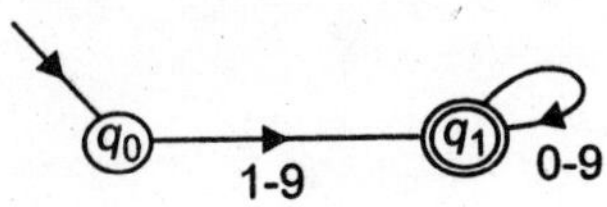

Alphabet $\Sigma = \{0,1, \ldots ,9\}$

(e) Set of signed Integers.

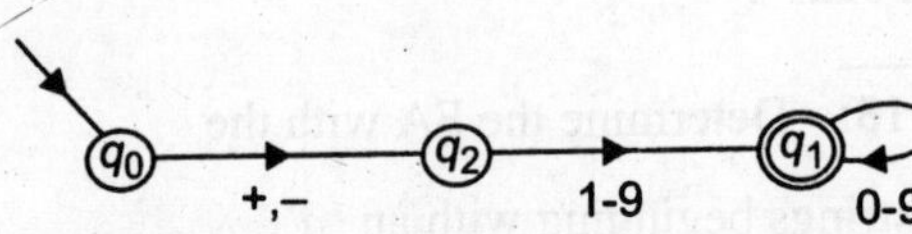

1.2 NON-DETERMINISTIC FINITE AUTOMATA (NFA)

Definition

A Nondeterministic Finite Automata (NFA) is defined by a 5-tuple

$$M = (Q, \Sigma, \delta, q_0, F)$$

where $Q, \Sigma, \delta, q_0, F$ are defined as follows:

Q = Finite set of internal states
Σ = Finite set of symbols called "Input alphabet"
$\delta = Q \times (\Sigma \cup \{\lambda\}) \rightarrow 2^Q$
$q_0 \in Q$ is the Initial states
$F \subseteq Q$ is a set of Final states

NFA differs from DFA in that, the range of δ in NFA is in the powerset 2^Q.

A string is accepted by an NFA if there is some sequence of possible moves that will put the machine in the final state at the end of the string.

Example 1.2.1: Obtain an NFA for a language consisting of all strings over {0,1} containing a 1 in the third position from the end.

Solution

q_1, q_2, q_3 are initial states

q_4 is the final state.

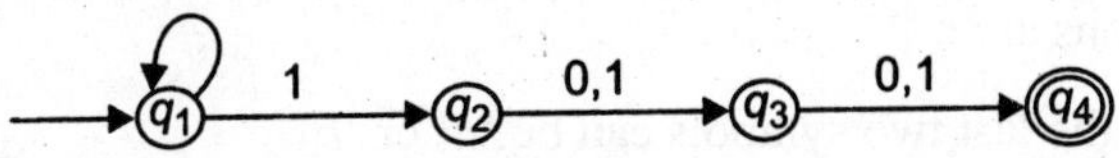

Please note that this is an NFA as $\delta(q_2,0) = q_3$ and $\delta(q_2,1) = q_3$.

Example 1.2.2: Determine an NFA accepting the language

(a) $L_1 = \{x \mid x \in \{a, b, c\}^*$ and x contains the pattern $abac\}$

(b) $L_2 = \{a^* \cup b^*\}$

Solution

(a)

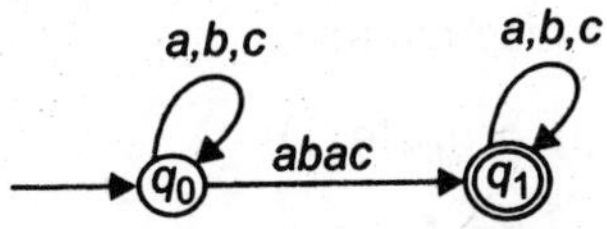

(b)

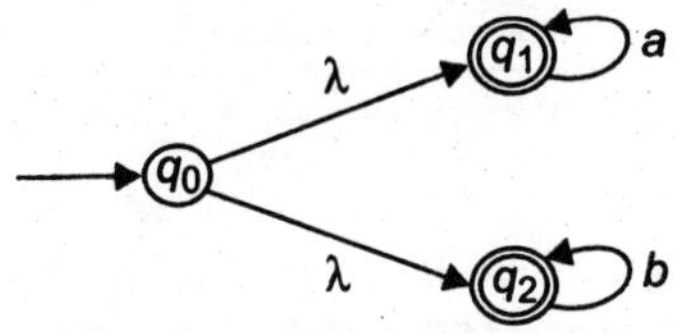

Example 1.2.3: Determine an NFA accepting all strings over $\{0,1\}$ which end in 1 but does not contain the substring 00.

Solution

The conditions to be satisfied are:

(a) String should end in a 1
(b) String should not contain 00.

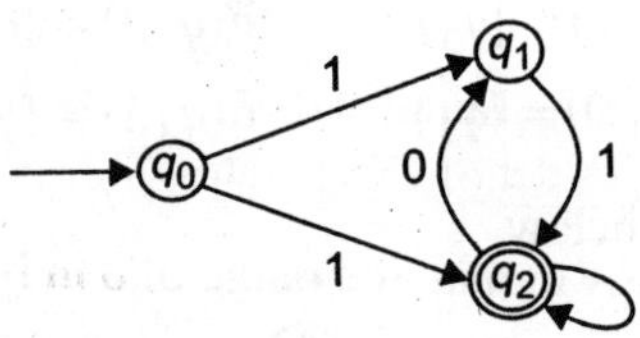

The NFA is shown in figure.

Example 1.2.4: Obtain an NFA which should accept a language L_A, given by $L_A = \{x \in \{a, b\}^* : |x| \geq 3$ and third symbol of x from the right is $\{\text{'}a\text{'}\}$.

Solution

The conditions are

(a) the last two symbols can be 'a' or 'b'.
(b) third symbol from the right is 'a'
(c) symbol in any position but for the last three position can be 'a' or 'b'.

The NFA is shown in fig. below.

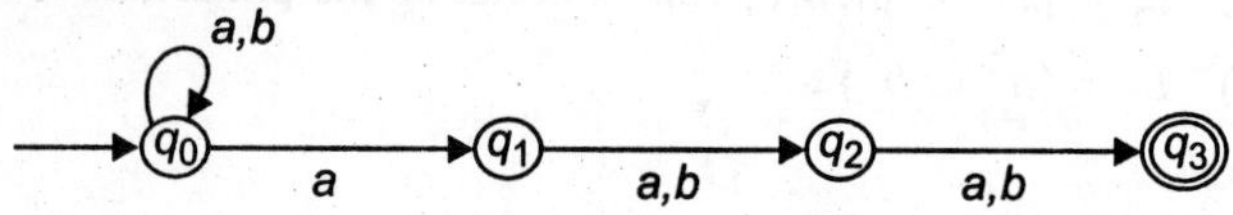

Example 1.2.5: Sketch the NFA state diagram for

$$M = (\{q_0, q_1, q_2, q_3\}, \{0,1\}, \delta, q_0, \{q_3\})$$

with the state table as given below.

δ	0	1
q_0	q_0, q_1	q_0, q_2
q_1	q_3	$\varnothing$
q_2	$\varnothing$	q_3
q_3	q_3	q_3

Solution

The NFA states are q_0, q_1, q_2 and q_3.

$$\delta(q_0,0) = \{q_0, q_1\} \qquad \delta(q_0,1) = \{q_0, q_2\}$$
$$\delta(q_1,0) = \{q_3\} \qquad \delta(q_2,1) = \{q_3\}$$
$$\delta(q_3,0) = \{q_3\} \qquad \delta(q_3,1) = \{q_3\}\ .$$

The NFA is as shown below.

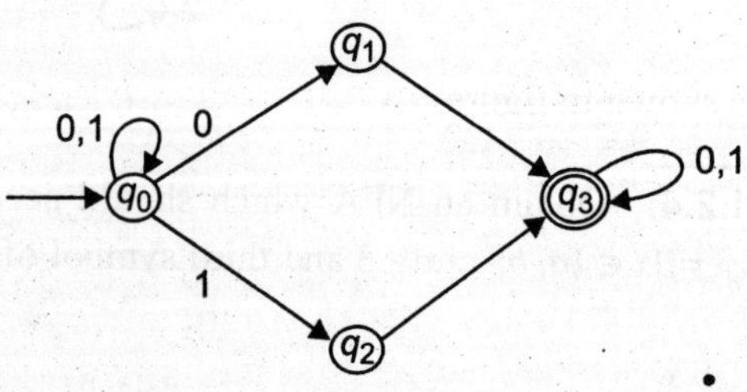

Example 1.2.6: Given L is the language accepted by NFA in Fig. Determine an NFA that accepts $L \cup \{a^5\}$.

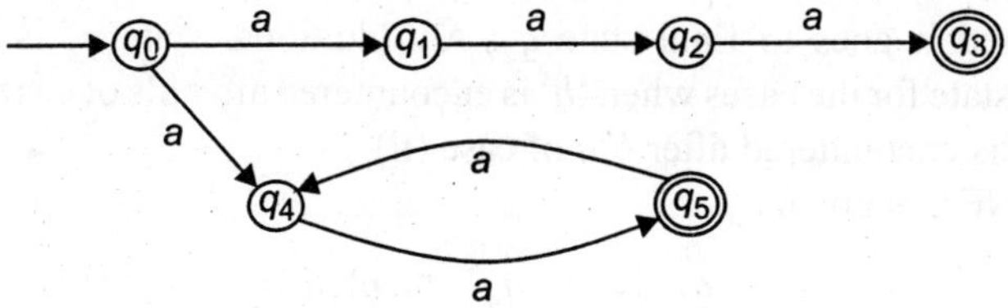

Solution

The language accepted by the given NFA is

$$L = \{a^3\} \cup \{a^n : n \text{ is odd}\}.$$

Now to make an NFA accepting the language:

$$L = \{a^3\} \cup \{a^n : n \text{ is odd}\} \cup \{a^5\}.$$

This is accomplished by adding two states after state q_3 viz., q_6 and q_7 as shown in fig.

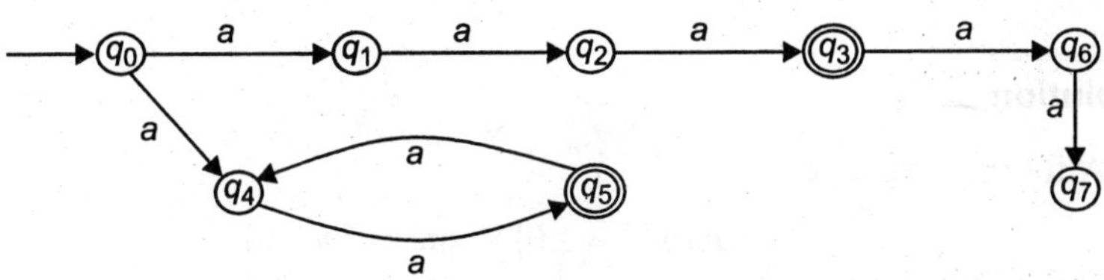

The NFA is given by

$$M = (\{q_0, q_1, q_2, q_3, q_4, q_5, q_6, q_7\}, \{a\}, \delta, q_0, \{q_3, q_5, q_7\})$$

Example 1.2.7: Find an NFA with four states for

$$L = \{a^n : n \geq 0\} \cup \{b^n a : n \geq 1\}$$

Solution

NFA for the language:

$$L = \{a^n : n \geq 0\} \cup \{b^n a : n \geq 1\}$$

For such a language two cases are to be considered.

Case (i): $a^n, n \geq 0$

q_0 goes to a state q_3 where all a's are absorbed. Hence a^n is accepted.

Case (ii): $b^n a : n \geq 1$

q_0 goes to a state q_1 where all b's are accepted and when an 'a' is encountered it goes to final state q_2. An additional state q_4 is added as a rejection state for the cases when 'b' is encountered after a's of case (i) or when 'a' or 'b' is encountered after $b^n a$ of case (ii).

The NFA is given by

$$M = (\{q_0, q_1, q_2, q_3, q_4\}, \{a, b\}, \delta, q_0, \{q_2, q_3\})$$

which is shown in the fig. below.

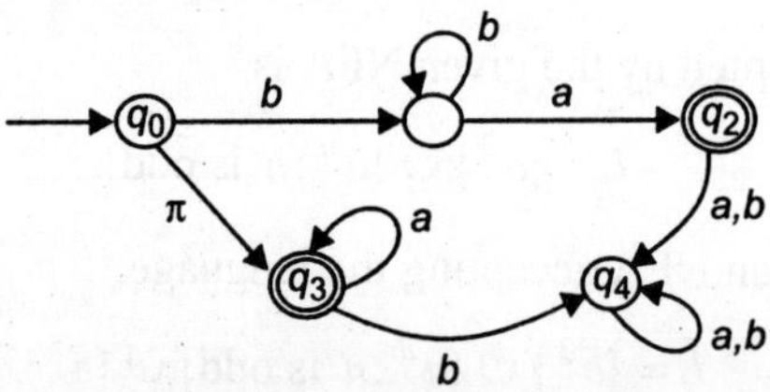

Example 1.2.8: Design an NFA with no more than five states for the set

$$\{abab^n : n \geq 0\} \cup \{aba^n : n \geq 0\}.$$

Solution

NFA for the language

$$L = \{abab^n : n \geq 0\} \cup \{aba^n : n \geq 0\}$$

is

$$M = (\{q_0, q_1, q_2, q_3, q_4\}, \{a, b\}, \delta, q_0, \{q_2, q_3, q_4\}).$$

Here the NFA is such that it accepts all strings of the type aba^n and $abab^n$ where $n \geq 0$.

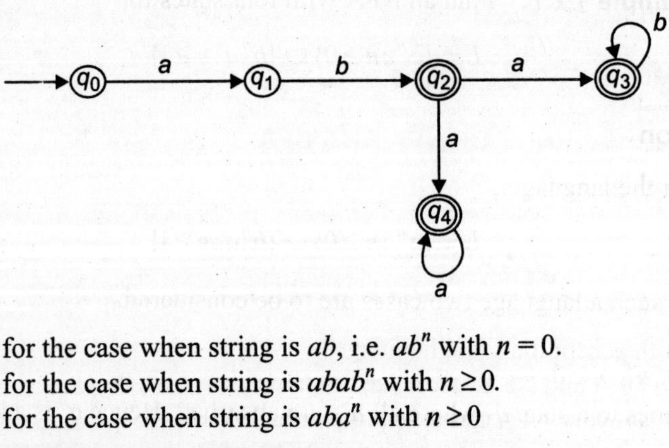

q_2 is for the case when string is ab, i.e. ab^n with $n = 0$.
q_3 is for the case when string is $abab^n$ with $n \geq 0$.
q_4 is for the case when string is aba^n with $n \geq 0$

This NFA is shown in the fig. above.

Example 1.2.9: Determine an NFA with three states that accepts the language $\{ab, abc\}^*$.

Solution:

NFA for the language

$$L = \{ab, abc\}^*$$

should be such that it accepts "*ab*" or "*abc*" in the first step and then this is looped with initial state so that any combination of "*ab*" and "*abc*" can be accepted.

Hence we have the NFA as

$$M = (\{q_0, q_1, q_2\}, \{a, b, c\}, \delta, q_0, \{q_1\})$$

which is shown below:

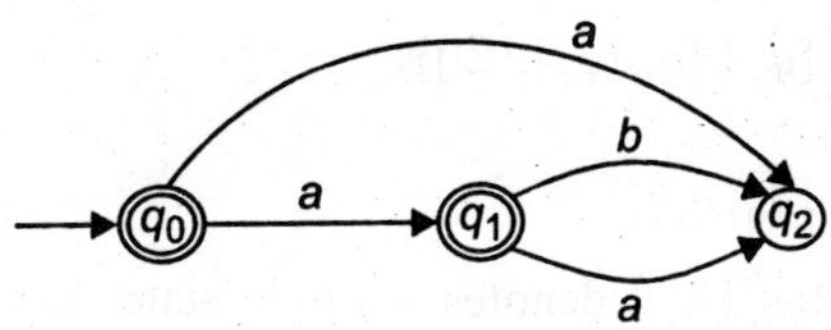

Example 1.2.10: Determine an NFA that accepts the language

$$L(aa^* (a + b)).$$

Solution:

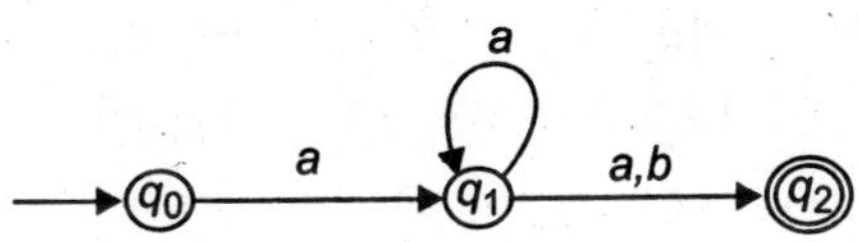

NFA is given by

$$M = (\{q_0, q_1, q_2\}, \{a, b\}, \delta, q_0, \{q_2\})$$

1.3 EQUIVALENCE OF NFA AND DFA

Definition

Two finite accepters M_1 and M_2 are equivalent iff

$$L(M_1) = L(M_2)$$

i.e., if both accept the same language.

Both DFA and NFA recognize the same class of languages. It is important to note that every NFA has an equivalent DFA.

Let us illustrate the conversion of NDA to DFA through an example.

Example 1.3.1: Determine a deterministic Finite State Automaton from the given Nondeterministic FSA.

$$M = (\{q_0, q_1\}, \{a, b\}, \delta, q_0, \{q_1\})$$

with the state table diagram for δ given below.

δ	a	b
q_0	$\{q_0, q_1\}$	$\{q_1\}$
q_1	$\varnothing$	$\{q_0, q_1\}$

Solution

Let $M' = (Q', \Sigma, \delta', q_0', F')$ be a determine. Finite state automaton (DFA), where

$$Q' = \{[q_0], [q_1], [q_0, q_1], [\varnothing]\},$$
$$q_0' = [q_0]$$

and $\quad F' = \{[q_1], [q_0, q_1]\}$

Please remember that [ ] denotes a single state. Let us now proceed to determine δ' to be defined for the DFA.

δ'	a	b
$[q_0]$	$[q_0, q_1]$	$[q_1]$
$[q_1]$	$\varnothing$	$[q_0, q_1]$
$[q_0, q_1]$	$[q_0, q_1]$	$[q_0, q_1]$
$\varnothing$	$\varnothing$	$\varnothing$

It is to be noted that

$$\delta'([q_0, q_1], a) = [q_0, q_1]$$

since
$$\delta'([q_0, q_1], a) = \delta(q_0, a) \cup \delta(q_1, a)$$
$$= \{q_0, q_1\} \cup \varnothing$$
$$= \{q_1, q_1\}$$

and
$$\delta'([q_0, q_1], b) = [q_0, q_1]$$

since
$$\delta([q_0, q_1], b) = \delta(q_0, b) \cup \delta(q_1, b)$$
$$= \{q_1\} \cup \{q_0, q_1\}$$
$$= \{q_0, q_1\}$$

Here any subset containing q_1 is the final state in DFA. This is shown as below.

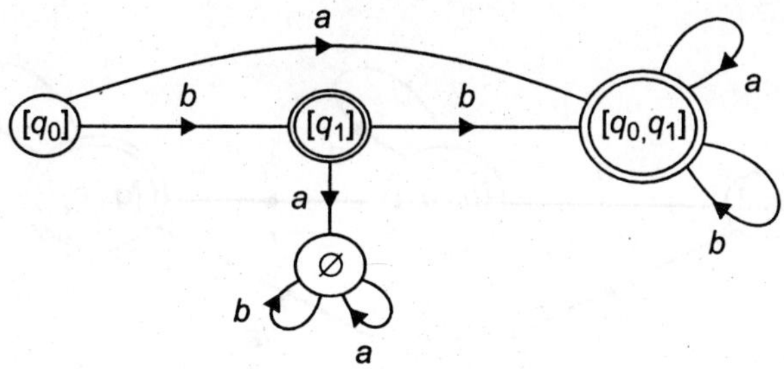

Example 1.3.2: Given the NDA as shown in Fig. (a), with δ as shown in Fig. (b).

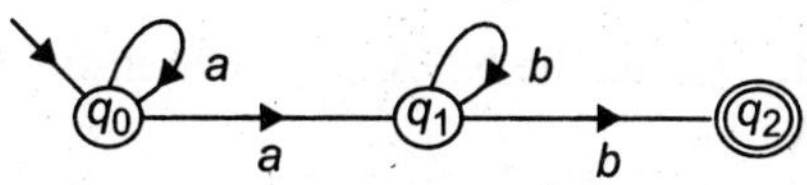

Fig. (a)

	a	b
q_0	$\{q_0, q_1\}$	$\varnothing$
q_1	$\varnothing$	$\{q_1, q_2\}$
q_2	$\varnothing$	$\varnothing$

Fig. (b)

Determine the equivalent DFA for the above given NDA.

Solution

Conversion of NDA to DFA is done through subset construction as shown in the State table diagram below.

	a	b
$[q_0]$	$[q_0, q_1]$	$\varnothing$
$[q_0, q_1]$	$[q_0, q_1]$	$[q_1, q_2]$
$[q_1, q_2]$	$\varnothing$	$[q_1, q_2]$
$\varnothing$	$\varnothing$	$\varnothing$

The corresponding DFA is shown below. Please note that here any subset containing q_2 is the final state.

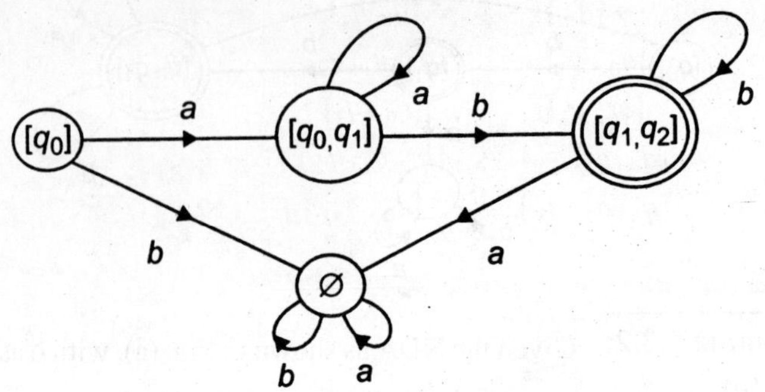

Example 1.3.3: Given the NDA as shown in fig. below, determine the equivalent DFA.

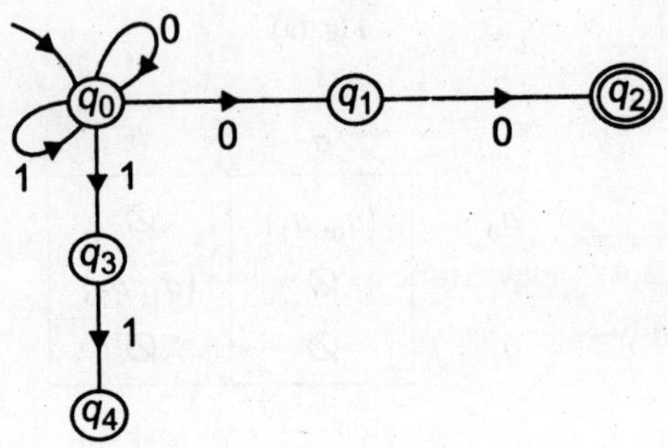

Solution

The given NDA has q_2 and q_4 as final states. It accepts strings ending in 00 or 11. The state table is shown below.

	0	1
q_0	$\{q_0, q_1\}$	$\{q_0, q_3\}$
q_1	$\{q_2\}$	$\varnothing$
q_2	$\varnothing$	$\varnothing$
q_3	$\varnothing$	$\{q_4\}$
q_4	$\varnothing$	$\varnothing$

The conversion of NDA to DFA is done through the subset construction.

δ′ is given by the following state table.

	0	1
→ $[q_0]$	$[q_0, q_1]$	$[q_0, q_3]$
$[q_0, q_1]$	$[q_0, q_1, q_2]$	$[q_0, q_3]$
$[q_0, q_3]$	$[q_0, q_1]$	$[q_0, q_3, q_4]$
$[q_0, q_1, q_2]$	$[q_0, q_1, q_2]$	$[q_0, q_3]$
$[q_0, q_3, q_4]$	$[q_0, q_1]$	$[q_0, q_3, q_4]$

Any state containing q_2 or q_4 will be a final state.

The DFA is shown below.

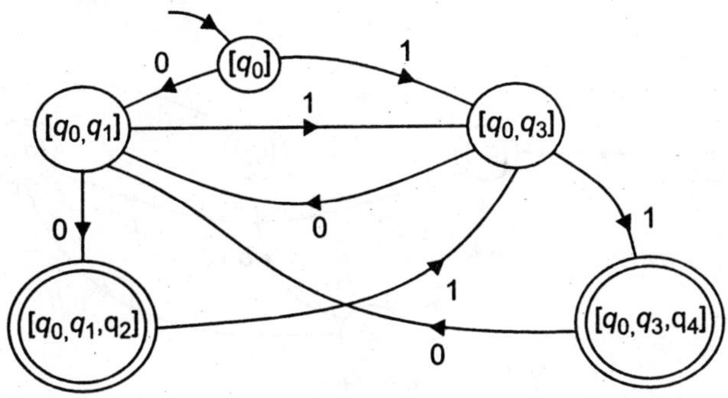

Example 1.3.4: Determine a NFA accepting $\{ab, ba\}$ and use it to find a DFA accepting it.

Solution

The state table is as shown below.

	a	b
q_0	q_1	q_2
q_1	∅	q_3
q_2	q_3	∅
q_3	∅	∅

The NFA is shown below.

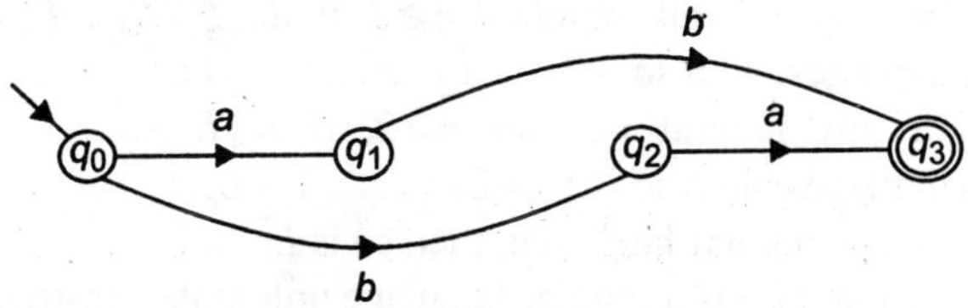

q_0 is the input state, q_3 is the final state.

The state table corresponding to the DFA is derived by using subset construction. State table for DFA is as shown below.

	a	b
$[q_0]$	$[q_1]$	$[q_2]$
$[q_1]$	$\varnothing$	$[q_3]$
$[q_2]$	$[q_3]$	$\varnothing$
$[q_3]$	$\varnothing$	$\varnothing$
$\varnothing$	$\varnothing$	$\varnothing$

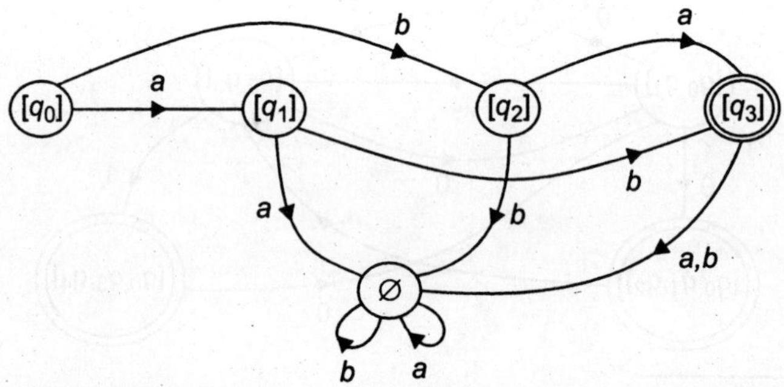

The DFA is as shown above.

1.4 REGULAR EXPRESSION

1.4.1 Regular Languages

The regular languages are those languages that can be constructed from the "big three" set operations viz., (a) Union (b) Concatenation (c) Kleene star.

A regular language is defined as follows.

Definition: Let Σ be an alphabet. The class of "regular languages" over Σ is defined inductively as follows:

(a) $\varnothing$ is a regular language
(b) For each $\sigma \in \Sigma$, $\{\sigma\}$ is a regular language
(c) For any natural number $n \geq 2$ if $L_1, L_2, \ldots\ldots L_n$ are regular languages, then so is $L_1 \cup L_2 \cup \ldots \ldots \cup L_n$.
(d) For any natural number $n \geq 2$, if $L_1, L_2, \ldots\ldots L_n$ are regular languages, then so is $L_1 \circ L_2 \circ \ldots \ldots \circ L_n$.
(e) If L is a regular language, then so is L^*.
(f) Nothing else is a regular language unless its construction follows from rules (a) to (e).

Examples:

(i) $\varnothing$ is a regular language (by rule (a))

(ii) $L = \{a, ab\}$ is a language over $\Sigma = \{a, b\}$ because, both $\{a\}$ and $\{b\}$ are regular languages by rule (b). By rule (d) it follows that $\{a\} \circ \{b\} = \{ab\}$ is a regular language. Using rule (c), we see that $\{a\} \cup \{ab\} = L$ is a regular language.

(iii) The language over the alphabet $\{0,1\}$ where strings contain an even number of 0's can be constructed by

$$(1^*((01^*)(01^*))^*)$$

or simply $1^*(01^*\ 01^*)^*$.

1.4.2 Regular Expressions

Regular expressions were designed to represent regular languages with a mathematical tool, a tool built from a set of primitives and operations.

This representation involves a combination of strings of symbols from some alphabet Σ, parantheses and the operators +, $\cdot$, and *.

A regular expression is obtained from the symbol $\{a, b, c\}$, empty string $\in$, and empty-set $\varnothing$ perform the operations +, $\cdot$ and * (union, concatenation and Kleene star).

Examples

$0 + 1$ represents the set $\{0, 1\}$

1 represents the set $\{1\}$

0 represents the set $\{0\}$

$(0 + 1)\ 1$ represents the set $\{01, 11\}$

$(a + b) \cdot (b + c)$ represents the set $\{ab, bb, ac, bc\}$

$$(0 + 1)^* = \in + (0 + 1) + (0 + 1)\ (0 + 1) + \cdots\cdots = \Sigma^*$$

$$(0 + 1)^+ = (0 + 1)\ (0 + 1)^* = \Sigma^+ = \Sigma^* - \{\varepsilon\}$$

1.4.3 Building Regular Expressions

Assume that $\Sigma = \{a, b, c\}$

Zero or more: a^* means "zero or more a's",

To say "zero or more ab's," i.e., $\{\lambda, ab, abab, \ldots\ldots\}$ you need to say $(ab)^*$.

One or more: Since a^* means "zero or more a's", you can use aa^* (or equivalently a^*a) to mean "one or more a's". Similarly to describe 'one or more ab's", that is $\{ab, abab, ababab, \ldots\ldots\}$, you can use $ab\ (ab)^*$.

Zero or one: It can be described as an optional 'a' with $(a + \lambda)$.

Any string at all: To describe any string at all (with $\Sigma = \{a, b, c\}$ you can use $(a+b+c)^*$.

Any nonempty string: This is written any character from $\Sigma = \{a, b, c\}$ followed by any string at all: $(a+b+c)(a+b+c)^*$

Any string not containing ....: To describe any string at all that does not contain an '*a*' (with $\Sigma = \{a, b, c\}$), you can use $(b+c)^*$.

Any string containing exactly one ....: To describe any string that contains exactly one '*a*' put "any string not containing an *a*", on either side of the '*a*' like: $(b+c)^* a(b+c)^*$.

1.4.4 Languages defined by Regular Expressions

There is a very simple correspondence between regular expressions and the languages they denote:

Regular expression	*L* (Regular Expression)
x, for each $x \in \Sigma$	$\{x\}$
λ	$\{\lambda\}$
$\varnothing$	$\{\ \}$
(r_1)	$L(r_1)$
r_1^*	$(L(r_1))^*$
$r_1 r_2$	$L(r_1)L(r_2)$
$r_1 + r_2$	$L(r_1) \cup L(r_2)$

1.4.5 Regular Expressions to NFA

(i) For any x in Σ, the regular expression denotes the language $\{x\}$. The NFA (with a single start state and a single final state) as shown below, represents exactly that language.

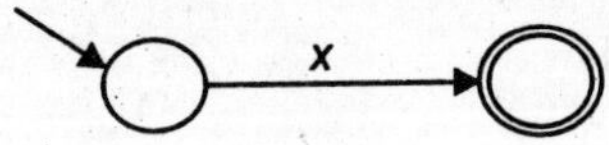

NFA for *x*

(ii) The regular expression λ denotes the language $\{\lambda\}$ that is the language containing only the empty string.

NFA for λ

(iii) The regular expression ∅ denotes the language ∅; no strings belong to this language, not even the empty string.

NFA for ∅

(iv) For juxtaposition, strings in $L(r_1)$ followed by strings in $L(r_2)$, we

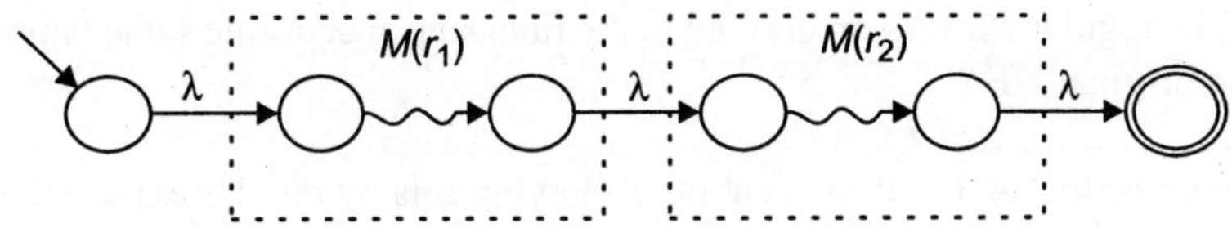

NFA for r_1r_2

chain the NFAs together as shown.

(v) The "+" denotes "or" in a regular expression, we would use an NFA with a choice of paths.

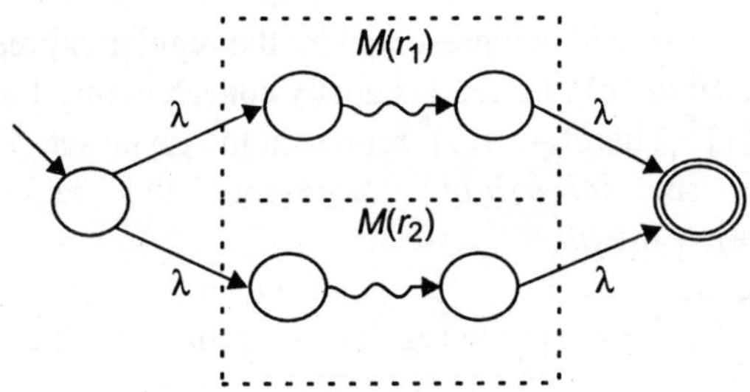

NFA for $r_1 + r_2$

(vi) The star (*) denotes zero or more applications of the regular expression, hence a loop has to be set up in the NFA.

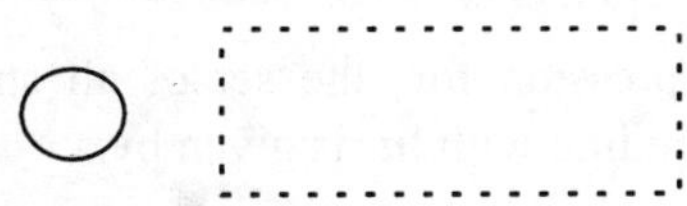

1.4.6 NFAs to Regular Expression

The basic approach to convert NFA, to Regular Expressions is as follows:

(i) If an NFA has more than one final state, convert it to an NFA with only one final state. Make the original final states nonfinal, and add a λ-transition from each to the new (single) final state.

(ii) Consider the NFA to be a generalised transition graph, which is just like an NFA except that the edges may be labeled with arbitrary regular expressions. Since the labels on the edges of an NFA may be either λ or members of each of these can be considered to be a regular expression.

(iii) Removes states one by one from the NFA, relabeling edge as you go, until only the initial and the final state remain.

(iv) Read the final regular expression from the two state automaton that results.

The regular expression derived in the final step accepts the same language as the original NFA.

Example 1.4.1: Represent the following sets by regular expression

(a) $\{\wedge, ab\}$

(b) $\{1, 11, 111, \ldots\ldots\}$

(c) $\{ab, a, b, bb\}$

Solution

(a) The set $\{\wedge, ab\}$ is represented by the regular expression $\wedge + ab$

(b) The set $\{1, 11, 111, \ldots\ldots\}$ is got by concatenating 1 and any element of $\{1\}^*$. Therefore $1(1)^*$ represent the given set.

(c) The set $\{ab, a, b, bb\}$ represents the regular expression $ab + a + b + bb$.

Example 1.4.2: Obtain the regular expressions for the following sets:

(a) The set of all strings over $\{a, b\}$ beginning and ending with 'a'.

(b) $\{b^2, b^5, b^8, \ldots\ldots\}$

(c) $\{a^{2n+1} \mid n > 0\}$

Solution

(a) The regular expression for 'the set of all strings over $\{a, b\}$ beginning and ending with 'a' is given by:

$$a\,(a + b)^* a$$

(b) The regular expression for $\{b^2, b^5, b^8, \ldots\ldots\}$ is given by:

$$bb\,(bbb)^*$$

(c) The regular expression for $\{a^{2n+1} \mid n > 0\}$ is given by:

$$a\,(aa)^*$$

Example 1.4.3: Obtain the regular expressions for the languages given by

(a) $L_1 = \{a^{2n}b^{2m+1} \mid n \geq 0, m \geq 0\}$
(b) $L_2 = \{a, bb, aa, abb, ba, bbb, \ldots\ldots\}$
(c) $L_3 = \{w \in \{0,1\}^* \mid w$ has no pair of consecutive zeros$\}$
(d) $L_4 = \{$strings of 0's and 1's ending in 00$\}$

Solution

(a) $L_1 = \{a^{2n}b^{2m+1} \mid n \geq 0, m \geq 0\}$ denotes the regular expression

$$(aa)^*(bb)^*b$$

(b) The regular expression for the language $L_2 = \{a, bb, aa, abb, ba, bbb, \ldots\ldots\}$

$$(a+b)^*\ (a+bb)$$

(c) The regular expression for the language $L_3 = \{w \in \{0,1\}^* \mid w$ has no pair of consecutive zeros$\}$ is given by

$$(1^*011^*)^*(0+\lambda)+1^*(0+\lambda)$$

(d) The regular expression for the language $L_4 = \{$strings of 0's and 1's beginning with 0 and ending with 1$\}$ is given by

$$0\ (0+1)^*1$$

Example 1.4.4: Describe the set represented by the regular expression $(aa+b)^*\ (bb+a)^*$

Solution

The given regular expression is

$$(aa+b)^*(bb+a)^*.$$

The English language description is as follows: "The set of all the strings of the form uv where a's are in pairs in u and b's are in pairs in v".

Example 1.4.5: Give Regular expressions for the following on $\Sigma = \{a, b, c\}$

(a) all strings containing exactly one a
(b) all strings containing no more than three a's
(c) all strings which contain at least one occurrence of each symbol in Σ.

(d) all strings which contain no runs of a's of length greater than two.
(e) all strings in which all runs of a's have lengths that are multiples of three.

Solution

(a) R.E $= (b+c)^* a (b+c)^*$ [for all strings containing exact one a]

(b) All strings containing no more than three a's: We can describe the string containing zero, one, two or three a's (and nothing else) as

$$(\lambda + a)(\lambda + a)(\lambda + a)$$

Now we want to allow arbitrary strings not containing a's at the places marked by X's:

$$X(\lambda + a)X(\lambda + a)X(\lambda + a)X$$

Therefore we put $(b+c)^*$ for each X.

$$(b+c)^* (\lambda + a)(b+c)^* (\lambda + a)(b+c)^* (\lambda + a)(b+c)^*$$

(c) *All strings which contain at least one occurrence of each symbol in* Σ:
Here we cannot assume the symbols are in any particular order. We have no way of saying "in any order', so we have to list the possible orders:

$$abc + acb + bac + bca + cab + cba$$

Let us put X in every place where we want to allow an arbitrary string:

$$XaXbXcX + XaXcXbX + XbXaXcX + XbXcXaX + XcXaXbX + XcXbXaX$$

Finally, we replace all X's with $(a+b+c)^*$ to get the final regular expression:

$$\begin{aligned}
&(a+b+c)^* a(a+b+c)^* b(a+b+c)^* c(a+b+c)^* +\\
&(a+b+c)^* a(a+b+c)^* c(a+b+c)^* b(a+b+c)^* +\\
&(a+b+c)^* b(a+b+c)^* a(a+b+c)^* c(a+b+c)^* +\\
&(a+b+c)^* b(a+b+c)^* c(a+b+c)^* a(a+b+c)^* +\\
&(a+b+c)^* c(a+b+c)^* a(a+b+c)^* b(a+b+c)^* +\\
&(a+b+c)^* c(a+b+c)^* b(a+b+c)^* a(a+b+c)^*
\end{aligned}$$

(d) *All strings which contain no runs of a's of length greater than two:* An expression containing no a, one a, or one aa:

$$(b+c)^* (\lambda + a + aa)(b+c)^*$$

But if we want to repeat this, we have to ensure to have least one non-a between repetitions:

$$(b+c)^*(\lambda+a+aa)(b+c)^*((b+c)(b+c)^*(\lambda+a+aa)(b+c)^*)^*$$

(e) *All strings in which all runs of* a*'s have lengths that are multiples of three:*

$$(aaa+b+c)^*$$

Example 1.4.6: Find regular expressions over $\Sigma = \{a, b\}$ for the language defined as follows:

(a) $L_1 = \{a^m b^m : m > 0\}$

(b) $L_2 = \{b^m ab^n : m > 0, n > 0\}$

(c) $L_3 = \{a^m b^m, m > 0, n > 0\}$

Solution

(a) Given $L_1 = \{a^m b^m : m > 0\}$,

L_1 has those words beginning with one or more a's followed by one or more b's.

Therefore the regular expression is

$$aa^*bb^* \text{ (or) } a^*ab^*b$$

(b) Given $L_2 = \{b^m ab^n : m > 0, n > 0\}$. This language has those words w whose letters are all b except for one 'a' that is not the first or last letter of w.

Therefore the regular expression is

$$bb^*abb^*$$

(c) Given $L_3 = \{a^m b^m, m > 0\}$.

There is no regular expression for this beginning as L_3 is not regular.

Example 1.4.7: Determine all strings in $L((a+b)^* b(a+ab)^*)$ of length less than four.

Solution

b, ab, bb, ba, aab, abb, bab, bbb, baa, bba, aba

Example 1.4.8: Find the regular expressions for the languages defined by

(i) $L_1 = \{a^n b^m : n \geq 1,\ m \geq 1,\ nm \geq 3\}$

(ii) $L_2 = \{ab^n w : n \geq 3, w \in \{a, b\}^+\}$

(iii) $L_3 = \{vwv : v, w \in \{a, b\}^*, |v| = 2\}$

(iv) $L_4 = \{w : |w| \bmod 3 = 0\}$

Solution:

(i) Regular Expression for $L_1 = \{a^n b^m : n \geq 1,\ m \geq 1,\ nm \geq 3\}$ is given by

$$aa\,(a^*)\,b(b^*) + a(a^*)\,bb\,(b^*)$$

(ii) Regular Expression for $L_2 = \{ab^n w : n \geq 3, w \in \{a, b\}^+\}$ is given by

$$abbb\,(b^*)\,(a+b)\,(a+b)^*$$

(iii) Regular Expression for $L_3 = \{vwv : v, w \in \{a, b\}^*, |v| = 2\}$ is given by

$$(a+b)\,(a+b)\,(a+b)^*\,(a+b)\,(a+b)$$

(iv) The regular expression for $L_4 = \{w : |w| \bmod 3 = 0\}$ is given by

$$(aaa + bbb + ccc\ + aab + aba + abb + bab + bba + cab + cba + cbb + caa)^*$$

1.5 TWO-WAY FINITE AUTOMATA

Two-way finite automata are machines that can read input string in either direction. This type of machines have a "read head", which can move left or right over the input string.

Like the finite automata, the two-way finite automata also have a finite set Q of states and they can be either deterministic (2DFA) or nondeterministic (2NFA).

They accept only regular sets like the ordinary finite automata. Let us assume that the symbols of the input string are occupying cells of a finite tape, one symbol per cell as shown in fig. The left and right endmarkers |— and —| enclose the input string. The endmarkers are not included in the input alphabet Σ.

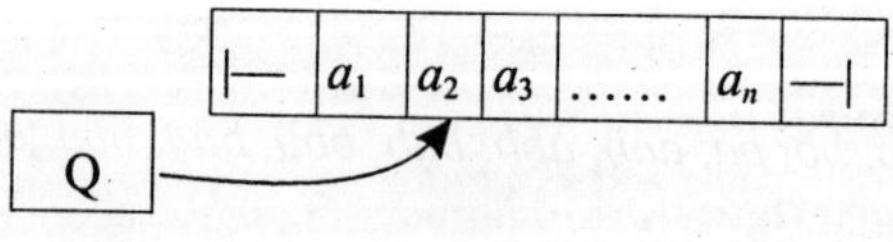

Definition

A 2DFA is an octuple

$$M = (Q,\ \Sigma, \vdash, \dashv, \delta, s, t, r)$$

where, Q is a finite set of states
Σ is a finite set of input alphabet.
$\vdash$ is the left endmarker, $\vdash\ \notin \Sigma$,
$\dashv$ is the right endmarker, $\dashv\ \notin \Sigma$,

$$\delta : Q \times (\Sigma \cup \{\vdash, \dashv\}) \rightarrow (Q \times \{L, R\}) \text{ is the transition function.}$$

$s \in Q$ is the start state,
$t \in Q$ is the accept state, and
$r \in Q$ is the reject state, $r \neq t$

such that for all the states q,

$$\delta(q, t) = (u, R) \text{ for some } u \in Q,$$
$$\delta(q, \dashv) = (v, L) \text{ for some } v \in Q$$

and for all symbols $b \in \Sigma \cup \{\vdash\}$

$$\delta(t, b) = (t, R), \qquad \delta(r, b) = (r, R)$$
$$\delta(t, \dashv) = (t, L), \qquad \delta(r, \dashv) = (r, L).$$

δ takes a state and a symbol as arguments and returns a new state and a direction to move the head i.e., if $\delta(p, b) = (q, d)$, then whenever the machine is in state p and scanning a tape cell containing symbol b, it moves its head one cell in the direction d and enters the state q.

1.6 FINITE AUTOMATA WITH OUTPUT

1.6.1 Definition

A finite-state machine $M = (Q, \Sigma, O, \delta, \lambda, q_0)$ consists of a finite set Q of states, a finite input alphabet Σ, a finite output alphabet O, a transition function δ that assigns to each state and input pair a new state, an output function λ that assigns to each state and input pair an output, and an initial state q_0.

Let $M = (Q, \Sigma, O, \delta, \lambda, q_0)$ be a finite state machine. A state table is used to denote the values of the transition function δ and the output function λ for all pairs of states and input.

1.6.2 Mealey Machine

Usually the finite automata have binary output, i.e., they accept the string or do not accept the string. This is basically decided on the basis of whether the final state is reached by the initial state. Removing this restriction, we are trying to consider a model where the outputs can be chosen from some other alphabet.

The values of the output function $F(t)$ in the most general case is a function of the present state $q(t)$ and present input $x(t)$.

$$F(t) = \lambda(q(t), x(t))$$

where λ is called the output function.

This model is called the "Mealey machine".

A "Mealey machine" is a six-tuple $(Q, \Sigma, O, \delta, \lambda, q_0)$ where all the symbols except λ have the same meaning as discussed in the sections above.

λ is the output function mapping $\Sigma \times Q$ into O.

1.6.3 Moore Machine

If the output function $F(t)$ depends only on the present state and is independent of the present input $q(t)$, then we have the output function $f(t)$ given by

$$F(t) = \lambda(q(t))$$

A Moore machine is a six-tuple $(Q, \Sigma, O, \delta, \lambda, q_0)$ with the usual meanings for symbols.

Example 1.6.1: Given state table as shown below that describes a finite-state machine with states $Q = \{q_0, q_1, q_2, q_3\}$, input alphabet $\Sigma = \{0,1\}$ and output alphabet $O = \{0, 1\}$, sketch the state diagram.

State	δ		λ	
	Input		Output	
	0	1	0	1
q_0	q_1	q_0	1	0
q_1	q_3	q_0	1	1
q_2	q_1	q_2	0	1
q_3	q_2	q_1	0	0

Solution

The given state table corresponds to finite-state machine with output. The corresponding state diagram is shown below.

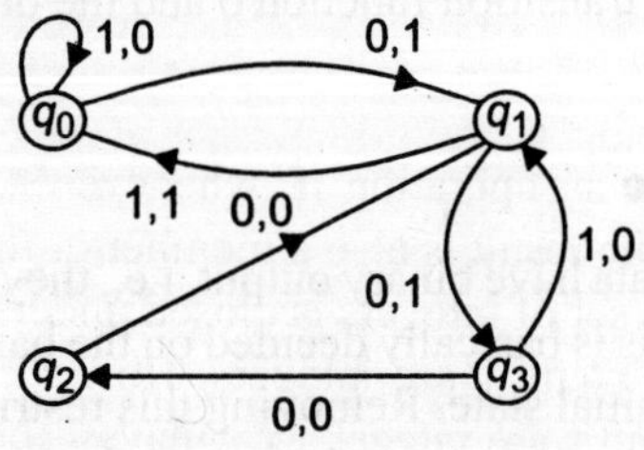

Example 1.6.2: Give examples for Moore and Mealy Models of finite automata with outputs.

Solution

State Table shown in Fig. (a) represents a Moore Machine and that of Fig. (b) shows a Mealey Machine.

	Current State	Next State δ (Input 0)	Next State δ (Input 1)	Output λ
Input →	q_0	q_3	q_1	0
	q_1	q_1	q_2	1
	q_2	q_2	q_3	0
	q_3	q_3	q_0	0

Fig. (a)

		Next State			
		Input 0		Input 1	
		State	Output	State	Output
Input →	q_1	q_3	0	q_2	0
	q_2	q_1	1	q_4	0
	q_3	q_2	1	q_1	1
	q_4	q_4	1	q_3	0

Fig. (b)

1.7 PROPERTIES OF REGULAR SETS (LANGUAGES)

A regular set (language) is a set accepted by a finite automaton.

1.7.1 Closure

A set is closed under an operation if, whenever the operation is applied to members of the set, the result is also a member of the set.

For example, the set of integers is closed under addition, because $x + y$ is an integer whenever x and y are integers. However, integers are not closed under division: if x and y are integers, x/y may or may not be an integer.

There are several operations defined on languages:

$L_1 \cup L_2$: strings in either L_1 or L_2.
$L_1 \cap L_2$: strings in both L_1 and L_2.
$L_1 L_2$: strings composed of one string from L, followed by one string from L_2.
$-L_2$: All strings (over the same alphabet) not in L_1.
L_1^* : Zero or more strings from L_1 concatenated together
$L_1 - L_2$: strings in L_1 that are not in L_2.
L_1^R : strings in L_1, reversed.

We shall show that the set of regular languages is closed under each of these operations.

1.7.2 Union, Concatenation, Negation, Kleene Star, Reverse

The general approach is as follows:

(i) Build automata (DFA or NFA) for each of the languages involved.
(ii) Show how to combine the automata in order to form a new automaton which recognizes the desired language.
(iii) Since the language is represented by NFA/DFA, we shall conclude that the language is regular.

Union of L_1 and L_2

(a) Create a new start state
(b) Make a λ-transition from the new start state to each of the original start states.

Concatenation of L_1 and L_2

(a) Put a λ-transition from each final state of L_1 to the initial state of L_2.
(b) Make the original final states of L_1 nonfinal.

1.7.3 Intersection and Set Difference

Just as with the other operations, it can be proved that regular languages are closed under intersection and set difference by starting with automata for the initial languages, and constructing a new automaton that represents the operation applied to the initial languages.

In this construction, a completely new machine is formed, whose states are labelled with an ordered pair of state names: the first element of each pair is a state from L_1 and the second element of each pair is a state from L_2.

(a) Begin by creating a start state whose label is (start state of L_1, start state of L_2).

(b) Repeat the following until no new arcs can be added:

  (1) Find a state (A, B) that lacks a transition for some x in Σ.
  (2) Add a transition on x from state (A, B) to state $(\delta(A, x), \delta(B, x))$. (If this state does not already exist, create it).

Negation of L_1

(a) Start with a complete DFA, not with an NFA
(b) Make every final state nonfinal and every nonfinal state final.

Kleene star of L_1

(a) Make a new start state; connect it to the original start state with a λ-transition.
(b) Make a new final state; connect the original final state (which becomes nonfinal) to it with λ-transitions.
(c) Connect the new start state and new final state with a pair of λ-transitions.

Reverse of L_1

(a) Start with an automaton with just one final state.
(b) Make the initial state final and final state initial.
(c) Reverse the direction of every arc.

The same construction is used for both intersection and set difference. The distinction is in how the final states are selected.

Intersection

Make a state (A, B) as final if both

(i) A is a final state in L_1 and
(ii) B is a final state in L_2

Set Difference

Mark a state (A, B) as final if A is a final state in L_1, but B is not a final state in L_2.

1.8 PUMPING LEMMA

1.8.1 Principle of Pumping Lemma

- If an infinite language is regular, it can be defined by a DFA.
- The DFA has some finite number of states (say).
- Since the language is infinite, some strings of the language should have length $> n$.

- For a string of length > n accepted by the DFA, the walk through the DFA must contain a cycle.
- Repeating the cycle an arbitrary number of times should yield another string accepted by the DFA.

The "pumping lemma" for regular languages is another way of showing that a given infinnite language is not regular. The proof is always done by "contradiction". The technique that is followed is as outlined below:

(i) Assume that the language L is regular.
(ii) By Pigeon-hole principle, any sufficiently long string in L should repeat some state in the DFA, and therefore, the walk contains a "cycle".
(iii) Show that repeating the cycle some number of times ("pumping" the cycle) yields a string that is not in L.
(iv) Conclude that L is not regular.

1.8.2 Applying the Pumping Lemma

Definition of Pumping Lemma

If L is an infinite regular language, then there exists some positive integer 'm' such that any string $w \in L$, whose length is 'm' or greater can be decomposed into three parts, xyz where

(i) $|xy|$ is less than or equal to m.
(ii) $|y| > 0$,
(iii) $w_i = xy^i z$ is also in L for all $i = 0, 1, 2, 3, \ldots\ldots$

To use this lemma, we need to show:

(i) For any choice of m,
(ii) For some $w \in L$ that we get to choose (and we will choose one of length at least 'm').
(iii) For any way of decomposing w into xyz, so long as $|xy|$ is not greater than m and y is not λ,
(iv) We can choose an i such that xy^iz is not in L.

Example 1.8.1: Prove that $L = \{a^n b^n : n \geq 0\}$ is not regular.

Solution

(i) We don't know m, but let us assume that there is one.
(ii) Choose a string $w = a^n b^n$, where $n > m$, so that any prefix of length 'm' consists only of a's.

(iii) We don't know the decomposition of w into xyz, but since $|xy| \le m$, xy must consist entirely of a's. Moreover, y cannot be empty.

(iv) Choose $i = 0$. This has the effect of dropping $|y|$ a's out of the string, without affectng the number of b's. The resultant string has fewer a's than b's, hence does not belong to L.

Therefore L is not regular.

Example 1.8.2: Prove that $L = \{a^n b^k \; : n > k \text{ and } n \ge 0\}$ is not regular.

Solution

(i) We do not know 'm', but assume there is one.

(ii) Choose a string $w = a^n b^k$, where $n > m$, so that any prefix of length 'm' consists entirely of a's, and $k = n - 1$, so that there is just one more a than b.

(iii) We do not know the decomposition of w into xyz, but since $|xy| \le m$, xy must consist entirely of a's. Moreover, y cannot be empty.

(iv) Choose $i = 0$. This has the effect of dropping $|y|$ a's out of the string, without affecting the number of b's. The resultant string fewer a's than before, so it has either fewer a's than b's, or the same number of each. Either way, the string does not belong to L, so L is not regular.

Example 1.8.3: Show that $L = \{a^n : n \text{ is a prime number}\}$ is not regular.

Solution

(i) We don't know m, but assume there is one.

(ii) Chose a string $w = a^n$ where n is a prime number and $|xyz| = n > m + 1$. (This can always be done because there is no largest prime number). Any prefix of w consists entirely of a's.

(iii) We do not know the decomposition of w into xyz but since $|xy| \le m$, it follows that $|z| > 1$. As usual, $|y| > 0$.

(iv) Since $|z| > 1$, $|xy| > 1$.. Choose $i = |xz|$. Then $|xy^i z| = |xz| + |y|\,|xz|$

$$= (1 + |y|)\,|xz|.$$

Since $(1 + |y|)$ and $|xz|$ are each greater than 1, the product must be a composite number.

Therefore $|xy^i z|$ is a composite number.

Hence L is not regular.

1.9 CLOSURE PROPERTIES OF REGULAR LANGUAGES

THEOREM 1: If L_1 and L_2 are regular over Σ, then $L_1 \cup L_2$ is regular i.e., union of two regular sets is also regular. [Regular sets are closed w.r.t. union].

Proof: As L_1 and L_2 are given to be regular; there exists finite automata $M_1 = (Q, \Sigma, \delta_1, q_1, F_1)$ and $M_2 = (Q_2, \Sigma, \delta_2, q_2, F_2)$ such that $L_1 = T(M_1)$ and $L_2 = T(M_2)$.

$$[T(M) = \{x \in \Sigma^* : \delta(q_0, x) \in F\}$$

is a language $L(M)$ accepted by M]

Let us assume that $Q_1 \cap Q_2 = \emptyset$.

Let us define NFA with $\in$-transitions as follows:

$$M_3 = (Q, \Sigma, \delta, q_0, F)$$

where

(i) $Q = Q_1 \cup Q_2 \cup \{q_0\}$ where q_0 is a new state not in $Q_1 \cup Q_2$

(ii) $F = F_1 \cup F_2$

(iii) δ is defined by $\delta(q_0, \in) = \{q_1, q_2\}$ (a)

$$\delta(q, a) = \begin{cases} \delta_1(q, a) \text{ if } q \in Q_1 \\ \delta_2(q, a) \text{ if } q \in Q_2 \end{cases} \quad \text{(b)}$$

It is obvious that $\delta(q_0, \in) = \{q_1, q_2\}$ induces $\in$-transitions either to the initial state q_1 of M_1 or initial state q_2 of M_2.

From (b), the transitions of M are the same as transitions M_1 or M_2 depending on whether q_1 or q_2 reached by $\in$-transitions from q_0.

Since $F = F_1 \cup F_2$, any string accepted by M_1 or M_2 accepted by M.

Therefore $L_1 \cup L_2 = T(M)$ and so is regular. □

THEOREM 2: If L is regular and $L \subseteq \Sigma^*$, then $\Sigma^* - L$ is also a regular set.

Proof: Let $L = T(M)$ where $M = (Q, \Sigma, \delta, q_0, F)$ is an FA.

Though $L \subseteq \Sigma^*$, $\delta(q, a)$ need not be defined as for all 'a' in Σ.

$\delta(q, a)$ is defined for some 'a' in Σ eventhough 'a' does not find a place in the strings accepted by M.

Let us now modify Σ, Q and δ as defined below.

(i) If $a \in \Sigma_1 - \Sigma$, then the symbol 'a' will not appear in any string of $T(M)$. Therefore we delete 'a' from Σ_1 and all transitions defined by the symbol 'a'. $T(M)$ is not affected by this).

(ii) If $\Sigma - \Sigma_1 \neq \emptyset$, we add a dead state d to Q. We define $\delta(d, a) = d$ for all 'a' in Σ and $\delta(d, a) = d$ for all q in Q and 'a' in $\Sigma - \Sigma_1$.

Once again $T(M)$ is not affected by this.

Let us consider M got after applying (i) and (ii) to Σ, Q and δ. We write the modified M as

$$(Q, \Sigma, \delta, q_0, F).$$

Let us now define a new automaton M' by

$$M' = (Q, \Sigma, \delta, q_0, Q - F).$$

We can see that $w \in T(M')$ iff $\delta(q_0, w) \in Q - F$ and $w \notin T(M)$. Therefore $\Sigma^* - L = T(M')$ and therefore regular. □

THEOREM 3: If L_1 and L_2 are regular, so is $L_1 \cap L_2$ [Regular sets are closed w.r.t. Intersection]

Proof: It is important to note that

$$L_1 \cap L_2 = (L_1^c \cup L_2^c)^c$$

If L_1 and L_2 are regular, then L_1^c, L_2^c are regular by theorem 1.

Therefore $(L_1^c \cup L_2^c)^c$ is regular by theorem 2.

Hence $L_1 \cap L_2$ is regular. □

1.10 MYHILL-NERODE THEOREM

1.10.1 Myhill-Nerode Relations

Isomorphism

Two DFAs given by $M = (Q_M, \Sigma, \delta_m, s_m, F_m)$ and $N = (Q_N, \Sigma, \delta_n, s_n, F_n)$ are said to be "isomorphic" if there is a one-to-one and onto mapping $f : Q_M \to Q_N$ such that

(i) $f(s_M) = s_N$,

(ii) $f(\delta_M(p, a)) = \delta_N(f(p), a)$ for all $P \in Q_M, a \in \Sigma$,

(iii) $p \in F_M$ *if* $f(p) \in F_N$.

Isomorphic automata accept same set.

Myhill-Nerode Relations

Let $R \subseteq \Sigma^*$ be a regular set, and let $M = (Q, \Sigma, \delta, s, F)$ be a DFA for R with no inaccessible states.

The automaton M induces an equivalence relation $\equiv_M$ on Σ^* defined by

$$x \equiv_M y \overset{def}{\Leftrightarrow} \hat{\delta}(s, x) = \hat{\delta}(s, y)$$

It is easy to show that the relation $\equiv_M$ is an equivalence relation, meaning it is reflexive, symmetric and transitive.

A few properties satisfied by $\equiv_M$ are as follows:

(a) It is a *right congruence:* for any $x, y \in \Sigma^*$ and $a \in \Sigma$,

$$x \equiv_M y \Rightarrow xa \equiv_M y_a$$

Proof: Assume $x \equiv_M y$.
Therefore we have

$$\begin{aligned}\hat{\delta}(s, xa) &= \delta(\hat{\delta}(s, x), a)\\ &= \delta(\hat{\delta}(s, y), a) \quad \text{(by assumption)}\\ &= \hat{\delta}(s, ya)\end{aligned}$$ □

(b) It refines R : for any $x, y \in \Sigma^*$,

$$x \equiv_M y \Rightarrow (x \in R \Leftrightarrow y \in R).$$

Proof: Since $\hat{\delta}(s, x) = \hat{\delta}(s, y)$, which is either an accept state or a reject state, so either both x and y are accepted or both are rejected. □

(c) It is of "Finite index": i.e., it has only finitely many equivalence class. This is because there is exactly one equivalence class

$$\{x \in \Sigma^* \mid \hat{\delta}(s, x) = q\}$$

corresponding to each state q of M.

Hence the equivalence relation $\equiv$ on Σ^* is a "Myhill-Herode relation" for R if it satisfies properties (a), (b) and (c). i.e., if it is a right congruence of finite index refining R.

1.10.2 Myhill-Nerode Theorem

Let $R \subseteq \Sigma^*$. The following statements are equivalent.

(i) R is regular
(ii) There exists a Myhill-Nerode relation for R
(iii) The relation $\equiv_R$ is of finite index.

(The proof is beyond the scope of this book).

Example 1.10.1: Using Myhill-Nerode Theorem verify whether $L = \{a^n b^n : n \geq 0\}$ is regular or not.

Solution

This is done by determining the $\equiv_R$-classes. If $k \neq m$, then $a^k \not\equiv_L a^m$, since

$a^k b^k \in L$ but $a^m b^k \notin L$. Hence there are infinitely many $\equiv_L$-classes, at least one for each $a^k, k \geq 0$.

Hence by Myhill-Nerode Theorem L is not regular. (The application of Myhill-Nerode theorem has been illustrated above).

GLOSSARY

Automaton: Abstract model of a digital computer.

Acceptor: Automaton whose output response is "Yes" or "No"

DFA: Deterministic Finite Automata.

NFA: Non-deterministic Finite Automata.

Regular Language: Language that can be constructed from the set operations—Union, Concatenation and Kleene star.

Regular expression: Mathematical tool built from a set of primitives and operations.

Two-way Finite Automata: Machines that can read input string in either direction.

Moore machine: Output function depends only on present state and independent of present input.

Mealey machine: Value of the output function is a function of the present state and present input in a Mealey Machine.

Pumping lemma: A way to show that an infinite language is not regular.

REVIEW QUESTIONS

1. Define the term 'Automata' with an example.
2. What are the types of Automaton?
3. Explain Deterministic automata with an example.
4. Explain Non-deterministic automaton with an example.
5. Distinguish between DFA and NFA.
6. Explain the terms:
   (a) State Table diagram
   (b) State Transition diagram.
7. Define Non-deterministic Finite automata.
8. Comment on the equivalence of NFA and DFA.
9. What are regular expressions?
10. Define a regular language.
11. Give examples for regular expressions.

12. Comment on the correspondence between regular expressions and the languages they denote.
13. How will you convert an NFA to a regular expression?
14. What do you mean by two way finite automata?
15. What do you mean by finite automata with output.
16. What do you mean by a Mealy machine?
17. What do you mean by a Moore machine?
18. Give examples for Moore and mealy models of finite automata with outputs.
19. State the properties of regular sets.
20. State the principle of pumping lemma.
21. Define Pumping lemma.
22. Explain the closure properties of Regular languages.
23. What is Isomorphism?
24. State the Myhill-Nerode relations.

EXERCISES

1. For $\Sigma = \{a, b\}$ construct DFA that accepts the following set of strings
   (a) all strings with exactly one 'a'
   (b) all strings with at least one 'a'
   (c) all strings with no more than three a's
   (d) all strings with at least one 'a' and exactly two b's.
   (e) $L = \{ w : |w| \bmod 3 = 0 \}$
   (f) $L = \{ w : |w| \bmod 5 \neq 0 \}$
2. Determine a DFA that accepts all strings on {0,1} except those containing the substring 001.
3. Obtain the NFA for a language defined by

$$L = \{a^n b^m / n, m \geq 1\}.$$

   and its associated state table diagram.
4. Construct an NFA for the state table given below.

δ	0	1
q_0	$\{q_0, q_1\}$	$\{q_3\}$
q_1	$\{q_0\}$	$\{q_1, q_3\}$
q_2	$\emptyset$	$\{q_0, q_2\}$
q_3	$\{q_1, q_2, q_3\}$	$\{q_1\}$

5. Obtain the language recognised by the NDA shown below.

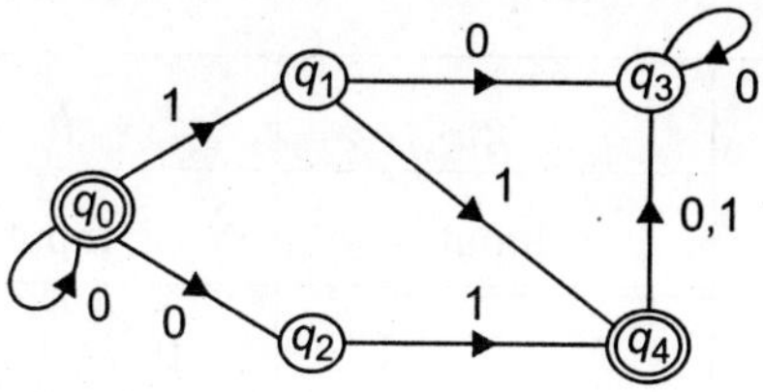

6. Convert the NDA to DFA given $M = (\{q_0, q_1, q_2\}, \{a, b\}, \delta, q_0, \{q_1\})$ with state table as given below

	a	b
q_0	$\{q_1, q_2\}$	$\varnothing$
q_1	$\varnothing$	$\{q_2\}$
q_2	$\varnothing$	$\{q_2\}$

7. Determine the DFA that accepts the language

$$L(aa^* + aba^* + b^*)$$

8. Determine the DFA that accepts the language

$$L(ab(a + ab^*(a + aa)).$$

9. Determine the regular expression for the languages accepted by the following automata:

(a)

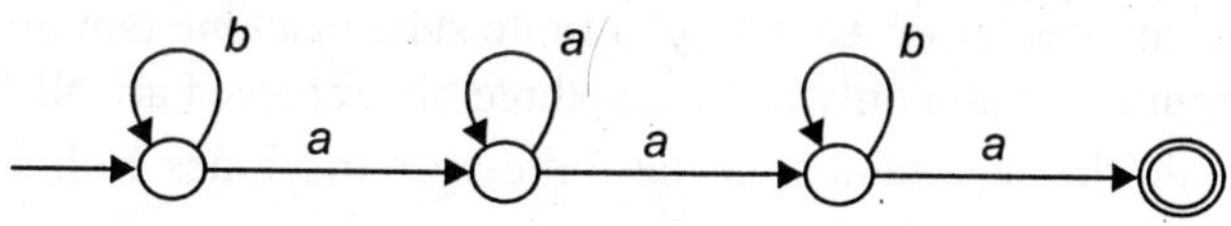

(b)

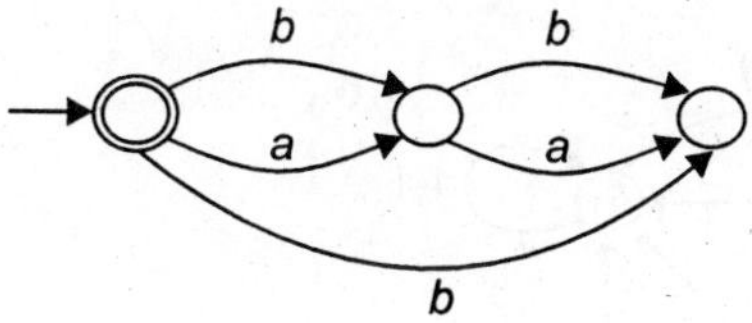

(c)

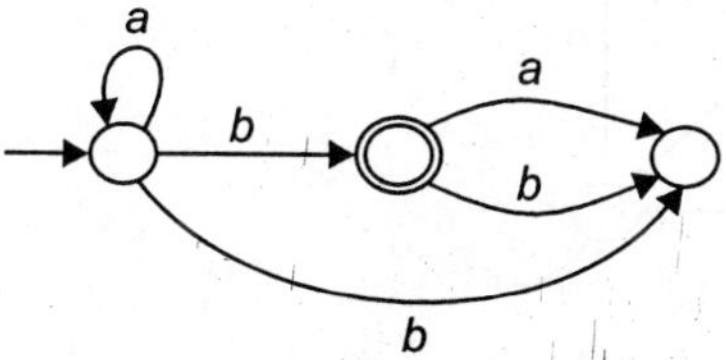

10. Construct the state diagram for the finite-state machine with the state table shown below.

	g		*h*	
	Input		Input	
State	0	1	0	1
s_0	s_1	s_0	1	0
s_1	s_3	s_0	1	1
s_2	s_1	s_2	0	1
s_3	s_2	s_1	0	0

11. Construct the state table for the finite-state machine with the state diagram shown below.

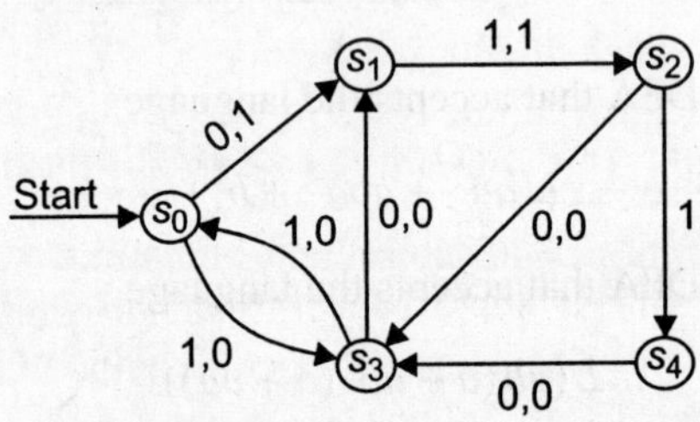

12. In a given coding algorithm, when three consecutive 1's appear in a message, the receiver of the message knows that there has been a transmission error. Construct a finite state machine that gives a 1 as its output but if and only if the last three bits received are all 1's.

13. Obtain the state tables for the finite-state machines with the following state diagrams.

(a)

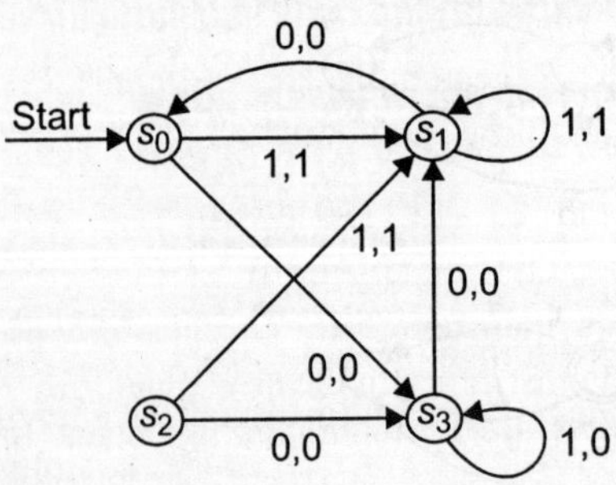

(b) 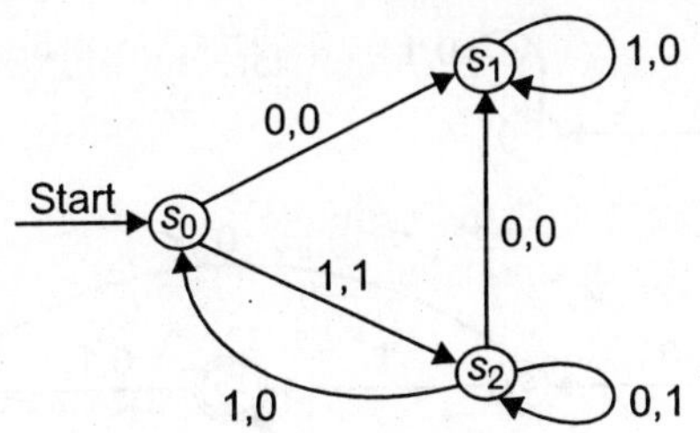

14. For the finite-state machine shown in problem (13), determine the output for each of the following input strings
    (a) 0111
    (b) 11011011
    (c) 01010101010
15. Construct a finite-state machine that delays an input string two bits, giving 00 as the first two bits of output.
16. Construct a finite state machine that determines whether the input string has a 1 in the last position and a 0 in the third to the last position read so far.
17. Construct the state table for the Moore machine with the state diagram shown below. Each input string to a Moore machine M produces an output string. The output corresponding to an input string $a_1, a_2, \ldots\ldots, a_k$ is the string $g(s_0)g(s_1) \ldots\ldots g(s_k)$ where $s_1 = f(s_{i-a}, a_i)$ for $i = 1, 2, \ldots\ldots k$.

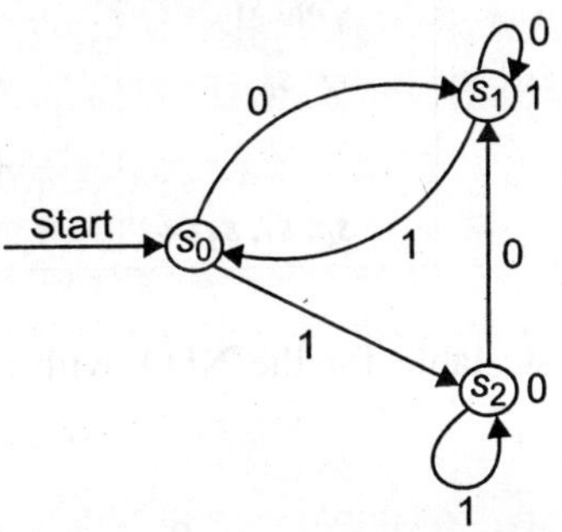

18. Determine the output generated by the Moore machine shown in problem (17), with each of the input strings shown below.

    (a) 0101 (b) 111111 (c) 11101110111
19. Construct a Moore machine that determines whether an input string contains an even or odd number of 1^s. The machine should give 1 as output if an even number of 1^s are in the string and 0 as output if an odd number of 1^s are in the string.
20. Obtain the languages recognized by each of the following Finite-state automata shown below.

(a) 

(b) 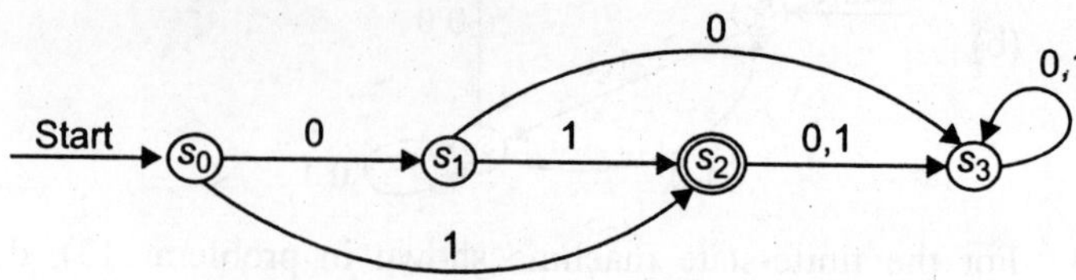

(c) 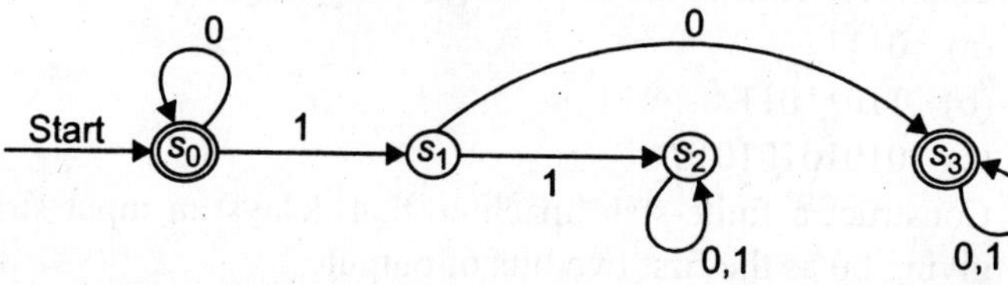

21. **Obtain the NDA with state table shown below.**

State	f Input 0	1
s_0	s_0, s_1	s_3
s_1	s_0	s_1, s_3
s_2		s_0, s_2
s_3	s_0, s_1, s_2	s_1

22. **Determine the state table for the NDA with state diagram as shown below.**

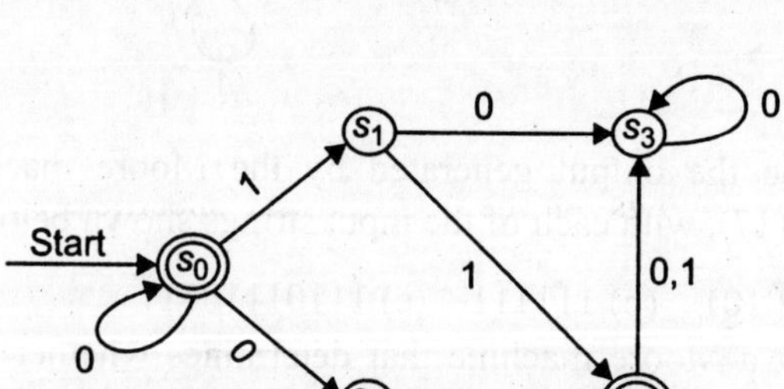

23. **Determine a DFA that recognizes the same language as the NDA shown in problem 2.2 (Determine the language first).**

24. **Determine the language recognized by the NDA shown below.**

(a) 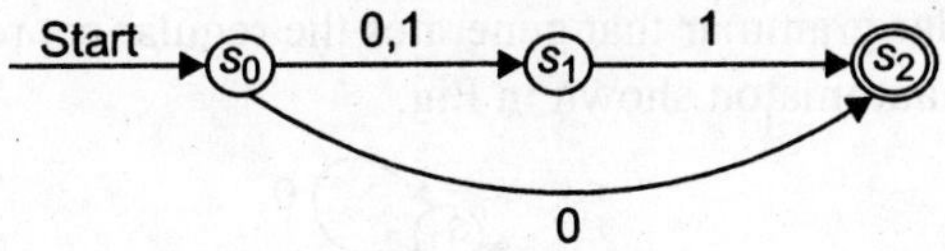

(b) 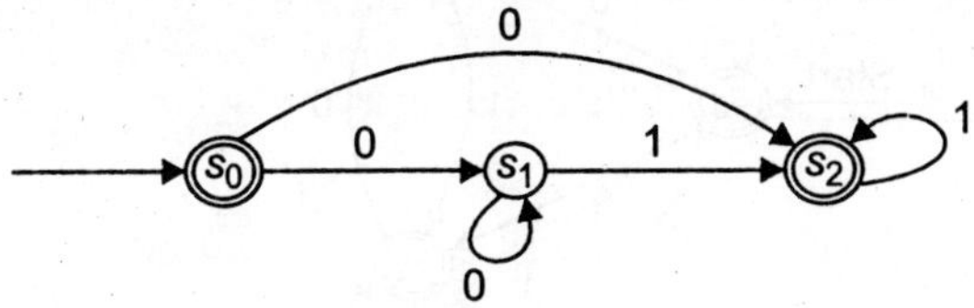

(c) 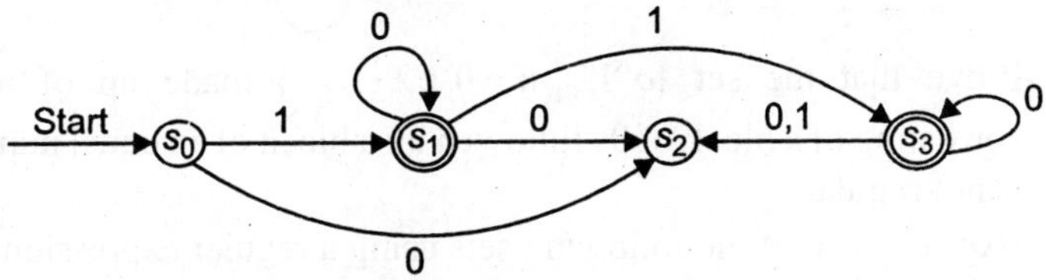

25. **Determine the languages recognized by the given DFA.**

(a) 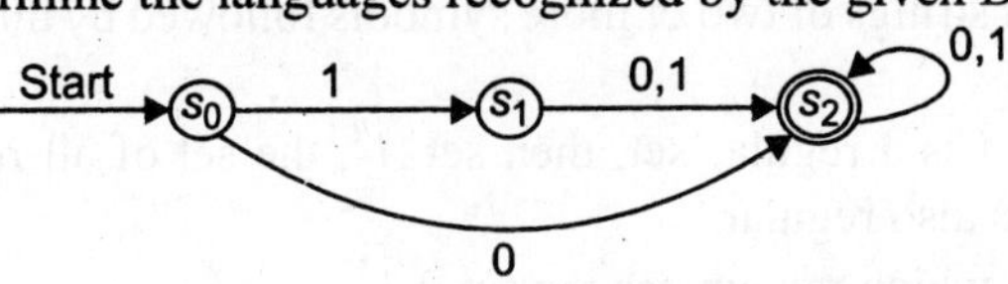

(b) 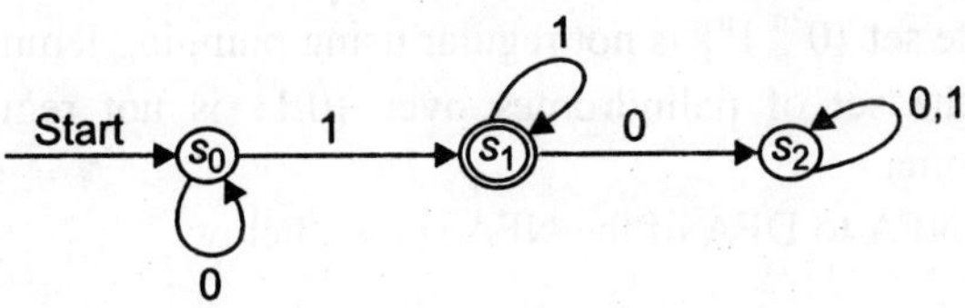

26. **Determine a DFA that recognizes each of the following**

   (a) $\{1^n \mid n = 1, 2, 3, \ldots\ldots\}$

   (b) $\{1, 00\}$

   (c) $\{0\}$

27. **Show that there is no finite-state automaton that recognizes the set of bit strings containing an equal number of 0^s and 1^s.**

28. **What are the strings in the regular sets specified by the regular expressions given below.**

   (a) 10^*

   (b) $(10)^*$

   (c) $0 \cup 01$

   (d) $0(0 \cup 1)^*$

   (e) $(0 * 1)^*$.

29. **Construct a NDA that recognizes the regular set $1^* \cup 01$.**

30. Determine a regular grammar that generates the regular set recognized by the finite state automaton shown in Fig.

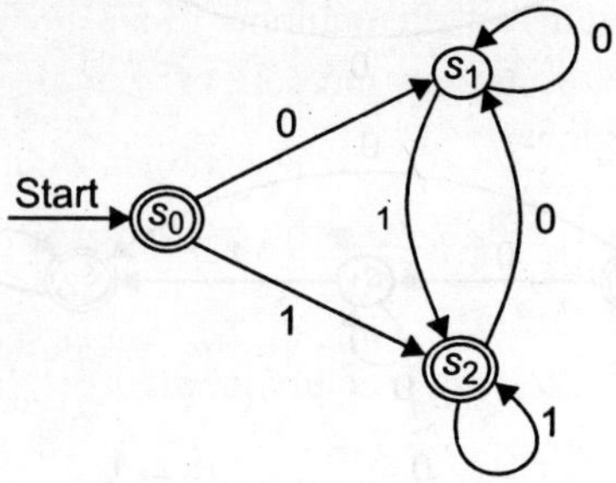

31. Prove that the set $\{o^n 1^n \mid n = 0, 1, 2, \ldots\ldots\}$ made up of all strings consisting of a block of 0s followed by a block of an equal number of 1^s, is not regular.

32. Express each of the following sets using a regular expression.
   (a) the set of strings of one or more 0s followed by a 1.
   (b) the set of strings of two or more symbols followed by three or more 0s.

33. Show that if A is a regular set, then set A^R, the set of all reversals of strings in A, is also regular.

34. Find an NDA which recognizes the set $0^* 1^*$.

35. Show that the set $\{0^{2n} 1^n\}$ is not regular using pumping lemma.

36. Show that the set of palindromes over $\{0,1\}$ is not regular using pumping lemma.

37. Convert the NFA to DFA of the NFA shown below.

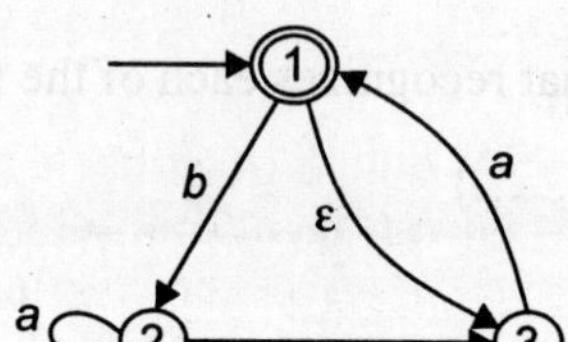

38. Convert the regular expression $(ab \cup a)^*$ to an NFA.

39. Convert the regular expression $(a \cup b)^* aba$ to an NFA.

40. Using pumping lemma show that the following languages are not regular.
   (a) $L_1 = \{0^n 1^n 2^n \mid n \geq 0\}$
   (b) $L_2 = \{a^{2^n} \mid n \geq 0\}$ (a^{2^n} means a string of 2^n a's).

41. Give regular expressions for each of the following subsets of $\{a, b\}^*$.
   (a) $\{x \mid x$ contains an even number of a's $\}$

(b) $\{x \mid x$ contains an odd number of b's$\}$
(c) $\{x \mid x$ contains an even number of a's or an odd number of b's$\}$
(d) $\{x \mid x$ contains an even number of a's and an odd number of b's$\}$

42. Give the DFA accepting the sets of strings matching the following regular expressions:
(a) $(000^* + 111^*)^*$
(b) $(01 + 10)(01 + 10)(01 + 10)$
(c) $(0 + 1(01^*0)^*1)^*$

43. Show that the following sets are not regular.
(a) $\{a^n b^m \mid n = 2m\}$
(b) $\{x \in \{a, b, c\}^* \mid x$ is a palindrome$\}$
(c) $\{x \in \{a, b, c\}^* \mid$ the length of x is a square$\}$

44. Consider the NFA shown below.

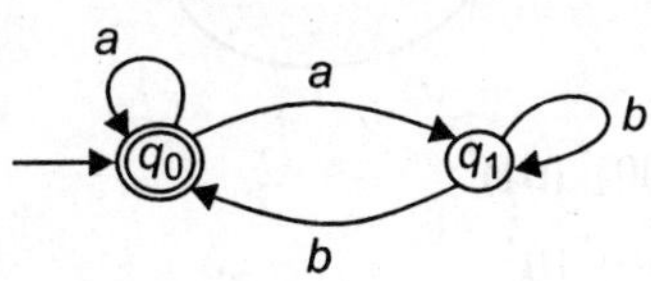

(a) Construct an equivalent DFA.
(b) Give an equivalent regular expression.

45. Convert the NDA to equivalent DFA for each of the following:

(a)
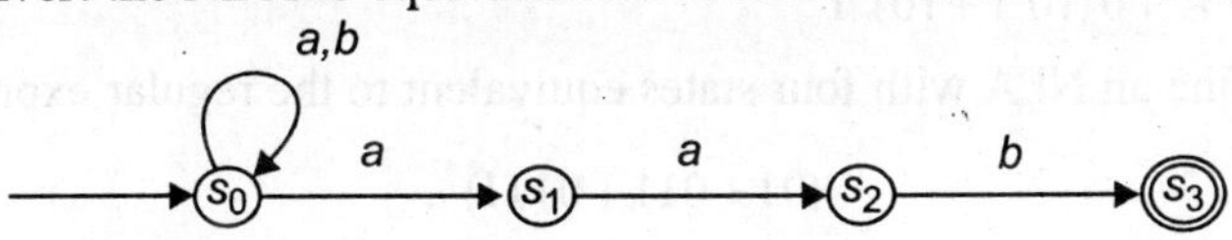

(b)
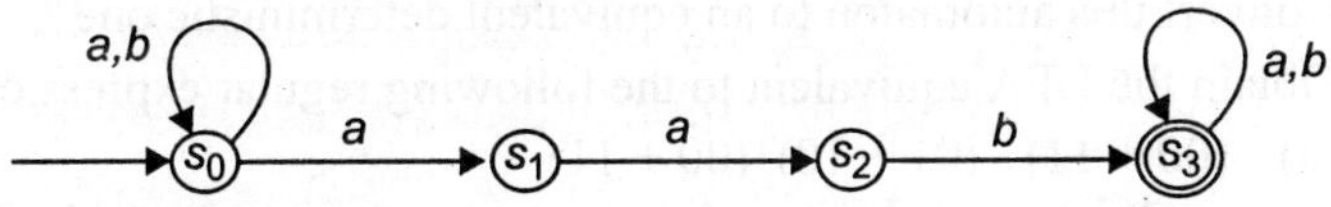

46. Give the regular expressions for each of the following subsets of $\{a, b\}^*$.
(a) $\{x \mid x$ does not contain the substring $a\}$
(b) $\{x \mid x$ does not contain the substring $ab\}$
(c) $\{x \mid x$ does not contain the substring $aba\}$

47. Match each NFA with an equivalent regular expression.

(a)
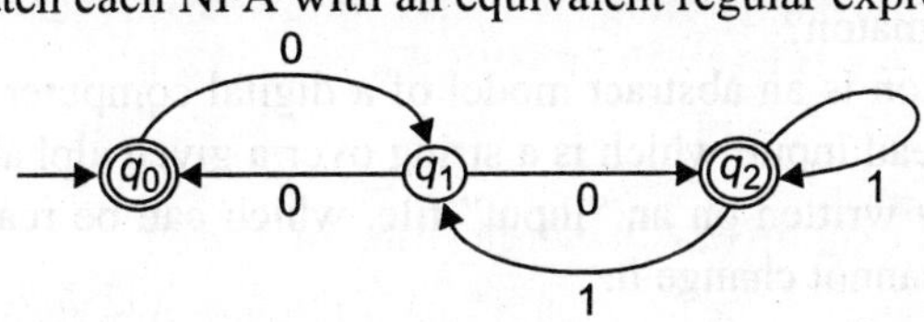

(b)

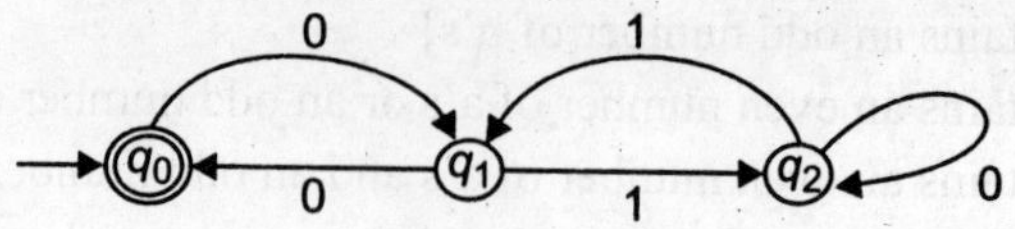

(c)

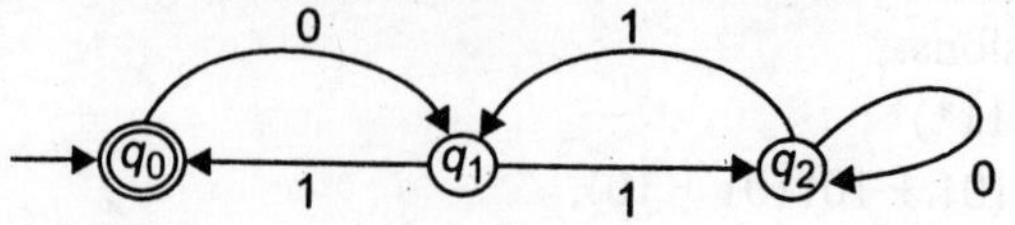

(d)

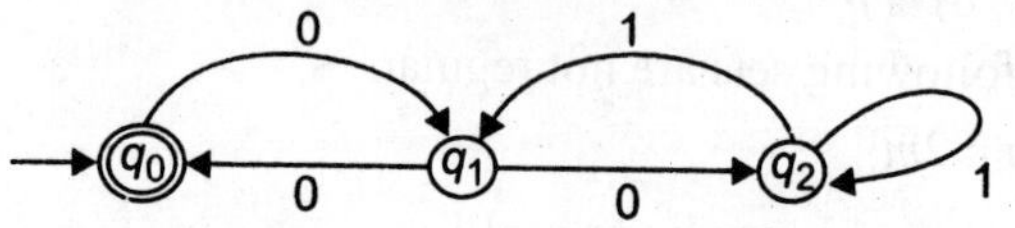

(e)

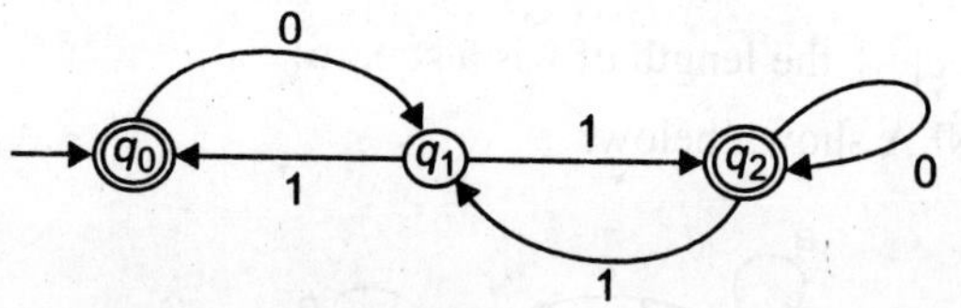

(i) $\in +0(01^*1+00)^*(01)^*$

(ii) $\in +0(10^*1+10)^*10^*$

(iii) $\in +0(10^*1+00)^*0$

(iv) $\in +0(01^*1+00)^*0$

(v) $\in +0(10^*1+10)^*1$

48. Define an NFA with four states equivalent to the regular expression

$$(01+011+0111)^*.$$

Convert this automaton to an equivalent deterministic one.

49. Obtain the DFA equivalent to the following regular expressions:

(a) $(00+11)^*\ (01+10)\ (00+11)^*$

(b) $(000)^*\ 1+(00)^*1$

(c) $(0\ (01)^*\ (1+00)+1\ (10)^*\ (0+11))^*$

SHORT QUESTIONS AND ANSWERS

1. What is an automaton?

An Automaton is an abstract model of a digital computer. It has a mechanism to read input, which is a string over a given alphabet. This input is actually written on an "input" file, which can be read by the automaton but cannot change it.

2. What are the types of Automaton?

(a) Deterministic Automata

(b) Non-deterministic Automata

3. What do you mean by deterministic automata?

If the internal state, input and contents of storage are known, it is possible to predict the future behaviour of the automaton. This is said to be deterministic automaton.

4. What do you mean by non-deterministic automata?

If the internal state, input and contents of storage are known, if it is not possible to predict the future behaviours of the automaton, it is said to be non-determine automaton.

5. Give the formal definition of Deterministic Finite Automaton (DFA).

A Deterministic Finite Automaton (DFA) is a *t*-tuple

$$M = (Q, \Sigma, \delta, q_0, F)$$

where

Q = Finite state of "internal states"

Σ = Finite state of symbols called 'Input Alphabet'.

$\delta : Q \times \Sigma \rightarrow Q$ = Transition function

$q_0 \in Q$ = Initial state

$F \subseteq Q$ = Set of Final states.

6. Define the transition function δ in DFA.

If $\delta(q_0, a) = q_1$, then if the DFA is in state q_0 and the current input symbol is a, the DFA will go into state q_1.

7. Give the formal definition of Non-deterministic Finite Automata (NFA).

A non-deterministic Finite Automata (NFA) is defined by a 5-tuple

$$M = (Q, \Sigma, \delta, q_0, F)$$

where $Q, \Sigma, \delta, q_0, F$ are defined as follows:

Q = Finite set of internal states

Σ = Finite set of symbols called 'Input alphabet'

$\delta = Q \times (\Sigma \cup \{\lambda\}) \rightarrow 2^Q$

$q_0 \in Q$ is the 'Initial state'

$F \subseteq Q$ is a set of Final states.

8. What is the difference between NFA and DFA in terms of the transition function δ?

NFA differs from DFA is that, the range of δ in NFA is in the powerset 2^Q.

9. When is a string accepted by an NFA?

A string is accepted by an NFA if there is some sequence of possible moves that will put the machine in the final state at the end of the string.

10. When are two finite acceptors M_1 and M_2 said to be equivalent?

Two finite acceptors M_1 and M_2 are said to be equivalent if

$$L(M_1) = L(M_2)$$

i.e., if both accept the same language.

11. Is it possible to convert every NFA into an equivalent DFA?

Yes, it is possible to convert every NFA into an equivalent DFA and vice-versa.

12. What are regular languages?

Regular languages are those languages that can be constructed from the three set operations (a) Union (b) Concatenation and (c) Kleene star.

13. Give the formal definition of a regular language.

Let Σ be an alphabet. The class of 'regular languages' over Σ is defined inductively as follows:

(a) $\varnothing$ is a regular language
(b) For each $\sigma \in \Sigma, \{\sigma\}$ is a regular language
(c) For any natural number $n \geq 2$ if $L_1, L_2, \ldots\ldots L_n$ are regular languages, then so is $L_1 \cup L_2 \ldots\ldots \cup L_n$.
(d) For any natural number $n \geq 2$ if $L_1, L_2, \ldots\ldots L_n$ are regular languages, then so is $L_1 \circ L_2 \circ \ldots\ldots \circ L_n$.
(e) If L is a regular language, then so is L^*.
(f) Nothing else is a regular language unless its construction follows from rules (a) to (e).

14. Give an example of a regular language.

The language over the alphabet {0, 1} whose strings contain an even number of 0's can be constructed by

$$1^*((01^*)(01^*))^*)$$

or simply $1^*(01^*01^*)^*$.

15. What is the motivation behind writing regular expressions?

Regular expresions were designed to represent regular languages with a mathematical tool, a tool built from a set of primitives and operations.

16. How are regular expressions formed?

A regular expression is obtained from the symbols {a, b, c}, empty string $\in$, and empty set $\varnothing$ performing the operations +, $\cdot$ and * (union concatenation and Kleene star).

17. What do the following regular expressions represent?

(a) $(0+1)\,1$ (b) $(a+b)\cdot(b+c)$ (c) $(0+1)^*$ (d) 0 (e) $(0+1)^+$

(a) $(0+1)\,1$ represents the set {01, 11}
(b) $(a+b)\cdot(b+c)$ represents the set $\{ab, bb, ac, bc\}$

(c) $(0 + 1)^*$ represents the following:

$$(0+1)^* = \in + (0+1) + (0+1)(0+1) + \cdots\cdots = \Sigma^*$$

(d) 0 represents the set { 0 }

(e) $(0+1)^+ = (0+1)(0+1)^* = \Sigma^+ = \Sigma^* - \{\in\}$

18. What are the languages defined by the following regular expressions?
(a) $\varnothing$ (b) $r_1 r_2$ (c) $r_1 + r_2$

(a) For $\varnothing$, the language is { }

(b) For $r_1 r_2$, the language is $L(r_1)L(r_2)$.

(c) For $r_1 + r_2$, the language is $L(r_1) \cup L(r_2)$.

19. Sketch the NFA for (a) $x \in \Sigma$ (b) λ (c) $\varnothing$.

(a) NFA for x: 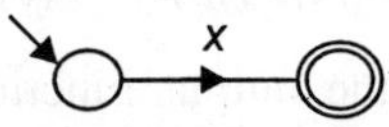

(b) NFA for λ: 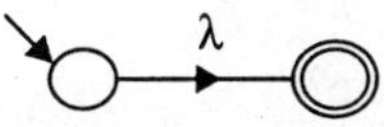

(c) NFA for $\varnothing$: 

20. What do you mean by two-way finite automata?

Two way-finite automata are machines that can read input string in either direction.

21. What is the kind of arrangement you have for the "read head" in a two-way automata machine?

These types of machines have a 'read head', which can move left or right over the input string.

22. State a common characteristic between Finite automata and two-way finite automata?

Both Finite automata and two-way finite automata have the same finite set Q of states. They accept only regular sets.

23. What are the types of two-way finite automata?

(a) 2DFA (Deteminististic)

(b) 2NFA (Non-deterministic)

24. Give the formal definition of a 2DFA (two-way DFA).

A 2DFA is an octuple

$$M = (Q, \Sigma, \vdash, \dashv, \delta, s, t, r)$$

where, Q is a fine set of states,

Σ is a finite set of input,

$\vdash$ is the left end marker, $\vdash \notin \Sigma$,

$\dashv$ is the right end marker, $\dashv \notin \Sigma$,

$\delta : Q \times (\Sigma \cup \{\vdash, \dashv\} \rightarrow (Q \times \{L, R\})$ is the transition function

$s \in Q$ is the start state,
$t \in Q$ is the accept state, and
$r \in Q$ is the reject state, $r \neq t$.

25. What is a Mealey Machine?

Usually the finite automata have binary output i.e., they accept the string or do not accept the string. This is basically decided on the basis of whether the final state is reached by the initial state. Removing this restrictin, we are trying to consider a model where the outputs can be chosen from some other alphabet. The value of the output function $F(t)$ in the most general case is a function of the present state $q(t)$ and present input $x(t)$.

$$F(t) = \lambda(q(t), x(t))$$

where λ is called the output function. This model is called the "Mealey Machine".

26. What is a Moore Machine?

If the output function $F(t)$ depends only on the present state and is independent of the present input $q(t)$, then we have the output function $F(t)$ given by

$$F(t) = \lambda(q(t))$$

A Moore machine is a six-tuple $(Q, \Sigma, 0, \delta, \lambda, q_0)$ with the usual meanings for symbols.

27. What is a regular set?

A set which is accepted by a finite automaton is called a regular set.

28. What is closure property of a regular set?

A set is closed under an operation if, whenever the operation is applied to members of the set, the result is also a member of the set.

29. State the meanings of the following operations made on languages:

(a) $L_1 \cup L_2$ (b) $L_1 \cap L_2$ (c) $-L_2$ (d) $L_1 - L_2$ (e) L_1^* (f) L_1^R.

(a) $L_1 \cup L_2$: Strings in either L_1 or L_2.
(b) $L_1 \cap L_2$: Strings in both L_1 and L_2.
(c) $-L_2$: All strings (over the same alphabet) not in L_1.
(d) $L_1 - L_2$: Strings in L_1 that are not in L_2.
(e) L_1^*: Zero or more strings from L_1 concatenated together.
(f) L_1^R: Strings in L_1, reversed.

30. What is meant by Pumping Lemma?

The Pumping Lemma for regular languages is another way of showing that a given infinite language is not regular.

31. What is the method of proof used by Pumping Lemma?

The proof is always done by contradiction.

32. State the principle of Pumping Lemma.

If an infinite language is regular,k it can be defined by a DFA. The DFA has some finite number of states (say n). Since the language is infinite, some strings of the language should have length $>n$. For a string of length $>n$ accepted by DFA, the walk through of the DFA must contain a cycle. Repeating the cycle an arbitrary number of times should yield aother string accepted by the DFA.

33. How will you show that a given infinite language is not regular using a Pumping Lemma?

(i) Assume that the language L is regular
(ii) By Pigeon-hole principle, any sufficiently long string in L should repeat some state in the DFA, and therefore, the walk contains a "cycle".
(iii) Show that repeating the cycle some number of times ("pumping" the cycle) yields a string that is not in L.
(iv) Conclude that L is not regular.

33. Give the formal definition of a Pumping Lemma.

If L is an infinite regular language, then there exists some positive integer 'm' such that any string $w \in L$, whose length is 'm' or greater can be decomposed into three parts, xyz where

(i) $|xy|$ is less than or equal to m
(ii) $|y| > 0$,
(iii) $w_i = xy^i z$ is also in L for all $i = 0, 1, 2, 3, \ldots\ldots$

34. Is the language $L = \{a^n b^n \ : n \geq 0\}$ regular or not.

The language L is not regular.

35. Are the following languages regular or not.

(a) $L = \{a^n b^k \ : n > k \text{ and } n \geq 0\}$

(b) $L = \{a^n \ : n \text{ is a prime number}\}$.

(a) Not regular
(b) Not regular.

36. State the closure property of Regular Languages.

(a) If L_1 and L_2 are regular over Σ, then $L_1 \cup L_2$ is regular, i.e., union of two regular sets is also regular. Regular sets are closed w.r.t. union.
(b) If L_1 and L_2 are regular, so is $L_1 \cap L_2$, i.e., regular sets are closed w.r.t. intersection.

37. State the Myhill-Nerode Theorem.

Let $R \subseteq \Sigma^*$. The following statements are equivalent

(i) R is regular

(ii) there exists a Myhill-Nerode relation for R.

(iii) the relation $\equiv_R$ is of finite index.

38. What is an acceptor?

Automaton whose output response is 'Yes' or 'No' is called an acceptor.

39. What is a regular expression?

It is a mathematical tool built from a set of primitive and operations.

40. What are the properties of regular sets?

(a) Closure
(b) Union
(c) Concatenation
(d) Negation
(e) Kleene star
(f) Intersection
(g) Set difference

Chapter 2

Context-Free Grammars

2.1 INTRODUCTION

2.1.1 Definition of CFG

A context-free grammar is a 4-tuple (V, T, S, P) where

(i) V is a finite set called the variables
(ii) T is a finite set, disjoint from V, called the terminals
(iii) P is a finite set of rules, with each rule being a variable and a string of variables and terminals, and
(iv) $S \in V$ is the start variable.

If u, v and w are strings of variables and terminals, and $A \to w$ is a rule of the grammar, we say that uAv yields uwv, written $uAv \Rightarrow uwv$.

2.1.2 Example of CFG

Given a grammar $G = (\{S\}, \{a, b\}, R, S)$.

The set of rules R is

$$S \to aSb$$
$$S \to SS$$
$$S \to \in$$

This grammar generates strings such as

abab, *aaabbb*, and *aababb*

If we assume that a is left paranthesis '(' and b is right paranthesis ')', then $L(G)$ is the language of all strings of properly nested parantheses.

2.1.3 Right-Linear Grammar

In general productions have the form:

$$(V \cup T)^+ \to (V \cup T)^*.$$

In right-linear grammar, all productions have one of the two forms:

$$V \to T^*V$$

or $$V \to T^*$$

i.e., the left hand side should have a single variable and the right hand side consists of any number of terminals (members of *T*) optionally followed by a single variable.

2.1.4 Right-Linear Grammars and NFAs

There is a simple connection between right-linear grammars and NFAs, as shown in the following illustration.

$A \to xB$

$A \to xyzB$

$A \to B$

$A \to x$

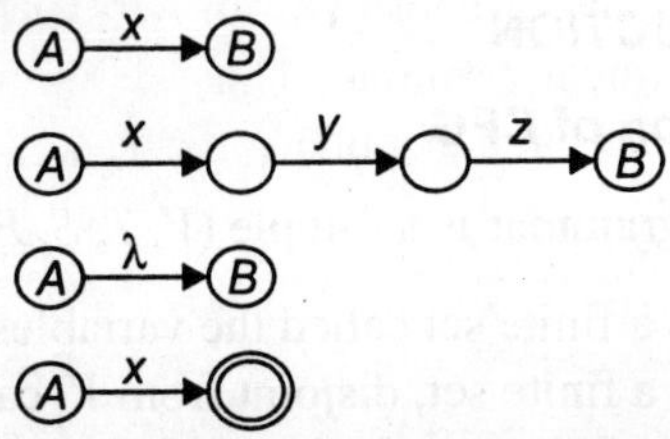

As an example of the correspondence between an NFA and a right linear grammar, the following automaton and grammar both recognize the set of set of strings consisting of an even number of 0's and an even number of 1's.

$S \to \lambda$

$S \to 0B$

$S \to 0A$

$A \to 0C$

$A \to 1S$

$B \to 0S$

$B \to 1C$

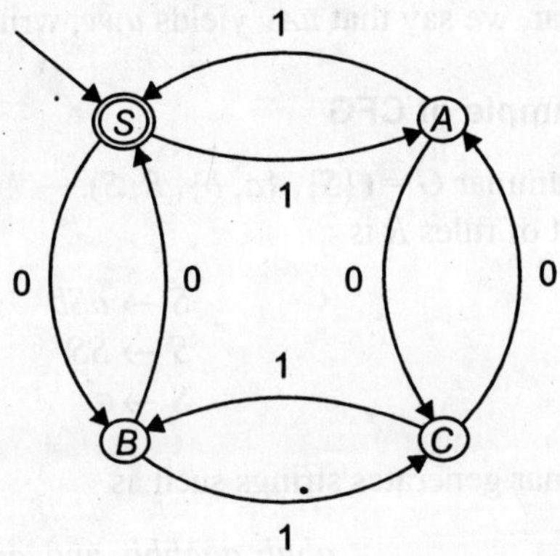

2.1.5 Left-Linear Grammar

In a left-linear grammar, all productions have one of the two forms:

$$V \to VT^*$$

or $$V \to T^*$$

i.e., the left hand side must consist of a single varibale, and the right-hand side consists of an optional single variable followed by one number of terminals.

2.1.6 Conversion of Left-linear Grammar into Right-Linear Grammar

Step	Method
(a) Construct a right-linear grammar for the different languages L^R.	Replace each production $A \rightarrow x$ of L with a production $A \rightarrow x^R$ and replace each production $A \rightarrow Bx$ with a production $A \rightarrow x^R B$
(b) Construct an NFA for L^R from the right-linear grammar. This NFA should have just one final state.	Refer to section 2.1.4 for deriving an NFA from a right-linear grammar.
(c) Reverse the NFA for L^R to obtain an NFA for L.	(i) Construct an NFA to recognize the language L. (ii) Ensure the NFA has only a single final state (iii) Reverse the direction of arcs (iv) Make the initial state final and final state initial
(d) Construct a right-linear grammar for L from the NFA for L.	This is the technique described in the previous section.

Example 2.1.1: Give some example of context-free languages.

Solution

(a) The grammar $G = (\{S\}, \{a, b\}, S, P)$ with productions

$$S \rightarrow aSa, \quad S \rightarrow bSb, \quad S \rightarrow \lambda$$

is context free.

$$S \Rightarrow aSa \Rightarrow aaSaa \Rightarrow aabSbaa \Rightarrow aabbaa$$

Thus we have $L(a) = \{ww^R : w \in \{a, b\}^*\}$.

This language is context free.

(b) The grammar G, with production rules given by

$$S \rightarrow abB,$$
$$A \rightarrow aaBb,$$
$$B \rightarrow bbAa,$$
$$A \rightarrow \lambda$$

is context free.

The language is

$$L(G) = \{ab(bbaa)^n bba(ba)^n : n \geq 0\}$$

Example 2.1.2: Construct right-and left-linear grammars for the language $L = \{a^n b^m : n \geq 2,\ m \geq 3\}$.

Solution

Right-Linear Grammar:

$$S \to aS$$
$$S \to aaA$$
$$A \to bA$$
$$A \to bbb$$

Left-Linear Grammar:

$$S \to Abbb$$
$$S \to Sb$$
$$A \to Aa$$
$$A \to aa$$

2.2 DERIVATION TREES

A 'derivation tree' is an ordered tree which the the nodes are labeled with the left sides of productions and in which the children of a node represent its corresponding right sides.

2.2.1 Definition of a Derivation Tree

Let $G = (V, T, S, P)$ be a CFG. An ordered tree is a derivation tree for G iff it has the following properties:

(i) The root of the derivation tree is S.

(ii) Each and every leaf in the tree has a label from $T \cup \{\lambda\}$.

(iii) Each and every interior vertex (a vertex which is no a leaf) has a label from V.

(iv) If a vertex has label $A \in V$, and its children are labeled (from left to right) $a_1, a_2, \ldots\ldots a_n$, then P must contain a production of the form

$$A \to a_1, a_2, \ldots \ldots a_n$$

(v) A leaf labeled λ has no siblings, that is, a vertex with a child labeled λ can have no other children.

2.2.2 Sentential Form

For a given CFG with productions $S \to aA, A \to aB, B \to bB, B \to a$. The derivation tree is as shown below.

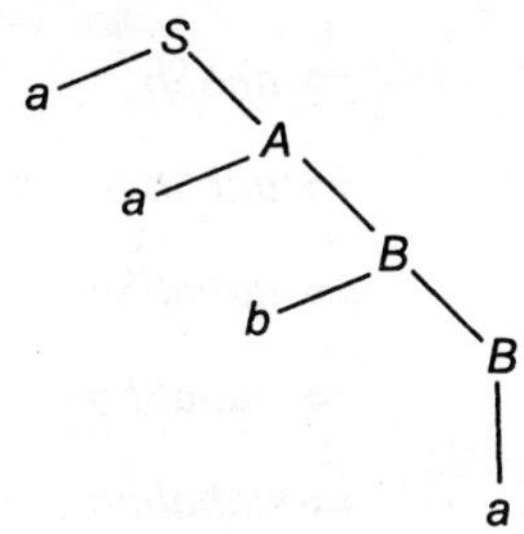

$$S \Rightarrow aA \Rightarrow aaB \Rightarrow aabB \Rightarrow aaba$$

The resultant of the derivation tree is the word $w = aaba$.
This is said to be in "Sentential Form".

2.2.3 Partial Derivation Tree

In the definition of derivation tree given, if every leaf has a label from $V \cup T \cup \{\lambda\}$ it is said to be "partial derivation tree".

2.2.4 Right Most/Left Most/Mixed Derivation

Consider the grammar G with production

$$\begin{Bmatrix} 1.\ S \to aSS \\ 2.\ S \to b \end{Bmatrix}$$

Now, we have

$$\begin{aligned} S &\overset{1}{\Rightarrow} aSS \\ &\overset{1}{\Rightarrow} aaSSS \\ &\overset{2}{\Rightarrow} aabSS \\ &\overset{1}{\Rightarrow} aabaSSS \\ &\overset{2}{\Rightarrow} aababSS \\ &\overset{2}{\Rightarrow} aababbS \\ &\overset{2}{\Rightarrow} aababbb \end{aligned}$$

(Left Most Derivation)

The sequence followed is "left most derivation", following "1121222", giving "*aababbb*".

$$\begin{aligned} S &\overset{1}{\Rightarrow} aSS \\ &\overset{2}{\Rightarrow} aSb \\ &\overset{1}{\Rightarrow} aaSSb \\ &\overset{2}{\Rightarrow} aabSb \\ &\overset{1}{\Rightarrow} aabaSSb \\ &\overset{2}{\Rightarrow} aabaSbb \\ &\overset{2}{\Rightarrow} aababbb \end{aligned} \qquad \text{(Mixed Derivation)}$$

The sequence 1212122 represents a "Mixed Derivation", giving "*aababbb*".

$$\begin{aligned} S &\overset{1}{\Rightarrow} aSS \\ &\overset{2}{\Rightarrow} aSb \\ &\overset{1}{\Rightarrow} aaSSb \\ &\overset{1}{\Rightarrow} aaSaSSb \\ &\overset{2}{\Rightarrow} aaSaSbb \\ &\overset{2}{\Rightarrow} aaSabbb \\ &\overset{2}{\Rightarrow} aababbb \end{aligned} \qquad \text{(Right Most Derivation)}$$

The sequence 1211222 represents a "Right Most Derivation", giving "*aababbb*".

Example 2.2.1: A grammar G which is context-free has the productions

$$\begin{aligned} S &\to aAB \\ A &\to Bba \\ B &\to bB \\ B &\to c. \end{aligned}$$

(The word $w = acbabc$ is derived as follows)

$$S \Rightarrow aAB \to a(Bba)B \Rightarrow acbaB \Rightarrow acba(bB) \Rightarrow acbabc.$$

Obtain the derivation tree.

Solution

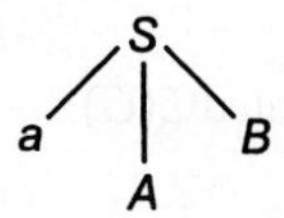

(a) $S \rightarrow aAB$

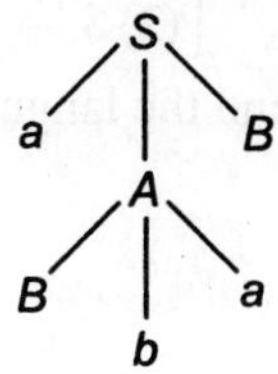

(b) $A \rightarrow Bba$

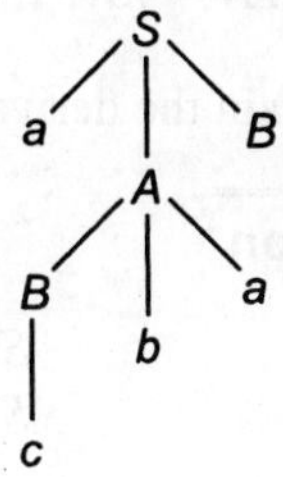

(c) $B \rightarrow c$

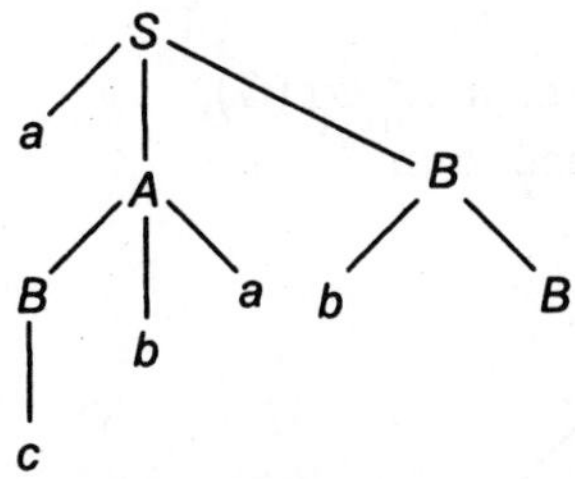

(d) $B \rightarrow bB$

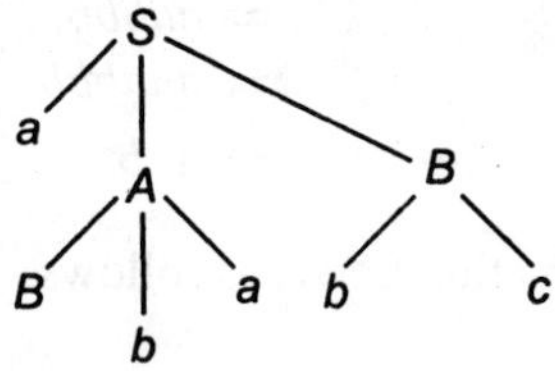

(e) $B \rightarrow c$

Example 2.2.2: A CFG given by productions is

$$S \rightarrow a,$$
$$S \rightarrow aAS,$$
$$\text{and} \quad A \rightarrow bS$$

Obtain the derivation tree of the word $w = abaabaa$.

Solution

$w = abaabaa$ is derived from S as

$$\begin{aligned} S \Rightarrow aAS \Rightarrow a(bS)S \Rightarrow abaS &\Rightarrow aba(aAS) \\ &\Rightarrow abaa(bs)S \\ &\Rightarrow abaabaS \\ &\Rightarrow abaabaa \end{aligned}$$

The derivation tree is sketched below.

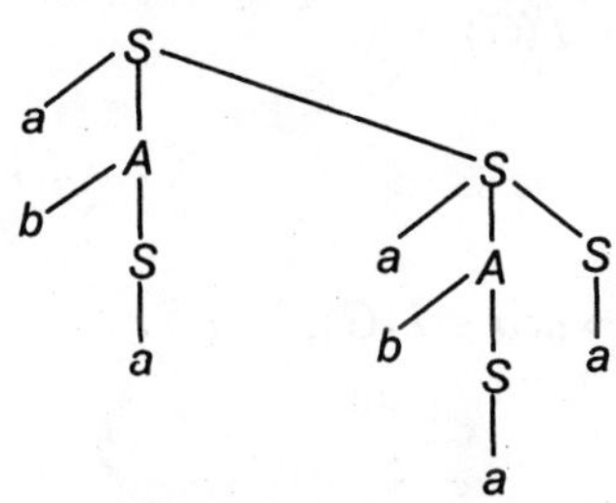

Example 2.2.3: Given a CFG given by $G = (N, T, P, S)$ with $N = \{S\}$, $T = \{a, b\}$, $P = \left\{\begin{matrix}(1)\, S \rightarrow aSb \\ (2)\, S \rightarrow ab\end{matrix}\right\}$.

Obtain the derivation tree and the language generated $L(G)$.

Solution

$$
\begin{aligned}
S &\Rightarrow ab && \text{i.e., } ab \in L(G) \\
S &\Rightarrow aSb && \\
&\Rightarrow aabb && \text{i.e., } a^2b^2 \in L(G) \\
S &\Rightarrow aSb && \\
&\Rightarrow aaSbb && \\
&\Rightarrow aaabbb && \text{i.e., } a^3b^3 \in L(G), \\
&\Rightarrow a^3b^3 && \text{and so on}
\end{aligned}
$$

Derivation tree is as follows.

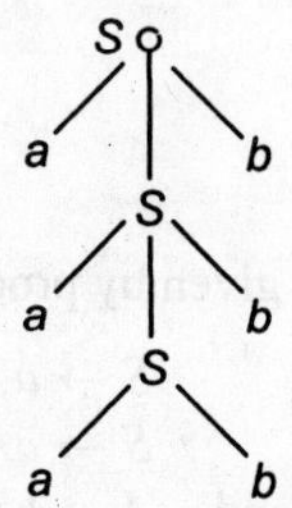

Language generated $L(G) = \{a^n b^n \mid n \geq 1\}$.

Example 2.2.4: Given a CFG $G = (N, T, P, S)$ with $N = \{S\}$, $T = \{a, b, c\}$ and $P = \left\{\begin{matrix}(1)\, S \rightarrow aSa \\ (2)\, S \rightarrow bSb \\ (3)\, S \rightarrow c\end{matrix}\right\}$.

Obtain the derivation tree and language generated $L(G)$.

Solution

(i) $S \Rightarrow c, \quad c \in L(G)$

(ii) $S \Rightarrow aSa \Rightarrow aca \in L(G)$

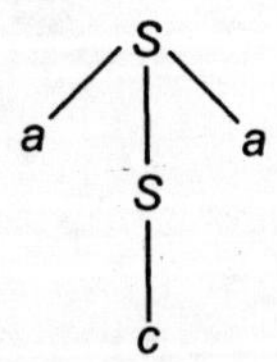

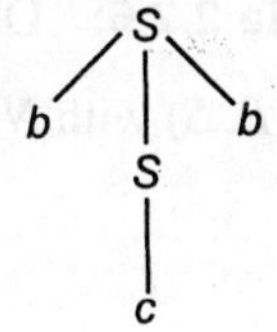

(iii) $S \Rightarrow bSb \Rightarrow bcb \in L(G)$

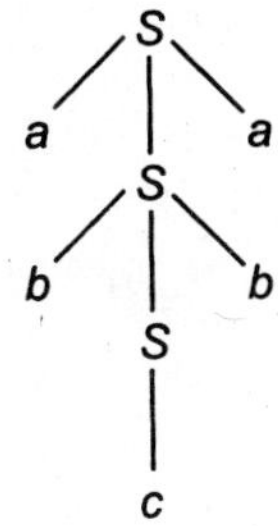

(iv) $S \Rightarrow aSa$
$\Rightarrow abSba$
$\Rightarrow abcba \in L(G)$

and so on.

Hence the language generated $L(G)$ is given by

$$L(G) = \{wcw^R \mid w \in \{a, b\}^*\}$$

where w^R = reversal of w

i.e., if $w = a_1 a_2 \ldots\ldots a_{n-1} a_n$
then $w^R = a_n a_{n-1} \ldots\ldots a_2 a_1$.

Example 2.2.5: Given $G = (N, T, P, S)$ with $N = \{E\}, S = E, T = \{id, +, *, c\}$

and P: 1. $E \rightarrow E + E$
2. $E \rightarrow E * E$.
3. $E \rightarrow (E)$
4. $E \rightarrow id$

Obtain the derivation tree.

Solution

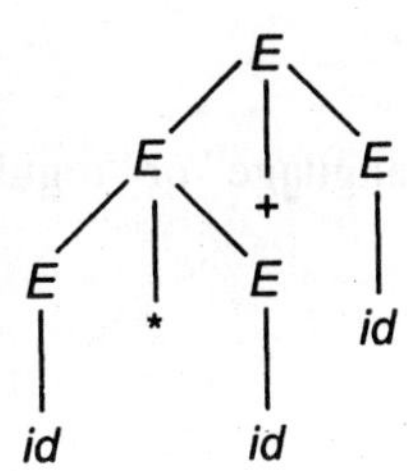

$\Rightarrow$ id * id + id

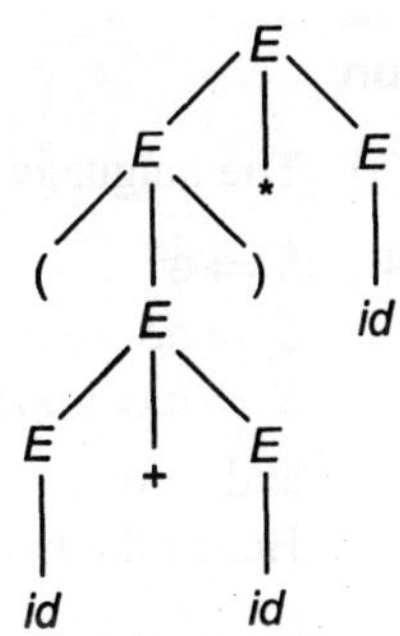

$\Rightarrow$ (id + id) * id

Example 2.2.6: Obtain the language generated $L(G)$ for a CFG given $G(N, T, P, S)$ with $N = \{S\}$, $T\{a\}$, $P: \begin{Bmatrix} 1.\ S \to SS \\ 2.\ S \to a \end{Bmatrix}$

Solution

$$S \Rightarrow a$$

$$\begin{aligned} S &\Rightarrow SS \\ &\Rightarrow aS \\ &\Rightarrow aa \end{aligned}$$

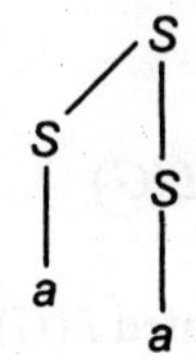

$S \Rightarrow SS \Rightarrow aS \Rightarrow aSS \Rightarrow aaS \Rightarrow aaa$ and so on....

Therefore the language generated is

$$L(G) = \{a^n \mid n \geq 1\}$$

Example 2.2.7: Obtain the language generated by each of the following production rules.

(a) $A \to a$, $A \to aB$, $A \to \in$

(b) $S \to aS$, $S \to \in$

(c) $A \to a$, $A \to aB$, $A \to \in$

(d) $A \to aS$, $S \to bS$, $S \to \in$

(e) $S \to aS$, $S \to bS$, $S \to a$

(f) $S \to ab$, $S \to bs$, $S \to a$, $S \to b$

Solution

(a) The language generated is a "type-3 language" or "regular set".

(b) $S \Rightarrow \in$

$S \Rightarrow aS \Rightarrow a$

$S \Rightarrow as \Rightarrow aaS \Rightarrow aa$

and so on.

Hence the language generated is

$$L(G) = \{a^n \mid n \geq 0\}$$

(c) $A \Rightarrow \epsilon$

$A \Rightarrow a$ $\quad L(G) = \{ww^R \mid w \in \{a,b\}^+\}$

$A \Rightarrow aB$

(d) $S \to aS$

$S \to bS$ $\quad L(G) = \{a,b\}^*$

$S \to \epsilon$ $\quad$ Language generated of any string of a,b

(e) $S \to aS$

$S \to bS$ $\quad L(G) = \{a,b\}^* a$

$S \to a$

(f) $S \to ab$

$S \to bS$ $\quad L(G) = \{a,b\}^+$.

$S \to a$

$S \to b$

Example 2.2.8: Given a CFG $G = (N, T, P, S)$

$$\text{with } N = \{S, A\},\ T = \{a, b\} \text{ and } P = \begin{Bmatrix} 1.\ S \to aS \\ 2.\ S \to aA \\ 3.\ A \to bA \\ 4.\ A \to b \end{Bmatrix}$$

Obtain the derivation tree and $L(G)$.

Solution

$S \Rightarrow aA \Rightarrow ab$

$S \Rightarrow aS \Rightarrow aaA \Rightarrow aab$

$S \Rightarrow aS \Rightarrow aaS \Rightarrow aaaA \Rightarrow aaabA \Rightarrow aaabb$

and so on ...

The derivation tree has been shown here in fig.

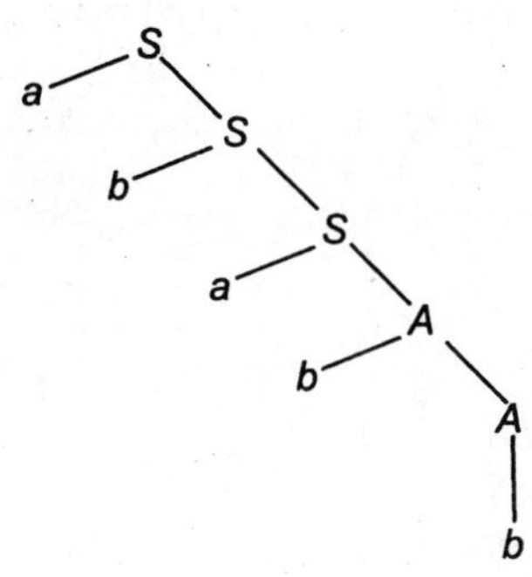

The language generated is

$$L(G) = \{a^n b^m \ n \geq 1,\ m \geq 1\}$$

Example 2.2.9: Given a CFG with

$$P = \begin{Bmatrix} 1.\ S \to aA \\ 2.\ A \to bS \\ 3.\ A \to b \end{Bmatrix}.$$ Obtain the derivation tree and $L(G)$.

Solution

$$S \Rightarrow aA \Rightarrow ab$$

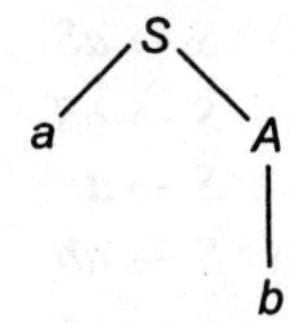

$$S \Rightarrow aA \Rightarrow abS \Rightarrow abaA \Rightarrow abab\ldots\ \ldots$$

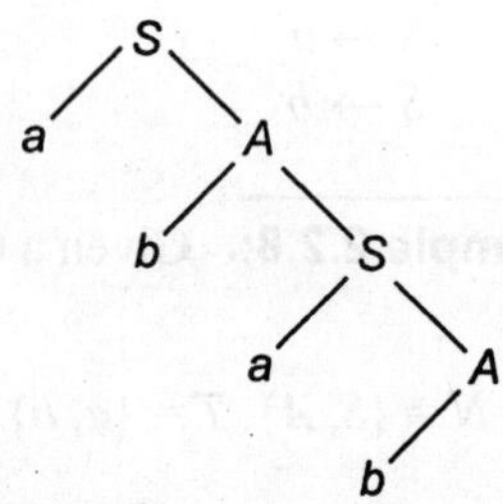

The derivation trees suggest *ab*, *abab*, ...
Therefore the language generated

$$L(G) = \{(ab)^n \mid n \geq 1\}$$

Example 2.2.10: Obtain the production rules for CFG given the language generated as

(a) $L(G) = \{w \mid w \in \{a, b\}^*,\ \times_a(w) = \times_b(w)\}$

(b) $L(G) = \{w \mid w \in \{a, b\}^*,\ \times_a(w) = 2\times_b(w)\}$

(c) $L(G) = \{w \mid w \in \{a, b\}^*,\ \times_a(w) = 3\times_b(w)\}$

Solution

(a) $S \to SaSbS$
$S \to \epsilon$
$S \to SbSaS$

(b) $S \to SaSaSbS$
$S \to SaSbSaS$
$S \to SbSaSaS$
$S \to \epsilon$

(c) $S \to SaSaSaSbS$
$S \to SaSaSbSaS$
$S \to SaSbSaSaS$
$S \to SbSaSaSaS$
$S \to \in$

Example 2.2.11: Given a grammar G with production rules

$$S \to aB$$
$$S \to bA$$
$$A \to aS$$
$$A \to bAA$$
$$A \to a$$
$$B \to bS$$
$$B \to aBB$$
$$B \to b$$

Obtain the (i) leftmost derivation, and (ii) rightmost derivation for the string "*aaabbabbba*".

Solution

(i) *Leftmost derivation:*

$$S \Rightarrow aB \Rightarrow aaBB \Rightarrow aaaBBB \Rightarrow aaabBB \Rightarrow aaabbB$$
$$\Rightarrow aaabbabB \Rightarrow aaabbabbB \Rightarrow aaabbabbbS \Rightarrow aaabbabbba$$
$$\Rightarrow aaabbabb$$

(ii) *Rightmost derivation:*

$$S \Rightarrow aB \Rightarrow aaBB \Rightarrow aaBbS \Rightarrow aaBbbA \Rightarrow aaaBBbba$$
$$\Rightarrow aaabBbba \Rightarrow aaabbSbba \Rightarrow aaabbaBbba \Rightarrow aaabbabbba$$

2.3 PARSING AND AMBIGUITY

2.3.1 Parsing

A grammar can be used in two ways:

(a) Using the grammar to generate strings of the language.
(b) Using the grammar to recognize the strings.

"Parsing" a string is finding a derivation (or a derivation tree) for that string.

Parsing a string is like recognizing a string. The only realistic way to recognize a string of a context-free grammar is to parse it.

2.3.2 Exhaustive Search Parsing

The basic idea of the "Exhaustive Search Parsing" is to parse a string w, generate all strings in L and check if w is among them.

Problem arises when L is an infinite language. Therefore a systematic approach is needed to achieve this, as it is required to know that no strings are overlooked. And also it is necessary so as to stop after a finite number of steps.

The idea of exhaustive search parsing for a string is to generate all strings of length no greater than $|w|$, and see if w is among them.

The restrictions that are placed on the grammar will allow us to generate any string $w \in L$ in at most $2|w| - 1$ derivation steps.

Exhaustive search parsing is inefficient. It requires time exponential in $|w|$.

There are ways to further restrict context free grammar so that strings may be parsed in linear or non-linear time (which methods are beyond the scope of this book).

There is no known linear or non-linear algorithm for parsing strings of a general context free grammar.

2.3.3 Topdown/Bottomup Parsing

Sequence of rules are applied in a leftmost derivation in Topdown parsing. (Refer to section 2.2.4.)

Sequence of rules are applied in a rightmost derivation in Bottomup parsing.

This is illustrated below.

Consider the grammar G with production

$$1.\ S \rightarrow aSS$$

$$2.\ S \rightarrow b.$$

The parse trees are as follows.

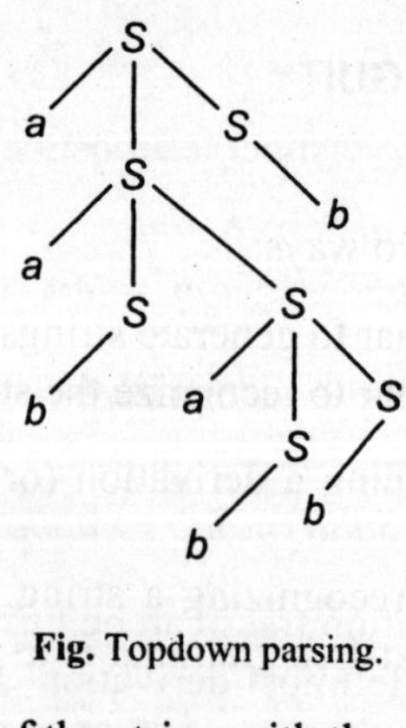

Fig. Topdown parsing.

aababbb $\rightarrow$ Left parse of the string with the sequence 1121222.

This is known as "Topdown Parsing."

"Right Parse" is the reversal of sequence of rules applied in a rightmost derivation.

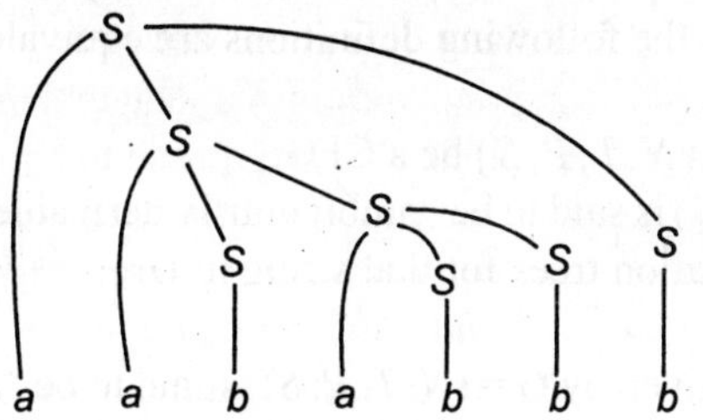

Fig. Bottom-up parsing.

aababbb $\rightarrow$ Right parse of the string with the sequence 2221121.
This is known as "Bottom-up Parsing."

2.3.4 Ambiguity

The grammar given by

$$G = (\{S\}, \{a, b\}, S, S \rightarrow aSb \mid bSa \mid SS \mid \lambda)$$

generates strings having an equal number of *a*'s and *b*'s.

The string "*abab*" can be generated from this grammar in two distinct ways, as shown in the following derivation trees:

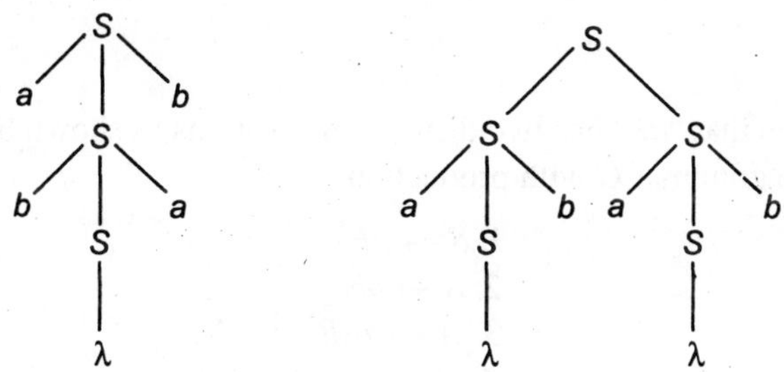

Similarly, "*abab*" has two distinct leftmost derivations:

$$S \Rightarrow aSb \Rightarrow abSab \Rightarrow abab$$
$$S \Rightarrow SS \Rightarrow aSbS \Rightarrow abS \Rightarrow abaSb \Rightarrow abab.$$

Also, "*abab*" has two distinct rightmost derivations:

$$S \Rightarrow aSb \Rightarrow abSab \Rightarrow abab$$
$$S \Rightarrow SS \Rightarrow SaSb \Rightarrow Sab \Rightarrow aSbab \Rightarrow abab$$

Each of the above derivation trees can be turned into a unique rightmost derivation, or into a unique leftmost derivation. Each leftmost or rightmost derivation can be turned into a unique derivation tree. These representations are largely interchangeable.

2.3.5 Ambiguous Grammars/Ambiguous Languages

Since derivation trees, leftmost derivations, and rightmost derivations are equivalent rotations, the following definitions are equivalent:

Definition: Let $G = (N, T, P, S)$ be a CFG.

A string $w \in L(G)$ is said to be "ambiguously derivable "if there are two or more different derivation trees for that string in G.

Definition: A CFG given by $G = (N, T, P, S)$ is said to be "ambiguous" if there exists at least one string in $L(G)$ which is ambiguously derivable. Otherwise it is unambiguous.

Ambiguity is a property of a grammar, and it is usually, but not always possible to find an equivalent unambiguous grammar.

An "inherantly ambiguous language" is a language for which no unambiguous grammar exists.

Example 2.3.1: Prove that the grammar

$$S \to aB \mid ab,$$
$$A \to aAB \mid a,$$
$$B \to ABb \mid b$$

is ambiguous.

Solution

It is easy to see that "*ab*" has two different derivations as shown below.

Given the grammar G with production

1. $S \to aB$
2. $S \to ab$
3. $A \to aAB$
4. $A \to a$
5. $B \to ABb$
6. $B \to b$

$$\left.\begin{array}{ll} \text{Using (2),} & S \Rightarrow ab \\ \text{Using (1),} & S \Rightarrow aB \Rightarrow ab \\ \text{and then (6).} & \end{array}\right\}$$

Example 2.3.2: Show that the grammar $S \to S \mid S,\ S \to a$ is ambiguous.

Solution

In order to show that G is ambiguous, we need to find a $w \in L(G)$, which is ambiguous.

Assume $w = abababa.$

The two derivation trees for $w = abababa$ is shown below in Fig. (a) and (b).

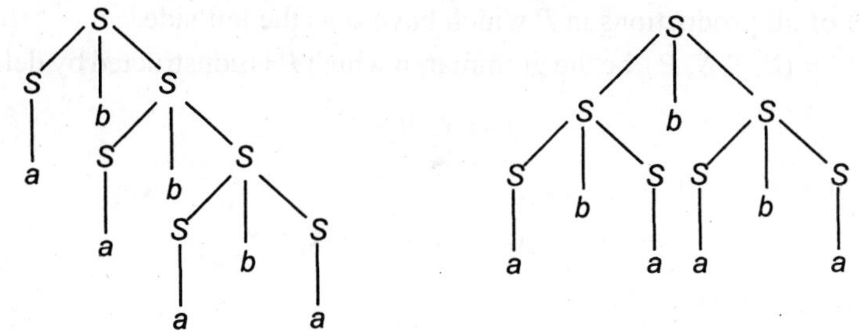

(a) (b)

Therefore, the grammar G is ambiguous.

Example 2.3.3: Show that the grammar G with production

$$S \to a \mid aAb \mid abSb$$
$$A \to aAAb \mid bS$$

is ambiguous.

Solution

$$S \Rightarrow abSb \quad (\because S \to abSb)$$
$$\Rightarrow abab \quad (\because S \to a)$$

Similarly,

$$S \Rightarrow aAb \quad (\because S \to aAb)$$
$$\Rightarrow abSb \quad (\because A \to bS)$$
$$\Rightarrow abab$$

Since '*abab*' has two different derivations, the grammar G is ambiguous.

2.4 SIMPLIFICATION OF CFG

2.4.1 Simplification of CFG-Introduction

In a Context Free Grammar (CFG), it may not be necessary to use all the symbols in $V \cup T$, or all the production rules in P while deriving sentences.

Let us try to eliminate symbols and productions in G which are not useful in deriving sentences.

Let $G = (V, T, S, P)$ be a context-free grammar. Suppose that P contains a production of the form

$$A \to x_1 \, B \, x_2.$$

Assume that A and B are different variables and that

$$B \to y_1 \mid y_2 \mid \cdots\cdots \mid y_n.$$

is the set of all productions in P which have B as the left side.

Let $\hat{G} = (V, T, S, \hat{P})$ be the grammar in which $\hat{P}$ is constructed by deleting

$$A \to x_1 \, B \, x_2$$

from P, and adding to it

$$A \to x_1 \, y_1 x_2 \mid x_1 \, y_2 x_2 \mid \cdots \mid x_1 \, y_n x_2.$$

Then $L(\hat{G}) = L(G)$.

Substitution Rule

A production $A \to x_1 B x_2$ can be eliminated from a grammar if we put in its place the set of productions in which B is replaced by all strings it derives in one step. In this result, it is necessary that A and B are different variables.

An illustration is given in examples 2.4.1 and 2.4.2.

2.4.2 Abolishing Useless Productions

In the grammar G with P,

$$S \to aSb \mid \lambda \mid A$$
$$A \to aA.$$

the production $S \to A$ does not play any role because A cannot be transformed into a terminal string. 'A' can occur in a string derived from S, this can never lead to a sentential form. Hence this production rule can be removed, which does not affect the language.

Definition: Let $G = (V, T, S, P)$ be a CFG.

A variable $A \in V$ is said to be "useful" iff there is at least one $w \in L(G)$ such that

$$S \stackrel{*}{\Rightarrow} xAy \stackrel{*}{\Rightarrow} w$$

with x, y in $(V \cup T)^*$, i.e., a variable is useful iff it occurs in at least one derivation.

Illustration: Consider the grammar G with P

$$S \to A$$
$$A \to aA \mid \lambda$$
$$B \to bA.$$

Here the variable B is said to be "useless", hence the production $B \to bA$ is also "useless". There is nó way to achieve $S \stackrel{*}{\Rightarrow} xBy$.

THEOREM: Let $G = (V, T, S, P)$ be a CFG. There exists an equivalent grammar $\hat{G} = (\hat{V}, \hat{T}, S, \hat{P})$ that does not contain any useless variables or productions.

Procedure: The first Part-A is to find G_1 using the algorithm.

Step 1: Set V_1 to $\varnothing$

Step 2: Repeat the following step until no more variables are added to V_1.
For every $A \in V$ for which P has a production of the form.

$$A \to x_1 x_2 \ldots\ldots x_n, \text{ with all } x_i. \text{ in } V_1 \cup T, \text{ add } A \text{ to } V_1.$$

Step 3: Take P_1 as all the productions in P whose symbols are all in $(V_1 \cup T)$.

Thus the grammar G_1 can be generated from G by the above algorithm. Here $G_1 = (V_1, T_2, S, P_1)$ such that V_1 contains only variables A for which

$$A \overset{*}{\Rightarrow} w \in T^*$$

The next step is to check whether every A for which $A \overset{*}{\Rightarrow} w = ab \ldots$ is added to V_1 before the procedure terminates.

Step below describes the second *Part B*.

"Dependency graph" is drawn to find all the variables that cannot be reached from the start symbol S. These variables are removed from the variable set and also all the productions involving the variables.

The resultant obtained is $\hat{G}$.

(a) Empty Production Removal

The productions of context-free grammars can be coerced into a variety of forms without affecting the expressive power of the grammars.

If the empty string does not belong to a language, then there is a way to eliminate the productions of the form $A \to \lambda$ from the grammar.

If the empty string belongs to a language, then we can eliminate λ from all productions save for the single production $S \to \lambda$. In this case we can also eliminate any ocurrences of S from the right-hand side of productions.

Let us illustrate this through the Example 2.4.4. Any production of a CFG of the form

$$A \to \lambda$$

is called a λ-production. Any variable A for which the derivation

$$A \overset{*}{\Rightarrow} \lambda \text{ is possible.}$$

is called "NULLABLE".

Let G be any CFG with λ not in $L(G)$. Then there exists an equivalent grammar $\hat{G}$ having no λ-productions.

Procedure to find CFG without λ-Productions

Step (i): For all productions $A \to \lambda$, put A into V_N.

Step (ii): Repeat the following steps until no further variables are added to V_N.

For all productions

$$B \to A_1 A_2 \ldots\ldots A_n.$$

where $A_1, A_2, A_3, \ldots\ldots, A_n$ are in V_N, put B into V_N.

To find $\hat{P}$, let us consider all productions in P of the form

$$A \to x_1 x_2 \ldots\ldots x_m, m \geq 1$$

for each $x_i \in V \cup T$.

For each such production of P, we put into $\hat{P}$ that production as well as all those generated by replacing nullable variables with λ in all possible combinations.

(If all x_i are nullable, the production $A \to \lambda$ is not put into $\hat{P}$).

Let us illustrate this procedure through an example as shown in example 2.4.5.

(b) Unit Productions Removal

Any production of a CFG of the form

$$A \to B$$

where $A, B \in V$ is called a "Unit-production". Having variable one on either side of a production is sometimes undesirable.

"Substitution Rule" is made use of in removing the unit-productions.

Given $G = (V, T, S, P)$, a CFG with no λ-productions, there exists a CFG $\hat{G} = (\hat{V}, \hat{T}, S, \hat{P})$ that does not have any unit-productions and that is equivalent to G.

Let us illustrate the procedure to remove unit-production through example 2.4.6.

Procedure to remove the unit productions:

Find all variables B, for each A such that

$$A \overset{*}{\Rightarrow} B$$

This is done by sketching a "depending graph" with an edge (C, D)

whenever the grammar has unit-production $C \to D$, then $A \overset{*}{\Rightarrow} B$ holds whenever there is a walk between A and B.

The new grammar $\hat{G}$, equivalent to G is obtained by letting into $\hat{P}$ all non-unit productions of P.

Then for all A and B satisfying $A \overset{*}{\Rightarrow} B$, we add to $\hat{P}$

$$A \to y_1 \mid y_2 \mid \ldots\ldots \mid y_n$$

where $B \to y_1 \mid y_2 \mid \ldots\ldots \mid y_n$ is the set of all rules in $\hat{P}$ with B on the left.

(c) Left Recursion Removal

A variable A is left-recursive if it occurs in a production of the form

$$A \to Ax$$

for any $x \in (V \cup T)^*$.

A grammar is left-recursive if it contains at least one left-recursive variable.

Every content-free language can be represented by a grammar that is not left-recursive.

Example 2.4.1: Given a grammar $G = (\{A, B\}, \{a, b, c\}, A, P)$ with productions

$$A \to a \mid aaA \mid abBc$$
$$B \to abbA \mid b.$$

obtain an equivalent grammar $\hat{G}$ such that both G and $\hat{G}$ would accept the string "*aaabbc*".

Solution

Given G as

$$A \to a \mid aaA \mid abBc \quad (1)$$
$$B \to abbA \mid b. \quad (2)$$

Making use of (2) in (1), we have the grammar $\hat{G}$ with productions

$$A \to a \mid aaA \mid ababbAc \mid abbc$$
$$B \to abbA \mid b.$$

$\hat{G}$ is equivalent to G.

Thus the string "*aaabbc*" is derived as

$$A \Rightarrow aaA \Rightarrow aaabBc \Rightarrow aaabbc \qquad \text{(with } G\text{)}$$

and

$$A \Rightarrow aaA \Rightarrow aaabbc \quad (\text{with } \hat{G})$$

since G and $\hat{G}$ are equivalent.

Example 2.4.2: Given a CFG as

$$G = (\{S, A, B, C, E\}, \{a, b, c\}, P, S)$$

with production P given by

$$\begin{aligned} &S \to AB \\ &A \to a \\ &B \to b \\ &B \to C \\ &E \to c \,/\, \lambda \end{aligned}$$

Obtain $L(G)$ and obtain an equivalent grammar $L(\hat{G})$ by eliminating useless terminals and productions.

Solution

$L(G)$ is obtained as follows:

$$S \Rightarrow AB \Rightarrow aB \Rightarrow ab.$$

Therefore, $L(G) = \{ab\}$.

Here $\hat{G} = (\{S, A, B\}, \{a, b\}, P', S).$

where P' has the production rules

$$\begin{aligned} &S \to AB \\ &A \to a \\ &B \to b \end{aligned}$$

We have eliminated C as it does not derive terminal string. E and C do not appear in any sentential form.

$E \to \lambda$ is a null production and hence eliminated. $B \to C$ simply replaces B by C.

Example 2.4.3: Given $G = (V, T, S, P)$ with P given by

$$\begin{aligned} &S \to aS \,|\, A \,|\, C \\ &A \to a \\ &B \to aa \\ &C \to aCb \end{aligned}$$

Eliminate the useless symbols and productions from G.

Solution

Here $V = \{S, A, B, C\}$. Let us determine the set of variables that can lead to a terminal string.

Since $A \to a$ and $B \to aa$, implies A and B belong to this set. Also S belongs to this set, since $S \Rightarrow A \Rightarrow a$.

But C does not belong to this set because C does not produce terminals since $C \to aCb$.

Thus C is removed and its corresponding productions are also removed.

$$S \to aS \mid A$$
$$A \to a$$
$$B \to aa$$

Here $V_1 = \{S, A, B\}$.

To eliminate the variables that cannot be reached from the start variable, a "*dependency graph*" is drawn and decided.

The dependency graph for $V_1 = \{S, A, B\}$ is drawn as below.

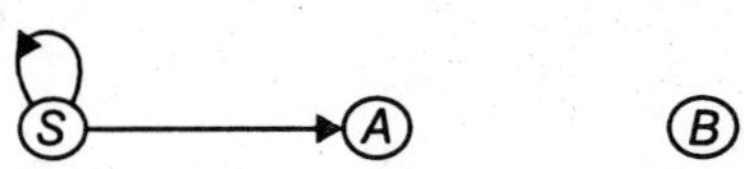

A variable is useful only if there is a path from the vertex labeled S to the vertex labeled with that variable.

From the above fig. it is obvious B is useless. Hence we have

$$\hat{G} = (\hat{V}, \hat{T}, S, \hat{P}) \text{ with } \hat{V} = \{S, A\},\ \hat{T} = \{a\} \text{ and } P \text{ given by}$$

$$S \to aS \mid A$$
$$A \to a.$$

Example 2.4.4: Given a CFG with P given by

$$S \to aS_1 b$$
$$S_1 \to aS_1 b \mid \lambda$$

obtain a new set of P for a grammar same as the given CFG.

Solution

The given grammar

$$S \to aS_1 b$$
$$S_1 \to aS_1 b \mid \lambda$$

generates the λ-free language given by

$$\{a^n b^n : n \geq 1\}$$

The λ-production in P viz.,

$$S_1 \to \lambda$$

is removed after adding new productions by substituting λ for S_1 where it occurs on the right. Hence we get

$$S \to aS_1b \mid ab$$
$$S_1 \to aS_1b \mid ab$$

which is the new set of P that produces the same language given by $\{a^n b^n : n \geq 1\}$.

Example 2.4.5: Determine a CFG without λ-production equivalent to the grammar given by P as

$$S \to ABaC, \quad A \to BC, \quad B \to b \mid \lambda, \quad C \to D \mid \lambda, \quad D \to d$$

Solution

Refer to the procedure outlined in section 2.4.2 to find CFG without λ-productions.

Step 1: The "Nullable variables" are A, B and C.

Step 2:

$$S \to ABaC \mid BaC \mid ABa \mid AaC \mid Aa \mid Ba \mid ac \mid a$$
$$A \to B \mid C \mid BC$$
$$B \to b$$
$$C \to D$$
$$D \to d$$

The above set of rules represent P' for the new CFG after elimination of λ-productions.

Example 2.4.6: Eliminate unit productions from the grammar G given by productions (P).

$$S \to AB$$
$$A \to a$$
$$B \to C \mid b$$
$$C \to D$$
$$D \to E$$
$$E \to a.$$

Solution

$A \to a,\ B \to b, E \to a$ are nonunit production. Therefore $\hat{P}$ will contain these productions.

Since $B \overset{*}{\Rightarrow} E$, and $E \to a$ is a non-unit production, include $B \to a$ in $\hat{P}$.

Since $C \overset{*}{\Rightarrow} E, D \Rightarrow E$, include $C \to a, D \to a$ in $\hat{P}$.

Hence we have the equivalent grammar without unit productions as $\hat{G}$ defined by

$$\hat{G} = (\{S, A, B, C, D, E\}, \{a, b\}, \hat{P}, S)$$

with $\hat{P}$ given by

$$\begin{aligned} S &\to AB \\ A &\to a \\ B &\to b \\ B &\to a \\ C &\to a \\ D &\to a \end{aligned}$$

Example 2.4.7: Given a CFG with P given by

$$\begin{aligned} S &\to AB \\ A &\to a \\ B &\to C \\ C &\to D \\ D &\to b. \end{aligned}$$

Eliminate the unit productions to obtain an equivalent grammar.

Solution

In the grammar defined by P, we have

$$\begin{aligned} B &\to C \\ C &\to D \end{aligned}$$

as unit-productions.

We can replace

$$\begin{aligned} B &\to C \\ C &\to D \end{aligned}$$

and $\qquad D \to b$

by $\qquad B \to b,$

we have $\hat{P}$ for an equivalent grammar given by

$$S \to AB$$
$$A \to a$$
$$B \to b$$

Example 2.4.8: Eliminate the unit-production from the CFG with P given by

$$S \to Aa \mid B$$
$$B \to A \mid bb$$
$$A \to a \mid bc \mid B.$$

Solution

From the given P we shall draw the dependency graph as follows.

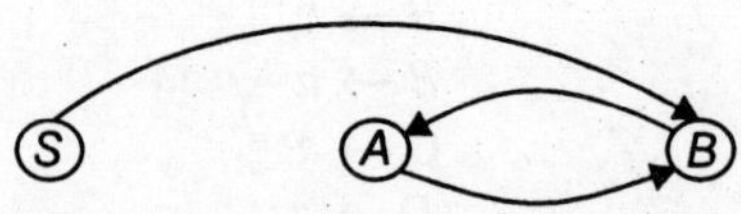

From this we see that

$$S \overset{*}{\Rightarrow} A$$
$$S \overset{*}{\Rightarrow} B$$
$$B \overset{*}{\Rightarrow} A$$
$$A \overset{*}{\Rightarrow} B$$

Therefore these rules are added to the original non-unit productions

$$S \to Aa$$
$$A \to a \mid bc \qquad \text{(from given } P\text{)}$$
$$B \to bb$$

the following new rules

$$S \to a \mid bc \mid bb$$
$$A \to bb$$
$$B \to a \mid bc$$

in order to obtain

$$S \to a \mid bc \mid bb \mid Aa$$
$$A \to a \mid bb \mid bc$$
$$B \to a \mid bb \mid bc$$

which is $\hat{P}$ for the new grammar generated equivalent to the given grammar.

Example 2.4.9: Given a CFG with P given by

$$S \to AB \mid a$$
$$A \to b$$

Eliminate the useless symbols to obtain an equivalent grammar.

Solution

Given
$$S \to AB \mid a$$
$$A \to b$$

B is a non-generating symbol. a and b generate themselves. S generates a and A generates b.

When B is eliminated, $S \to AB$ is eliminated. Therefore we have

$$S \to a$$
$$A \to b$$

S and a are only reachable from S. Therefore we eliminate A and b, therefore we have

$$S \to a$$

as the new $\hat{P}$ for equivalent grammar.

Example 2.4.10: Given the CFG with P given by

$$S \to AB$$
$$A \to aAA \mid \lambda$$
$$B \to bBB \mid \lambda.$$

Eliminate the λ-productions to obtain $\hat{P}$ for an equivalent CFG.

Solution

A and B are "Nullable Symbols" as they have λ-productions. S is also "Nullable", because it has the production $S \to AB$, which has only "Nullable symbols", A and B.

For $S \to AB$, we have three ways viz.,

$$S \to AB \mid A \mid B$$

For $A \to aAA$, we have four ways viz.,

$$A \to aAA \mid aA \mid aA \mid a$$

For $B \to bBB$, we have three ways viz.,

$$B \to bBB \mid bB \mid b$$

Therefore, the new set of productions $\hat{P}$ for the grammar equivalent to the given CFG is

$$S \to AB \mid A \mid B$$
$$S \to aAA \mid aA \mid a$$
$$B \to bBB \mid bB \mid b.$$

2.5 NORMAL FORMS

Two kinds of normal forms viz., Chomsky Normal Form and Greibach Normal Form (GNF) are considered here.

2.5.1 Chomsky Normal Form (CNF)

Any context-free language L without any λ-production is generated by a grammar is which productions are of the form $A \to BC$ or $A \to a$, where $A, B \in V_N$, and $a \in V_T$.

Procedure to find Equivalent Grammar in CNF

(i) Eliminate the unit productions, and λ-productions if any,

(ii) Eliminate the terminals on the right hand side of length two or more.

(iii) Restrict the number of variables on the right hand side of productions to two.

Proof:

For Step (i): Apply the following theorem:

"Every context free language can be generated by a grammar with no useless symbols and no unit productions".

At the end of this step the RHS of any production has a single terminal or two or more symbols. Let us assume the equivalent resulting grammar as $G = (V_N, V_T, P, S)$.

For Step (ii): Consider any production of the form

$$A \to y_1 y_2 \;\ldots\ldots\; y_m, \quad m \geq 2.$$

If y_1 is a terminal, say 'a', then introduce a new variable B_a and a production

$$B_a \to a$$

Repeat this for every terminal on RHS.

Let P' be the set of productions in P together with the new productions

$B_a \to a$. Let V_N' be the set of variables in V_N together with B_a's introduced for every terminal on RHS.

The resulting grammar $G_1 = (V_N', V_T, P', S)$ is equivalent to G and every production in P' has either a single terminal or two or more variables.

For step (iii): Consider $A \to B_1 B_2 \ldots\ldots B_m$

where B_i's are variables and $m \geq 3$.

If $m = 2$, then $A \to B_1, B_2$ is in proper form.

The production $A \to B_1 B_2 \ldots\ldots B_m$ is replaced by new productions

$$A \to B_1 D_1,$$
$$D_1 \to B_2 D_2,$$
$$\ldots\ldots \quad \ldots\ldots$$
$$\ldots\ldots \quad \ldots\ldots$$
$$D_{m-2} \to B_{m-1} B_m$$

where $D_i'S$ are new variables.

The grammar thus obtained is G_2, which is in CNF.

Example 2.5.1: Obtain a grammar in Chomsky Normal Form (CNF) equivalent to the grammar G with productions P given

$$S \to aAbB$$
$$A \to aA \mid a$$
$$B \to bB \mid b.$$

Solution

(i) There are no unit productions in the given set of P.

(ii) Amongst the given productions, we have

$$A \to a,$$
$$B \to b$$

which are in proper form.

For $S \to aAbB$, we have

$$S \to B_a A B_b B,$$
$$B_a \to a$$
$$B_b \to b.$$

For $A \to aA$, we have

$$A \to B_a A$$

For $B \to bB$, we have

$$B \to B_b B.$$

Therefore, we have G_1 given by

$$G_1 = (\{S, A, B, B_a, B_b\}, \{a, b\}, P', S)$$

where P' has the productions

$$S \to B_a AB_b B$$
$$A \to B_a A$$
$$B \to B_b B$$
$$B_a \to a$$
$$B_b \to b$$
$$A \to a$$
$$B \to b$$

(iii) In P' above, we have only

$$S \to B_a AB_b B$$

not in proper form.

Hence we assume new variables D_1 and D_2 and the productions

$$S \to B_a D_1$$
$$D_1 \to AD_2$$
$$D_2 \to B_b B$$

Therefore the grammar in Chomsky Normal Form (CNF) is G_2 with the productions given by

$$S \to B_a D_1,$$
$$D_1 \to AD_2,$$
$$D_2 \to B_b B,$$
$$A \to B_a A,$$
$$B \to B_b B,$$
$$B_a \to a,$$
$$B_b \to b,$$
$$A \to a,$$

and $$B \to b.$$

Example 2.5.2: Obtain a grammar in Chomsky Normal Form (CNF) equivalent to the grammar G with productions P given by

$$S \to ABa$$
$$A \to aab$$
$$B \to AC$$

Solution

(i) The given set P does not have any unit productions or λ-productions.

(ii) None of the given rules is in proper form.

For $S \to ABa$, we have

$$S \to ABB_a$$

and $$B_a \to a$$

For $A \to aab$, we have

$$A \to B_aB_aB_b$$

and $$B_b \to b.$$

For $B \to Ac$, we have

$$B \to AB_c$$

and $$B_c \to c$$

Therefore G_1 has a set of productions P' given by

$$\begin{aligned} S &\to ABB_a \\ A &\to B_aB_aB_b \\ B &\to AB_c \\ B_a &\to a \\ B_b &\to b \\ B_c &\to c \end{aligned}$$

(iii) In P' above, we have

$$\begin{aligned} S &\to ABB_a \\ A &\to B_aB_aB_b \end{aligned}$$

not in proper form.

Hence we assume new variables D_1 and D_2 and the productions

$$\begin{aligned} S &\to AD_1, \\ D_1 &\to BB_a, \\ A &\to B_aD_2, \\ D_2 &\to B_aB_b. \end{aligned}$$

Thus the grammar in Chomsky Normal Form (CNF) is G_2 given by the productions given by

$$\begin{aligned} S &\to AD_1, \\ D_1 &\to BB_a, \\ A &\to B_aD_2, \\ D_2 &\to B_aB_b, \end{aligned}$$

$$B \to AB_c,$$
$$B_a \to a,$$
$$B_b \to b,$$
and $$B_c \to c.$$

Example 2.5.3: Reduce the given CFG with P given by

$$S \to abSb \mid a \mid aAb \quad \text{and} \quad A \to bS \mid aAAb$$

to Chomsky Normal Form (CNF).

Solution

(i) There are neither λ-productions nor unit product in the given set of P.

(ii) Among the given productions, we have

$$S \to a$$

in proper form.

For $S \to abSb$, we have

$$S \to B_a B_b S B_b, \quad B_a \to a, \quad \text{and } B_b \to b.$$

For $S \to aAb$, we have

$$S \to B_a A B_b.$$

For $A \to bS$, we have

$$A \to B_b S.$$

For $A \to aAAb$, we have

$$A \to B_a A A B_b.$$

Therefore, we have G_1 given by

$$G_1 = (\{S, A, B_a, B_b\}, \{a, b\}, P', S)$$

which has P' given by

$$S \to B_a B_b S B_b$$
$$S \to B_a A B_b$$
$$A \to B_a A A B_b$$
$$A \to B_b S$$
$$B_a \to a$$
$$B_b \to b$$
and $$S \to a.$$

(iii) In P' above, we have

$$S \to B_a B_b S B_b$$
$$S \to B_a A B_b$$

and $A \to B_a AAB_b$

not in proper form.

Hence we assume new variables D_1, D_2, D_3, D_4 and D_5 with productions given as below:

For $S \to B_a B_b SB_b$, we have

$$S \to B_a D_1, \quad D_1 \to B_b D_2, \quad D_2 \to SB_b$$

For $S \to B_a AB_b$, we have

$$S \to B_a D_3$$
$$D_3 \to AB_b$$

For $A \to B_a AAB_b$, we have

$$A \to B_a D_4$$
$$D_4 \to AD_5$$
$$D_5 \to AB_b$$

Therefore, the grammar in Chomsky Normal Form (CNF) is G_2 with production given by

$$S \to B_a D_1$$
$$D_1 \to B_b D_2$$
$$D_2 \to SB_b$$
$$S \to B_a D_3$$
$$D_3 \to AB_b$$
$$A \to B_a D_4$$
$$D_4 \to AD_5$$
$$D_5 \to AB_b$$
$$A \to B_b S$$
$$B_a \to a$$
$$B_b \to b$$

and $S \to a.$

Example 2.5.4: Obtain the grammar G given by P as $S \to a \mid b \mid cSS$.

Solution

(i) There are no λ-productions and no unit productions in given P.

(ii) Among the given productions,

$$S \to a$$

and $S \to b$

are in proper form.

For $S \rightarrow cSS$, we have

$$S \rightarrow B_c SS.$$
$$B_c \rightarrow c.$$

Therefore we have G_1 given by

$$G_1 = (\{S_*\}, \{a, b, c\}, P', S)$$

which has P' given by

$$S \rightarrow B_c SS$$
$$B_c \rightarrow c$$
$$S \rightarrow a$$
$$S \rightarrow b$$

(iii) In P' above, we have

$$S \rightarrow B_c SS$$

not in proper form.
Hence we have new variable D_1 and new productions,

$$S \rightarrow B_c D_1$$
$$D_1 \rightarrow SS$$

Therefore the grammar in Chomsky Normal Form (CNF) is G_2 with productions given by

$$S \rightarrow B_c D_1$$
$$D_1 \rightarrow SS$$
$$B_c \rightarrow c$$
$$S \rightarrow a$$

and $\quad S \rightarrow b.$

2.5.2 Greibach Normal Form

In Chomsky's Normal Form (CNF), restrictions are put on the length of right sides of a production, whereas in Greibach Normal Form (GNF), restriction are put on the positions in which terminals and variables can appear.

GNF is useful in simplifying some proofs and making constructions such as Push Down Automaton (PDA) accepting a CFG.

Definition: A context-free grammar is said to be in Greibach Normal Form (GNF) if all productions have the form

$$A \rightarrow ax,$$

where $a \in T$ and $x \in V^*$.

For a grammar in GNF, the RHS of every production has a single terminal followed by a string of variables.

The procedure of getting a grammar in GNF is beyond the scope of this book.

GLOSSARY

CFG: Context-Free Grammar.

Left-Linear Grammar: All productions are either of the form

$$V \to VT^*$$

or

$$V \to T^*$$

Right-Linear Grammar: All productions are either of the form

$$V \to T^*V$$

or

$$V \to T^*$$

Parsing: Finding a derivation of the string.

Topdown Parsing: Sequence of rules applied in the leftmost derivation

Bottomup Parsing: Sequence of rules applied in a rightmost derivation.

Ambiguous Grammar: A CFG is said to be "ambiguous" if there exists at least one string in the language of the CFG which is ambiguously derivable. Otherwise it is unambiguous.

Useless Production: A production rule not affecting the language

Unit Production: Any production of a CFG of the form $A \to B$ where $A, B \in V$ is called a Unit-Production.

Chomsky Normal Form: A CFG without any λ-productions is generated by a grammar in which productions are of the form $A \to BC$ or $A \to a$, where $A, B \in V_N$ and $a \in V_T$.

REVIEW QUESTIONS

1. Define the term: Context-Free Grammar (CFG).
2. Give an example of a CFG.
3. What do you mean by a right linear grammar?
4. Show the relationship existing between right-linear grammars and NFAs. Give an example.
5. What is a left-linear grammar?
6. Compare right-linear grammar with left-linear grammar.
7. Give some examples of Context-free languages.
8. What are derivation Trees?

9. Define 'derivation tree'.
10. When is an ordered tree said to be a derivation tree?
11. What do you mean by sentential form?
12. What is a partial derivation tree?
13. Explain (a) Rightmost (b) Leftmost and (c) Mixed derivation.
14. What do you mean by the terms
    (a) Parsing
    (b) Ambiguity.
15. What do you mean by exhaustive search parsing?
16. Distinguish between top-down and bottom-up parsing.
17. Define the terms:
    (a) Ambiguous Grammar (b) Ambiguous Language.
18. What do you mean by inherantly ambiguous language?
19. Explain the method of simplifying a CFG.
20. State the substitution rule.
21. How will you abolish useless production in CFG?
22. What do you mean by empty production removal? Explain with an example.
23. State the procedure to find CFG without λ-productions.
24. What do you mean by unit production removal?
25. What do you mean by left recursion removal?
26. What are the kinds of Normal Forms?
27. What do you mean by Chomsky Normal Form (CNF)?
28. State the procedure to find equivalent grammar in CNF.
29. What do you mean by Greibach Normal Form (GNF).
30. When is a CFG said to be in GNF?

EXERCISES

1. Generate the Context-Free Grammars that give the following languages.
   (a) $\{w \mid w \text{ contains at least three 1s}\}$
   (b) $\{w \mid w \text{ starts and ends with the same symbol}\}$
   (c) $\{w \mid \text{the length of } w \text{ is odd}\}$
   (d) $\{w \mid w = w^R$, that is, w is a palindrome$\}$
2. Determine the CFG that generates the following languages.
   (a) The set of strings over the alphabet {a, b} with twice as many a's as b's.
   (b) The complement of the language $\{a^n b^n \mid n \geq 0\}$
3. Determine a derivation tree of $a * b + a * b$ given that $a * b + a * b$ is in $L(G)$ where G is given by the productions $S \rightarrow S + S \mid S * S \mid a \mid b$.

4. Given grammar G with productions

$$S \to aB \mid bA,\ A \to a \mid aS \mid bAA,\ B \to b \mid bs \mid aBB.$$

For the string *aaabbabbba*, find a rightmost derivation, leftmost derivation and parse tree.

5. Obtain the derivation tree for the string a^2b^2c in the grammar $G = (N, T, P, S)$ where $N = (x_0, x_1)$, $T = (a, b, c)$, $S = x_0$, $P = \{x_0 \to ax_0 \mid bx_1, x_1 \to bx_1 \mid c\}$.

6. Obtain a CFG that generates the language $L = \{a^i b^j c^k \mid i, j, k \geq 0$ and either $i = j$ or $j = k\}$. Is the grammar you have generated ambiguous?

7. Let G_A and G_B be context-free grammars, generating the languages $L(G_A)$ and $L(G_B)$, respectively. Show that there is a context-free grammar generating each of the following sets.

(a) $L(G_A) \cup L(G_B)$ (b) $L(G_A)L(G_B)$ (c) $L(G_A)^*$.

8. Given $V = \{S, A, B, a, b\}$ and $T = \{a, b\}$. Determine whether $G = (V, T, S, P)$ is a type 0 grammar but not a type 1 grammar, a type 1 grammar but not a type 2 grammar, or a type 2 grammar but not a type 3 grammar if P, the set of productions is

(a) $S \to aAB,\ A \to Bb,\ B \to \lambda;$ (b) $S \to ABa,\ AB \to a;$
(c) $S \to bA,\ A \to B,\ B \to a;$ (d) $S \to bA,\ A \to b,\ S \to \lambda;$
(e) $S \to aA,\ A \to bB,\ B \to b,\ B \to \lambda.$

9. Given G is a grammar with $V = \{a, b, c, S\}, T = \{a, b, c\}$, starting symbol S, and productions $S \to abS$, $S \to bcS$, $S \to bbS$, $S \to a$ and $S \to cb$. Construct derivation trees for:

(a) *bcbba*
(b) *bbbcbba*
(c) *bcabbbbbcb*.

10. For a grammar G with productions

$$S \to aAS \mid a$$
$$A \to SbA \mid SS \mid ba.$$

Show that $S \overset{*}{\Rightarrow} aabbaa$ and construct a derivation tree for *aabbaa*.

11. Obtain a CFG for generating all integers.

12. Given the grammar G:

$$S \to aAD$$
$$A \to aB \mid bAB$$
$$B \to b$$
$$D \to d$$

Reduce the grammar G to Chomsky Normal Form.

13. Obtain a grammar in Chomsky Normal Form equivalent to $S \to aAbB, A \to aA \mid a, B \to bB \mid b$.
14. Convert the following NFA to DFA.

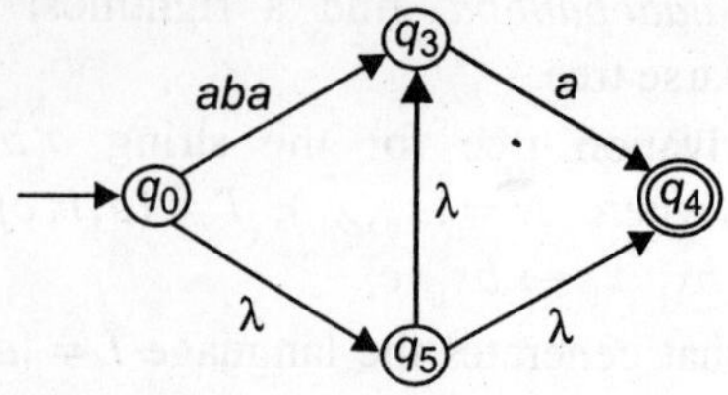

15. Prove that for every NFA there is an equivalent NFA that has only one final state.
16. Given $M = (\{q_0, q_1\}, \{0,1\}, \Delta, q_0, \{q_1\})$ is an NFA with

$$\Delta = \{(q_0,0,q_0),(q_0,0,q_1),(q_0,1,q_1),(q_1,1,q_0),(q_1,1,q_1)\}$$

Draw the state transition diagram for M. Convert to a DFA using subset construction.
17. Show that the grammar with productions $S \to aSb \mid SS \mid \lambda$, is ambiguous.
18. Show that the grammar

$$S \to aSbS \mid bSaS \mid \lambda$$

is ambiguous.
19. Give the derivation tree for $(((a + b) * c)) + a + b$, using the grammar

$$
\begin{aligned}
&G = (V, T, E, P)\\
&V = \{E, T, F, I\}\\
&E \to T\\
&T \to F\\
&F \to I\\
&E \to E + T\\
&T \to T * F\\
&F \to (E),\\
&I \to a \mid b \mid c
\end{aligned}
$$

20. Eliminate useless productions from

$$
\begin{aligned}
&S \to a \mid aA \mid B \mid C\\
&A \to aB \mid \lambda\\
&B \to Aa\\
&C \to cCD,\\
&D \to ddd
\end{aligned}
$$

21. Show that the two grammars

$$
\begin{aligned}
&S \to abAaA \mid abAbb \mid ba,\\
&A \to aaa
\end{aligned}
$$

and $S \to abAB \mid ba,$
$A \to aaa,$
$B \to aA \mid bb$

are equivalent.

22. Eliminate all the λ-productions from

$$S \to AaB \mid aaB,$$
$$A \to \lambda$$
$$B \to bbA \mid \lambda.$$

23. Say whether the following grammars are in CNF:
(a) $S \to AS \mid a,$ $A \to SA \mid b$ (b) $S \to AS \mid AAS,$ $A \to SA \mid aa.$

24. Convert the grammar $S \to aSb \mid ab$ into Chomsky Normal Form.

25. Convert the grammar with productions

$$S \to abAB,$$
$$A \to bAB \mid \lambda,$$
$$B \to BAa \mid A \mid \lambda$$

into Chomsky Normal Form.

26. Give a grammar with no ∈- or unit productions generating the set $L(G) - \{\in\}$, where G is the grammar

$$S \to aSbb \mid T,$$
$$T \to bTaa \mid S \mid \in.$$

27. Give grammars in Chomsky Normal Form for the following CFGs.
(a) $\{a, b\}^*$-(palindromes)
(b) $\{a^k b^m c^n \mid k, m, n \geq 1, 2k \geq n\}$
(c) $\{a^n b^k a^n \mid k,\ n \geq 1\}$
(d) $\{a^n b^{2n} c^k \mid k, n \geq 1\}.$

SHORT-QUESTIONS AND ANSWERS

1. Define a Context-Free Grammar (CFG).

A context-free grammar is a 4-tuple (*V*, *T*, *S*, *P*) where

(i) *V* is a finite set called the variables
(ii) *T* is a finite set, disjoint from *V*, called the terminals.
(iii) *P* is a finite set of rules, with each rule being a variable and a string of variables and terminals, and
(iv) $S \in V$ is the start variable.

If u, v and w are strings of variables and terminals and $A \to w$ is a rule of the grammar, we say that uAv yields uwv, written $uAv \Rightarrow uwv$.

2. Give an example of CFG.

Given a grammar of $G = (\{S\}, \{a, b\}, R, S)$. The set of rules R is

$$S \to aSB$$
$$S \to SS$$
$$S \to \in$$

This grammar generates strings such as *abab*, *aaabbb* and *aababb*.

3. What is a left linear grammar?

A grammar is which all productions are either of the form

$$V \to VT^*$$

or

$$V \to T^*$$

is called a left linear grammar.

4. What is right linear grammar?

A grammar is which all productions are either of the form

$$V \to T^*V$$

or

$$V \to T^*$$

is called a right linear grammar.

5. What do you mean by Parsing?

Finding a derivation of the string is called Parsing.

6. What are derivation trees?

A derivation tree is an ordered tree in which the nodes are labeled with the left sides of productions and in which the children of a node represent its corresponding right sides.

7. What do you mean by sentential form?

The resultant of the derivation tree is a word something like w = *aaba* for a CFG with productions $S \to aA, A \to aB, B \to bB$, $B \to a$. This word is said to be in sentential form.

8. Sketch the derivation tree for the CFG given by $S \to aA, A \to aB$, $B \to bB, B \to a$.

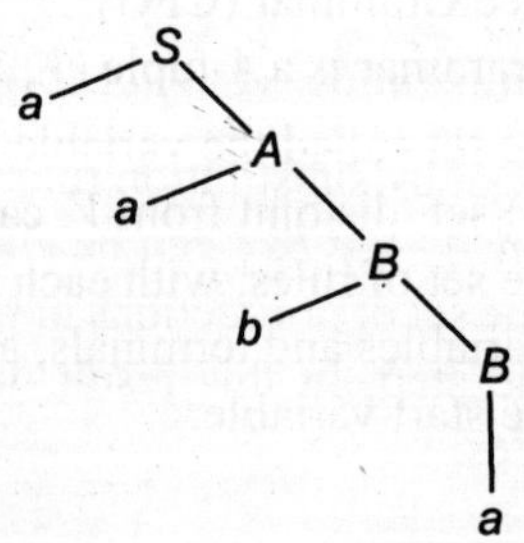

9. What is a partial derivation tree?

In the definition of derivation tree given, if every leaf has a label from $V \cup T \cup \{\lambda\}$ then it is said to be a partial derivation tree.

10. What do you mean by Topdown Parsing?

The sequence of rules being applied in the leftmost derivation is referred to as Topdown Parsing.

11. What is meant by bottomup Parsing?

Sequence of rules applied in a rightmost derivation is referred to as bottom-up parsing.

12. What is an ambiguous grammar?

A CFG is said to be ambiguous if there exists at least one string in the language of the CFG which is ambiguously derivable. Otherwise it is unambiguous.

13. What is meant by a useless production?

A production which does not affect a language is called a useless production.

14. What is an Unit Production?

Any production of a CFG of the form $A \to B$ where $A, B \in V$ is called a Unit Production.

15. What do you mean by exhaustive search parsing?

To parse a string w, that generates all strings in L and check if w is among them is called exhaustive search parsing.

16. Give the formal definition of an ambiguous CFG.

Let $G = (N, T, P, S)$ be a CFG. A string $w \in L(G)$ is said to be "ambiguously derivable" if there are two or more different derivation trees for that string in G.

17. What is an inherantly ambiguous language?

A language for which no unambiguous grammar exists, is called an inherantly ambiguous language.

18. Give examples for ambiguous grammars.

(a) A CFG which has the production rules

$S \to SbS, S \to a$ is ambiguous.

(b) A CFG which has the production rules

$S \to a \mid aAb \mid abSb,\ A \to aAAb \mid bS$ is ambiguous.

19. What do you mean by substitution rule?

A production $A \to x_1 B x_2$ can be eliminated from a grammar if we put in its place the set of productions in which B is replaced by all strings it derives in one step. In this result, it is essential that A and B are different variables.

20. Give the formal definition of a useful production.

Let $G = (V, T, S, P)$ be a CFG. A variable $A \in V$ is said to be 'useful' iff there is at least one $w \in L(G)$ such that.

$$S \overset{*}{\Rightarrow} xAy \overset{*}{\Rightarrow} w$$

with x, y in $(V \cup T)^*$, i.e., a variable is useful if it occurs in at least one derivation.

21. Give an example of a grammar with useless production.

In the grammar G with production rules P given by

$$S \to aSb \mid \lambda \mid A$$
$$A \to aA$$

The production $S \to A$ does not play any role because 'A' cannot be transformed into a terminal string. 'A' can occur in a string derived from S, this can never lead to a sentential form.

22. Determine whether the grammar G with P

$$S \to A$$
$$A \to aA \mid \lambda$$
$$B \to bA$$

has a useless production?

Here the variable B is "useless", therefore $B \to bA$ is also useless.

There is no way to achieve $S \overset{*}{\Rightarrow} xBy$. Therefore $B \to bA$ is a useless production.

23. What is a λ-production?

Any production of a CFG of the form

$$A \to \lambda$$

is called a λ-production.

24. When is a variable said to be "nullable"?

Any variable A for which the derivation

$$A \overset{*}{\Rightarrow} \lambda$$

is possible is called "Nullable".

25. Write a procedure to find CFG without λ-productions

(i) For all production $A \to \lambda$, put A into V_N.

(ii) Repeat the following steps until no further variables are added to V_N.

For all productions

$$B \to A_1 A_2 \;\ldots\ldots\; A_n$$

where $A_1, A_2, A_3, \ldots\ldots A_n$ are in V_N, put B into V_N.

26. What is meant by a Unit Production?

Any production of a CFG of the form

$$A \rightarrow B$$

where $A, B \in V$ is called a 'Unit Production'.

27. State the procedure to remove the unit productions.

(i) Find all variables B, for each A such that

$$A \overset{*}{\Rightarrow} B$$

This is done by sketching a "dependency graph" with an edge (C, D) whenever the grammar has unit production $C \rightarrow D$, then $A \overset{*}{\Rightarrow} B$ holds whenever there is a walk between A and B.

(ii) The new grammar $\hat{G}$, equivalent to G is obtained by letting into $\hat{P}$ all non-unit productions of P.

(iii) Then for all A and B satisfying $A \overset{*}{\Rightarrow} B$, we add to $\hat{P}$

$$A \rightarrow y_1 \mid y_2 \mid \ldots\ldots \mid y_n$$

where $B \rightarrow y_1 \mid y_2 \mid \ldots\ldots \mid y_n$ is the set of all rules in $\hat{P}$ with B on the left.

28. What do you mean by left recursion?

A variable A is left-recursive if it occurs in a production of the form

$$A \rightarrow Ax$$

for any $x \in (V \cup T)^*$.

A grammar is left-recursive if it contains at least one left-recursive variable.

29. Can every CF language be represented by a grammar that is not left-recursive?

YES.

30. What are the kinds of Normal Forms?

There are two kinds of Normal Forms viz.,

(a) Chomsky Normal Form (CNF)
(b) Greibach Normal Form (GNF)

31. What do you mean by Chomsky Normal Form?

A CFG without any λ-production is generated by a grammar in which productions are of the form $A \rightarrow BC$ or $A \rightarrow a$, where $A, B \in V_N$ and $a \in V_T$.

32. Differentiate between Chomsky's Normal Form (CNF) and Greibach Normal Form (GNF).

In CNF, restrictions are put on the length of right sides of production, whereas in Greibach Normal Form (GNF), restrictions are put on the positions in which terminals and variables can appear.

33. What is meant by Greibach Normal Form?

A CFG is said to be in Greibach Normal Form if all productions have the form

$$A \rightarrow ax$$

where $a \in T$ and $x \in V^*$.

Chapter 3

Pushdown Automata

3.1 DEFINITIONS

Let us consider a finite automata which accepts the language

$$L_1(M) = \{a^m b^n \mid m, n \geq 1\}.$$

We see that M moves from q_0 to q_1, on the occurence of a's. On seeing 'b', M moves from q_1 to q_2 and continues to be in the state q_2 on getting more b's.

Assume that the input string is given by

$$a^m b^n,$$

then the resulting state is final state and so M accepts $a^m b^n$.

Consider the language $L_2(M) = \{a^n b^n \mid n \geq 1\}$ where the number of b's and a's are equal. The FA constructed for L_1 differs from that of L_2.

For the language $L_1(M) = \{a^m b^n \mid m, n \geq 1\}$ there is not necessity to remember the number of a's. The following have to be remembered.

(a) Whether the first symbol is 'b' (to reject the string)
(b) Whether 'a' follows 'b' (to reject the string)
(c) Whether 'a' follows 'a' and 'b' follows 'b' (to accept the string).

We know that FA has only a finite number of states, M cannot remember the number of a's in $a^n b^n$ where 'n' is larger than the number of states of M.

The FA does not accept the sets of the form $\{a^n b^n \mid n \geq 1\}$. This is taken care by a "PUSHDOWN AUTOMATA".

Let us illustrate a Pushdown Automata (PDA) model.

3.1.1 Nondeterministic PDA (Definition)

An NPDA is defined by the 7-tuple

$$M = (Q, \Sigma, \Gamma, \delta, q_0, Z, F)$$

where
Q = Finite set of internal states of the control unit
Σ = Input alphabet
Γ = Finite set of symbols called "Stack alphabet"

δ : $Q \times (\Sigma \cup \{\lambda\}) \times \Gamma \rightarrow$ finite subsets of $Q \times \Gamma^*$ is the transition function

q_0 = Initial state of the control unit $\in Q$

Z = Stack start symbol

$F \subseteq Q$ = Set of Final states.

The arguments of δ are the current state of the control unit, the current input symbol, and the current symbol on the top of the stack.

The result is a set of pairs (q, x)

where q = next state of the control unit

x = string that is put on top of the stack in place of the single symbol there before.

The 'stack' is an additional component available as part of PDA. The 'stack' increases its memory. With respect to $\{a^n b^n \mid n \geq 1\}$, we can store a's in the stack. When the symbol 'b' is encountered, an 'a' from the stack can be removed. If the stack becomes empty on the completion of processing a given string, then the PDA accepts the string.

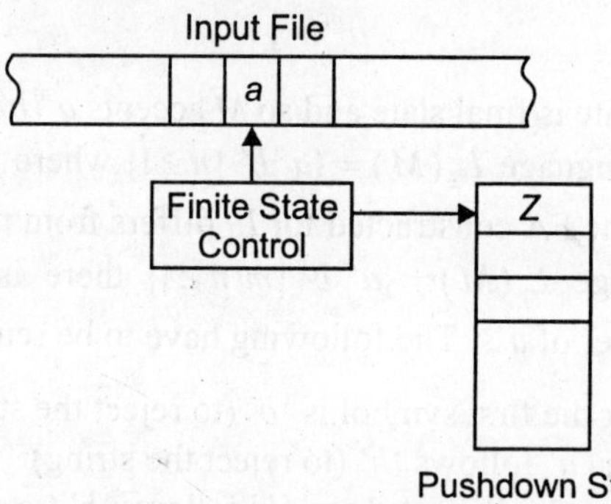

Fig. Model of Pushdown Automaton (PDA)

3.1.2 Transition Functions for NPDA

The transition function for an NPDA has the form

$$\delta : Q \times (\Sigma \cup \{\lambda\}) \times \Gamma \rightarrow \text{Finite subsets of } Q \times \overline{\Gamma}$$

δ is now a function of three arguments.

The first two arguments are the same as before:

(i) the state

(ii) either λ, or a symbol from the input alphabet.

The third argument is the symbol on top of the stack. Just as the input symbol is "consumed" when the function is applied, the stack symbol is also "consumed" (removed from the stack).

Note that while the second argument may be λ, rather than a member of the input alphabet (so that no input symbol is consumed), there is no such option for the third argument.

δ always consumes a symbol from the stack, no move is possible if the stack is empty.

There may also be a λ-transition, where the second argument may be λ, which means that a move that does not consume an input symbol is possible. No move is possible if the stack is empty.

Example: Consider the set of transition rules of an NPDA given by

$$\delta(q_1, a, b) = \{(q_2, cd), (q_3, \lambda)\}$$

If at any time the control unit is in state q_1, the input symbol read is 'a', and the symbol on the top of stack is 'b', then one of the following two cases can occur:

(a) The control unit tends to go into the state q_2 and the string 'cd' replaces 'b' on top of the stack.

(b) The control unit goes into state q_3 with the symbol b removed from the top of the stack.

In the deterministic case, when the function δ is applied, the automaton moves to a new state $q \in Q$ and pushes a new string of symbols $x \in \Gamma^*$ onto the stack. As we are dealing with nondeterministic pushdown automaton, the result of applying δ is a finite set of (q, x) pairs.

3.1.3 Drawing NPDAs

NPDAs are not usually drawn. However, with a few minor extensions, we can draw an NPDA similar to the way we draw an NFA.

Instead of labeling an are with an element of Σ, we can label arcs with $a|x, y$ where $a \in \Sigma, x \in \Gamma$ and $y \in \Gamma^*$.

Let us consider the NPDA given by

$$(Q = \{q_0, q_1, q_2, q_3\},\ \Sigma = \{a, b\},\ \Gamma = \{0, 1\}, \delta, q_0, Z = 0, F = \{q_3\})$$

where
$$\delta(q_0, a, 0) = \{(q_1, 10), (q_3, \lambda)\}$$
$$\delta(q_0, \lambda, 0) = \{(q_3, \lambda)\}$$
$$\delta(q_1, a, 1) = \{(q_1, 11)\}$$
$$\delta(q_1, b, 1) = \{(q_2, \lambda)\}$$
$$\delta(q_1, b, 1) = \{(q_2, \lambda)\}$$
$$\delta(q_2, \lambda, 0) = \{(q_3, \lambda)\}$$

This NPDA is drawn as follows.

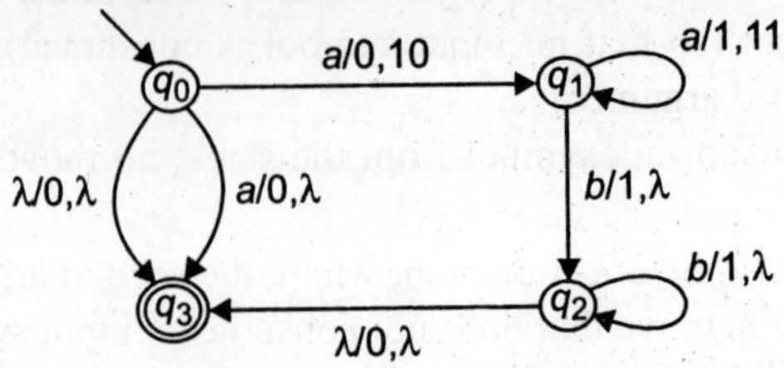

Please note that the top of the stack is considered to be the left, so that, for example, if we get an '*a*' from the starting position, the stack changes from '0' to '10.'.

3.1.4 Execution of NPDA

Assume that someone is in the middle of stepping through a string with a DFA, and we need to take over and finish the job. There are two things that are required to be known:

(a) the state of the DFA is in, and
(b) what the remaining input is.

But if the automaton is an NPDA we need to know one more viz., contents of the stack.

Instantaneous Description of a PDA

The Instantaneous description of a PDA is a triplet (q, w, u),

where q = current state of the automaton
w = unread part of the input string
u = stack contents (written as a string, with the leftmost symbol at the top of the stack).

Let the symbol "$\vdash$" denote a move of the NPDA, and suppose that $\delta(q_1, a, x) = \{(q_2, y), \ldots\}$, then the following is possible:

$$(q_1, aW, xz) \vdash (q_2, W, yz)$$

where W indicates the rest of the string following '*a*' and Z indicates the rest of the stack contents underneath the x.

This notation tells that in moving from state q_1 to state q_2, an '*a*' is consumed from the input string aW, and the x at the top (left) of the stack xZ is replaced with y, leaving yZ on the stack.

3.1.5 Accepting Strings with an NPDA

Assume that you have the NPDA given by

$$M = (Q, \Sigma, \Gamma, \delta, q_0, z, F).$$

To recognize string w, begin with the instantaneous assumption

$$(q_0, w, z)$$

where q_0 = start state
w = entire string to be processed, and
z = start stack symbol.

Starting with this instantaneous description, make zero or more moves, just as is done with an NFA.

There are two kinds of moves that can be made:

(a) *λ-Transitions:* If you are in state q_1, x is the top (leftmost) symbol in the stack, and

$$\delta(q_1, \lambda, x) = \{(q_2, w_2), \ldots\ldots\}$$

then you can replace the symbol x with the string w_2 and move to q_2.

(b) *Nonempty transitions:* If you are in the state q_1, 'a' is the next unconsumed input symbol, x is the top (leftmost) symbol in the stack, and

$$\delta(q_1, a, x) = \{(q_2, w_2), \ldots\ldots\}$$

then you can remove the 'a' from the input string, replace the symbol x with the string w_2, and move to state q_2.

If you are in the final state when you reach the end of the string (and may be make some λ-transition after reaching the end), then the string is accepted by the NPDA. It does not matter what is on the stack.

3.1.6 An Example of NPDA Execution

Let us consider the NPDA given by

$$\delta(q_0, a, 0) = \{(q_1, 10), (q_3, \lambda)\}$$
$$\delta(q_0, \lambda, 0) = \{(q_3, \lambda)\}$$
$$\delta(q_1, a, 1) = \{(q_1, 11)\}$$
$$\delta(q_1, b, 1) = \{(q_2, \lambda)\}$$
$$\delta(q_2, b, 1) = \{(q_2, \lambda)\}$$
$$\delta(q_1, \lambda, 0) = \{(q_3, \lambda)\}$$

It is possible for us to recognize the string "*aaabbb*" using the following sequence of "Moves":

$$\begin{aligned}(q_0, aaabbb, 0) &\vdash (q_1, aabbb, 10)\\ &\vdash (q_1, abbb, 110)\\ &\vdash (q_1, bbb, 1110)\\ &\vdash (q_2, bb, 110)\\ &\vdash (q_2, b, 10)\\ &\vdash (q_2, \lambda, 0)\end{aligned}$$

3.1.7 Accepting Strings with NPDA (Formal Version)

The notation "$\vdash$" is used to indicate a single move of an NPDA.

"$\vdash^*$" is used to indicate a sequence of zero or more moves.

"$\vdash^+$" is used to indicate a sequence of one or more moves.

If $M = (Q, \Sigma, \Gamma, \delta, q_0, Z, F)$ is an NPDA, then the language accepted by M, L(M), is given by

$$L(M) = \{w \in \Sigma^* : (q_0, w, z) \overset{*}{\vdash} (p, \lambda, u), p \in F, u \in \Gamma^*\}.$$

Example 3.1.1: Construct a Push Down Automata (PDA) accepting $\{a^n b^m a^n \mid m, n \geq 1\}$ by empty store.

Solution

The PDA which will accept

$$\{a^n b^m a^n \mid m, n \geq 1\}$$

is given below

$$\text{PDA} = (\{q_0, q_1\}, \{a, b\}, \{a, z_0\}, \delta, q_0, z_0; \phi)$$

where δ is given by

(1) $\delta(q_0, a, z_0) = \{(q_0, a z_0)\}$
(2) $\delta(q_0, a, a) = \{(q_0, aa)\}$
(3) $\delta(q_0, b, a) = \{(q_1, a)\}$
(4) $\delta(q_1, b, a) = \{(q_1, a)\}$
(5) $\delta(q_1, a, a) = \{(q_1, \lambda)\}$
(6) $\delta(q_1, \lambda, z_0) = \{(q_1, \lambda)\}$

Therefore we can see that we start storing a's till b occurs ((1) and (2)). When the current input symbol is b, the state changes, but no change in PDS occurs ((3)). Once all the b's in the input string acts over ((4)), the remaining a's are erased ((5)).

Using (6), z_0 is erased.

Therefore we have

$$(q_0, a^n b^m a^n, z_0) \overset{*}{\vdash} (q_1, \lambda, z_0) \vdash (q_1, \lambda, \lambda)$$

Therefore we see that $a^n b^m a^n \in N$ (PDA).

Example 3.1.2: Construct a PDA accepting $\{a^n b^{2n} \mid n \geq 1\}$ by empty store.

Solution

The PDA that will accept $\{a^n\ b^{2n} \mid n \geq 1\}$ is given by

$$\text{PDA} = (\{q_0, q_1, q_2\}, \{a, b\}, \{a, z_0\}, \delta, q_0, z_0, \phi)$$

where δ is given by

$$\begin{aligned}
\delta(q_0, a, z_0) &= \{(q_1, a\, z_0)\} \\
\delta(q_1, a, a) &= \{(q_1, a\, a)\} \\
\delta(q_1, b, a) &= \{(q_2, a)\} \\
\delta(q_2, b, a) &= \{(q_1, \lambda)\} \\
\delta(q_1, \lambda, z_0) &= \{(q_1, \lambda)\}
\end{aligned}$$

Example 3.1.3: Obtain the PDA accepting $\{a^m\ b^m\ c^n \mid m, n \geq 1\}$ by empty store.

Solution

The PDA which will accept $\{a^m\ b^m\ c^n \mid m, n \geq 1\}$ by empty store is given below.

$$\text{PDA} = (\{q_0, q_1\}, (a, b, c\}, \{z_0, z_1\}, \delta, q_0, z_0, \phi)$$

where δ is given by

$$\begin{aligned}
\delta(q_0, a, z_0) &= \{(q_0, z, z_0)\} \\
\delta(q_0, a, z_1) &= \{(q_0, z_1 z_1)\} \\
\delta(q_0, b, z_1) &= \{(q_1, \lambda)\} \\
\delta(q_1, b, z_1) &= \{(q_1, \lambda)\} \\
\delta(q_1, c, z_0) &= \{(q_1, z_0)\} \\
\delta(q_1, \lambda, z_0) &= \{(q_1, \lambda)\}
\end{aligned}$$

When an 'a' is read z_1 is added. When a 'b' is read then z_1 is removed.

Example 3.1.4: Construct a PDA accepting $\{a^n\ b^m\ a^n \mid m, n \geq 1\}$ by final state.

Solution

THEOREM: If $A = (Q, \Sigma, \Gamma, \delta, q_0, z_0, F)$ is a PDA accepting L by null store, we can find a PDA

$$B = (Q', \Sigma, \Gamma', \delta_B, q_0', z_0', F')$$

which accept L by final state, i.e.,

$$L = N(A) = T(B).$$

Using the above theorem, we have

$$B = (\{q_0, q_1, q_0', q_f\}, \{a, b\}, \{a, z_0, z_0'\}, \delta, q_0', z_0', \{q_f\})$$

where δ is given by

$$\delta(q_0', \lambda, z_0') = \{(q_0, z_0\, z_0')\}$$

$$\delta(q_0, \lambda, z_0') = \{(q_f, \lambda)\} = \delta(q_0, \lambda, z_0')$$
$$\delta(q_1, \lambda, z_0') = \{(q_f, \lambda)\} = \delta(q_1, \lambda, z_0')$$
$$\delta(q_0, a, z_0) = \{(q_0, a\, z_0)\}$$
$$\delta(q_0, a, a) = \{(q_0, aa)\}$$
$$\delta(q_0, b, a) = \{(q_1, a)\}$$
$$\delta(q_1, b, a) = \{(q_1, a)\}$$
$$\delta(q_1, a, a) = \{(q_f, \lambda)\}$$
$$\delta(q_1, \lambda, z_0) = \{(q_1, \lambda)\}$$

Example 3.1.5: Given $L = \{a^m\, b^n \mid n < m\}$.

Derive (i) a context-free grammar that accepts L
(ii) a PDA accepting L by empty store
(iii) a PDA accepting L by final state.

Solution

(i) Given $L = \{a^m\, b^n \mid n < m\}$
CFG is given by $G = (\{S\}, \{a, b\}, P, S)$, where productions P are

$$\left.\begin{array}{l} S \to aSb \\ S \to aS \\ S \to a \end{array}\right\}$$

(ii) The PDA that will accept $L(G)$ by empty store is given by

$$A = (\{q\}, \{a, b\}, \{S, a, b\}, \delta, q, S, \phi),$$

where δ is defined by the rule:
$\delta(q, \lambda, S) = \{(q, aSb), (q, aS), (q, a)\}$
$\delta(q, a, a) = \delta(q, b, b) = \{(q, \lambda)\}$

(iii) $B = (Q', \Sigma, \Gamma', \delta_B, q_0', z_0', F')$, where
$Q' = \{q_0, q_0', q_f\}, \Gamma' = \{S, a, b, z_0'\}, F = \{q_f\}$.
δ_B is given by
$\delta_B(q_0', \lambda, z_0') = \{(q_1, z_0\, z_0')\}$
$\delta_B(q, \lambda, S) = \{(q, aSb), (q, aS), (q, a)\}$
$\delta_B(q, a, a) = \{(q, \lambda)\} = \delta_B(q, b, b)$
$\delta_B(q_1, \lambda, z_0') = \{(q_f, \lambda)\}$
where
$\delta_B(q, a, S) = \delta(q, a, S) = \phi$ and
$\delta_B(q, b, S) = \delta(q, b, S) = \phi$.

3.2 RELATIONSHIP BETWEEN PDA AND CONTEXT FREE LANGUAGES

3.2.1 Simplifying CFGs

The productions of context-free grammars can be coerced into a variety of forms without affecting the expressive power of the grammar.

(a) Empty Production Removal

If the empty string does not belong to a language, then there is no way to eliminate production of the form $A \to \lambda$ from the grammar.

If the empty string belongs to a language, then we can eliminate λ from all productions same for the single productions $S \to \lambda$. In this case we can eliminate any occurrences of S from the right-hand-side of productions.

(b) Unit Production Removal

We can eliminate productions of the form $A \to B$ from a CFG.

(c) Left Recursion Removal

A variable A is left-recursive if it occurs in a production of the form

$$A \to Ax$$

for any $x \in (V \cup T)^*$. A grammar is left-recursive if it contains at least one left-recursive variable.

Every CFL can be represented by a grammar that is not left-recursive.

3.2.2 Normal Forms of Context-Free Grammars

(a) Chomsky Normal Form

A grammar is in Chomsky Normal form if all productions are of the form

$$A \to BC$$

or

$$A \to a$$

where A, B and C are variables and 'a' is a terminal. Any context-free grammar that does not contain λ can be put into Chomsky Normal Form.

(b) Greibach Normal Form (GNF)

A grammar is in Greibach Normal Form if all productions are of the form

$$A \to ax$$

where 'a' is a terminal and $x \in V^*$.

Grammars in Greibach Normal Form are much longer than the CFG from which they were derived. GNF is useful for proving the equivalence of NPDA and CFG.

Thus GNF is useful in converting a CFG to NPDA.

3.2.3 CFG to NPDA

For any context-free grammar in GNF, it is easy to build an equivalent nondeterministic pushdown automaton (NPDA).

Any string of a context-free language has a leftmost derivation. We set up the NPDA so that the stack contents "corresponds" to this sentential form: every move of the NPDA represents one derivation step.

The sentential form is

(The characters already read) + (symbols on the stack)
– (Final z (initial stack symbol)

In the NPDA, we will construct, the states that are not of much importance. All the real work is done on the stack. We will use only the following three states, irrespective of the complexity of the grammar.

(i) start state q_0 just gets things initialized. We use the transition from q_0 to q_1 to put the grammar's start symbol on the stack.

$$\delta(q_0, \lambda, Z) \rightarrow \{(q_1, Sz)\}$$

(ii) State q_1 does the bulk of the work. We represent every derivation step as a move from q_1 to q_1.

(iii) We use the transition from q_1 to q_f to accept the string

$$\delta(q_1, \lambda, z) \rightarrow \{(q_f, z)\}$$

Example Consider the grammar $G = (\{S, A, B\}, \{a, b\}, S, P)$, where

$$P = \{S \rightarrow a, S \rightarrow aAB, A \rightarrow aA, A \rightarrow a, B \rightarrow bB, B \rightarrow b\}$$

These productions can be turned into transition functions by rearranging the components.

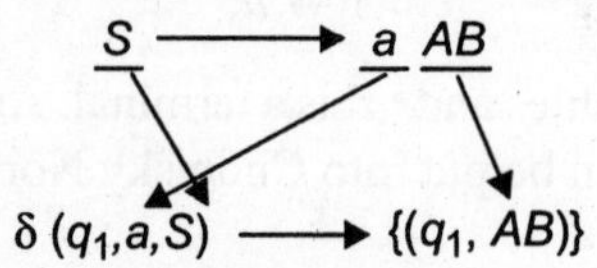

Thus we obtain the following table:

(Start)	$\delta(q_0, \lambda, z) \rightarrow \{(q_1, Sz)\}$
$S \rightarrow a$	$\delta(q_1, a, S) \rightarrow \{(q_1, \lambda)\}$
$S \rightarrow aAB$	$\delta(q_1, a, S) \rightarrow \{(q_1, AB)\}$
$A \rightarrow aA$	$\delta(q_1, a, A) \rightarrow \{(q_1, A)\}$
$A \rightarrow a$	$\delta(q_1, a, A) \rightarrow \{(q_1, \lambda)\}$
$B \rightarrow bB$	$\delta(q_1, b, B) \rightarrow \{(q_1, B)\}$
$B \rightarrow b$	$\delta(q_1, b, B) \rightarrow \{(q_1, \lambda)\}$
(finish)	$\delta(q_1, \lambda, z) \rightarrow \{(q_f, z)\}$

For example, the derivation

$$S \Rightarrow aAB \Rightarrow aaB \Rightarrow aabB \Rightarrow aabb$$

maps into the sequence of moves

$$\begin{aligned}(q_0, aabb, z) &\vdash (q_1, aabb, Sz)\\ &\vdash (q_1, abb, ABz)\\ &\vdash (q_1, bb, Bz)\\ &\vdash (q_1, b, Bz)\\ &\vdash (q_1, \lambda, z)\\ &\vdash (q_2, \lambda, \lambda)\end{aligned}$$

3.2.4 NPDA to CFG

(a) We have shown that for any CFG, an equivalent NPDA can be obtained. We shall show also that, for any NPDA, we can produce an equivalent CFG. This will establish the equivalence of CFGs and NFDAs.

We shall assert without proof that any NPDA can be transformed into an equivalent NPDA which has the following form:

(i) The NPDA has only one final state, which it enters if and only if the stack is empty.
(ii) All transitions have the form

$$\delta(q, a, A) = \{c_1, c_2, c_3, \ldots\ldots\}$$

where each c_i has one of the two forms

$$(q_j, \lambda)$$

or $$(q_j, BC)$$

(b) When we write a grammar, we can use any variable names we choose. As in programming languages, we like to use "meaningful" variable names.

When we translate an NPDA into a CFG, we will use variable names that encode information about both the state of the NPDA and the stack content variable names will have the form

$$[q_i A q_j],$$

where q_i and q_j are states and A is a variable.

The "meaning" of the variable $[q_i Aq_j]$ is that the NPDA can go from state q_i with Ax on the stack to state q_j with x on the stack.

Each transition of the form $\delta(q_i, a, A) = (q_j, \lambda)$ results in a single grammar rule.

Each transition of the form

$$\delta(q_i, a, A) = \{q_j, BC)$$

results is a multitude of grammar rules, one for each pair of states q_x and q_y in the NPDA.

3.2.5 Deterministic Pushdown Automata

A Non-deterministic finite acceptor differs from a deterministic finite acceptor in two ways:

(i) The transition function δ is single-valued for a DFA, but multi-valued for an NFA.
(ii) An NFA may have λ-transitions.

A non-deterministic pushdown automaton differs from a pushdown automaton in the following ways:

(i) The transition function δ is at most single-valued for a DPDA, multi-valued for an NPDA.
Formally: $|\delta(q_1, a, b)| = 0$ or 1, for every $q \in Q, a \in \Sigma \cup \{\lambda\}$, and $b \in \Gamma$.
(ii) Both NPDA and DPDA may have λ-transitions; but a DPDA may have a λ-transition only if no other transition is possible.
Formally: If $|\delta(q, \lambda, b)| \neq \varnothing$, then $\delta(q, c, b) = \varnothing$ for every $c \in \Sigma$.

A deterministic CFL is a language that can be recognized by a DPDA. The deterministic context-free languages are a proper subset of the context-free languages.

3.3 PROPERTIES OF CONTEXT FREE LANGUAGES

3.3.1 Pumping Lemma for CFG

A "Pumping Lemma" is a theorem used to show that, if certain strings belong to a language, then certain other strings must also belong to the language.

Let us discuss a Pumping Lemma for CFL.

We will show that, if L is a context-free language, then strings of L that are at least 'm' symbols long can be "pumped" to produce additional strings in L. The value of 'm' depends on the particular language.

Let L be an infinite context-free language. Then there is some positive integer 'm' such that, if S is a string of L of Length at least 'm', then

(i) $S = uvwxy$ (for some u, v, w, x, y)
(ii) $|vwx| \leq m$
(iii) $|vx| \geq 1$
(iv) $uv^iwx^iy \in L$.

for all non-negative values of i.

It should be understood that

(i) If S is sufficiently long string, then there are two substrings, v and x, somewhere in S. There is stuff (u) before v, stuff (w) between v and x, and stuff (y), after x.

(ii) The stuff between v and x won't be too long, because $| vwx |$ can't be larger than m.

(iii) Substrings v and x won't both be empty, though either one could be.

(iv) If we duplicate substring v, some number (i) of times, and duplicate x the same number of times, the resultant string will also be in L.

3.3.2 Definitions

A variable is useful if it occurs in the derivation of some string. This requires that

(a) the variable occurs in some sentential form (you can get to the variable if you start from S), and

(b) a string of terminals can be derived from the sentential form (the variable is not a "dead end").

A variable is "recursive" if it can generate a string containing itself. For example, variable A is recursive if

$$S \overset{*}{\Rightarrow} uAy$$

for some values of u and y.

A recursive variable A can be either

(i) "Directly Recursive", i.e., there is a production

$$A \rightarrow x_1 A x_2$$

for some strings $x_1, x_2 \in (T \cup V)^*$, or

(ii) "Indirectly Recursive", i.e., there are variables x_i and productions

$$\begin{aligned} &A \rightarrow X_1 \ldots \\ &X_1 \rightarrow \ldots X_2 \ldots \\ &X_2 \rightarrow \ldots X_3 \ldots \\ &X_N \rightarrow \ldots A \ldots \end{aligned}$$

3.3.3 Proof of Pumping Lemma

(a) Suppose we have a CFL given by L. Then there is some context-free Grammar G that generates L. Suppose

(i) L is infinite, hence there is no proper upper bound on the length of strings belonging to L.

(ii) L does not contain λ.

(iii) G has no productions or λ-productions.

There are only a finite number of variables in a grammar and the productions for each variable have finite lengths. The only way that a grammar can generate arbitrarily long strings is if one or more variables is both useful and recursive.

Suppose no variable is recursive.

Since the start symbol is nonrecursive, it must be defined only in terms of terminals and other variables. Then since those variabls are non recursive, they have to be defined in terms of terminals and still other variables and so on. After a while we run out of "other variables" while the generated string is still finite. Therefore there is an upperbond on the length of the string which can be generated from the start symbol. This contradicts our statement that the language is finite.

Hence, our assumption that no variable is recursive must be incorrect.

(b) Let us consider a string X belonging to L.

If X is sufficiently long, then the derivation of X must have involved recursive use of some variable A.

Since A was used in the derivation, the derivation should have started as

$$S \overset{*}{\Rightarrow} uAy$$

for some values of u and y. Since A was used recursively the derivation must have continued as

$$S \overset{*}{\Rightarrow} uAy \overset{*}{\Rightarrow} uvAxy$$

Finally the derivation must have eliminated all variables to reach a string X in the language.

$$S \overset{*}{\Rightarrow} uAy \overset{*}{\Rightarrow} uvAxy \overset{*}{\Rightarrow} uvwxy = x$$

This shows that derivation steps

$$A \overset{*}{\Rightarrow} vAx$$

and

$$A \overset{*}{\Rightarrow} w$$

are possible. Hence the derivation

$$A \overset{*}{\Rightarrow} vwx$$

must also be possible.

It should be noted here that the above does not imply that a was used recursively only once. The * of $\overset{*}{\Rightarrow}$ could cover many uses of A, as well as other recursive variables.

There has to be some "last" recursive step. Consider the longest strings that can be derived for v, w and x without the use of recursion. Then there is a number 'm' such that $|vwx| < m$.

Since the grammar does not contain any λ-productions or unit productions, every derivation step either introduces a terminal or increases the length of the sentential form. Since $A \overset{*}{\Rightarrow} vAx$, it follows that $|vx| > 0$.

Finally, since $uvAxy$ occurs in the derivation, and $A \overset{*}{\Rightarrow} vAx$ and $A \overset{*}{\Rightarrow} w$ are both possible, it follows that uv^iwx^iy also belongs to L.

This completes the proof of all parts of Lemma.

3.3.4 Usage of Pumping Lemma

The Pumping Lemma can be used to show that certain languages are not context free.

Let us show that the language

$$L = \{a^ib^ic^i \mid i > 0\}$$

is not context-free.

Proof: Suppose L is a context-free language.

If string $X \in L$, where $|X| > m$, it follows that $X = uvwxy$, where $|vwx| \leq m$.

Choose a value i that is greater than m. Then, wherever vwx occurs in the string $a^ib^ic^i$, it cannot contain more than two distinct letters it can be all a's, all b's, all c's, or it can be a's and b's, or it can be b's and c's.

Therefore the string vx cannot contain more than two distinct letters; but by the "Pumping Lemma" it cannot be empty, either, so it must contain at least one letter.

Now we are ready to "pump".

Since $uvwxy$ is in L, uv^2wx^2y must also be in L. Since v and x can't both be empty,

$$|uv^2wx^2y| > |uvwxy|,$$

so we have added letters.

Both since vx does not contain all three distinct letters, we cannot have added the same number of each letter.

Therefore, uv^2wx^2y cannot be in L.

Thus we have arrived at a "contradiction".

Hence our original assumption, that L is context free should be false. Hence the language L is not context-free. □

Example 3.3.1: Check whether the language given by

$$L = \{a^m b^m c^n : m \leq n \leq 2m\}$$

is a CFL or not.

Solution

Let $s = a^n b^n c^{2n}$, n being obtained from Pumping Lemma.

Then $s = uvwxy$, where $1 \leq |vx| \leq n$.

Therefore, vx cannot have all the three symbols a, b, c.

If you assume that vx has only a's and b's then we can shoose i such that $uv^i wx^i y$ has more than $2n$ occurrence of a or b and exactly $2n$ occurences of c.

Hence $uv^i wx^i y \notin L$, which is a contradiction. Hence L is not a CFL.

Example 3.3.2: "If L is regular and $L \subseteq \Sigma^*$, then $\Sigma^* - L$ is also a regular set"—Prove this theorem.

Proof: Let $L = T(M)$ where $M = (Q, \Sigma, \delta, q_0, F)$ is a Finite Automata.

We modify Σ, Q and δ as follows:

(a) If $a \in \Sigma_1 - \Sigma$, then the symbol 'a' will not appear in any string of $T(M)$.
Therefore we can delete 'a' from Σ_1 and all transitions defined by 'a'.
Here $T(M)$ is not affected.

(b) If $\Sigma - \Sigma_1 \neq \varnothing$, we can add a dead state d to Q. Let us define $\delta(d, a) = d$, for all 'a' in Σ and $\delta(q, a) = d$, for all q in Q and a in $\Sigma - \Sigma_1$.
Hence also $T(M)$ is not affected.

Let us consider M obtained by applying (a) and (b) to Σ, Q and δ.

The new M is now written as $(Q, \Sigma, \delta, q_0, F)$. Let us define a new automaton 'M'' such that $M' = (Q, \Sigma, \delta, Q, F)$, where M' differs from M only in its final states.

There $w \in T(M')$ iff $\delta(q_0, w) \in Q - F$ and $w \notin T(M)$.

Therefore, $\Sigma^* - L = T(M')$ is regular. □

Example 3.3.3: Prove that the language L given by

$$L = \{a^n b^n \mid n \geq 0,\ n \neq 1000\}$$

is context-free.

Proof: Let us assume that

$$L_A = \{a^{1000}b^{1000}\}.$$

Then, since L_1 is finite, it is regular.

It is obvious that

$$L = \{a^n b^n \mid n \geq 0\} \cap \overline{L_1}.$$

According to the *theorem:* "If L_1 is a CFL and L_2 is a regular language, $L_1 \cap L_2$ is context-free", we have the following.

By closure of regular languages under complementation and closure of context free languages under regular intersection, the language L given by

$$L = \{a^n b^n \mid n \geq 0,\ n \neq 1000\}$$

is context-free. □

Example 3.3.4: Check whether the language given by

$$L = \{w \in \{a, b, c\}^* \mid n_a(w) = n_b(w) = n_c(w)\}$$

is not context-free.

Proof: If L is assumed to be context-free, then

$$L \cap L(a^* b^* c^*) = \{a^n b^n c^n \mid n \geq 0\}.$$

which is also context-free.

But it is a fact that the latter is not context-free.

Therefore we conclude that

$$L = \{w \in \{a, b, c\}^* \mid n_a(w) = n_b(w) = n_c(w)\}$$

is not context-free. □

Example 3.3.5: Determine whether the language given by $L = \{a^{n^2} \mid n \geq 1\}$ is context-free or not.

Solution

Let us assume that

$$s = a^{n^2}.$$

$s = uvwxy$, where $1 \leq |vx| \leq n$. which is true

since, $|vwx| \leq n$ (by Pumping Lemma)

Let $|vx| = m,\ m \leq n$.

By Pumping Lemma, uv^2wx^2y is in L.

Since
$$|uv^2wx^2y| > n^2,$$
$$|uv^2wx^2y| = k^2.$$

where $k \geq n+1$.

But $|uv^2wx^2y| = n^2 + m < n^2 + 2n + 1$.

Therefore, $|uv^2wx^2y|$ lies between n^2 and $(n+1)^2$.

Hence, $uv^2wx^2y \notin L$, which is a contradiction.

Therefore, $\{a^{n^2} : n \geq 1\}$ is not context-free.

3.4 DECISION ALGORITHMS

THEOREM: Given L is a regular set, i.e., a language accepted by a finite automaton. There exists a constant 'n' such that if 's' in any string in L and $|s| \geq n$, then $s = uvw$ such that $|uv| \leq n, |v| \geq 1$ and for all $i \geq 0,\ uv^iw \in L$.

Proof: Let us assume that $L = T(M)$ where $M = (Q, \Sigma, \delta, q_0, F)$ and 'n' be the number of states in Q.

Let $w = a_1a_2 \ldots\ldots a_m \in L$ where $m \geq c$

and $\delta(q_0, q_1, q_2, \ldots\ldots a_i) = q_i$.

Since $m \geq n$, the number of states, the sequences $q_0, q_1, \ldots\ldots q_m$ will have some repeated states.

Hence there are two integers j and k, $0 \leq j < k < n$ such that $q_i = q_k$.

Let us assume that k is least in the chosen pair (j, k).

For this we have

(a) $q_i = q_k$

(b) if $0 < 1 < k$, then $q_i \neq q_j$ for all $0 \leq i < 1$, therefore $q_0, q_1, \ldots\ldots q_{k-1}$ are distinct states in Q and $k \leq n$.

Let $u = a_1a_2 \ldots\ldots a_j$; $v = a_{j+1} \ldots\ldots, a_k$ and $w = a_{k+1}, \ldots\ldots, a_n$.

Therefore $s = uvw$ (as shown in Fig.).

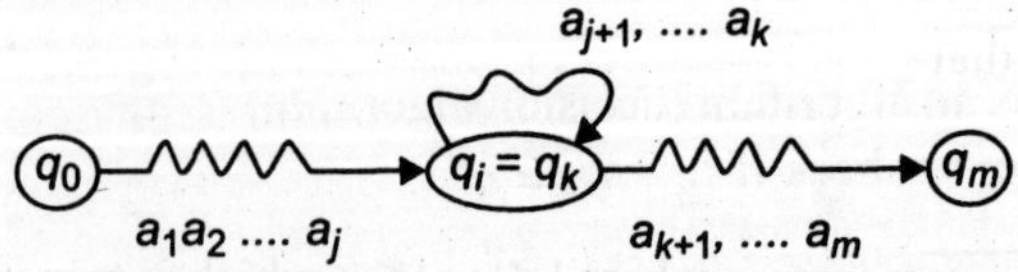

Since $\delta(q_i, v) = q_k = q_j, \delta(q_j, v^i) = q_j$.

Therefore $\delta(q_0, uv^iw) = q_m \in F$.

This illustrates that $uv^i w \in L$, for all $i \geq 0$.
Since $uv = a_1 a_2 \ldots\ldots a_k$ and

$$k \leq n, |uv| \leq n.$$

Hence, $|v| \geq 1$. □

THEOREM: The set of strings that is accepted by a finite automaton which has 'n' state is

(a) nonempty if and only if M accepts some string of length less than n.
(b) infinite, if an only if M accepts some string of length k where $n \leq k < 2n$.

Thus there is a *DECISION ALGORITHM*, to find out whether M accepts zero, a finite number, or an infinite number of strings.

Algorithm (i): Let us give an algorithm to decide if $T(M) = \varnothing$.
Let us consider the strings of length less than n. Test if any of these strings is in $T(M)$. If so, $T(M) = \varnothing$. Otherwise, $T(M)$ is empty.

Algorithm (ii): Let us give an algorithm to decide if $T(M)$ is infinite.
Let us consider the strings of length k, where $n \leq k \leq 2n-1$. Test if any such string is found in $T(M)$. If so, $T(M)$ is infinite, otherwise $T(M)$ is finite.

Example 3.4.1: Prove that there exists an algorithm to find if two finite automata M_1 and M_2 accept the same language.

Proof: Let us assume that

$$L_1 = T(M_1) \text{ and}$$
$$L_2 = T(M_2).$$

Let us define $L = (L_1 - L_2) \cup (L_2 - L_1)$.

The language L is regular.

Let us assume that M is a finite automaton such that $L = T(M)$.

Now, if $L = \varnothing$, iff $L_1 = L_2$.

Since there is an algorithm (decision algorithm) to test if L is a empty, we have an algorithm to check if $L_1 = L_2$. □

Example 3.4.2: Check whether the language defined by

$$L = \{a^p = p \text{ is a prime number}\} \text{ is regular or not.}$$

Solution

Let us assume that $L = T(M)$, where the automaton M has n states.

If p is a prime number greater than n, consider

$$z = a^p \in L.$$

By using pumping lemma, $s = uvw$ and $uv^i w \in L$ for $i \geq 1$.

Also $$uv^{P+1}w \in L.$$

But $|uv^{P+1}w| = |uvw| + |v^P| = p + pm$ where $m = |v|$.

This is a contradiction as we see that $p + pm$ cannot be prime.

Therefore the language L is not prime.

Example 3.4.3: Construct a deterministic Pushdown Automata to accept $L_{()}$, the language of nested, balanced parantheses.

Solution

The idea is to store all left parantheses on the stack and then pop them off as each one matches a right parantheses.

Let us define

$$M = (\{q_0, q_1\}, \{(\ ,\ )\}, \delta, q_0, \{q_1\})$$

where δ is given in the table below.

Table: Transition Table for DPDA.

Transition Number	Current state	Input symbol	Stack Top	New state	Input op	Stack op
1	q_0	(	>	q_0	+	push (
2	q_0	(	(	q_0	+	push (
3	q_0	)	(	q_0	+	pop
4	q_0	>	>	q_1	0	0
5	q_0	>	(	q_2	0	0
6	q_0	)	>	q_2	0	0

Transitions (1) and (2) are used to push opening parantheses on the stack; transition (3) is used to to match a closing paranthesis with an open one on the stack; (4) accepts the input, and (5) and (6) send the machine into a rejecting state, which halts the machine.

Consider M on input (( ) ( )):

$$(q_0, [1, ((\,)(\,))], [1, \lambda] \underset{M}{\vdash} (q_0, [2, ((\,)(\,))], [1, (])$$

$$\underset{M}{\vdash} (q_0, [3, ((\,)(\,))], [1, ((])$$

$$\underset{M}{\vdash} (q_0, [4, ((\,)(\,))], [1, (])$$

$$\underset{M}{\vdash} (q_0, [5, ((\,)(\,))], [1, (])$$

$$\underset{M}{\vdash} (q_0, [6, ((\,)(\,))], [1, (])$$

$$\underset{M}{\vdash} (q_0, [7, ((\,)(\,))], [1, \lambda])$$

$$\underset{M}{\vdash} (q_1, [7, ((\,)(\,))], [1, \lambda])$$

Therefore,

$$(q_0[1, ((\,)(\,)], [1, \lambda]) \overset{*}{\underset{M}{\vdash}} (q_1, [7, ((\,)(\,)], [1, \lambda])$$

and since q_1 is an accepting state, all input has been read, and the stack is empty, we have $((\,)(\,)) \in L(M)$.

Let us consider M on the input string ( )). We get the following computations.

$$(q_0, [1, (\,)], [1, \lambda] \underset{M}{\vdash} (q_0, [2, (\,))], [1, (])$$

$$\underset{M}{\vdash} (q_0, [3, (\,))], [1, \lambda])$$

$$\underset{M}{\vdash} (q_2, [3, (\,))], [1, \lambda])$$

No further transitions of M can be applied, q_2 is not an accepting state, and so $(\,)) \notin L_{()}$.

GLOSSARY

NDPDA: Non-deterministic Pushdown automata

PDA: Pushdown automata

Transition Function of NPDA: Are of the form

$$\delta = Q \times (\Sigma \cup \{\lambda\}) \times \Gamma$$

These are finite subsets of $Q \times \Gamma^*$.

Stack: One additional component available as part of PDA.

More of NPDA: $\vdash$ denotes a move of NPDA.

PDA: Has (q, w, u),

where q = current state of automaton
w = unreal part of input string
u = stack contents.

Simplifying CFG: Done either through (i) Empty Production removal (ii) Unit production removal (iii) Left recursion removal.

DPDA: Deterministic PDA, which has a transition function as single-valued for DFA and has λ-transitions.

Pumping Lemma: Theorem used to show that if certain strings belong to a language, then certain other strings must also belong to the language.

Decision Algorithm: To find out if M accepts zero, a finite number, or an infinite number of strings.

REVIEW QUESTIONS

1. Define a Pushdown automata.
2. Define a Nondeterministic Pushdown automata.
3. State the general form of transition function for an NPDA.
4. Give the instantaneous description of a PDA.
5. Explain how the strings are accepted with an NPDA.
6. What are the kinds of moves that can be made while accepting strings with an NPDA?
7. Explain the terms (a) λ-transitions (b) Non-empty transitions
8. Give an example of NPDA execution.
9. State the relationship between PDA and context free languages.
10. Explain: (a) Empty Production removal (b) Unit Production removal.
11. What are the Normal forms of CFGs?
12. How will you convert a CFG to NPDA?
13. How will you convert a NPDA to CFG?
14. What do you mean by deterministic pushdown automata?
15. State the properties of Context free languages.
16. State the pumping lemma for CFG.
17. Give the proof for pumping lemma.
18. State the usuage of pumping lemma.
19. What are decision algorithms?
20. State the usefulness of decision algorithms.

EXERCISE

1. Construct a Pushdown automata (PDA) accepting the language

$$L = \{0^i 1^i \mid i \geq 0\} \cup \{0^j 1^{2j} \mid j \geq 0\}.$$

2. For $\Sigma = \{0,1\}$, design DPDAs to accept the following languages:
   (a) 0^*
   (b) $\{0^i 1^i 0^j 1^j \mid i, j \geq 0\}$
   (c) $\{0^{2i} 1^i \mid i \geq 1\}$
   (d) $\{0^m 1^n \mid m \neq n\}$
3. Define the concepts of string and language acceptance for PDAs.
4. For $\Sigma = \{0,1\}$, design PDA to accept the following languages:
   (a) $\{xx \mid x \in \{0,1\}^*\}$
   (b) $\{x \mid x \in \{0,1\}^*$ and $x = x^R\}$
   (c) $\{0^m 1^n \mid n \leq m \leq 2n\}$
   (d) $\{0^m 1^n \mid 3n \leq m \leq 7n\}$
5. Construct a PDA accepting $\{a^n b^{3n} \mid n \geq 1\}$ by empty store.
6. Obtain the PDA accepting $\{a^m b^n c^n \mid m, n \geq 1\}$ by empty store.
7. Obtain the PDA accepting $\{a^m b^n c^n \mid m, n \geq 1\}$ by final state.
8. Given $L = \{a^n b^m \mid m < n\}$. Derive
   (a) a CFG that accepts L
   (b) a PDA accepting L by empty store
   (c) a PDA accepting L by final state.
9. Construct a PDA accepting $L = \{wcw^T : w \in \{a,b\}^*\}$ by final state.
10. Construct a PDA accepting $L = \{wcw^T : w \in \{a,b\}^*\}$ by empty store.
11. If the PDA $A = \{Q, \Sigma, \Gamma, \delta, q_0, Z_0, F)$ accepts L by final state, prove that there exists another PDA B accepting L by empty store, i.e., $T(A) = T(B) = L$.
12. Find PDA accepting the following sets by final state
    (a) $\{x \in \{a,b\}^* : n_a(x) > n_b(x)\}$
    (b) $x \in \{a,b\}^* : n_a(x) < x_b(x)\}$
13. Design a PDA recognizing the set L of all non-palindromes over $\{a,b\}$.
14. Construct a PDA equivalent to the CFG.

$$S \to 0BB, \quad B \to 0S, \quad B \to 1S, \quad B \to 0$$

15. Construct a CFG accepting $L = \{a^m b^n \mid n < m\}$ and construct a PDA accepting L by empty store.

16. Construct a PDA accepting L by empty store where

$$L = \{a^j b^n a^n \mid n \geq 1, j \geq 0\}$$

17. Construct a PDA accepting $\{a^j b^n c^n : n \geq 1, j \geq 1\}$ by final state.
18. Constuct a CFG generating $\{a^n b^n \mid n \geq 1\} \cup \{a^m b^{2m} \mid m \geq 1\}$. Using this CFG, construct a PDA accepting the given set by empty store.
19. Using Pumping lemma show that the language $L = \{a^i b^i c^i \mid i \geq 0\}$ is not context free.
20. Using Pumping lemma show that the language

$$L = \{a^m b^n c^p \mid 0 \leq m \leq n \leq p\}$$

is not a CFL.

21. Using Pumping Lemma prove that the language $L = \{ww \mid w \in \{0,1\}^*$ is not a CFL.
22. Consider the set of all strings over $\{a, b\}$ with no more than twice as many a's as b's:

$$\{x \in \{a, b\}^* \mid \# a(x) \leq 2 \# b(x)\}$$

(a) Give a CFG for this set, and prove that it is correct.

(b) Give a PDA for this set. Show sample runs on the input strings *aabbaa, aaabbb* and *aaabaa.*

23. Consider the set

$$a^* b^* c^* — \{a^n b^n c^n \mid n \geq 0\}$$

the set of all strings of a's followed by b's followed by c's such that the number of a's, b's and c's are not all equal.

(a) Give a CFG for the set, and prove that your grammar is correct.

(b) Give an equivalent PDA.

24. Show that $\{a, b\}^* — \{a^n b^{n^2} \mid n \geq 0\}$ is not context free.

SHORT QUESTIONS AND ANSWERS

1. What is PDA and NDPDA?

PDA means Push Down Automata and NDPDA means non-deterministic Push Down Automata.

2. Define an NDPDA.

An NDPDA is defined by the 7-tuple

$$M = (Q, \Sigma, \Gamma, \delta, q_0, Z, F)$$

where Q = Finite set of internal states of the control unit

Σ = input alphabet

Γ = Finite set of symbols called 'stack alphabet'.

$\delta : Q \times (\Sigma \cup \{\lambda\}) \times \Gamma \rightarrow$ Finite subsets of $Q \times \Gamma^*$ is the transition function.

q_0 = Initial state of the control unit $\in Q$

Z = Stack start symbol

$F \subseteq Q \rightarrow$ Set of Final states.

3. What is the data structure used in a Push Down Automaton?

   Stack is the data structure used in a PDA.

4. What is the general form of a transition function of an NPDA?

   $\delta : Q \times (\Sigma \cup \{\lambda\}) \times \Gamma \rightarrow$ Finite subsets of $Q \times \Gamma^*$. where δ has now three arguments:

   (a) the state
   (b) either λ, or a symbol from the input alphabet.
   (c) symbol on the top of the stack.

5. State the requirements for execution of an NPDA.

   (a) The state of the DFA is in
   (b) What the remaining input is.

6. Given an instantaneous description of a PDA.

   The instantaneous description of a PDA is a triplet (q, w, u), where

   q = current state of the automaton

   w = unreal part of the input string

   u = stack contents (written as a string, with the leftmost symbol at the top of the stack).

7. What are the types of moves that are made while accepting strings with an NPDA?

   (a) λ-transition.
   (b) Non-empty transition.

8. What do you mean by a λ-transition in PDA?

   If you are in a state q_1, x is the top (leftmost) symbol in the stack, and

$$\delta(q_1; \lambda, x) = \{(q_2, w_2), \ldots\}$$

   then you can replace the symbol x with the string w_2 and move to q_2.

9. What are non-empty transitions in an NPDA?

   If you are in the state q_1, 'a' is the next unconsumed input symbol, x is the top (leftmost) symbol in the stack, and

$$\delta(q_1, a, x) = \{(q_2, w_2), \ldots\}$$

   then you can remove the 'a' from the input string, replace the symbol x with the string w_2, and move to the state q_2.

10. State the meanings of $\vdash$, $\overset{*}{\vdash}$ and $\overset{+}{\vdash}$ while accepting strings with NPDA.

    $\vdash$ is used to indicate a single move of an NPDA

    $\overset{*}{\vdash}$ is used to indicate a sequence of zero or more moves

    $\overset{+}{\vdash}$ is used to indicate a sequence removal in a PDA.

11. What is meant by Empty Production removal in a PDA?

    If the empty string does not belong to a language, the there is no way to eliminate production of the from $A \to \lambda$ from the grammar. If the empty string belongs to a language, then we can eliminate λ from all productions for the single production $S \to \lambda$. In this case we can eliminate any occurrences of S from the right hand side of productions.

12. What is meant by unit production removal in PDA?

    Eliminating productions of the form $A \to B$ from a CFG is called a unit production removal in PDA.

13. What is meant by left recursion removal in PDA?

    A variable A is left recursive if it occurs in a production of the form

$$A \to Ax$$

    for any $x \in (V \cup T)^*$. A grammar is left-recursive if it contains at least one left-recursive variable. Every CFL can be represented by a grammar that is not left-recursive.

14. What are the Normal Forms of CFGs?

    (a) Chomsky Normal Form.

    (b) Greibach Normal Form.

15. How is an NPDA built from a CFL?

    Any string of a CFL has a leftmost derivation. NPDA is set up so that the stack contents corresponds to this sentential form, every move of the NPDA represents one derivation step.

16. How is the sentential form obtained while converting a CFG into an NPDA?

    The sentential form is obtained as

    [The characters already read] + [symbols on the stack] – [Final z (initial stack symbol)]

17. What are the two ways in which deterministic pushdown finite acceptor differs from a non-deterministic finite acceptor?

    (a) The transition function δ is single-valued for a DFA, but multi-valued for an NFA.

    (b) An NFA may have λ-transitions.

18. What are the ways in which a non-deterministic pushdown automaton differs from a Pushdown automata

(a) The transition function δ is at most single-valued for a DPDA, multi-valued for an NPDA.
Formally: $|\delta(q, a, b)| = 0$ or l,
for every $q \in Q$, $a \in \Sigma \cup \{\lambda\}$, and $b \in \Gamma$.

(b) Both NPDA and DPDA may have λ-transitions, but a DPDA may have a λ-transition only if no other transition is possible.
Formally: If $\delta(q, \lambda, b) \neq \varnothing$, then $\delta(q, c, b) = \varnothing$ for every $c \in \Sigma$.

19. State the Pumping Lemma for Context Free Grammars.

Let L be an infinite context-free language. Then there is some positive integer 'm' such that, if S is a string of L of length at least 'm', then

(i) $S = uvwxy$ (for some u, v, w, x, y)
(ii) $|vwx| \leq m$
(iii) $|vx| \geq 1$
(iv) $uv^i wiy \in L$, for all non-negative values of i.

20. State one usage of a Pumping Lemma.

The Pumping Lemma can be used to show that certain languages are not context free.

21. What is a decision algorithm?

The set of strings that is accepted by a finite automaton M which has 'n' state is

(a) non empty, if and only if M accepts some string of length less than n.
(b) infinite, if and only if M accepts some string of length k where $n \leq k \leq 2n$.

22. State the use of decision algorithm:

It is used to find out whether a finite automaton M accepts zero, a finite number, or an infinite number of strings.

23. What are the ways to simplify a CFG to an NPDA?

(a) Empty Production Removal
(b) Unit Production Removal
(c) Left Recursion Removal.

24. How is a 'move' of an NPDA denoted?

$\vdash$ denotes a move of NPDA.

Chapter 4

Turing Machines

4.1 TURING MACHINE MODEL

4.1.1 What is a Turing Machine?

A Turing Machine is like a Pushdown Automaton. Both have a finite-state machine as a central component, both have additional storage.

A Pushdown Automaton uses a "stack" for storage whereas a Turing Machine usea a "tape", which is actually infinite in both the directions. The tape consists of a series of "squares", each of which can hold a single symbol. The "tape-head", or "read-write head", can read a symbol from the tape, write a symbol to the tape and move one square in either direction.

There are two kinds of Turing Machine available.

(a) Deterministic Turing Machine.
(b) Non-deterministic Turing Machine.

We will discuss about Deterministic Machines only. A Turing Machine does not read "input", unlike the other automata. Instead, there are usually symbols on the tape before the Turing Machine begins, the Turing Machine might read some. all, or none of these symbols. The initial tape may, if desired, be thought of as "input".

"Acceptors" produce only a binary (accept/reject) output. "Transducers" can produce more complicated results. So far all our previous discussions were only with acceptors. A Turing Machine also accepts or rejects its input. The results left on the tape when the Turing Machine finshes can be regarded as the "output" of the computation. Therefore a Turing Machine is a "Transducer".

4.1.2 Definition of Turing Machines

A Turing Machine M is a 7-tuple

$$(Q, \Sigma, \Gamma, \delta, q_0, \#, F)$$

where Q is a set of states

Σ is a finite set of symbols, "input alphabet".

Γ is a finite set of symbols, "tape alphabet".

δ is the partial transition function

$\# \in T$ is a symbol called 'blank'
$q_0 \in Q$ is the initial state
$F \subseteq Q$ is a set of final states

As the Turing machine will have to be able to find its input, and to know when it has processed all of that input, we require:

(a) The tape is initially "blank" (every symbol is #) except possibly for a finite, contiguous sequence of symbols.
(b) If there are initially nonblank symbols on the tape, the tape head is initially positioned on one of them.

This emphasises the fact that the "input" viz., the non-blank symbols on the tape does not contain #.

4.1.3 Transition Function, Instantaneous Description and Moves

The "*Transition Function*" for Turing Machine is given by

$$\delta : Q \times \Gamma \rightarrow Q \times \Gamma \times \{L, R\}$$

When the machine is in a given state (Q) and reads a given symbol (Γ) from the tape, it replaces the symbol on the tape with some other symbol (Γ), goes to some other state (Q), and moves the tape head one square left (L) or right (R).

An "*Instantaneous Description*" or "*Configuration*" of a Turing machine requires.

(a) the state the Turing machine is in
(b) the contents of the tape
(c) the position of the tape head on the tape.

This is written as a string of the form

$$x_i \ldots\ldots x_j q_m x_k \ldots\ldots x_l$$

where the x's are the symbols on the tape, q_m is the current state, and the tape head is on the square containing x_k (the symbol immediately following q_m).

The "*Move*" of a Turing machine can therefore be expressed as a pair of instantaneous descriptions, separated by a symbol "$\vdash$".

For example, if

$$\delta(q_5, b) = (q_8, c, R)$$

then a possible move can be

$$abbabq_5babb \ \vdash \ abbabcq_8abb$$

4.1.4 Programming a Turing Machine

As we have the "productions" as the control theme of a grammar, the "transitions" are the central theme of a Turing machine. These transitions are given as a table or list of S-tuples, where each tuple has the form

(current state, symbol read, symbol written, direction, next state)

Creating such a list is called "programming" a Turing machine.

A Turing machine is often defined to start with the read head positioned over the first (leftmost) input symbol. This is not really necessary, because if the Turing machine starts anywhere on the nonblank portion of the tape, it is simple to get to the first input symbol.

For the input alphabet $\Sigma = \{a, b\}$, the following program fragment does the trick, then goes to state q_1.

$$(q_0, a, a, L, q_0)$$
$$(q_0, b, b, L, q_0)$$
$$(q_0, \#, \#, R, q_1)$$

4.1.5 Turing Machines as Acceptors

A Turing machine halts when it no longer has available moves. If it halts in a final state, it accepts its input, otherwise it rejects its input.

A Turing machine $T = (Q, \Sigma, \Gamma, \delta, q_0, \#, F)$ accepts a language L(M), where

$$L(M) = (w \in \Sigma^+ : q_0 w \overset{*}{\vdash} x_i q_f x_j \text{ for some } q_f \in F, x_i, x_j \in \Gamma^*),$$

with the assumption that the Turing machine starts with its tape head positioned on the leftmost symbol.

A Turing Machine accepts its input if it halts in a final state. There are two ways this could fail to happen:

(a) The Turing machine could halt in a nonfinal state or
(b) The Turing machine could never stop i.e., it enters an "infinite loop".

4.1.6 How to Recognize a Language

This machine will match strings of the form

$$\{a^n b^n : n \geq 0\}$$

q_1 is the only "final state".
q_4 (which has no available moves at all) serves as an "error state".

Current state	Symbol read	Symbol written	Direction	Next state
Find the left end of the input				
q_0	a	a	L	q_0
q_0	b	b	L	q_0
q_0	#	#	R	q_1
If leftmost symbol is "a", erase it, if "b" fail				
q_1	a	#	R	q_2
q_1	b	#	R	q_4
Find the right end of the input				
q_2	a	a	R	q_2
q_2	b	b	R	q_2
q_2	#	#	L	q_3
Erase the "b" at the left end of the input				
q_3	b	#	L	q_0

The basic operation of this machine is a loop:

```
q0: move all the way to the left
q1: erase on 'a'
q2: move all the way to the right
q3: Erase a 'b'
Repeat
```

If the string is not of the form $\{a^n b^n : n \geq 0\}$, it will finally either

(a) See an 'a' in nonfinal state q_3, and halt, or
(b) see a 'b' in final state q_1, move to nonfinal state q_4, and halt.

4.1.7 Turing Machines as Transducers

To use a Turing machine as a transducer, treat the entire nonblank portion of the initial tape as input, and treat the entire nonblank portion of the tape when the machine halts as output.

A Turing machine defines a function $y = f(x)$ for strings $x, y \in \Sigma^*$ if

$$q_0 x \overset{*}{\vdash} q_f y$$

where q_f is the final state.

A function index is "Turing computable" if there exists a Turing machine that can perform the above task.

Example 4.1.1: Design a Turing machine that accepts the set of all even palindromes over {0,1}.

Solution

There are various steps involved in processing even length palindromes. The TM scans the first symbol of input tape (0 or 1), erases it and changes state (q_1, or q_2). TM scans the remaining part without changing the tape symbol until it encounters b. The read/write head moves to the left. If the rightmost symbol tallies with the leftmost symbol (which can be erased but remembered), the rightmost symbol is erased. Otherwise TM halts. The read/write head moves to the left until b is encountered. The above steps are repeated after changing the states suitably. The transition table is as shown below.

Present State	Input Symbol		
	0	1	b
$\rightarrow q_0$	bRq_1	bRq_2	bRq_7
q_1	$0Rq_1$	$1Rq_1$	bLq_3
q_2	$0Rq_1$	$1Rq_2$	bLq_4
q_3	bLq_5		
q_4		bLq_6	
q_5	$0Lq_5$	$1Lq_5$	bRq_0
q_6	$0Lq_6$	$1Lq_6$	bRq_0
q_7			

Example 4.1.2: Given $\Sigma = \{0,1\}$, design a Turing machine that accepts the language denoted by the regular expression 00^*.

Solution

Let us start at the left end of the input, we read each symbol and check that it is a 0. If it is, then we continue by moving right. If a blank is reached without seeing anything else other than 0, we terminate and accept the string.

If the input contains a 1 anywhere, the string is not in $L(00^*)$, and so we halt in a nonfinal state. In order to keep track of computation, two internal states $Q = \{q_0, q_1\}$ and the final state $F = \{q_1\}$ are enough.

Transition function is taken as

$$\delta(q_0, 0) = (q_0, 0, R)$$
$$\delta(q_0, \square) = (q_1, \square, R).$$

The head will move to the right, as long as 0 appears under the read-write head. If any time a 1 is read, the machine will halt in the nonfinal state q_0, since $\delta(q_0,1)$ is undefined.

Example 4.1.3: Design a Turing machine that accepts

$$L = \{a^n b^n \mid n \geq 0\}.$$

Solution

Assume that q_1 is the "final state".

q_4 (which has no available moves at all) serves as an "error state".

Current state	Symbol read	Symbol written	Direction	Next state
Find the left end of the input				
q_0	a	a	L	q_0
q_0	b	b	L	q_0
q_0	#	#	R	q_1
If leftmost symbol is "a", erase it, if "b", fail				
q_1	a	#	R	q_2
q_1	b	#	R	q_4
Find the right end of the input				
q_2	a	a	R	q_2
q_2	b	b	R	q_2
q_2	#	#	L	q_3
Erase the "b" at the left end of the input				
q_3	b	#	L	q_0

The basic operation of this machine is a loop:

```
q0: Move all the way to the left
q1: Erase an 'a'.
```

```
q2: Move all the way to the right
q3: Erase a "b".
Repeat
```

If the string is not of the form $\{a^n b^n \mid n \geq 0\}$ it will finally either

(a) see an 'a' in nonfinal state q_3, and halt, or
(b) see a 'b' in final state q_1, move to nonfinal state q_4, and halt.

Example 4.1.4: What does the Turing Machine described by the 5-tuples $(q_0,0,q_0,0,R), (q_0,1,q_1,0,R)$, (q_0,B,q_2,B,R), $(q_1,0,q_1,0,R)$, $(q_1,1,q_0,1,R)$ and (q_1,B,q_2,B,R) do when given a bit string as input?

Solution

If the tape contains at least one 1, the machine changes every other 1 to a 0 starting at the first 1, and halts when it reches the first blank symbol. If the tape is blank initially the machine halts without changing the tape. If the nonblank portion of the tape contains all 0s, the machine moves successively through these 0s and halts.

Example 4.1.5: Let T be the Turing machine defined by the five tuples: $(q_0, 0, q_1, 1, R)$, $(q_0, 1, q_1, 0, R)$, $(q_0, B, q_1, 0, R)$, $(q_1, 0, q_2, 1, L)$, $(q_1, 1, q_1, 0, R)$, $(q_1, B, q_2, 0, L)$. For each of the following initial tapes, determine the final tape when T halts, assuming that T begins in initial position.

(a)

...	B	B	0	0	1	1	B	B	...	...	...

(b)

...	B	B	B	B	B	B	B	B	...	...	...

Solution

(a) The nonblank portion of the tape contains the string 1111 when the machine halts.
(b) The nonblank portion of the tape contains the string 00 when the machine halts.

4.2 COMPLETE LANGUAGES AND FUNCTIONS

A Turing machine has an output function, the contents of the input tape after processing, a given input string can be viewed as the result of computation. Therefore a Turing machine is seen as a computer of functions, from integers to integers.

Let us now look at the procedure to compute functions $f(n_1, n_2, \ldots\ldots n_k)$ where $n_1, n_2, \ldots\ldots, n_k$ are non-negative integers.

(a) Represent the integers $n_1, n_2, \ldots\ldots, n_k$ in unary i.e., n_1 is written as 0^{n_1} etc. The input $(n_1, n_2, \ldots, n_k)$ is represented by $0^{n_1}10^{n_2}\ldots\ldots10^{n_k}$ where the 1's are used to separate the unary representation of $n_1, n_2, \ldots\ldots, n_k$.

(b) After several moves, if the Turing Machine halts (either in a final state or in any other state) and has 0^m in the input tape, then $F(n_1, n_2, \ldots\ldots, n_k) = m$.

Example 4.2.1: Design a Turing machine to add two given integers.

Solution

Assume that m and n are positive integers. Let us represent the input as $0^m B 0^n$.

If the separating B is removed and 0's come together we have the required output, $m + n$ is unary.

(i) The separating B is replaced by a 0.

(ii) The rightmost 0 is erased i.e., replaced by B.

Let us define $M = (\{q_0, q_1, q_2, q_3, q_4\}, \{0\}, \{0, B\}, \delta, q_0, \{q_4\})$. δ is defined by Table shown below.

State	Tape Symbol	
	0	B
q_0	$(q_0, 0, R)$	$(q_1, 0, R)$
q_1	$(q_1, 0, R)$	(q_2, B, L)
q_2	(q_3, B, L)	—
q_3	$(q_3, 0, L)$	(q_4, B, R)

M starts from ID $q_0 0^m B 0^n$, moves right until seeking the blank B. M changes state to q_1. On reaching the right end, it reverts, replaces the rightmost 0 by B. It moves left until it reaches the beginning of the input string. It halts at the final state q_4.

Example 4.2.2: Design a Turing Machine that copies strings of 1's.

Solution

Follow the following steps:

(a) Replace every 1 by an x.
(b) Find the rightmost x and replace it with 1.
(c) Travel to the right end of the current nonblank region and create a 1 there.
(d) Repeat steps (b) and (c) until there are no more x's.

The Transition function is given by

$$\delta(q_0,1) = (q_0, x, R),$$
$$\delta(q_0,\square) = (q_1, \square, L),$$
$$\delta(q_1, x) = (q_2, 1, R),$$
$$\delta(q_2,1) = (q_2, 1, R),$$
$$\delta(q_2,\square) = (q_1, 1, L),$$
$$\delta(q_1,1) = (q_1, 1, L),$$
$$\delta(q_1,\square) = (q_3, \square, R).$$

where q_3 is the only final state.

Example 4.2.3: Design a Turing Machine that multiplies two positive integers in unary notation.

Solution

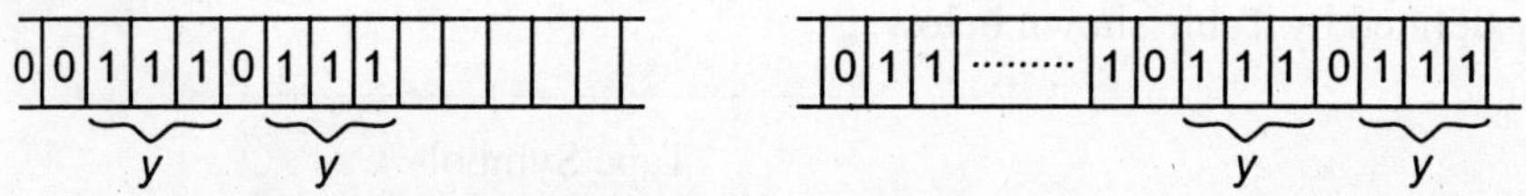

Assume that the initial and final tape contents are to be as indicated in figure above. Multiplication is visualized as a repeated copying of the multiplicand y for each 1 in the multiplies x, whereby the string y is added the appropriate number of times to the partially computed product. The steps involved in the process are:

(i) Repeat the following steps until x contains no more 1's—find a 1 in x and replace it with another symbol a. Replace the leftmost 0 by 0y.
(ii) Replace all a's with 1's.

Example 4.2.4: Design a Turing Machine that recognizes the set of bit strings which have a 1 as their second bit i.e., the regular set $(0 \vee 1)1(0 \vee 1)^*$.

Solution

We would like to have a Turing machine, which, starting at the leftmost nonblank tape cell, moves right, and determines whether the second symbol is a 1. If the second symbol is 1, the machine should more into a final state. If the second symbol is not a 1, the machine should not halt or it should halt in a non-final state.

To construct such a machine, we include the five-tuples $(q_0, 0, q_1, 0, R)$ and $(q_0, 1, q_1, 1, R)$ to read in the first symbol and put the Turing machine in state q_1.

Next, we include the five-tuples $(q_1, 0, q_2, 0, R)$ and $(q_1, 1, q_3, 1, R)$ to read in the second symbol and either move to state q_2 if this symbol is a 0, or to state q_3 if this symbol is a 1.

We do not want to recognize strings that have a 0 as their second bit, so q_2 should not be a final state. We want q_3 to be a final state. Therefore we can include the 5-tuple $(q_2, 0, q_2, 0, R)$. As we do not want to recognize the empty string nor a string with one bit, we also include the 5-tuples $(q_0, B, q_2, 0, R)$ and $(q_1, B, q_2, 0, R)$.

The Turing machine T consisting of seven 5-tuples given above will terminate in the final state q_3 if and only if the bit string has at least two bits and the second bit of the input string is a 1. If the bit string contains fewer than two bits or if the second bit is not a 1, the machine will terminate in the non final state q_2.

4.3 MODIFICATION OF TURING MACHINES

Two automata are said to be equivalent if they accept the same language. Two transducers are said to be equivalent if they compute the same function.

A class of automata e.g., Standard Turing machines is equivalent to another class of automata e.g., nondeterministic Turing machines, if for each transducer in one class, an equivalent transducer can be found in another class.

At each move of a Turing machine, the tape head may move either left or right. We can augment this with a "Stay option", i.e., we will add "don't move" to the set $\{L, R\}$.

"Turing machines with a stay option are equivalent to Standard Turing Machines."

4.3.1 *N*-Track Turing Machine

An N-track Turing Machine is one in which each square of the tape holds an ordered n-tuple of symbols from the tape alphabet. This can be thought of as a Turing machine with multiple tape heads, all of which move in lock-step mode.

"N-Track Turing machines are equivalent to standard Turing machines".

4.3.2 Semi-infinite tape/Offline/Multitape/ND Turing Machines

(a) A Turing machine may have a "*semi-infinite tape*", the nonblank input is at the extreme left end of the tape.
Turing machines with semi-infinite tape are equivalent to Standard Turing machines.

(b) An "*Offline Turing Machine*" has two tapes. One tape is read-only and contains the input, the other is read-write and is initially blank.
Offline Turing machines are equivalent to Standard Turing machines".

(c) A "*Multi-tape Turing Machine*" has a finite number of tapes, each with its own independently controlled tape head.
"Multi-tape Turing Machines are equivalent to Standard Turing Machines".

(d) A "*Nondeterministic Turing Machine*" is one in which the DFA controlling the tape is replaced with an NFA.

"Nondeterministic Turing machines are equivalent to Standard Turing Machines."

4.3.3 Multidimensional/Two-state Turing Machine

A "*Multidimensional Turing Machine*" has a Multidimensional "tape", for example, a two-dimensional Turing Machine would read and write on an infinite plane divided into squares, like a checkerboard. Possible directions that the tape head could move might be labelled $\{N, E, S, W\}$. A three-dimensional turing machine machine might have possible directions $\{N, E, S, W, V, D\}$ and so on.

"Multidimensional Turing Machines are equivalent to Standard Turing Machines".

A "*Binary Turing Machine*" is one whose tape alphabet consists of exactly two symbols.

Binary Turing machines are equivalent to Standard Turing Machines.

A "Two-state Turing Machine" is one that has only two states. Two-state Turing machines are equivalent to Standard Turing Machines.

4.4 CHURCH–TURING'S THESIS

Alan Turing defined Turing machines in an attempt to formalize the notion of an "effective producer" which is usually called as 'algorithm' these days.

Simultaneously mathematicians were working independently on the same problem.

Emil Post → Production Systems
Alonzo Church → Lambda Calculus

Noam Chomsky → Unrestricted Grammars
Stephen Kleene → Recursive function Theory
Raymond Smullyn → Formal Systems.

All of the above formalisms were proved equivalent to one another. This led to

(a) *Turing's Thesis (Weak Form):* A Turing machine can compute anything that can be computed by a general-purpose digital computer.
(b) *Turing's Thesis (Strong Form):* A Turing machine can compute anything that can be computed.

The strong form of Turing's Thesis cannot be proved it states a relationship between mathematical concepts and the "real world".

4.4.1 Counting

Two sets can be put into a one-to-one corresponding if and only if they have exactly the same number of elements.

Example:

{red,	yellow,	green,	blue}
↕	↕	↕	↕
{apple,	banana,	cucumber,	plum}

One-to-one correspondence with a subset of natural numbers can be done as:

{red,	yellow,	green,	blue}
↓	↓	↓	↓
{1,	2,	3,	4}

4.4.2 Recursive and Recursively Enumerable Language

There are three possible outcomes of executing a Turing machine over a given input.

The Turing machine may

(i) Halt and accept the input
(ii) Halt and reject the input, or
(iii) Never halt.

A language is "*recursive*" if there exists a Turing machine that accepts every string of language and rejects every string over the same alphabet that is not in the language.

If a language L is recursive, then its complement L should also be recursive.

A language is "recursively enumerable" if there exists a Turing machine that accepts every string of the language, and does not accept strings that are not in the language. Strings which are not in the language may be rejected or may cause the Turing machine to go into an infinite loop.

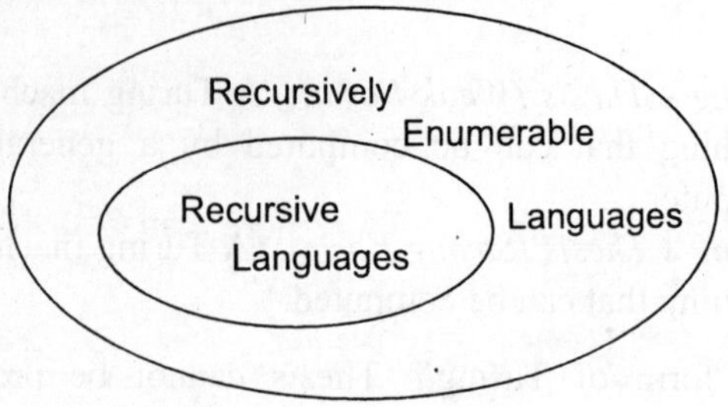

Every Recursive language is also recursively enumerable. But it is not clear if every recursively enumerable language is also recursive.

Turing Machines are not "recursive". The terminology is borrowed from recursive function theory.

4.4.3 Enumerating Strings in a Language

To enumerate a set is to place the elements of the set in a one-to-one correspondence with the natural numbers. The set of all strings over an alphabet is denumerable. Let us assume that a string is a number is an $|\Sigma|$ -ary number system. The strings in a language from a subset of the set of all strings over Σ. But is it possible to enumerate the strings in a language?

If a language is recursive, then there exists a Turing machine for it that is guaranteed to halt. We can generate the strings of Σ^* in a shortest first order to guarantee that every finite string will be generated, test the string with the Turing machine, and if the Turing machine accepts the string, assign that string the next available natural number. We can also enumerate the recursively enumerable languages. We have a Turing machine that will halt and accept any string that belongs to the language; the trick is to avoid getting hung up on strings that cause the Turing machine to go into an infinite loop. This is done using "Time sharing". Let us illustrate this now.

```
w: = Ø;  N: = 0;
for i: = 1 to χ0 do {
   add the next string in Σ* to set W;
   initialize a Turing machine for this new string;
   for each string in set W do {
      let the Turing machine for it make one more;
      if the Turing machine halts {
         accept or reject the string as appropriate;
         if the string is accepted {
            N: = N + 1;
```

```
            let this be string N of the language;
        }
        remove the string from set W;
    }
```

4.4.4 Non-recursively Enumerable Languages

A Language is a subset of Σ^*. A language is "any" subset of Σ^*. We have shown that Turing machines are enumerable. Since recursively enumerable laguages are those whose strings are accepted by a Turing machine, the set of recursively enumerable languages is also enumerable. The power set of an infinite set is not enumerable i.e., it has more than χ_0 subsets. Each of these subsets represent a language. Hence there should be languages that are not computable by a Turing machine.

According to Turing Thesis, a Turing machine can compute any effective procedure. Therefore there are languages that cannot be defined by any effective procedure. It is possible to find a non-recursively enumerable language *X* by a process called "diagonalisation".

4.5 UNDECIDABILITY

4.5.1 Halting Problem

The input to a Turing machine is a string. Turing machines themselves can be written as strings. Since these strings can be used as input to other Turing machines.

A "Universal Turing machine" is one whose input consists of a description *M* of some arbitrary Turing machine, and some input w to which machine *M* is to be applied, we write this combined input as $M + w$. This produces the same output that would be produced by M. This is written as

$$\text{Universal Turing Machine } (M + w) = M(w).$$

As a Turing machine can be represented as a string, it is fully possible to supply a Turing machine as input to itself, for example $M(M)$. This is not even a particularly bizarre thing to do for example, suppose you have written a C prettyprinter in C, then used the Prettyprinter on itself. Another common usage is Bootstrapping—where some convenient languages used to write a minimal compiler for some new language L, then used this minimal compiler for L to write a new, improved compiler for language L. Each time a new feature is added to language L, you can recompile and use this new feature in the next version of the compiler. Turing machines sometimes halt, and sometimes they enter an infinite loop. A Turing machine might halt for one input string, but go into an infinite loop when given some other string.

The halting problem asks: "It is possible to tell, in general, whether a given machine will halt for some given input?" If it is possible, then there is an effective procedure to look at a Turing machine and its input and determine whether the machine will halt with that input. If there is an effective procedure, then we can build a Turing machine to implement it.

Suppose we have a Turing machine "WillHalt" which, given an input string $M + w$, will halt and accept the string if Turing machine M halts on input w and will halt and reject the string if Turing machine M does not halt on input w. When viewed as a Boolean function, "WillHalt (M, w)" halts and returns "TRUE" in the first case, and (halts and) returns "FALSE" in the second.

THEOREM: Turing Machine "WillHalt (M, w)" does not exist.

Proof: This theorem is proved by contradiction.

Suppose we could build a machine "WillHalt".

Then we can certainly build a second machine,

"LoopIfHalts", that will go into an infinite loop if and only if "WillHalt" accepts its input:

```
Function LoopIfHalts (M, w):
  if WillHalt (M, w) then
    while true do {  }
  else
    return false;
```

We will also define a machine "LoopIfHaltOnItSelf" that, for any given input M, representing a Turing machine, will determine what will happen if M is applied to itself, and loops if M will halt in this case.

```
Function LoopIfHaltsOnItself (M):
    return LoopIfHalts (M, M):
```

Finally, we ask what happens if we try:

```
Function Impossible:
    return LoopIfHaltsOnItself (LoopIfHaltsOnItself):
```

This machine, when applied to itself, goes into an infinite loop if and only if it halts when applied to itself. This is impossible. Hence the theorem is proved.

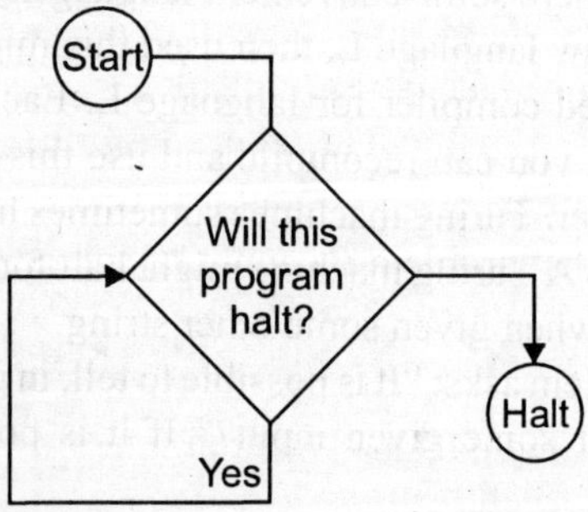

4.5.2 Implications of Halting Problem

(a) Programming

The Theorem of "Halting Problem" does not say that we can never determine whether or not a given program halts on a given input.

Most of the times, for practical reasons, we could eliminate infinite loops from programs. Sometimes a "meta-program" is used to check another program for potential infinite loops, and get this meta-program to work most of the time.

The theorem says that we cannot ever write such a meta-program and have it work all of the time. This result is also used to demonstrate that certain other programs are also impossible.

The basic outline is as follows:

(i) If we could solve a problem X, we could solve the Halting problem
(ii) We cannot solve the Halting Problem
(iii) Therefore, we cannot solve problem X.

(b) Artificial Intelligence (AI)

It has been tried to use the Halting Problem as an argument against the possibility of intelligent computers. The argument is as follows:

(i) There are things computer cannot do
(ii) We can do those things
(iii) Therefore, we must be superior to computers.

The first premise given above is definitely TRUE. The second premise is generally supported by displaying a program which solves some subset of the Halting Problem, then describing a nice trick which is not incorporated into the program, that solves a slightly larger subset. There may well be valid arguments against the possibility of AI. This is not one of them.

4.5.3 Reduction to Halting Problem

In order to reduce a problem P to the Halting problem, look at the following steps:

(i) Assume that you have an effective procedure—either a Turing machine or any kind of algorithm to solve problem P.
(ii) Show how to use the program for P to solve the Halting problem.
(iii) Conclude that problem P cannot be solved.

State Entry Problem

This problem otherwise called "dead code problem" is to determine whether Turing machine M, when given input w, ever enters state q. The only way a

Turing machine *M* halts is if it enters a state q for which some transition function $\delta(q_i, a_i)$ is undefined. Add a new final state *z* to the Turing machine, and add all these missing transitions to lead to state *z*. Now use the assumed state-entry procedure to test if state z, is ever entered when *M* is given input w. This will let us know if the original machine *M* halts. We conclude that it should not be possible to build the assumed state-entry procedure.

Some unsolvable Problems are as follows:

(i) Does a given Turing machine *M* halts on all input?
(ii) Does Turing machine *M* halt for any input?
(iii) Is the language *L*(*M*) finite?
(iv) Does *L*(*M*) contain a string of length *k*, for some given *k*?
(v) Do two Turing machines M_1 and M_2 accept the same language?

It is very obvious that if there is no algorithm that decides, for an arbitrary given Turing machine *M* and input string *w*, whether or not *M* accepts *w*. These problems for which no algorithms exist are called "UNDECIDABLE" or "UNSOLVABLE".

4.5.4 Post's Correspondence Problem

Let Σ be a finite alphabet, and let *A* and *B* be two lists of nonempty strings over Σ, with $|A|=|B|$, i.e.,

$$A = (w_1, w_2, w_3, \ldots\ldots w_k)$$

and
$$B = (x_1, x_2, x_3, \ldots\ldots x_k)$$

Post's Correspondence Problem is the following.

Does there exist a sequence of integers $i_1, i_2, \ldots\ldots i_m$ such that $m \geq 1$ and

$$w_{i1}\, w_{i2}\, w_{i3} \ \ldots\ldots\ w_{im} = x_{i1} x_{i2} x_{i3} \ \ldots\ldots\ x_{im}\,?$$

Example: Suppose *A* = (*a*, *abaaa*, *ab*) and *B* = (*aaa*, *ab*, *b*). Then the required sequence of integers is 2, 1, 1, 3 giving

$$abaaa\ a\ a\ ab = abaaa\ aaa\ b.$$

This example has a solution. It will turn out that Post's correspondence problem is insolvable in general.

Example 4.5.1: Prove that if L_1 is not recursive, and there is a reduction from L_1 to L_2, then L_2 is also not recursive.

Solution

Assume that L_2 is recursive, as decided by Turing machine M_2 and let *T* be the Turing machine that computes the reduction τ.

Then the Turing machine TM_2 would decide L_1. But L_1 is undeciable—a contradiction.

4.6 RICE'S THEOREM

A Turing machine (TM) is a way to describe a language and the decision problem can be interpreted as belonging to the general class of problems:

"Given a Turing machine, does L(TM) have the property P"?

In this case P is the property of containing the null string.

THEOREM: "If P is a property of languages that is satisfied by some but not all recursively enumerable languages, then the decision problem.

D: Given a TM, does L(TM) have property P is unsolvable."

Proof: Assume that P is a nontrivial language property. Starting with Turing machine TM, an arbitrary instance of Accepts (∧). (Which is the other unsolvable problem), we need to find an instance TM′ of D so that the answer for TM and TM′ are the same.

The machine TM′ is constructed so that the first things it does it to move its tape head past the input string and execute TM on input ∧. What TM′ does with its original input after that depends on the outcome of Accepts (∧).

We would like TM′ to proceed with its original input as if its goal were to accept some original input as if its goal were to accept some language L_A so that it halts if and only if the original input is in L_A. Also we would want TM′ to proceed as if it were accepted as a different language L.

In order to get everything right, we want L_A to be a language satisfying P and L_B to be a language not satisfying P and L_B to be a language not satisfying P. This ensures that if TM′ is a yes-instance of D if and only if TM is a yes-instance of Accepts (∧).

The problem that exists here is that if TM does not accept ∧, then it will go into infinite loop. Then TM′ could not accept anything. Therefore L_B is an empty language. Therefore if TM crashed on input ∧, then TM′ also crashes. If ∅ happens to be a language not satisfying the property P, then we have exactly what we want.

The choice of the language L_A is arbitrary subject to the condition L_A must satisfy P; then we have such a language L_A, since P is nontrival.

Therefore it is proved that if P is any nontrivial property not satisfied by the empty language, then D is unsolvable, which proves the Rice's Theorem. □

GLOSSARY

Turing machine: Finite-state machine with storage.

Types of TM: Deterministic TM, non-deterministic TM

Transition function of TM: $\delta : Q \times \Gamma \to Q \times \Gamma \times \{L, R\}$

Configuration of TM: Requires

(i) state of TM

(ii) contents of the tape

(iii) position of the tape head on the tape.

Move of a TM: Pair of instantaneous descriptions, separated by $\vdash$.

Programming a TM: Creating current state, symbol read, symbol written, direction, next state.

Transducer: TM is used as a Tranducer by treating the entire nonblank portion of the initial tape as input, and treating the entire nonblank portion of the tape when the machine halts as output.

N-Track Turing machine: One in whch each square of the tape holds an ordered n-tuple of symbols from the tape alphabet.

Semi-infinite tape TM: TM having an semi-infinite tape, with the non-blank input at the extreme left of the tape.

Offline TM: TM having two tapes, one tape is read-only and has the input, the other is read-write and is initially blank.

Multi-tape TM: TM having finite number of tapes, each having its own independently controlled tape head.

Standard TM: Multi-tape TMs are called so.

Binary TM: One whose tape alphabet consists of exactly two symbols.

Turing Thesis (Weak form): TM can compute anything that can be. computed by a general-purpose digital computer.

Turing Thesis (Strong Form): TM can compute anything that can be computed.

Recursively enumerable (R.E.): Language is R.E. if there exists a TM that accepts every string of the language and does not accept strings that are not in the language.

REVIEW QUESTIONS

1. What is a Turing machine?
2. What are the types of Turing machines?
3. Give the definition of a Turing machine.
4. Define the term 'Transition function' of a TM.
5. Define the term 'Instantaneous description' of a TM.
6. Define the term 'move' in a TM.
7. What are the requirements of the 'configuration' of a TM?
8. How will you program a Turing machine?
9. Explain "Turing machine as acceptors".

10. How will you recognize a language in a TM?
11. How are Turing machines used as Transducers?
12. Explain what do you mean by an N-Track Turing machine?
13. Explain the following terms
    (a) Semi-infinite tape
    (b) Offline Turing machine
    (c) Multitape Turing machine
    (d) Nondeterministic "Multidimensional Turing Machine"
14. What do you mean by "Multidimensional Turing Machine"?
15. What do you mean by a binary TM?
16. State the Church-Turing Thesis.
17. State the weak form and strong form of Turing's Thesis.
18. What do you mean by Recursively enumerable languages?
19. How will you enumerate strings in language?
20. What are non-recursively enumerable languages?
21. What do you mean by Undecidability?
22. What do you mean by the Halting problem?
23. What is an Universal Turing machine?
24. State the implications of Halting problem.
25. What do you mean by Post's Correspondence problem?

EXERCISES

1. Design a Turing machine which recognizes the language consisting of all strings of 0s whose length is a power of 2. i.e., it decides the language $L = \{0^{2^n} \mid n \geq 0\}$.
2. Design a Turing machine which recognizes the language $L = \{w\# w \mid w \in \{0,1\}^*\}$.
3. Design a Turing machine which recognizes the language $L = \{a^i b^j c^k \mid i \times j = k \text{ and } i, j, k \geq 1\}$.
4. Design a deterministic Turing machine (DTM) to accept the language $L = \{a^i b^i c^i \mid i \geq 0\}$.
5. Define a DTMs to accept the following languages. Specify the 5-tuple in each. (Use multi-tape machine if necessary).
   (a) $\{xx \mid x \in \{0,1\}^*\}$
   (b) $\{x \mid x \in \{0,1\}^* \text{ and } x = x^R\}$
6. Design DTMs to compute the following functions. (Input number can be in unary, i.e., n is encoded as 1^n).
   (a) Successor function: $f : N \rightarrow N$ where $f(n) = n + 1$.

(b) $f: N \times N \to N$ such that $f(a, b) = \lceil a / b \rceil$
(c) $f: N \to N$ such that $f(n) = \lceil \log_2 n \rceil$

7. Define Nondeterministic Turing machines to accept the following languages.
   (a) $\{xx \mid x \in \{0,1\}^*\}$
   (b) $\{x \mid x \in \{0,1\}^* \text{ and } x = x^R\}$
8. Define a multiheaded Turing machine, a model in which each tape can have k tape heads. Prove that a Deterministic Turing Machine (DTM) with one work tape can simulate a two-headed Turing machine.
9. Design a Turing machine which computes the function $f(n_1, n_2) = \min(n_1, n_2)$ for all non-negative integers n_1 and n_2.
10. Design a Turing machine which computes the function $f(n) = 3$ if $n \geq 5$ and $f(n) = 0$ if n =0, 1, 2, 3 or 4.
11. Construct a Turing machine which computes the function $f(n) = n \bmod 5$.
12. Design a Turing machine which recognizes the set $\{0^n 1^n 2^n \mid n \geq 0\}$.
13. Design a TM that recognizes the set of all bit strings that contain an even number of 1^s.
14. Construct a TM that recognizes the set of all bit strings which end with a 0.
15. Design a Turing machine with tape symbols 0, 1 and B that given a bit string as input, replaces all but the leftmost 1 on the tape with 0s and does not change any of the other symbols on the tape.
16. Design a TM with tape symbols 0, 1 and B that replaces the first 0 with a 1 and does not change any of the other symbols on the tape.
17. Design a TM that recognizes the set

$$\{0^{2n} 1^n \mid n \geq 0\}.$$

18. Show that the recursiveness problem of Type-0 grammars is unsolvable.
19. Show that the problem of determining whether or not a TM over $\{0,1\}$ will print ever the symbol 1, with a given tape configuration is unsolvable.
20. Show that there exists a TM for which the halting problem is unsolvable.

SHORT QUESTIONS AND ANSWERS

1. What is a Turing machine?

   A finite-state machine with storage is called a Turing machine.
2. What is the analogy between a Turing machine and a Push Down

Automaton?

Both have a finite-state machine as a central component, both have additional storage.

3. What are the types of Turing machines?
   (a) Deterministic Turing machine.
   (b) Non-deterministic Turing machine.
4. Define a Turing machine.

   A Turing machine is a 7-Tuple

$$(Q, \Sigma, \Gamma, \delta, q_0, \#, F)$$

where Q is a set of states
Σ is a finite set of symbols, "Input alphabet"
Γ is a finite set of symbols, "Tape alphabet"
δ is the partial transition function
$\# \in T$ is a symbol called 'blank'
$q_0 \in Q$ is the initial state
$F \subseteq Q$ is a set of final states

5. Define the Transition Function for Turing Machine (TM)

$$\delta : Q \times \Gamma \rightarrow Q \times \Gamma \times \{L, R\} \text{ is the transition function.}$$

When a machine is in a given state (Q) and reads a given symbol (Γ) from the tape, it replaces the symbol on the tape with some other symbol (Γ), goes to some other state (Q), and moves the tape head one square left (L) or right (R).

6. State the requirements of an instantaneous description or configuration of a TM.

   TM requires:
   (a) the state the TM is in
   (b) the contents of the tape
   (c) the position of the tape head on the tape.
7. How is move of a Turing machine expressed?

   It is expressed as a pair of instantaneous descriptions, separated by a symbol $\vdash$.
8. What do you understand by "programming" a Turing machine?

   Creating a list:

   (current state, symbol read, symbol written, direction, next state) is called 'Programming' a Turing machine.
9. What are the reasons for a TM not accepting its input?
   (a) The TM could halt in a nonfinal state.
   (b) The TM could never stop i.e., it enters an "infinite loop".
10. How is a Turing machine used as a Transducer?

To use a Turing machine as a Transducer, treat the entire nonblank portion of the initial tape as input, and treat the entire nonblank portion of the tape when the machine halts as output.

11. When is a function f said to be "Turing computable"?

A Turing machine defines a function $y = f(x)$ for strings $x, y \in \Sigma^*$ if

$$q_0 x \overset{*}{\vdash} q_f y$$

where q_f is the final state.

A function f is 'Turing Computable" if there exists a Turing machine that can perform the above task.

12. When are two automata said to be equivalent?

Two automata are said to be equivalent if they accept the same language.

13. When are two transducers said to be equivalent?

Two transducers are said to be equivalent if they compute the same function.

14. What do you mean by standard Turing machines?

At each move of a Turing machine, the tape head may move either left or right. We can augment this with a 'stay' option, i.e. we will add "don't move" to the set {L, R}.

Turing machines with a stay option are equivalent to Standard Turing Machines.

15. What is an *N*-Track Turing machine?

A TM in which each square of the tape holds an ordered *n*-tuple of symbols from the tape alphabet is said to be an *N*-Track Turing Machine.

16. What is a semi-infinite tape Turing Machine?

A Turing machine having a semi-infinite tape, with the non-blank input at the extreme left of the tape is called so.

17. What is an offline Turing machine?

A Turing machine having two tapes, one tape being read-only and has the input, the other being read-write that is initially blank is called an offline Turing machine.

18. What is a multi-tape Turing machine?

A Turing machine with finite number of tapes, each having its own independently controlled tape head is called a multi-tape TM.

19. What are standard Turing Machines?

Multi-tape Turing machines are called standard Turing Machines.

20. What is a binary Turing Machine?

A Turing machine whose tape alphabet having exactly two symbols is a binary Turing Machine.

21. What is the 'weak form' of Turing Thesis?

"A Turing machine can compute anything that can be computed by a general-purpose digital computer." This is the weak form of Turing Thesis.

22. What is the 'strong form' of Turing Thesis?

"A Turing Machine can compute anything that can be computed". This is the strong form of Turing Thesis.

23. When is a language said to be recursively enumerable?

A language is recursively enumerable if there exists a Turing machine that accepts every string of the language, and does not accept strings that are not in the language.

24. What is the Post's correspondence problem?

Let Σ be a finite alphabet, and let A and B be the lists of nonempty strings over Σ, with $|A| = |B|$, i.e.,

$$A = (w_1, w_2, \ldots\ldots w_k)$$

and

$$B = (x_1, x_2, \ldots\ldots x_k).$$

Post's correspondence problem is the following:

"Does there exist a sequence of integers $i_1, i_2, \ldots i_m$ such that $m \geq 1$ and

$$w_{i1} w_{i2} w_{i3} \ldots\ldots w_{im} = x_{i1}\, x_{i2} x_{i3} \ \ldots\ldots\ x_{im}\ ?"$$

Chapter 5

Chomsky Hierarchy

5.1 CONTEXT SENSITIVE GRAMMARS AND LANGUAGES

A context-sensitive Language is a language generated by a context sensitive grammar.

Definition 1: A context-sensitive grammar is one whose productions are all of the form

$$xAy \rightarrow xvy$$

where $A \in v$ and $x, v, y \in (V \cup T)^*$.

"Context-sensitive" implies the fact that the actual string modification is given by $A \rightarrow v$, while the x and y provide the context in which the rule may be applied.

Definition 2: A context-sensitive grammar is one whose productions are all of the form

$$x \rightarrow y$$

where $x, y \in (V \cup T)^+$, and $|x| \leq |y|$.

This type of grammar is called "Non-contracting" as the derivation steps never decrease the length of the sentential form.

This definition given above is mostly used. The two kinds of grammar are almost equivalent generating the same languages with only the exception: One kind of grammar permits languages to contain the empty string, while the other doesn't.

A language L is context-sensitive if there exists a context sensitive grammar G such that either $L = L(G)$ or $L = L(G) \cup \{\lambda\}$.

Example 5.1.1: Show that the language $L = \{a^n b^n c^n \mid n \geq 1\}$ is a context-sensitive language.

Solution

Let us prove this by showing a context-sensitive grammar fc the language.

A kind of grammar is

$$\begin{aligned} S &\rightarrow abc \mid aAbc, \\ Ab &\rightarrow bA, \\ Ac &\rightarrow Bbcc, \\ bB &\rightarrow Bb, \\ aB &\rightarrow aa \mid aa\,A \end{aligned}$$

Let us see how this works by looking at the derivation of $a^3b^3c^3$.

$$\begin{aligned} S &\Rightarrow aAbc \Rightarrow abAc \Rightarrow abBbcc \\ &\Rightarrow aBbbcc \Rightarrow aaAbbcc \Rightarrow aabAbcc \\ &\Rightarrow aabbAcc \Rightarrow aabbBbccc \\ &\Rightarrow aabBbbccc \Rightarrow aaBbbbccc \\ &\Rightarrow aaabbbccc. \end{aligned}$$

This uses the variables A and B. Since the language is not context-free, it is said to be context-sensitive language.

5.2 LINEAR BOUNDED AUTOMATA

A Turing machine has an infinite supply of blank tape. A linear-bounded automaton is a Turing machine whose tape is only αn squares long, where 'n' is the length of the input string and α is a constant associated with the particular linear-bounded automaton.

THEOREM (I): For every context-sensitive language L there exists a linear-bounded automaton M such that $L = L(M)$, i.e., M accept exactly the strings of L.

THEOREM (II): For every language L accepted by a linear-bounded automaton that produces exactly L or $L - \{\lambda\}$, depending on the definition of context sensitive grammar.

5.3 RELATIONSHIP OF OTHER GRAMMARS

THEOREM (I): Every context-free language is context-sensitive.

Proof: The productions of a context-free language have the form $A \rightarrow v$. The productions of a context-sensitive language have the form $xAy \rightarrow xvy$, where x and y are permitted to be λ.

Hence the result. □

THEOREM (II): There exists a context-sensitive language that is not context-free.

Proof: The language $\{a^n b^n c^n \mid n \geq 0\}$ is not context-free (which could be proved using a pumping lemma).

It can be shown that it is context-sensitive by providing an approprite grammar.

The productions of one such grammar is given here.

$$S \rightarrow aABC \quad S \rightarrow aBC \quad A \rightarrow aABC$$
$$A \rightarrow aBC \quad CB \rightarrow BC \quad aB \rightarrow ab$$
$$bB \rightarrow bb \quad bC \rightarrow bc \quad cC \rightarrow cc$$

□

THEOREM (III): Every context-sensitive language is recursive.

Proof: A context-sensitive grammar is noncontracting. Moreover, for any integer n there are only a finite number of sentential forms of length n. Therefore, for any string w we could set a bound on the number of derivation steps required to generate w, hence a bound on the number of possible derivations. The string w is in the language if and only if one of these derivations produces w.

5.4 THE CHOMSKY HIERARCHY

The Chomsky Hierarchy, as originally defined by Noam Chomsky, comprises four types of languages and their associated grammars and machines.

Language	Grammar	Machine	Example
Regular language	Regular grammar —Right-linear grammar —Left-linear grammar	Deterministic or Nondeterministic finite-state acceptor	a^*
Context-free language	Context-free grammar	Nondeterministic pushdown automaton	$a^n b^n$
Context-sensitive language	Context sensitive grammar	Linear-bounded automaton	$a^n b^n c^n$
Recursively enumerable language	Unrestricted grammar	Turing machine	Any computable function

5.5 EXTENDING THE CHOMSKY HIERARCHY

So far we have discussed about other types of languages besides those in the "classical Chomsky hierarchy. For example, we noted that deterministic pushdown automaton were less powerful than nondeterministic pushdown automata. The table below shows a table of some of the language classes we have covered that fit readily into the hierarchy.

Language	Machine
Regular language	Deterministic or Non-deterministic finite-state acceptor
Deterministic context-free language	Deterministic Pushdown Automaton
Context-free language	Non-deterministic pushdown Automaton
Context-Sensitive language	Linear-bounded Automaton
Recursive language	Turing machine that halts
Recursively enumerable language	Turing machine

It should be noted that not all language classes fit into a hierarchy. When linear languages are considered, they fit neatly between the regular languages and the context-free languages. However there are languages that are linear but not deterministic context-free, and there are languages that are deterministic context-free but not linear.

5.6 UNRESTRICTED GRAMMAR

The grammars in the Chomsky hierarchy allows productions of the form

$$\alpha \to \beta$$

where α and β are arbitrary strings of grammar symbols, with $\alpha \neq \lambda$.

These types of grammars as called "Unrestricted grammars". The 4-tuple notation $G = (V, T, P, S)$ is used for unrestricted grammars also.

$$L(G) = \{w \mid w \text{ is in } T^* \text{ and } S \overset{*}{\Rightarrow} w\}$$

$\overset{*}{\Rightarrow}$ denotes the reflexive and transitive closure of the relation $\Rightarrow$.

THEOREM (I): If L is $L(G)$ for unrestricted grammar $G = (V, T, P, S)$, then L is an r.e. language.

THEOREM (II): If L is an r.e. language, then $L = L(G)$ for some unrestricted grammar G.

5.7 RANDOM-ACCESS MACHINE

A randon access machine is defined as follows:

Data Types: The only data type supported is the Natural Numbers 0, 1, 2, 3, ... But the numbers may be very large.

Variables: An orbitrary number of variables are allowed. Each variable is capable of holding a single natural number. All variables are initialized to 0.

Tests: The only test allowed is <variable> = 0.

Statements: There are the following types of statements in the language:

(a) if <test> then <statement> else <statement>;
(b) while <test> do <statements>;
(c) <variable> : = <variable> +1; (increment)
(d) <variable>: = <variable> –1; (decrement)

It is to be noted that decrementing a variable whose value is already zero has no effect.

Statements to be executed in sequence (<statement>; <statement>; <statement>; ...... are allowed and parantheses are used to group a sequence of statement into a single statement. This language is very equivalent in power to a Turing machine. This can be proved by using the language to implement a Turing machine, and then using a Turing machine to enulate the language.

This language is so powerful to compute anything that can be computed in any programming language.

GLOSSARY

Context sensitive language: Language generated by a context-sensitive grammar.

Context-sensitive grammar: It is one whose productions are of the form

$$xAy \rightarrow xVy$$

where $A \in V$ and $x, v, y \in (V \cup T)^*$.

Linear Bounded automata (LBA): It is a TM whose tape is only αn squares long, where 'n' is the length of input string and α is a constant associated with the LBA.

Chomsky hierarchy: Has 4 types of languages viz.,

(a) Regular language
(b) Context-free language
(c) Context-sensitive language
(d) Recursively enumerable language.

Unrestricted grammar: Production of the form $\alpha \to \beta$ where α, β are arbitrary strings of grammar symbols, with $\alpha \neq \lambda$ forms unrestricted grammar.

REVIEW QUESTIONS

1. What do you mean by a context-sensitive grammar?
2. What do you mean by a context-sensitive language?
3. What do you mean Linear bounded automata?
4. Prove: "Every context-free language is context-sensitive".
5. Prove: "There exists a context-sensitive language that is not context-free".
6. Prove: "Every context-sensitive language is recursive".
7. Given an example for
   (a) Regular language (b) Context-free language.
8. Give an example for
   (a) Context-sensitive language (b) Recursively enumerable language.
9. What do you mean by Chomsky hierarchy of languages?
10. What are the machines corresponding to each of the following?
    (a) Recursively enumerable language
    (b) Context sensitive language
    (c) Context-free language
    (d) Regular language.
11. What do you mean by unrestricted grammar?
12. What do you mean by a random access machine?

EXERCISES

1. Check whether the language given by

   $$L = \{a^n b^n \mid n \geq 1\}$$

   is a context-sensitive language or not.
2. Check whether the language

   $$L = \{1^n 0^n \mid n \geq 1\}$$

   is a context-sensitive language or not.
3. Explain the Chomsky hierarchy of languages with an example.
4. Explain the concept of unrestricted grammar with examples.
5. Show that every context-free language is context sensitive.

6. Prove that exists a context-sensitive language that is not context-free.
7. Show that every context sensitive language is recursive.

SHORT QUESTIONS AND ANSWERS

1. What is a context-sensitive language?

   A language generated by a context-sensitive grammar is called a context-sensitive language.
2. Define a context sensitive grammar.

   A context-sensitive grammar is one whose productions are all of the form

$$xAy \to xVy$$

   where $A \in v$ and $x, v, y \in (V \cup T)^*$.
3. Give an alternative definition of context-sensitive grammar.

   A context-sensitive grammar is one whose productions are all of the form

$$x \to y$$

   where $x, y \in (V \cup T)^+$ and $|x| \leq |y|$.
4. What is meant by "non-contracting" grammar?

   Grammar is which the derivation steps never decrease the length of the sentential form is called a 'non-contracting' grammar.
5. When is a language said to be context sensitive?

   A language L is context-sensitive if there exists a content-sensitive grammar G, such that either $L = L(G)$ or $L = L(G) \cup \{\lambda\}$
6. Give an example for a context-sensitive language.

   $L = \{a^n b^n c^n \mid n \geq 1\}$ is an example of a context-sensitive language.
7. What is a linear bounded automata?

   A linear bounded automaton is a Turing machine whose tape is only αn squares long, where 'n' is the length of the input string and α is a constant.
8. Say True or False: "Every context-free language is context-sensitive."

   TRUE.
9. Say True or False: "There exists a context-sensitive language that is not context-free."

   TRUE.
10. Say True or False: "Every context-sensitive language need not be recursive".

    FALSE, every context-sensitive language is recursive.

11. Give an example of a regular language
    a^*.
12. Give an example of a context-free language?
    $a^n b^n$.
13. Give an example of a context-sensitive language
    $a^n b^n c^n$.
14. Give an example of a recursively enumerable language.
    Any computable function is an example.
15. What are kinds of regular grammars?
    (a) Right-linear grammar.
    (b) Left-linear grammar.
16. Give an example of a machine which applies context-free language.
    Nondeterministic Pushdown Automaton
17. Give an example of a machine which applies context-sensitive language. ·
    Linear Bounded Automaton
18. Give an example of a machine which applies recursively enumerable language.
    Turing machine.
19. What is the grammar corresponding to a recursively enumerable language.
    Unrestricted grammar.
20. What are the languages the Chomsky Hierarchy describes?
    (a) Regular language
    (b) Context-free language
    (c) Context-sensitive language
    (d) Recursively enumerable language.
21. What are Unrestricted grammars?
    The grammars in the Chomsky hierarchy allows productions of the form

$$\alpha \rightarrow \beta$$

where α and β are arbitrary strings of grammar symbols, with $\alpha \neq \lambda$. These grammars are called 'Unrestricted grammars".

22. Mention the types of statements in the language of a random access machine.
    (a) if <test> then <statement> else <statement>;
    (b) while <test> do <statement>;
    (c) <variable>: = <variable> + 1; (increment)
    (d) <variable>: = <variable> – 1; (decrement)

Chapter 6

Computability

6.1 FORMAL SYSTEMS

The necessary properties of a satisfactory formal system are as follows:

(a) *Completeness:* It should be possible either to prove or disprove any proposition that can be expressed in the system.

(b) *Consistency:* It should not be possible to both prove and disprove a proposition in the system.

Consistency becomes crucial if it becomes possible to prove and disprove some proposition in the system, which means the same can be done for every proposition in the system.

In the late 1800's there were a lot of mathematicians who were working on a method of putting together all of mathematics, starting from the axions of set theory.

In fact, sets can have other sets as members. In 1901 Bertrand Russel discovered the Russel's Paradox:

Russel's Paradox

"Consider the set of all sets that do not have themselves as a member. Is this set a member of itself?"

This problem was tried to be resolved by the way of defining "type". This theory of types though not accepted fully have paved way for new philosophies of mathematics.

Godel was able to express proofs as numbers like considering a computer program to be a very large binary number. Godel proved the following result:

> "If it is possible to prove, within a formal system, that the system is consistent, then the formal system is not, in fact, consistent."

Equivalently, we can say,

> "If a formal system is consistent, then it is impossible to prove (within the system) that it is consistent."

This particular result shows that any attempt to prove mathematics consistent is foredoomed to failure. It is still possible to prove a system consistent by logical arguments outside that system, provided the outer system is known to be consistent.

6.2 RECURSIVE FUNCTION THEORY

It is seen that a sufficiently powerful formal system cannot be both consistent and complete as proved by Godel. Simple arithmetic on integers is an example of a system that is "sufficiently powerful". It is always preferred to give up completeness rather than consistency, because in a consistent system any proposition can be proven.

Ideally, we wanted to have an algorithmic theorem proving procedure to distinguish between the provable propositions and unprovable ones. Alan Turing invented Turing machines in an attempt to solve this problem. With the halting problem, Alan Turing had shown that it is not possible to distinguish between soluable and insolvable problems. Similar results were arrived at by other scientists. Church invented "Recursive Function Theory".

6.3 PRIMITIVE RECURSIVE FUNCTIONS

This section describes the basic ideas behind recursive function theory.

The Recursive functions are described over the natural numbers $I = \{0, 1, 2, 3, ...\}$. Recursive functions are looked at as "Pure Symbol Systems". Numbers are not used in the system, rather, we use the system to construct both numbers and arithmetical functions on numbers. Its a different numbering system, in the same way as Roman numerals are different. The correspondence is as given below.

$$z(x) = 0,\ s(z(x)) = 1,\ s(s(z(x))) = 2, ...$$

In order to translate to decimal, just count the number of s's surrounding the central $z(x)$.

(a) *Zero Function:* $z(x) = z(y)$, for all $x, y \in I$. This is our "zero"; it is written as a function so we don't have to introduce constants into the system.

(b) *Successor Function s(x):* This function informally means $x + 1$. Formally, it does not return a value. It just lies there, the result of $s(x)$ is $s(x)$.

(c) *Projector Function:*

$$p_1(x) = x$$
$$p_1(x, y) = x$$
$$p_2(x, y) = y$$

These projector functions are a way of extracting one of the parameters and discarding the rest. We define only P_1 and P_2 as only functions of no more than two arguments are only discused.

Definition: A total function f over N is primitive recursive if (i) it is any one of the three initial functions [zero function, successor function and Projector Function] or (ii) it can be got by applying composition and recursion finite number of times to the set of initial functions. This is dealt with in the subsequent sections.

Example 6.3.1: How are the following functions defined.

(a) Zero function $Z(x)$
(b) Successor function $S(x)$
(c) Projection function $P_i^n(x)$.

Solution

(a) Zero function $Z(x) = 0$
(b) Successor function $S(x) = x + 1$
(c) Projection function $P_i^n(x_1, x_2, \ldots\ldots x_n) = x_i$

Example 6.3.2: How are the following functions defined?

(a) nil (x)
(b) cons $a(x)$
(c) cons $b(x)$

Solution

(a) nil $(x) = \lambda$
(b) cons $a(x) = ax$
(c) cons $b(x) = bx$

Example 6.3.3: Find out the values of

(a) $Z(80)$
(b) $P_2^4(2,3,7,6)$
(c) $P_3^4(2,3,6,7)$
(d) $S(78)$

With Z as the zero function, S as the successor function and U as the projection function.

Solution

(a) $Z(80) = 0$ since zero function $Z(x) = 0$.

(b) We know that $P_i^n(x_1, x_2, \ldots\ldots, x_n) = x_i$.

Therefore we have

$$P_2^4(2,3,7,6) = 3$$

(c) $P_3^4(2,3,6,7) = 6$

(d) $S(x) = x + 1$.

Therefore $S(78) = 78 + 1 = 79$.

Example 6.3.4: Obtain the values of

(a) nil $(ababab)$

(b) cons $a(baba)$

(c) cons $b(ababab)$

with the usual definitions of functions over Σ.

Solution

(a) nil $(ababab) = \lambda$

(b) cons $a(baba) = ababa$

(c) cons $b(ababab) = bababab$.

Example 6.3.5: Check whether the following functions are Total functions or not. If a function is not total, specify the arguments for which the function is defined.

(a) $f(x) = x/4$ over N

(b) $f(x) = x^2 - 9$ over N

(c) $f(x) = x + 4$ over N

(d) $f(x) = x^2$ over N

(e) $f(x) = 5x^3 + 2x^2 + 6$ over N.

Solution

(a) $f(x) = x/4$ over N.

The function is defined for all natural numbers divisible by 4.

(b) $f(x) = x^2 - 9$ over N.

The function is defined for all $x \geq 3$.

(c) $f(x) = x + 4$ over N.

The function is defined for all natural numbers.

(d) $f(x) = x^2$ over N.

The function is defined for all natural numbers.

(e) $f(x) = 5x^3 + 2x^2 + 6$.

The function is defined for all natural numbers.

6.4 COMPOSITION AND RECURSION

If g_1, g_2, g_3 and h are previously defined functions, these functions can be combined to form new functions. These functions can be combined only in precisely defined ways.

(a) *Composition:* $f(x, y) = h(g_1(x, y), g_2(x, y))$. This allows us to use functions as arguments to functions.

(b) *Primitive Recursion*: This is a structured "recursive routine" with the form:

$$f(x,0) = g_1(x)$$
$$f(x, s(y)) = h(g_2(x, y), g_3(f(x, y)))$$

"A primitive recursive function is a function formed from the functions z, s, p_1 and p_2 by using only composition and primitive recursion".

The recursion should be guaranteed to terminate. In order to ensure this, the function should carry along an extra parameter that is "decremented" every time the function is called [$s(x)$ replaced by x], and halts the recursion when it reaches "zero" ($z(x)$), i.e.,

$$f(\ldots\ldots, z(x)) = \ldots\ldots$$
$$f(\ldots\ldots, s(x)) = \ldots\ldots f(\ldots\ldots, x), \ldots\ldots$$

The recursive function should appear only once in the definitions (RHS of the definition). This in fact, avoids various forms of "fancy" recursion.

Examples: The following examples show how these can be used to define more complicated functions.

(a) *Addition of two numbers:* According to the form, it is:

$$\text{add }(x, z(x)) = g_1(x)$$
$$\text{add }(x, s(y)) = h(g_2(x, y), g_3(\text{add }(x, y)))$$

By choosing $g_1 = p_1, g_2 = p_1, g_3 = s$ and $h = p_2$, we get

$$\text{add }(x, z(x)) = p_1(x)$$
$$\text{add }(x, s(y)) = p_2(p_1(x, y), s(\text{add }(x, y)))$$

which simplifies to

$$\text{add }(x, z(x)) = x$$
$$\text{add }(x, s(y)) = s(\text{add }(x, y)).$$

As an example, add (3, 2) works as follows:

$$\text{add }(s(s(s(z(x)))), s(s(z(x))))$$
$$\text{s(add }(s(s(s(z(x)))), s(z(x))))$$
$$s(s(\text{add}(s(s(s(z(x)))), z(x))))$$
$$s(s(s(s(s(z(x)))))).$$

(b) *Multiplication of Two Numbers:* The new feature is the use of a previously defined function, add, in the definition of a new function. We skip the step of playing around with the p_i functions to pick out the right parts, and go to the simplified form.

$$\text{multiply }(x, s(z(x))) = x$$
$$\text{multiply }(x, s(y)) = \text{add}(x, \text{multiply }(x, y))$$

(c) *Predecessor of a Number:* The important catch here is that it will not be able to drop below zero, so effectively $0 - 1 = 0$. In order to show this, we write a dot above the minus sign and call it "monus". The function is easy to define:

$$\text{pred }(z(x)) = z(x)$$
$$\text{pred }(s(x)) = x$$

(d) *Subtraction:*

$$\text{subtract }(x, z(x)) = x$$
$$\text{subtract }(x, s(y)) = \text{pred }(\text{subtract }(x, y)).$$

Example 6.4.1: Given

$$g_1 = (x, y) = x + y,$$
$$g_2 = (x, y) = 3xy$$
$$g_3 = (x, y) = 12x$$

and $h(x, y, z) = x + y + z$ are functions over N. Obtain the composition of h with g_1, g_2, g_3.

Solution

$$h(f_1(x, y); f_2(x, y); f_3(x, y)) = h(x + y, 3xy, 12x)$$
$$= x + y + 3xy + 12x.$$

Therefore the composition of h with g_1, g_2 and g_3 is given by a function

$$f(x, y) = x + y + 3xy + 12x.$$

Example: Given $f_1 = x_1^2 x_2^2$, $f_2 = \lambda$, $f_3 = 5x_1x_2$ all defined over Σ with the pair (x_1, y_1) and $g(x_1, x_2, x_3) = 5x_2x_3$; again defined over Σ. Obtain the composition of g with f_1, f_2 and f_3.

Solution

$$\begin{aligned} g(f_1, f_2, f_3) &= g(x_1^2 x_2^2, \lambda, 5x_1x_2) \\ &= 5\lambda(5x_1x_2) \\ &= 25x_1x_2. \end{aligned}$$

Therefore the composition of g with f_1, f_2 and f_3 is given by

$$h(x_1, x_2) = 25x_1x_2.$$

Example 6.4.2: Prove that the function $f_{\text{add}}(x, y) = x + y$ is primitive recursive.

Solution

A function f of $(n + 1)$ variables is defined by recursion if there exists a function g of 'n' variables, and a function h of $(n + 2)$ variables and f is defined as follows:

$$f(x_1, x_2, \ldots\ldots x_n, 0) = g(x_1, x_2, \ldots\ldots x_n) \tag{1}$$

$$f(x_1, x_2, \ldots\ldots x_n, y+1) = g(x_1, x_2, \ldots\ldots x_n, y, f(x_1, x_2, \ldots\ldots x_n, y)) \tag{2}$$

$f_{\text{add}}(x, y)$ is a function of two variables. In order that $f_{\text{add}}(x, y)$ is defined by recursion, we require a function 'g' of a single variable and a function 'h' of three variables.

$$f_{\text{add}}(x, 0) = x + 0 = x \tag{3}$$

Comparing $f_{\text{add}}(x, 0)$ with the left hand side of (1), we have

$$g(x) = x = p_1'(x) \tag{4}$$

(Note that p is the projector function).

Also we have

$$f_{\text{add}}(x, y+1) = x + (y+1) = (x+y) + 1 = f_{\text{add}}(x, y) + 1 \tag{5}$$

Comparing this with L.H.S. of equation (2), we have

$$\begin{aligned} h(x, y, f(x, y)) &= f_{\text{add}}(x, y) + 1 \\ &= s(f_{\text{add}}(x, y)) \\ &= s(p_3^3(x, y, f_{\text{add}}(x, y))) \end{aligned}$$

Let us assume $h(x, y, z) = s(p_3^3(x, y, z))$.

From (4) we have

$$g = p_1'(x).$$

Therefore we have h that is got from the initial functions p_3^3 and s by composition and f_{add} is got by recusion using g and h.

Hence we see here that f_{add} is got by applying composition and recursion finite number of times to initial functions p_1^1, p_3^3 and s.

Therefore $f_{\text{add}}(x, y) = x + y$ is "primitive recursive".

Example 6.4.3: Show that the function $f(x) = x^2$ is primitive recursive.

Solution

Given $f(x) = x^2$.

$$\begin{aligned} f(x+1) &= (x+1)^2 = x^2 + 2x + 1 \\ &= f(x) + s(s(z(x))) \cdot p_1'(x) + s(z(x)). \end{aligned}$$

Thus we have $f(x)$ shown to be obtained by recursion and addition of primitive recursive functions.

Example 6.4.4: Prove that the function given by the signum function

$$\text{sgn}(x) = \begin{cases} 0, & x = 0 \\ 1, & x > 0 \end{cases}$$

is primitive recursive.

Solution

Given that the signum function

$$\text{sgn}(x) = \begin{cases} 0, & x = 0 \\ 1, & x > 0 \end{cases}$$

Now,

$$\begin{aligned} \text{sgn}(0) &= z(0) \\ \text{sgn}(x+1) &= s(z(p_2^2(x, \text{sgn}(x)))) \end{aligned}$$

Therefore the given signum function is primitive recursive.

Example 6.4.5: Prove that the function

$$f(x, y) = \max(x, y)$$

is primitive recursive.

Solution

Given

$$f(x) = \text{Max}(x, y)$$
$$= y + (x \dot{-} y)$$

where $\dot{-}$ represents "Monus" given by

$$\left.\begin{array}{l}\text{pred}\,(z(x)) = z(x)\\ \text{pred}\,(s(x)) = x\end{array}\right\}.$$

Therefore the given function $f(x, y)$ is primitive recursive.

Example 6.4.6: Prove that the function $R(x, y)$ = Remainder (x/y) is primitive recursive.

Solution

When $y = 0$, $R(x, y) = R(x, 0) = 0$. When y is increased in its value by 1, the remainder $R(x, y)$ also increases by 1.

When $y = x$, we have $R(x, y) = 0$.

Therefore we have

$$R(x, y+1) = s(R(x, y)) * \text{sgn}\,(x \dot{-} s(R(x, y))).$$

where s is the successor function, $\dot{-}$ represents the monus function (defined in the usual way) and sgn (x) represents the signum function.

Therefore we have the remainder function defined by

$$R(x,0) = 0$$

$$R(x, y+1) = s(r(x, y)) * \text{sgn}\,(x \dot{-} s(R(x, y))).$$

Hence the function $R(x, y)$ = Remainder (x / y) is primitive recursive, as it obtained by applying composition and recursion to known primitive functions.

Example 6.4.7: Show that the characteristic function $\chi_{\{0\}}(x)$ defined by

$$\chi_{\{0\}}(x) = \begin{cases} 0, & x \neq 0 \\ 1, & x = 0 \end{cases}$$

is primitive recursive.

Solution

Given the characteristic function

$$\chi_{\{0\}}(x) = \begin{cases} 0, & x \neq 0 \\ 1, & x = 0 \end{cases}$$

i.e.

$$\chi_{\{0\}}(0) = 1$$
$$\chi_{\{0\}}(x+1) = \chi_{\{0\}}\,\mathrm{sgn}(p_R(x))$$

where predecessor function $p_R(x)$ is given by

$$p_R(x) = \begin{cases} x-1, & x \neq 0 \\ 0, & x = 0 \end{cases}$$

Since we are able to represent the function as a combination of the primitive functions, it is proved to be primitive recursive.

Example 6.4.8: Show that the function $p_R(x)$, the predecessor function given by

$$p_R(x) = \begin{cases} x-1, & x \neq 0 \\ 0, & x = 0 \end{cases}$$

is primitive recursive.

Solution

Given the predecessor function

$$p_R(x) = \begin{cases} x-1, & x \neq 0 \\ 0, & x = 0 \end{cases}$$

We have

$$p_R(0) = 0$$
$$p_R(y+1) = p_1^2(y, p_R(y))$$

(Note: p_R represents predecessor function and p_1^2 represents projector function).

Thus the given predecessor function $p_R(x)$ is defined by recursion using an initial function (projector function).

Hence we have the function to be primitive recursive.

Example 6.4.9: Prove that the function

$$g(x, y) = x^y$$

is primitive recursive.

Solution

Given $g(x, y) = x^y$.

We have $g(x, y)|_{y=0} = g(x,0) = x^0 = 1.$

and

$$\begin{aligned} g(x, y+1) &= x \cdot g(x, y) \\ &= p_1^3(x, y, g(x, y)) * p_3^3(x, y, g(x, y)) \end{aligned}$$

Thus we have been able to represent the given function as a combination of initial function. Therefore the given function is primitive recursive.

Example 6.4.10: Show that the function given by

$$\text{Abs}(x) = \begin{cases} x, & x \geq 0 \\ -x, & x < 0 \end{cases}$$

is primitive recursive.

Solution

Given the absolute value function as

$$\text{Abs}(x) = \begin{cases} x, & x \geq 0 \\ -x, & x < 0 \end{cases}$$

We are able to write

$$\text{Abs}(x - y) = (x \dot{-} y) + (y \dot{-} x)$$

Hence the function is primitive recursive as we have been able to represent the Absolute function as a combination of initial function/or function (monus) defined in terms of initial function.

Example 6.4.11: Prove that the characteristic function of a finite subset of N is primitive recursive.

Solution

Let us initially prove that the characteristic function

$$\chi_{\{0\}}(x) = \begin{cases} 0, & x \neq 0 \\ 1, & x = 0 \end{cases}$$

is primitive recursive.

i.e.
$$\chi_{\{0\}}(0) = 1$$
$$\chi_{\{0\}}(x+1) = \chi_{\{0\}}\,\text{sgn}(p_R(x))$$

where predecessor function $p_R(x)$ is given by

$$p_R(x) = \begin{cases} x-1, & x \neq 0 \\ 0, & x = 0 \end{cases}$$

Hence $\chi_{\{0\}}(x)$ is primitive recursive.

Now, we have

$$\chi_{\{\alpha_1,\alpha_2,\ldots\alpha_n\}} = \chi_{\{\alpha_1\}} + \chi_{\{\alpha_2\}} + \cdots\cdots + \chi_{\{\alpha_n\}}.$$

Since we have proved that $\chi_{\{\alpha_1\}}$ is primitive recursive and also the fact that the sum of primitive functions is also primitive recursive, it is proved that the characteristic function of a finite subset of N is primitive recursive. Hence proved.

6.5 ACKERMANN'S FUNCTION

Ackermann's function is an example of a function that is mu-recursive but not primitive recursive. Mu-recursive functions are said to have the power of a Turing machine. It is defined as follows:

$$A(0, y) = y+1$$
$$A(x,0) = A(x-1,1)$$
$$A(x, y) = A(x-1, A(x, y-1))$$

It is otherwise defined as

$$A(0, y) = y+1$$
$$A(x+1,0) = A(x,1)$$
$$A(x+1, y+1) = A(x, A(x+1, y))$$

$A(x, y)$ can be computed for every (x, y). Hence $A(x,y)$ is a total function. But Ackermann's function is not primitive recursive but recursive.

Example 6.5.1: Calculate A(1, 1) and A(1, 2) where A(x, y) represents Ackermann's function.

Solution

We have Ackermann's function given by

$$A(0, y) = y+1 \quad (1)$$
$$A(x+1,0) = A(x,1) \quad (2)$$
$$A(x+1, y+1) = A(x, A(x+1, y)) \quad (3)$$

Therefore, to calculate $A(1, 1)$, we have

$$\begin{aligned} A(1,1) &= A(0+1, 0+1) \\ &= A(0, A(1,0)) \quad \text{(using (3))} \\ &= A(0, A(0,1)) \quad \text{(using (2))} \\ &= A(0,2) \quad \text{(using (1))} \\ A(1,1) &= 3 \quad \text{(using (1))} \end{aligned}$$

$$\begin{aligned} A(2,2) &= A(1+1, 1+1) \\ &= A(1, A(2,1) \quad \text{(using (3))} \end{aligned}$$

Now,

$$\begin{aligned} A(2,1) &= A(1+1, 0+1) \\ &= A(1, A(2, 0) \quad \text{(using (3))} \\ &= A(1, A(1,1)) \quad \text{(using (2))} \\ &= A(1, A(1,1)) \\ &= A(1,3) \\ &= A(0+1, 2+1) \\ &= A(0, A(1,2)) \quad \text{(using (3))} \\ &= \mathrm{A}(0,4) \\ \mathrm{A}(2,1) &= 5. \end{aligned}$$

Therefore,

$$\begin{aligned} A(2,2) &= A(1, A(2,1)) \\ &= A(1,5) \end{aligned}$$

Now,

$$\begin{aligned} A(1,5) &= A(0+1, 4+1) \\ &= A(0, A(1, 4)) \quad \text{(Using (3))} \\ &= 1 + A(1, 4) \quad \text{(Using (1))} \\ &= 1 + A(0+1, 3+1) \\ &= 1 + A(0, A(1,3)) \\ &= 1 + 1 + A(1,3) \\ &= 1 + 1 + 1 + A(1,2) \\ &= 1 + 1 + 1 + 4 \\ A(1,5) &= 7. \end{aligned}$$

Therefore $A(2, 2) = 7$.

GLOSSARY

Formal system: Should be complete and consistent.

Completeness: Should be possible either to prove or disprove any proposition that can be expressed in the system.

Consistency: Should not be possible to both prove and disprove a proposition in the system.

Russel's Paradox: Consider the set of all sets that do not have themselves as a member. Is this set a member of itself?

Primitive Recursive function: Total function is primitive recursive if (a) it is any one of three initial functions (zero function, successor function and Projector function) or (b) it can be got by applying composition and recursion finite number of times to the set of initial functions.

Initial functions: Zero function, successor function and projector function.

Composition of functions: Allows us to use functions as arguments to functions.

$$f(x, y) = h(g_1(x, y), g_2(x, y))$$

Ackermann's function:

$$\begin{aligned} A(0, y) &= y+1 \\ A(x,0) &= A(x-1,1) \\ A(x, y) &= A(x-1, A(x, y-1)) \end{aligned}$$

REVIEW QUESTIONS

1. What are formal systems?
2. Define (a) Completeness (b) Consistency in Formal Systems.
3. State the Russel's Paradox.
4. What are recursive functions?
5. Give examples for recursive functions.
6. What is a primitive recursive function?
7. Give examples for primitive recursive function.
8. Explain composition of functions.
9. What do you mean by primitive recursion?
10. What is Ackermann's function?

EXERCISES

1. Obtain the values of
   (a) $Z(90)$
   (b) $p_2^5(2,3,7,8,6)$
   (c) $p_3^7(1,2,3,4,5,6,7)$
   (d) $S(82)$.
2. Obtain the values of
   (a) nil (*abababab*)
   (b) cons *a*(*ababab*)
   (c) cons *b*(*abababa*)

3. Determine whether the following functions are total functions or not. If a function is not total, specify the arguments for which the function is defined.
   (a) $f(x) = \frac{x}{9}$ over N
   (b) $f(x) = x^2 - 25$ over N
   (c) $f(x) = 3x^2 + 2x + 5$ over N
   (d) $f(x) = x + 8$ over N.
4. Given $g_1(x, y) = x + 2y$, $g_2(x, y) = 2xy$ and $g_3(x, y) = 6x$ and $h(x, y, z) = 2x + y + z$ are functions over N. Obtain the composition of h with g_1, g_2 and g_3.
5. Given $f_1 = 2x_1^2 x_2^2$, $f_2 = \lambda$, $f_3 = 2x_1 x_2$ all defined over Σ. With the pair (x_1, y_1) and $g(x_1, x_2, x_3) = 15x_2 x_3$ again defined over Σ. Obtain the composition of g with f_1, f_2 and f_3.
6. Show that the function $f_{mult}(x, y) = xy$ is primitive recursive.
7. Show that the function $f(x, y) =$ Min (x, y) is primitive recursive.
8. Show that the function $Q(x, y) =$ Quotient (x/y) is primitive recursive.
9. Show that the function $p(x) = \begin{cases} 2x - 1, & x \neq 0 \\ 0, & x = 0 \end{cases}$ is primitive recursive.
10. Check whether the function $g(x, y) = x^{y^2}$ is primitive recursive or not.
11. Show that the function $f(x) = x/2$ is partial recursive function over N.
12. Prove that the function

$$f(x) = \begin{cases} 4x & \text{if } x \text{ is perfect square} \\ 4x + 1 & \text{otherwise} \end{cases}$$

is primitive recursive.

13. Compute $A(2, 4)$ and $A(3, 3)$ when $A(x, y)$ is Ackermann's function.

SHORT QUESTIONS AND ANSWERS

1. What are the properties of a formal system?
   (a) Completeness
   (b) Consistency
2. Define the term 'completeness' of a formal system.
   It could be either to prove or disprove any proposition that can be expressed in the system.
3. Define the term 'consistency' of a formal system.
   It should not be possible to both prove and disprove a proposition in the system.

4. What is Russel's Paradox?
   "Consider the set of all sets that do not have themselves as a member. Is this set a member of itself?"
5. What is Godel's proof of numbers about.
   "If it is possible to prove within a formal system that the system is consistent, then the formal system is not, in fact consistent."
6. What are the different primitive recursive functions?
   (a) Zero function
   (b) Successor function
   (c) Projector function
7. What is a zero function?

$$z(x) = z(y), \text{ for all } x, y \in I$$

   This is our "zero", it is written as a function so we don't have to introduce constants into the system.
8. What is a successor function?
   This function informally means $x + 1$. Formally, it does not return a value.
9. What is a Projector function?

$$p_1(x) = x$$
$$p_1(x, y) = x$$
$$p_2(x, y) = y$$

   These functions are a way of extracting one of the parameters and discarding the rest.
10. What is a primitive recursive function?
    A Total function f over N is primitive recursive if (a) it is any one of the three initial functions [zero function, successor function and projector function] or (b) it can be got by applying composition and recursion finite number of times so the set of initial functions.
11. What do you mean by composition of functions?
    Use of function as arguments to functions represent composition of functions.

$$f(x, y) = h(g_1(x, y), g_2(x, y))$$

12. What is primitive recursion?
    This is a structured "recursive routine" with the form

$$f(x,0) = g_1(x)$$
$$f(x, s(y)) = h(g_2(x, y), g_3(f(x, y)))$$

    A primitive recursive function is formed from the functions z, s, p_1 and p_2 by using only composition and primitive recursion.

13. Give examples for primitive recursive functions

(a) $f_{add}(x, y) = x + y$

(b) $f(x) = x^2$

(c) $\text{sgn}(x) = \begin{cases} 0, & x = 0 \\ 1, & x > 0 \end{cases}$

14. Are the following functions primitive recursive?

(a) $R(x, y) =$ Remainder (x/y).

(b) $f(x, y) =$ Max (x, y)

(a) YES

(b) YES

15. Are the following functions primitive recursive?

(a) $p_R(x) = \begin{cases} x-1, & x \neq 0 \\ 0, & x = 0 \end{cases}$

(b) $\chi_{\{0\}}(x) = \begin{cases} 0, & x \neq 0 \\ 1, & x = 0 \end{cases}$

(a) YES

(b) YES

16. Give an example of a function that is mu-recursive but not primitive recursive.

Ackermann's function.

17. Define the Ackermann's function.

$$\begin{aligned} A(0, y) &= y+1 \\ A(x+1,0) &= A(x,1) \\ A(x+1, y+1) &= A(x, A(x+1, y)) \end{aligned}$$

18. Is Ackermann's function recursive/primitive recursive?

It is recursive not primitive recursive.

19. What is a formal system?

A system which is complete and consistent is a formal system.

20. What are the initial functions?

(a) Zero function.

(b) Successor function.

(c) Projector function.

Chapter 7

Complexity Theory

7.1 INTRODUCTION

There are two kinds of measures with Complexity Theory: (a) time and (b) space.

(i) *Time Complexity:* It is a measure of how long a computation takes to execute. As far as Turing machine is concerned, this could be measured as the number of moves which are required to perform a computation. In the case of a digital computer, this could be measured as the number of machine cycles which are required for the computation.

(ii) *Space Complexity:* It is a measure of how much storage is required for a computation. In the case of a Turing machine, the obvious measure is the number of tape squares used, for a digital computer, the number of bytes used.

It is to be noted that both these measures functions of a single input parameter, viz., "size of the input", which is defined in terms of squares or bytes. For any given input size, different inputs require different amounts of space and time. Thus it will be easier to discuss about the "average case" or for the "worst case". It is usually interesting to look at the worst-case complexity because

(a) It may be difficult to define an "average case"
(b) Usually easier to compute worst-case complexity.

Order Statistic

In Complexity theory, equations are subjected to extreme simplifications.

If an algorithm takes exactly $50n^3 + 5n^2 - 5n + 56$ machine cycles, where 'n' is the size of the input, then we shall simplify this to $O(n^3)$. This is called the "order statistic".

It is customary to (a) drop all terms except the highest-ordered one (b) drop the co-efficient of the highest-ordered term.

For very large values of n, the effect of the highest-order term completely swamps the contribution of lower-ordered term. Tweaking the code can improve the coefficients, but the order statisfic is a function of the algorithm itself.

Example 7.1.1: Given $P(n) = a_0 + a_1 n + a_2 n^2 + \cdots + a_m n^m$. Show that

$$P(n) = O(n^m).$$

Solution

Let $b_0 = |a_0|, b_1 = |a_1|, \ldots\ldots b_m = |a_m|$.
Then for $n \geq 1$,

$$P(n) \leq b_0 + b_1 n + b_2 n^2 + \cdots\cdots + b_m n^m = \left(\frac{b_0}{n^m} + \frac{b_1}{n^{m-1}} + \cdots\cdots + b_m\right) n^m$$

$$\leq (b_0 + b_1 + \cdots\cdots + b_m) n^m = M n^m$$

where $$M = |a_0| + |a_1| + \cdots\cdots + |a_m|.$$

Therefore $$P(n) = O(n^m).$$

Example 7.1.2: Find the order of the following polynomials:

(a) $f_1(n) = 5n^3 + 3n + 1$
(b) $f_2(n) = n^5 - 400n^2$

Solution

(a) $(f_1(n)) = O(n^3)$.
(b) $f_2(n) = O(n^5)$.

7.2 POLYNOMIAL-TIME ALGORITHMS

A polynomial-time algorithm is an algorithm whose execution time is either given by a polynomial on the size of the input, or can be bounded by such a polynomial. Problems which can be solved by a polynomial-time algorithm are called "tractable" problems. As an example, most algorithms on arrays can use the array size, *n*, as the input size. In order to find the largest element in any array requires a single pass through the array, so the algorithm which does this is of $O(n)$, or it is a "linear time" algorithm.

Sorting algorithms take $O(n \log n)$ or $O(n^2)$ time. Bubble sort takes linear time in the least case, but $O(n^2)$ time in the average and worst cases. Heapsort takes $O(n \log n)$ time in all cases. Quicksort takes $O(n \log n)$ time on average, but $O(n^2)$ time in the worst case.

As far as $O(n \log n)$ is concerned, it must be noted that the base of the logarithms is irrelevant, as the difference is a constant factor, which is ignored.

All programming tasks we know have polynomial solutions. It is not due to the reason that all practical problems have polynomial-time solutions.

Rather, it is because the day-to-day problems are one for which there is no known practical solution.

7.3 NON-DETERMINISTIC POLYNOMIAL TIME ALGORITHMS

A nondeterministic computation is viewed as:

(i) when a choice point is reached, an infallible oracle can be consulted to determine the right option.

(ii) When a choice point is reached, all choices are made and computation can proceed simultaneously.

A Non-deterministic Polynomial Time Algorithm is one that can be executed in polynomial time on a nondeterministic machine. The machine can either consult an oracle in constant time, or it can spawn an arbitrarily large number of parallel processes, which is obviously a nice machine to have.

Summary to common time complexities:

Complexity	Verbal Description	Feasilality
$O(1)$	constant time	feasible
$O(\log n)$	log time	feasible
$O(n)$	linear time	feasible
$O(n \log n)$	log linear time	feasible
$O(n^2)$	quadratic time	sometimes feasible
$O(n^3)$	cubic time	less often feasible
$O(2^n)$	exponential time	rarely feasible

7.4 INTEGER BIN PACKING

Assume we are given a set of n integers. Our task is to arrange these integers into two piles or bins, so that the sum of the integers in one pile is equal to the sum of the integers in the other pile.

For example, given the integers

$$\{19, 23, 32, 42, 50, 62, 77, 88, 89, 105, 114, 123, 176\}$$

These numbers sum to 1000. Can they be divided into two bins, bin A and bin B, such that the sum of the integers in each bin is 500?

There is an obvious nondeterministic algorithm: For each number, put it in the correct bin. This requires linear time.

There is also a fairly easy deterministic algorithm. There are 13 numbers ($n = 13$), so form the 13-bit binary number 0000000000000.

For *i* ranging from 1 to 13: if bit i is zero, put integer *i* into bin A; if bit *i* is one, put integer *i* into bin B. Test the resultant arrangement.

If we don't have a solution yet, add 1 to the binary number and try again. If we reach 1111111111111, we will stop and conclude that there is no solution.

This is fairly simply algorithm; the only problem is that it takes $O(2^n)$ time, that is, "exponential time". In the above example, we may need to try as many as 2^{13} arrangements. This is fine for all small values of n (such as 13), but becomes unreasonable for large values of *n*.

We could find many shortcuts for problems such as this, but the best we can do is improve the coefficients. The time complexity remains $O(2^n)$. Problems that require exponential time are referred to as "Intractable" problems.

There are many variants to this problem.

- We can have multiple bins.
- We can have a single bin, and the object is to pack as much as possible into it.
- We can pack objects with multiple dimensions (volume and weight, for example).

7.5 BOOLEAN SATISFIABILITY

Assume we have *n* Boolean variables, viz., A, B, C, ... and an expression in the propositional Calculus i.e., we can use and, or and not to form the expression. Is there an assignment of truth values to the variables, (for example, A = true, B = true, C = false), that will make the expression true?

Here is a nondeterministic algorithm to solve the problem: For each Boolean variable, assign if the proper truth value. This is a linear algorithm. We can find a deterministic algorithm for this problem in much the same way as we did for the integer bin problem. Effectively, the idea is to set up a systematic procedure to try every possible assignment of truth values to variables. The algorithm terminates when a satisfactory solution is found, or when all 2^n possible assignments have been tried. Again, the deterministic solution requires exponential time.

Example 7.5.1: Check whether the boolean formula

$$\varnothing = (\bar{x} \wedge y) \vee (x \wedge \bar{z})$$

is satisfiable or not.

Solution

A Boolean formula is satisfiable if some assignment of 0s and 1s to the variables makes the formula evaluate to 1.

When $x = 0, y = 1$ and $z = 0$, we have

$$\varnothing = (1 \wedge 1) \vee (0 \wedge 1)$$
$$= 1 \vee 1$$
$$\varnothing = 1$$

Therefore the Boolean formula is satisfiable.

Example 7.5.2: Check whether the formula

$$(x \vee y) \wedge (x \vee \overline{y}) \wedge (\overline{x} \vee y) \wedge (\overline{x} \vee \overline{y})$$

is satisfiable or not?

Solution

(***Hint:*** Proceed in the same way as the previous problem).

7.6 ADDITIONAL NP PROBLEMS

The following problems have a polynomial-time solution, but an exponential-time solution on a deterministic machine. There are literally hundreds of additional examples.

(a) *The Travelling Salesman Problem (TSP):* A salesman starting in Texas, wants to visit every capital city in the United States, returning to Texas as his last stop. In what order should he visit the capital cities so as to minimize the total distance travelled?

(b) *The Hamiltonian Circuit Problem:* Every capital city has direct air flights to at least some capital cities. Our intrepid salesman wants to visit all the capitals, and return to his starting point, taking only direct air flights. Can he find a path that lets him do this?

(c) *Linear Programming:* We have on hand X amount of butter, Y amount of flour, Z eggs etc. We have cookie recipies that use varying amounts of these ingredients. Different kinds of cookies bring different prices. What mix of cookies should we make in order to maximize profits?

7.7 NP-COMPLETE PROBLEMS

All the known NP problems have a remarkable characteristic: They are all reducible to one another. What this means is that, given any two NP problems *X* and *Y*,

(a) There exists a polynomial-time algorith to restate a problem of type *X* as a problem of type *Y*, and
(b) There exists a polynomial-time algorithm to translate a solution to a type *Y* problem back into a solution for the type *X* problem.

This is what the "complete" refers to when we talk about NP-complete problems. What this means is that, if anyone ever discovers a polynomial-time algorithm for any of these problems, then there is an easily-derived polynomial-time algorithm for all of them. This leads to the question.

Does P = NP?

No one has ever found a deterministic polynomial-time algorithm for any of these problems (or the hundreds of others like them). However, no one has ever succeeded in proving that no deterministic polynomial time algorithm exists, either. The status for some years now is this: most computer scientists don't think a polynomial-time algorithm can exist, but no one knows for sure.

GLOSSARY

Measures of complexity: Time and space

Time complexity: Measure of how long a computation takes to execute.

Space complexity: Measure of how much storage is required for a computation.

Kinds of complexity analysis: (a) average case (b) worst case (c) best case

Polynomial time algorithm: An algorithm whose execution time is either given by a polynomial on the size of the input, or can be bounded by such a polynomial.

Heapsort complexity: $O(n \log n)$ at all times.

Quicksort complexity: $O(n \log n)$ time an average, $O(n^2)$ time in the worst case.

Nondeterministic Polynomial time algorithm: One that can be executed in polynomial time on a non-deterministic machine.

NP problem: How a polynomial-time solution, but an exponential time solution on a deterministic machine.

TSP: Travelling salesman problem.

REVIEW QUESTIONS

1. What is meant by complexity theory?
2. What do you mean by Time complexity?
3. What do you mean by space complexity?
4. Define order-statistic in complexity theory?
5. Define O-notation (Big O).
6. What do you mean by Polynomial Time algorithms?
7. What do you mean by non-polynomial time algorithms?

8. State some of the common time complexities.
9. Discuss the feasibility of the following complexicities
   (a) $O(1)$ (b) $O(\log n)$ (c) $O(n)$ (d) $O(n \log n)$
   (e) $O(n^2)$ (f) $O(n^3)$ (g) $O(2^n)$ (h) $O(2^{n^2})$
10. What are heuristic algorithms?
11. Explain the following intractable problems
    (a) Integer Bin packing
    (b) TSP
12. What do you mean by Boolean satisfiablity?
13. What are P-class problems?
14. What are NP-class problems?
15. When are problems said to be NP-complete?
16. Give examples for
    (a) class-P
    (b) class-NP Problems.

EXERCISE

1. Prove the following
   (a) $n^2 + 100 \log n$ is $O(n^2)$
   (b) $n!$ is $O(n^n)$
   (c) 3^n is $O(n!)$
2. Given $f(n) = 5n^2 + n$ and $g(n) = O(n^2)$. Is the statement $f(n) - g(n) = O(n)$ valid?
3. Determine the order of the following polynomials
   (a) $f_a(n) = 100n^2 + 3n - 1$
   (b) $f_b(n) = 5n^5 - 4n^4 - 200n^2$.
4. Discuss the feasibility of algorithms with following time complexities.
   (a) $O(\log n)$ (b) $O(n \log n)$ (c) $O(n^2)$
5. Discuss the feasibility of algorithms with following time complexities.
   (a) $O(n^3)$ (b) $O(2^n)$ (c) $O(n!)$
6. Explain Boolean satisfiability with an example.
7. Verify whether the following formula

$$(x \wedge \bar{y}) \vee (\bar{x} \wedge y)$$

is Boolean satisfiable or not.

SHORT QUESTIONS AND ANSWERS

1. What are the measures of Complexity Theory?

   (a) Time (b) Space

2. What is meant by time complexity?

   It is a measure of how long a computation takes to execute.

3. What is meant by space complexity?

   It is a measure of how much storage is required for a computation.

4. How do you measure space complexity in a Turing machine?

   It is the number of tape squares used.

5. How do you measure space complexity in a digital computer?

   It is the number of bytes used in a digital computer which is a measure of space complexity.

6. What are the different cases of complexities?

   (a) averge case

   (b) best case

   (c) worst case.

7. What is order statistic?

   In complexity theory, equations are subjected to extreme simplifications.

   If an algorithm takes exactly $50n^3 + 5n^2 - 5n + 56$ machine cycles, where 'n' is the size of the input, then we shall simplify this to $O(n^3)$. This is called "order statistic".

8. Determine the order of the polynomials

   (a) $f_1(n) = 10n^3 + 6n + 1$

   (b) $f_2(n) = n^5 - 2n^2$

   (a) $f_1(n) = O(n^3)$

   (b) $f_2(n) = O(n^5)$

9. What is a Polynomial time algorithm?

   An algorithm whose execution time is either given by a polynomial on the size of the input or can be by bounded by such polynomial is a polynomial time algorithm.

10. What are tractable problems?

    Problems which can be solved by a polynomial time algorithm are called tractable problems.

11. What do you mean by saying that an algorithm is an $O(n)$ algorithm?

    It means it is a linear time algorithm.

12. What are the time complexities of sorting algorithms?

    $O(n \log n)$ or $O(n^2)$.

13. Mention the time complexities of a bubble sort in (a) best case (b) average case and (c) worst case?
    (a) Best case: $O(n)$
    (b) Average case: $O(n^2)$
    (c) Worst case: $O(n^2)$.
14. Mention the time complexities of Quicksort algorithm in (a) best case (b) average case and (c) worst case.
    (a) Best case: $O(n \log n)$
    (b) Average case: $O(n \log n)$
    (c) Worst case: $O(n^2)$
15. Discuss the feasibility of the following complexities:
    (a) $O(2^n)$ (b) $O(n^3)$ (c) $O(n^2)$.
    (a) $O(2^n) \rightarrow$ rarely feasible
    (b) $O(n^3) \rightarrow$ less often feasible
    (c) $O(n^2) \rightarrow$ sometimes feasible
16. Discuss the feasibility of the following complexities.
    (a) $O(n \log n)$ (b) $O(n)$ (c) $O(1)$
    (a) $O(n \log n) \rightarrow$ feasible
    (b) $O(n) \rightarrow$ feasible
    (c) $O(1) \rightarrow$ feasible
17. What is a non-deterministic Polynomial Time algorithm?
    It is the one that can be executed in polynomial time on a non-deterministic machine.
18. What are the view points of a non-deterministic computation?
    (a) When a choice point is reached, an infallible oracle can be consulted to determine the right option.
    (b) When a choice point is reached, all choices are made and computation can proceed simultaneously.
19. Name some of the intractable problems.
    (a) Integer Bin packing
    (b) Knapsack problem
    (c) Travelling Salesman Problem
20. What is 'integer bin packing' problem?
    Assume we are given a set of n integers. Our task is to arrange these integers into two piles or bins, so that the sum of the integers in one pile is equal to the sum of the integers in the other pile.
21. What is Boolean satisfiability?
    A Boolean formula is satisfiable if some assignment of 0s and 1s to the variables makes the formula evaluate to 1.

22. Name some of the NP problems.
    (a) Travelling salesman problem
    (b) Hamiltonian Circuit problem.
23. What is the TSP problem?
    "A salesman starting in a certain city, wants the visit every capital city in a country, returning to the city where he started. In what order should be visit the capital cities so as to minimize the total distance travelled?" This is the TSP.
24. Mention a remarkable characteristic of all NP Problems.
    All NP problems are reducible to one another.
25. Is P = NP?
    No one has proved or disproved that P = NP.

Chapter 8

Propositions and Predicates

8.1 PROPOSITIONS

Mathematics is the study of the properties of mathematical structures. A mathematical structure is defined by a set of "axioms". An "axiom" is a true statement about the properties of the structure.

"Logic" is the discipline that deals with the methods of reasoning. It gives a set of rules and techniques to determine whether a given argument is valid or not. True assertions which can be inferred from the truth of axioms are called "theorems". A "proof" of a theorem is an argument that establishes that the theorem is true for a specified mathematical structure.

A "proposition" or "statement" is any declarative sentence which is true (T) or false (F). We refer to T or F as the truth value of the statement. Propositional calculus is the calculus of propositions.

Some illustrations below explain the concept well.

(a) The sentence "$3 + 3 = 6$" is a statement, since it can be either true or false. Since it happens to be a true statement, its truth value is T.

(b) The sentence "$2 = 0$" is also a statement, but its truth value is F.

(c) "It will rain tomorrow" is a proposition. For its truth value, we shall have wait for tomorrow.

(d) "Solve the following equation for y" is not a statement, since it cannot be assigned any truth value whatsoever. It is an imperative, or command, rather than a declarative statement.

(e) *The Liar's Paradox:* "This statement is false" gets us into a bind: If it were true, then since it is declaring itself to be false, it must be false. On the other hand, if it were false, then its declaring itself false is a lie, so it is true! In other words, if it is true, then it is false, and if it is false, then it is true, and we go around in circles. We get out of this bind by refusing to accord it the privileges of statementhood. In other words it is not a statement. An equivalent pseudo statement is "I am lying", so we call this liar's paradox.

Such sentences are called "self-referential" sentences, since they refer to themselves.

We use the letters $p, q, r, s,$ ...... for propositions. Thus for example, we might decide that P should stand for the proposition "The earth is round". Then we shall write

p: "the earth is round"

to express this. We read this

p is the statement "the earth is round".

8.1.1 Connectives

In order to make use of some keywords like and, 'or', 'not', etc. which are called "sentential connectives", it is required to have some ground rules before making use of them. Let us now discuss about the different forms of connectives.

(a) *Negation (NOT):* The negation of p is the statement $\sim p$, which is read as "not P". Its truth value is defined by the following truth table.

p	$\sim p$
T	F
F	T

where p is the statement, T and F represent 'True' and 'False' respectively.

Illustration

(i) Given $p = "3+3=6"$, we have

$$\sim p = "3+3 \neq 6".$$

Note that $\sim p$ is false in this case, since p is true.

(ii) If p = "2 = 0", then we have

$$\sim p: "1 \neq 0".$$

$\sim p$ is true in this case, since p is false.

(iii) If p = "I loved either Nirmala or Padmaja".
then we have

$\sim p$: "I loved neither Nirmala nor Padmaja".

Here p is a hypothetical statement (but which was true!)

(iv) If p = "All the doctors in this town are crooks", then we have

$\sim p$ = "Not all the doctors in this town are crooks"

or

$\sim p$ = "At least one of the doctors in this town is not a crook".

It is very important to be careful while negating a statement involving the words "All" or "Some". The use of these "quantifiers" is the subject of "Predicate calculus". $\sim p$ is also written as $\neg\, p$.

(b) *Conjunction* (*AND*): The conjunction of p and q is the statement $p \wedge q$, which is read as "p and q", whose truth value is defined by the following truth table.

p	q	$p \wedge q$
T	T	T
T	F	F
F	T	F
F	F	F

If p and q columns are listed, all four possibile combinations of truth values for p and q, and in the $p \wedge q$ column we find the associated truth value for $p \wedge q$.

Illustration

(i) If p = "I am clever"
and q = "You are strong".
Therefore we have

$p \wedge q$ = "I am clever and you are strong".

(ii) If p = "The galaxy will at last wind up in a black hole"
and q = "3 + 3 = 6", then we have

$p \wedge q$: "This galaxy will at last wind up in a black hole and $3 + 3 = 6$".

and $p \wedge (\sim q)$: "This galaxy will at last windup in a black hole and $3 + 3 \neq 6$."

(iii) If p = "This chapter is boring".
and q = "Logic is a boring subject".

Let us see how the statement "This chapter is definitely not boring even though logic is a boring subject" is expressed in logical form.

The first clause is the negation of p, so is $\sim p$. The second clause is simply stating the (false) claim that logic is a boring subject, and thus amounts to q.

The phrase "even though" is a colourful way of saying that both clauses are ture, and so the whole statement is just $(\sim p) \wedge q$.

(c) *Disjunction* (*OR*): The disjunction of p and q is the statement $p \vee q$, which is read as "p or q", whose truth value is defined by the following truth table.

p	q	$p \vee q$
T	T	T
T	F	T
F	T	T
F	F	F

Note that the only way for the whole statement to be false is for both p and q to be false. Hence we say that $p \vee q$ means "p and q are not both false".

Illustration

(i) If p : I am clever
and q : You are strong

then $p \vee q$ = I am clever or you are strong.

Mathematicians have settled on "Inclusive or": $p \vee q$ means p is true or q is true or both are ture.

(ii) If p : The butler did it.
and q : The cook did it.
then we have

$p \vee q$: either the butler or the cook did it.

(iii) If p : The butler did it
q : The cook did it
r : The lawyer did it, then we have

$(p \vee q) \wedge (\sim r)$: Either the butler or the cook did it, but not the lawyer.

(d) *Implication* (*Conditional/ if .... then*): The conditional $p \Rightarrow q$, read as "if p, then q" or "p implies q", is defined by the following truth table.

p	q	$p \Rightarrow q$
T	T	T
T	F	F
F	T	T
F	F	T

The arrow $\Rightarrow$ is the "conditional" operator, and in $p \Rightarrow q$ the statement p is called the "antecedent" or "hypothesis", and q is called the "consequent", or "conclusion".

Illustration

(i) If p and q are both true, then $p \Rightarrow q$ is true. For example, "if $2+2=4$, then the sun rises in the East"

Here: p : "$2+2=4$" and q : "the sun rises in the east".

(ii) If p is true and q is false, then $p \Rightarrow q$ is false. For example:

"When it rains, I carry an umbrella". Here p : It is raining; q : I carry an umbrella.

If it is raining then I carry an umbrella. Now there are lot of days when it rains (p is true) and I forget to bring my umbrella (q is false). On any of those days the statement $p \Rightarrow q$ is clearly false.

(e) *Biconditional* (*If and only if........*)*:* The Biconditional $p \Leftrightarrow q$, which is read as "p if and only if p" or "p is equivalent to q" is defined by the following truth table.

p	q	$p \Leftrightarrow q$
T	T	T
T	F	F
F	T	F
F	F	T

From the truth table, we see that for $p \Leftrightarrow q$ to be true, both p and q must have the same truth values; otherwise it is false.

The statement $p \Leftrightarrow q$ is defined to be the statement $(p \Rightarrow q) \wedge (q \Rightarrow p)$. For this reason, the double headed arrow $\Leftrightarrow$ is called the "biconditional".

Each of the following is equivalent to the biconditional $p \Leftrightarrow q$

(i) p if and only if q

(ii) p is necessary and sufficient for q.

(iii) p is equivalent to q.

Illustration

(i) The statement "$2+2=6$ if and only if Gregory is Alexander the Great", is true since the given statement has the form $p \Leftrightarrow q$, where

p: "$2+2=6$" and

q : "Gregory is Alexander the Great"

Since both statements are false, the biconditional $p \Leftrightarrow q$ is true.

(ii) Consider the statement:

"I teach mathematics if and only if I am paid a large amount of money".

Some of the equivalent ways of phrasing this sentence are:

"My teaching Mathematics is necessary and sufficient for me to be paid a large amount of money".

"For me to teach Mathematics it is necessary and sufficient that I be paid a large sum of money".

Example 8.1.1: Express the following statements in symbolic form, with

p : Jalaney is good.
q : Padmaja is good.

(a) Jalaney is good and Padmaja is not good.
(b) Jalaney and Padmaja are both good.
(c) Neither Jalaney nor Padmaja are good.
(d) It is not true that Jalaney and Padmaja are both good.

Solution

(a) $p \wedge \neg q$
(b) $p \wedge q$
(c) $\neg p \wedge \neg q$
(d) $\neg (p \wedge q)$

Example 8.1.2: Express the following statements in symbolic form.

(a) Jack and Jill went behind the hill
(b) If either Naveena takes Maths or Nirmala takes Physics, then Anju will take English.
(c) If there is a ticket available, I will travel by this train
(d) There is either a fault with Raju or Mohan.

Solution

(a) p : Jack went behind the hill
q : Jill went behind the hill.
Then we have the given statement in symbolic form as

$$\boxed{p \wedge q}$$

(b) p : Naveena takes Maths
q : Nirmala takes physics
r : Anju takes English
Then the given statement is written as

$$(p \wedge q) \Rightarrow r$$

(c) p : Ticket is available
q : I will travel by this train.

$$p \Rightarrow q$$

is the given statement in symbolic form.

(d) p : There is a fault with Raju.
q : There is a fault with Mohan.

$$p \vee q$$

is the given statement is symbolic form.

Example 8.1.3: Given
p : Triangle PQR is isosceles
q : Triangle PQR is equilateral
r : Triangle PQR is equiangular.

Translate each of the following into a statement in English.

(a) $q \Leftrightarrow p$
(b) $\neg p \Leftrightarrow \neg q$
(c) $q \Leftrightarrow r$
(d) $p \wedge 7q$
(e) $r \Rightarrow p$.

Solution

(a) $q \Leftrightarrow p$
Triangle *PQR* is equilateral if and only if it is isoscles

(b) $\neg p \Leftrightarrow \neg q$
Triangle *PQR* is not isosciles if and only if it is not equilateral.

(c) $q \Leftrightarrow r$
Triangle *PQR* is equilateral if and only if it is equiangular

(d) $p \wedge \neg q$
Triangle *PQR* is isosceles and it is not equilateral.

(e) $r \Rightarrow p$
If Triangle *PQR* is equiangular then it is isosceles.

Example 8.1.4: Given

p : It is cold;
q : 12 + 5 = 200
and r : It rains.

Express the following in symbolic form.

(a) It is cold only if 12 + 5 = 200.
(b) A necessary condition for it to be cold is that 12 + 5 = 200.
(c) A sufficient condition for it to be cold is that 12 + 5 = 200.
(d) It rains and 12 + 5 is not 200.
(e) It never rains when 12 + 5 = 200.

Solution

(a) $p \Leftrightarrow q$
(b) $p \Leftrightarrow q$
(c) $q \Leftrightarrow p$
(d) $r \wedge \neg p$
(e) $q \Rightarrow \neg r$

Example 8.1.5: Let

p : prices are high,
q : wages are increasing.

Express the following in verbal form.
(a) $p \wedge q$ (b) $\neg p \wedge \neg q$ (c) $\neg (p \wedge q)$
(d) $p \vee \neg q$ (e) $\neg(\neg p \vee \neg q)$.

Solution

(a) $p \wedge q$: Prices are high and wages are increasing
(b) $\neg p \wedge \neg q$: Prices are not high and wages are not increasing
(c) $\neg (p \wedge q)$: It is not that prices are high and wages are increasing
(d) $p \vee \neg q$: Prices are high or the wages are not increasing
(e) $\neg (\neg p \vee \neg q)$: It is not that prices are not high or wages are not increasing.

Example 8.1.6: Determine the truth of the following:

(a) 5 < 6 and 6 is a positive integer.
(b) 5 > 6 or 6 is a positive integer
(c) If 5 > 6, then 100 is a prime number
(d) If 10 > 6, then 100 is a prime number.

Solution

(a) T ; (b) T; (c) T; (d) F.

Example 8.1.7: If p, q, r are three statements, with truth values 'True', 'True', 'False' respectively, find the truth values of the following:

(a) $p \vee q$ (b) $p \wedge r$ (c) $(p \vee q) \wedge r$ (d) $p \wedge (\neg r)$
(e) $(p \wedge \neg q) \wedge (\neg r)$ (f) $p \Rightarrow r$ (g) $p \Rightarrow (q \Leftrightarrow (r \Rightarrow s))$.

Solution

Given $p : T;$ $q : T;$ $r : F$

(a) $p \vee q$

p	q	$p \vee q$
T	T	T

True

(b) $p \wedge r$

p	r	$p \wedge r$
T	T	T

False

(c) $(p \vee q) \wedge r$

p	q	r	$p \vee q$	$(p \vee q) \wedge r$
T	T	F	T	F

False

(d) $p \wedge (\neg r)$

p	r	$\neg r$	$p \wedge (\neg r)$
T	F	T	T

True

(e) $(p \wedge \neg q) \wedge (\neg r)$

p	$\neg q$	$p \wedge \neg q$	$\neg r$	$(p \wedge \neg q) \wedge (\neg r)$
T	F	F	T	F

False

(f) $p \Rightarrow r$

p	r	$p \Rightarrow r$
T	F	F

False

(g) $p \Rightarrow (q \Leftrightarrow (r \Rightarrow s))$

p	q	r	s	$r \Rightarrow s$	$q \Leftrightarrow (r(\Leftrightarrow)s)$	$p \Rightarrow (q \Rightarrow (r \Rightarrow s))$
T	T	F	F	T	T	T

True

Example 8.1.8: Construct the truth table for

$$(\neg p \vee q) \wedge (\neg q \vee p).$$

Solution

p	q	$\neg p$	$\neg q$	$\neg p \vee q$	$\neg q \vee p$	$[(\neg p \vee q) \wedge (\neg q \vee p)$
T	T	F	F	T	T	T
T	F	F	T	F	T	F
F	T	T	F	T	F	F
F	F	T	T	T	T	T

Example 8.1.9: Determine the Truth Table for $\neg(\neg p \wedge \neg q)$.

p	q	$\neg p$	$\neg q$	$\neg p \wedge \neg q$	$\neg(\neg p \wedge \neg q)$
T	T	F	F	F	T
T	F	F	T	F	T
F	T	T	F	F	T
F	F	T	T	T	F

Example 8.1.9: Using truth tables, show that if $P \Leftrightarrow Q$ is true, then $P \Rightarrow Q$ and $Q \Rightarrow P$ are both true. Conversely, show that if $P \Rightarrow Q$ and $Q \Rightarrow P$ are both true, then $P \Leftrightarrow Q$ is true.

Solution

P	Q	$P \Leftrightarrow Q$	$P \Rightarrow Q$	$Q \Rightarrow P$	
T	T	T	T	T	—①
T	F	F	F	T	
F	T	F	T	F	
F	F	T	T	T	—②

From ① and ②, it is obvious that if $P \Leftrightarrow Q$ is true, then $P \Rightarrow Q$ and $Q \Rightarrow P$ is true.

From the above truth table, from ① & ②, it is seen that if $P \Rightarrow Q$ and $Q \Rightarrow P$ are true also $P \Leftrightarrow Q$ is true.

8.1.2 Tautology, Contradiction and Contingency

(a) *Tautology:* A Tautology is a propositional form whose truth value is true for all possible values of its propositional variables.

Example: $p \vee \neg p$.

(b) *Contradiction:* A contradiction or absurdity is a propositional form which is always false.

Example: $p \wedge \neg p$.

(c) *Contingency:* A propositional form which is neither a tautology nor a contradiction is called a contingency.

Example 8.1.10: Show that $P \Rightarrow Q$ has the same truth value as $\neg P \vee Q$ for all truth values of P and Q, i.e., show that $(P \Rightarrow Q) \Leftrightarrow (\neg P \vee Q)$ is a tautology.

Solution

P	Q	$\neg P$	$P \Rightarrow Q$	$\neg P \vee Q$	$(P \Rightarrow Q) \Leftrightarrow (\neg P \vee Q)$
T	T	F	F	T	T
T	F	F	F	F	T
F	T	T	T	T	T
F	F	T	T	T	T

From the truth table it is clear that $P \Rightarrow Q$ has the same truth value as $\neg P \vee Q$.

Also it is seen that $(P \Rightarrow Q) \Leftrightarrow (\neg P \vee Q)$ has all truth values to be "True". Therefore it is a "Tautology".

Example 8.1.11: Establish whether the following propositions are tautologies, contingencies or contradictions.

(a) $P \vee \neg P$
(b) $P \wedge \neg P$
(c) $P \Rightarrow \neg(\neg P)$
(d) $\neg(P \wedge Q) \Leftrightarrow (\neg P \vee \neg Q)$

Solution

(a) $P \vee \neg P$.

P	$\neg P$	$P \vee \neg P$
T	F	T
F	T	T

All truth values are True.
Therefore, it is a "Tautology".

(b) $P \wedge \neg P$

P	$\neg P$	$P \wedge \neg P$
T	F	F
F	T	F

All truth values are False.
Therefore, it is a "contradiction".

(c) $P \Rightarrow \neg(\neg P)$

P	$\neg P$	$\neg(\neg P)$	$P \Rightarrow \neg(\neg P)$
T	F	T	T
F	T	F	T

All truth values are "True".
Therefore, it is a "Tautology".

(d) $\neg(P \wedge Q) \Leftrightarrow (\neg P \vee \neg Q)$

P	Q	$P \wedge Q$	$\neg(P \wedge Q)$	$\neg P$	$\neg Q$	$\neg P \vee \neg Q$	$\neg(P \wedge Q) \Leftrightarrow (\neg P \vee \neg Q)$
T	T	T	F	F	F	F	T
T	F	F	T	F	T	T	T
F	T	F	T	T	F	T	T
F	F	F	T	T	T	T	T

All truth values are "True".
Therefore, it is a "Tautology".

Example 8.1.12: Establish whether the following propositions are tautologies, contingencies or contradictions.

(a) $\neg(P \vee Q) \Leftrightarrow (\neg P \wedge \neg Q)$
(b) $(P \Rightarrow Q) \Leftrightarrow (\neg Q \Rightarrow \neg P)$
(c) $(P \Rightarrow Q) \Leftrightarrow (\neg Q \Rightarrow \neg P)$
(d) $[P \wedge (Q \vee R)] \Rightarrow [(P \wedge Q) \vee (P \wedge R)]$.

Solution

(a) $\neg(P \vee Q) \Leftrightarrow (\neg P \wedge \neg Q)$
Tautology
(b) $(P \Rightarrow Q) \Leftrightarrow (\neg Q \Rightarrow \neg P)$
Tautology
(c) $(P \Rightarrow Q) \wedge (Q \Rightarrow P)$

P	Q	$P \Rightarrow Q$	$Q \Rightarrow P$	$(P \Rightarrow Q) \wedge (Q \Rightarrow P)$
T	T	T	T	T
T	F	F	T	F
F	T	T	F	F
F	F	T	T	T

Some values are True, some are False.
Therefore, it is a "Contingency".
(d) $[P \wedge (Q \vee R)] \Rightarrow [(P \wedge Q) \vee (P \wedge R)]$.
It can be shown to be a "tautology".

Example 8.1.13: Let P be the proposition "It is snowing".
Let Q be the proposition "I will go to town".
Let R be the proposition "I have time".

(a) Using logical connectives, write a proposition which symbolizes each of the following:

(i) If it is not snowing and I have time, then I will go to town.
(ii) I will go to town only if I have time.
(iii) It isn't snowing.
(iv) It is snowing, and I will not go to town.

(b) Write a sentence in English corresponding to each of the following propositions:

(i) $Q \Leftrightarrow (R \wedge \neg P)$
(ii) $R \wedge Q$
(iii) $(Q \Rightarrow R) \wedge (R \Rightarrow Q)$
(iv) $\neg(R \wedge Q)$.

Solution

(a) (i) $(\neg P \wedge R) \Rightarrow Q$
(ii) $R \Rightarrow Q$
(iii) $\neg P$
(iv) $P \wedge \neg Q$

(b) (i) $Q \Leftrightarrow (R \wedge \neg P)$.
I will go to town, if and only if I have time and it is not snowing.
(ii) $R \wedge Q$.
I have time and I will go to town.
(iii) $(Q \Rightarrow R) \wedge (R \Rightarrow Q)$.
I will go to town if I have time and if I have time, I will go to town.
(iv) $\neg (R \vee Q)$.
It is not that I have time or I will go to town.

Example 8.1.14: How many rows are needed for the truth table of the formula $(p \wedge \neg q) \Leftrightarrow ((\neg r \wedge s) \Rightarrow t)$?

Solution

Given p, q, r, s, t as propositions.
∴ Number of rows needed in Truth Table = $2^5 = 32$.

Example 8.1.15: If $p_1, p_2, \ldots\ldots p_n$ are primitive propositions and $\varnothing(p_1, p_2, \ldots\ldots p_n)$ is a formula which contains at least one occurrence of each $p_i\,(1 \le i \le n)$, how many rows are needed to construct the truth table for $\varnothing$?

Solution

Given $p_1, p_2, \ldots\ldots p_n$ as propositions. Therefore number of rows needed in Truth Table = 2^n (for n elements).

8.1.3 Logical Identities

If two propositional forms are logically equivalent one can be substituted for the other in any proposition in which they occur. Table below shows a list of important equivalences, which are called "identities." The symbols P, Q, and R represent arbitrary propositional forms. The symbol "1" is used to represent either a "tautology" or a true proposition. Similarly, "0" represents a false proposition or a contradiction.

Table. Logical Identities

1.	$P \Leftrightarrow (P \vee P)$	Idempotence of $\vee$
2.	$P \Leftrightarrow (P \wedge P)$	Idempotence of $\wedge$
3.	$(P \vee Q) \Leftrightarrow (Q \vee P)$	Commutativity of $\vee$
4.	$(P \wedge Q) \Leftrightarrow (Q \wedge P)$	Commutativity of $\wedge$
5.	$[(P \vee Q) \vee R] \Leftrightarrow [P \vee (Q \vee R)]$	Associativity of $\vee$
6.	$[(P \wedge Q) \wedge R] \Leftrightarrow [P \wedge (Q \wedge R)]$	Associativity of $\wedge$
7.	$\neg(P \vee Q) \Leftrightarrow (\neg P \wedge \neg Q)$	DeMorgan's Laws
8.	$\neg(P \wedge Q) \Leftrightarrow (\neg P \vee \neg Q)$	
9.	$[P \wedge (Q \wedge R)] \Leftrightarrow [(P \wedge Q) \vee (P \wedge R)]$	Distributivity of $\wedge$ over $\vee$
10.	$[P \vee (Q \wedge R)] \Leftrightarrow [(P \vee Q) \wedge (P \vee R)]$	Distributivity of $\vee$ over $\wedge$
11.	$(P \vee 1) \Leftrightarrow 1$	
12.	$(P \wedge 1) \Leftrightarrow P$	
13.	$(P \vee 0) \Leftrightarrow P$	
14.	$(P \wedge 0) \Leftrightarrow 0$	
15.	$(P \vee \neg P) \Leftrightarrow 1$	
16.	$(P \wedge \neg P) \Leftrightarrow 0$	
17.	$P \Leftrightarrow \neg(\neg P)$	Double Negation
18.	$(P \Rightarrow Q) \Leftrightarrow (\neg P \vee Q)$	Implication
19.	$(P \Leftrightarrow Q) \Leftrightarrow [(P \Rightarrow Q) \wedge (Q \Rightarrow P)]$	Equivalence
20.	$[(P \wedge Q) \Rightarrow R] \Leftrightarrow [P \Rightarrow (Q \Rightarrow R)]$	Exportation
21.	$[(P \Rightarrow Q) \wedge (P \Rightarrow \neg Q)] \Leftrightarrow \neg P$	Absurdity
22.	$(P \Rightarrow Q) \Leftrightarrow (\neg Q \Rightarrow \neg P)$	Contrapositive

All the above identities can be proved by constructing truth tables.
The following table gives a list of tautologies which are implications.

Table. Logical Implications

1.	$P \Rightarrow (P \vee Q)$	Addition
2.	$(P \wedge Q) \Rightarrow P$	Simplification
3.	$(P \wedge (P \Rightarrow Q)] \Rightarrow Q$	Modus Ponens
4.	$[(P \Rightarrow Q) \wedge \neg Q] \Rightarrow \neg P$	Modus Tollens
5.	$[\neg P \wedge (P \vee Q)] \Rightarrow Q$	Disjunctive Syllogism
6.	$[(P \Rightarrow Q) \wedge (Q \Rightarrow R)] \Rightarrow (P \Rightarrow R)$	Hypothetical Syllogism
7.	$(P \Rightarrow Q) \Rightarrow [(Q \Rightarrow R) \Rightarrow (P \Rightarrow R)]$	
8.	$[(P \Rightarrow Q) \wedge (R \Rightarrow S) \Rightarrow [(P \wedge R) \Rightarrow (Q \wedge S)]$	
9.	$[(P \Leftrightarrow Q) \wedge (Q \Leftrightarrow R)] \Rightarrow (P \Leftrightarrow R)$	

Example 8.1.15: State the converse and contrapositive of the following statements:

(a) If it rains, I am not going.
(b) I will stay only if you go.
(c) If you get 8 pounds, you can bake the cake.
(d) I can't complete the task if I don't get more help.

Solution

(a) Converse: If I don't go, then it rains.
Contrapositive: If I go, then it does not rain.
(b) Converse: If you go then I will stay
Contrapositive: If you go I will not stay
(c) Converse: If you can bake the cake you get 8 pounds.
Contrapositive: If you cannot bake the cake you don't get 8 pounds.
(d) Converse: I don't get more help if I can't complete the task.
Contrapositive: I can complete the the task if I get more help.

Example 8.1.16: For each of the following expressions, use identities to find equivalent expressions which use only $\wedge$ and $\neg$ and are as simple as possible.

(a) $P \vee Q \vee \neg R$
(b) $P \vee [(\neg Q \wedge R) \Rightarrow P]$
(c) $P \Rightarrow (Q \Rightarrow P)$

Solution

(a) $P \vee Q \vee \neg R \Leftrightarrow \neg(\neg P \wedge \neg Q) \vee \neg R$
$\Leftrightarrow \neg((\neg P \wedge \neg Q) \wedge R)$
$\Leftrightarrow \neg(\neg P \wedge \neg Q \wedge R)$
(b) $P \vee [(\neg Q \wedge R) \Rightarrow] \Leftrightarrow \neg(\neg P \wedge \neg[(\neg Q \wedge R) \Rightarrow P])$
$\Leftrightarrow \neg(\neg P \wedge \neg(\neg(\neg Q \wedge R) \vee P)]$
$\Leftrightarrow \neg(\neg P \wedge ((\neg Q \wedge R) \wedge \neg P)]$
(c) $P \Rightarrow (Q \Rightarrow P) \Leftrightarrow P \Rightarrow (\neg Q \vee P)$
$\Leftrightarrow \neg P \vee (\neg Q \vee P)$
$\Leftrightarrow (\neg P \vee P) \vee \neg Q$
$\Leftrightarrow 1 \vee \neg Q$
$\Leftrightarrow 1$

Example 8.1.17: For each of the following expressions, use identities to find equivalent expressions which use only $\vee$ and $\neg$ and are as simple as possible.

(a) $(P \wedge Q) \wedge \neg P$
(b) $[P \Rightarrow (Q \vee \neg R)] \wedge \neg P \wedge Q.$

Solution

(a) $(P \wedge Q) \wedge \neg P \Leftrightarrow \neg[\neg(P \wedge Q) \vee P]$

$$\Leftrightarrow \neg[\neg P \vee \neg Q \vee P]$$

(b) $[P \Rightarrow (Q \vee \neg R)] \wedge \neg P \wedge Q$

$$\Leftrightarrow [\neg P \vee (Q \vee \neg R)] \wedge (\neg P \wedge Q)$$
$$\Leftrightarrow \neg P \vee (Q \vee \neg R) \wedge \neg P \wedge Q$$
$$\Leftrightarrow (\neg P \wedge \neg P \wedge Q) \vee (Q \wedge (\neg P \wedge Q)) \vee (\neg R \wedge (\neg P \wedge Q))$$
$$\Leftrightarrow (\neg P \wedge Q) \vee (Q \wedge \neg P) \vee (\neg P \wedge Q \wedge \neg R) \vee [(Q \wedge \neg P)(1 \wedge \neg R)]$$
$$\Leftrightarrow \neg (P \vee \neg Q).$$

Example 8.1.18: Establish the following tautologies by simplifying the left side to the form of the right side:

(a) $[(P \wedge Q) \Rightarrow P) \Leftrightarrow 1]$
(b) $\neg(\neg(P \vee Q) \Rightarrow \neg P) \Leftrightarrow 0$
(c) $[(P \Rightarrow \neg P) \wedge (\neg P \Rightarrow P)] \Leftrightarrow 0$

Solution

(a) $[(P \wedge Q) \Rightarrow P] \Leftrightarrow \neg(P \wedge Q) \vee P$

$$\Leftrightarrow \neg P \vee \neg Q \vee P$$
$$\Leftrightarrow (P \vee \neg P) \vee \neg Q$$
$$\Leftrightarrow 1 \vee \neg Q$$
$$\Leftrightarrow 1$$

(b) $\neg(\neg(P \vee Q) \Rightarrow \neg P$

$$\Leftrightarrow \neg[(P \vee Q) \vee \neg P]$$
$$\Leftrightarrow \neg[P \vee \neg P) \vee Q]$$
$$\Leftrightarrow \neg[1 \vee Q]$$
$$\Leftrightarrow \neg[1]$$
$$\Leftrightarrow 0$$

(c) $[(P \Rightarrow \neg P) \wedge (\neg P \Rightarrow P)]$

$$\Leftrightarrow [(\neg P \vee \neg P) \wedge (P \vee P)]$$
$$\Leftrightarrow \neg P \wedge P$$
$$\Leftrightarrow 0$$

Example 8.1.19: Using the truth table of $\Rightarrow$, relate the following assertion to the logical operator $\Rightarrow$: "If you start with a false assumption, you can prove anything you like".

Solution

P	Q	$P \Rightarrow Q$
T	T	T
T	F	F
F	T	T
F	F	T

Suppose P is false.

Then $P \Rightarrow Q$ is true for any proposition Q. If we know $P \Rightarrow Q$ as true, and accept P as true, then we can infer the truth of Q.

Q may or may not be true (as seen in truth table).

Example 8.1.20: The Sheffer stroke, or nand operator, is defined by the following truth table:

P	Q	$P \mid Q$
0	0	1
0	1	1
1	0	1
1	1	0

Nand is an acronym for not and, $P \mid Q$ is logically equivalent to $\neg (P \wedge Q)$.

Show that (a) $P \mid P \Leftrightarrow \neg P$

(b) $(P \mid P) \mid (Q \mid Q) \Leftrightarrow P \vee Q$

(c) $(P \mid Q) \mid (P \mid Q) \Leftrightarrow P \wedge Q$.

Solution

P	Q	$P \wedge Q$	$\neg (P \wedge Q)$
T	T	T	F
T	F	F	T
F	T	F	T
F	F	F	T

$P \mid Q \Leftrightarrow \neg (P \wedge Q)$. (NAND).

(a) $P|P \Leftrightarrow \neg P$ (To prove)

We know $P|Q \Leftrightarrow \neg(P \wedge Q)$

$$P|P \Leftrightarrow \neg(P \wedge P)$$
$$\Leftrightarrow \neg P.$$

Hence proved.

(b) $(P|P)|(Q|Q) \Leftrightarrow P \vee Q$ (To prove)

We have from (a), $P|P \Leftrightarrow \neg P$

$$Q|Q \Leftrightarrow \neg Q$$
$$(P|P)|(Q|Q)$$
$$\Leftrightarrow \neg P|\neg Q$$
$$\Leftrightarrow \neg(\neg P \wedge \neg Q)$$
$$\Leftrightarrow P \vee Q.$$

Hence proved.

(c) $(P|Q)|(P|Q) \Leftrightarrow P \wedge Q$ (To prove)

$P|Q = \neg(P \wedge Q)$

$$(P|Q)|(P|Q)$$
$$\Leftrightarrow [\neg(P \wedge Q)]|[\neg(P \wedge Q)]$$
$$\Leftrightarrow \neg[[\neg(P \wedge Q) \wedge [\neg(P \wedge Q))]$$
$$\Leftrightarrow \neg[(P \vee Q) \wedge (P \vee Q)$$
$$\Leftrightarrow \neg(P \vee Q)$$
$$\Leftrightarrow P \wedge Q.$$

Hence proved.

Example 8.1.21: Establish the following implications:

(a) $\neg P \Rightarrow (P \Rightarrow Q)$
(b) $\neg(P \Rightarrow Q) \Rightarrow P$
(c) $\neg Q \wedge (P \Rightarrow Q) \Rightarrow \neg P$

Solution

(a) $\neg P \Rightarrow (P \Rightarrow Q)$

P	Q	$\neg P$	$P \Rightarrow Q$	$\neg P \Rightarrow (P \Rightarrow Q)$
T	T	F	T	T
T	F	F	F	T
F	T	T	T	T
F	F	T	T	T

∴ It is a Tautology.

Hence proved.

(b) $\neg(P \Rightarrow Q) \Rightarrow P$

P	Q	$P \Rightarrow Q$	$\neg(P \Rightarrow Q)$	$\neg(P \Rightarrow Q) \Rightarrow P$
T	T	T	F	T
T	F	F	T	T
F	T	T	F	T
F	F	T	F	T

$\therefore$ It is a tautology.
Hence proved.

(c) $\neg Q \wedge (P \Rightarrow Q) \Rightarrow \neg P$

P	Q	$\neg Q$	$P \Rightarrow Q$	$\neg P$	$\neg Q \wedge (P \Rightarrow Q)$	$\neg Q \wedge (P \Rightarrow Q) \Rightarrow \neg P$
T	T	F	T	F	F	T
T	F	T	F	F	F	T
F	T	F	T	T	F	T
F	F	T	T	T	T	T

$\therefore$ It is a tautology.
Hence proved.

Example 8.1.22: Show that

$$((P \vee Q) \wedge \neg(\neg P \wedge (\neg Q \vee \neg R))) \vee (\neg P \wedge \neg Q) \vee (\neg P \wedge \neg R)$$

is a tautology.

Solution

$$((P \vee Q) \wedge \neg(P \wedge (\neg Q \vee \neg R))) \vee (\neg P \wedge \neg Q) \vee (\neg P \wedge \neg R)$$
$$\Leftrightarrow ((P \vee Q) \wedge \neg(\neg P \wedge \neg(Q \wedge R)) \vee \neg(P \vee Q) \vee (\neg(P \vee R))$$
$$\Leftrightarrow ((P \vee Q) \wedge (P \vee (Q \wedge R)) \vee \neg(P \vee Q) \vee \neg(P \vee R)$$
$$\Leftrightarrow [(P \vee Q) \wedge ((P \vee Q) \vee \neg[(P \vee Q) \wedge (P \vee R)]$$
$$\Leftrightarrow [(P \vee Q) \wedge (P \vee R)] \vee \neg(P \vee (Q \wedge R))$$
$$\Leftrightarrow [P \vee (Q \wedge R)] \vee \neg[P \vee (Q \wedge R)]$$
$$\Leftrightarrow T$$

Hence the given formula is a tautology.

Example 8.1.23: Show that $(P \rightarrow Q) \wedge (R \rightarrow Q)$ and $(P \vee R) \rightarrow Q$ are equivalent formulae.

Solution

$$\begin{aligned}(P \to Q) \wedge (R \to Q) &\Leftrightarrow (\neg P \vee Q) \wedge (\neg R \vee Q)\\ &\Leftrightarrow (\neg P \wedge \neg R) \vee Q\\ &\Leftrightarrow \neg (P \vee R) \vee Q\\ &\Leftrightarrow (P \vee R) \to Q\end{aligned}$$

Hence proved.

Example 8.1.24: Prove that

$$\neg (P \wedge Q) \to (\neg P \vee (\neg P \vee Q)) \Rightarrow (\neg P \vee Q).$$

$$\begin{aligned}\neg (P \vee Q) \to (\neg P \vee (\neg P \vee Q))\\ &\Rightarrow (P \wedge Q) \vee [\neg P \vee (\neg P \vee Q)]\\ &\Rightarrow (P \wedge Q) \vee (\neg P \vee Q)\\ &\Rightarrow (P \wedge Q) \vee \neg P \vee Q\\ &\Rightarrow ((P \wedge Q) \vee \neg P) \vee Q\\ &\Rightarrow ((P \vee \neg P) \wedge (Q \vee \neg P) \vee Q\\ &\Rightarrow (T \wedge (Q \vee \neg P)) \vee Q\\ &\Rightarrow (Q \vee \neg P) \vee Q\\ &\Rightarrow Q \vee \neg P\\ &\Rightarrow \neg P \vee Q\end{aligned}$$

Hence proved.

Example 8.1.25: Show that $S \vee R$ is tautologically implied by $(P \vee Q) \wedge (P \to R) \wedge (Q \to S)$.

Solution

Assume that $(P \vee Q) \wedge (P \to R) \wedge (Q \to S)$ has the truth value T.

$(P \vee Q), (P \to R)$ and $(Q \to S)$ all have truth value T. As the truth value of $P \vee Q$ is T, either P has Truth value T or Q have truth value T.

Suppose P has the value T. As $P \to R$ has truth value T, R should have truth value T. On the other hand suppose Q has the truth value T. As $Q \to S$ has truth value T, S should have truth value T. Thus either R has truth value T or S has truth value T, i.e., $R \vee S$ has truth value T.

Therefore $(P \vee Q) \wedge (P \to R) \wedge (Q \to S)$ is tautologically implied by $S \vee R$.

8.2 LOGICAL INFERENCE

Rule P : A premise may be introduced at any point in the derivation.

Rule T : A formula S may be introduced in a derivation if S is tautologically implied by any one or more of the preceding formula in the derivation.

Rule CP : If we can derive S from R and a set of premises, then we an derive $R \to S$ from the set of premises alone. (Deduction Theorem).

Rules of Inference

Implications:

I_1 $P \wedge Q \Rightarrow P$ (Simplification)
I_2 $P \wedge Q \Rightarrow Q$
I_3 $P \Rightarrow P \vee Q$ (addition)
I_4 $Q \Rightarrow P \vee Q$
I_5 $\neg P \Rightarrow P \to Q$
I_6 $Q \Rightarrow P \to Q$
I_7 $\neg (P \to Q) \Rightarrow P$
I_8 $\neg (P \to Q) = \neg Q$
I_9 $P, Q \Rightarrow P \wedge Q$
I_{10} $\neg P, P \vee Q \Rightarrow Q$ (disjunctive syllogism)
I_{11} $P, P \to Q \Rightarrow Q$ (Modus Ponens)
I_{12} $\neg Q, P \to Q \Rightarrow \neg P$ (Modus Tollens)
I_{13} $P \to Q, Q \to R \Rightarrow P \to R$ (Hypothetical Syllogism)
I_{14} $P \vee Q, P \to R, Q \to R \Rightarrow R$ (dilemma)

Equivalences

E_1 $\neg\neg P \Leftrightarrow P$ (double Negation)
E_2 $P \wedge Q \Leftrightarrow Q \wedge P$ (Commutative laws)
E_3 $P \vee Q \Leftrightarrow Q \vee P$
E_4 $(P \wedge Q) \wedge R \Leftrightarrow P \wedge (Q \wedge R)$ (Associative laws)
E_5 $(P \vee Q) \vee R \Leftrightarrow P \vee (Q \vee R)$
E_6 $P \vee (Q \wedge R) \Leftrightarrow (P \vee Q) \wedge (P \vee R)$ (Distributive law)
E_7 $P \wedge (Q \wedge R) \Leftrightarrow (P \wedge Q) \vee (P \wedge R)$
E_8 $\neg (P \wedge Q) \Leftrightarrow \neg P \vee \neg Q$ (De Morgan's laws)
E_9 $\neg (P \vee Q) \Leftrightarrow \neg P \wedge \neg Q$
E_{10} $P \vee P \Leftrightarrow P$
E_{11} $P \wedge P \Leftrightarrow P$
E_{12} $R \vee (P \wedge \neg P) \Leftrightarrow R$
E_{13} $R \wedge (P \vee \neg P) \Leftrightarrow R$
E_{14} $R \vee (P \vee \neg P) \Leftrightarrow T$

E_{15} $R \wedge (P \wedge \neg P) \Leftrightarrow F$

E_{16} $P \rightarrow Q \Leftrightarrow \neg P \vee Q$

E_{17} $\neg (P \rightarrow Q) \Leftrightarrow P \wedge \neg Q$

E_{18} $P \rightarrow Q \Leftrightarrow \neg Q \rightarrow \neg P$

E_{19} $P \rightarrow (Q \rightarrow R) \Leftrightarrow (P \wedge Q) \rightarrow R$

E_{20} $\neg (P \Leftrightarrow Q) \Leftrightarrow P \Leftrightarrow \neg Q$

E_{21} $P \Leftrightarrow Q \Leftrightarrow (P \rightarrow Q) \wedge (Q \rightarrow P)$

E_{22} $(P \Leftrightarrow Q) \Leftrightarrow (P \wedge Q) \vee (\neg P \wedge \neg Q)$

Example 8.2.1: Show that $R \vee S$ follows logically from the premises $C \vee D, (C \vee D) \rightarrow \neg H, \neg H \rightarrow (A \wedge \neg B)$ and $(A \wedge \neg B) \rightarrow (R \vee S)$.

Solution

1. $C \vee D \rightarrow \neg H$ — P
2. $\neg H \rightarrow (A \wedge \neg B)$ — P
3. $C \vee D \rightarrow (A \wedge \neg B)$ — Using Hyp. Syll in (1), (2)
4. $(A \wedge \neg B) \rightarrow (R \vee S)$ — P
5. $(C \vee D) \rightarrow (R \vee S)$ — Using Hyp. Syll. in (3), (4)
6. $C \vee D$ — P
7. $R \vee S$ — Modus Ponens

Example 8.2.2: Show that $S \vee R$ is tautologically implied by

$$(P \vee Q) \wedge (P \rightarrow R) \wedge (Q \rightarrow S).$$

Solution

1. $P \vee Q$ — P
2. $\neg P \rightarrow Q$ — $(\because P \rightarrow P \Leftrightarrow (\neg P \vee Q))$
3. $Q \rightarrow S$ — P
4. $\neg P \rightarrow S$ — (2), (3), Hyp. Syll.
5. $\neg S \rightarrow P$ — (From (4), using $(P \rightarrow Q \Leftrightarrow \neg Q \rightarrow \neg P)$)
6. $P \rightarrow R$ — P
7. $\neg S \rightarrow R$ — (5), (6) & Hyp. Syll.
8. $S \vee R$

Example 8.2.3: Show that $R \wedge (P \vee Q)$ is a valid conclusion from the premises $P \vee Q, Q \rightarrow R, P \rightarrow M$ and $\neg M$.

Solution

1.	$P \rightarrow M$	P
2.	$\neg M$	P
3.	$\neg P$	(1), (2), Modus Tollens
4.	$P \vee Q$	P
5.	Q	Simplification of (4)
6.	$Q \rightarrow R$	P
7.	R	Modus Ponens
8.	$R \wedge (P \vee Q)$	$(\because P, Q \Rightarrow P \wedge Q)$

Hence proved.

Example 8.2.4: Demonstrate that S is a valid inference from the premises $P \rightarrow \neg Q, Q \vee R, \neg S \rightarrow P$ and $\neg R$.

Solution:

1.	$Q \vee R$	P
2.	$\neg R$	P
3.	Q	(1), (2), Disj. Syll.
4.	$P \rightarrow \neg Q$	P
5.	$\neg P$	(3), (4), Contrapositive, Modus Tollens
6.	$\neg S \rightarrow P$	P
7.	S	(5), (6), Modus Tollens

Example 8.2.5: Show that $\neg Q, P \rightarrow Q \Rightarrow \neg P$.

Solution

1.	$P \rightarrow Q$	P
2.	$\neg Q \rightarrow \neg P$	T, (1) and contra positive $[P \rightarrow Q \Leftrightarrow \neg Q \rightarrow \neg P]$
3.	$\neg Q$	P
4.	$\neg P$	T, (2), (3) and Modus Ponens. $[P \rightarrow Q, P \Rightarrow Q]$

Example 8.2.5: Show that $R \vee S$ is a valid conclusion from the premises $C \vee D, C \vee D \rightarrow \neg H, \neg H \rightarrow (A \wedge \neg B)$ and $(A \wedge \neg B) \rightarrow (R \vee S)$.

Solution

1.	$C \vee D$	P
2.	$C \vee D \to \neg H$	P
3.	$\neg H$	(1), (2), Modus Ponens
4.	$\neg H \to (A \wedge \neg B)$	P
5.	$A \wedge \neg B$	(3), (4), Modus Ponens
6.	$(A \wedge \neg B) \to (R \vee S)$	P
7.	$R \vee S$	(5), (6), Modus Ponens

Example 8.2.6: State whether the following argument is valid or not. If valid, give proof. If not valid, give counter example.

If a baby is hungry the baby cries.
If the baby is not mad, then he does not cry.
If a baby is mad, then he has a red face.
Therefore, if a baby is hungry, then he has a red face.

Solution

H : Baby is hungry
C : Baby cries
M : Baby is mad
R : Baby has a red face.

Given:
$$H \to C$$
$$\neg M \to \neg C$$
$$\underline{M \to R}$$
$$\therefore H \to R$$

Verification:

1.	$H \to C$	Premise
2.	$\neg M \to \neg C$	Premise
3.	$C \to M$	(2), Contrapositive
4.	$H \to M$	(1), (3), Hyp. Syll.
5.	$M \to R$	Premise
6.	$H \to R$	(4), (5), Hyp. Syll.

Example 8.2.7: State whether the following argument is valied or not.

"If Nixon is not re-elected, then Tulsa will lose its air base. Nixon will be re-elected if and only if Tulsa votes for him. If Tulsa keeps its air base, Nixon will be re-elected. Therefore, Nixon will be re-elected".

Solution

R : Nixon is re-elected
L : Tulsa will lost its air base
V : Tulsa votes for Nixon

Given:

$$\left.\begin{array}{ll}(1) & \neg R \to L \\ (2) & R \leftrightarrow V \\ (3) & \neg L \to R\end{array}\right\} \text{Premises}$$

$\therefore$ R

(1) and (3) are equivalent.

$$(\neg L \to R) \wedge (R \leftrightarrow V) \Rightarrow R$$

L	R	V	$(\neg L \to R)$	$(R \leftrightarrow V)$	$(\neg L \to R) \wedge (R \leftrightarrow V)$	$(\neg L \to R) \wedge (R \leftrightarrow V) \Rightarrow R$
T	T	T	T	T	T	T
T	T	F	T	F	F	T
T	F	T	F	F	F	T
T	F	F	F	F	F	T
F	T	T	T	T	T	T
F	T	F	T	F	F	T
F	F	T	T	F	F	T
F	F	F	T	F	T	F

Therefore the given implication is "*not a Tautology.*" Therefore the argument is not valid.

Example 8.2.8: For each of the following sets of premises, list the relevant conclusions which can be drawn and the rules of inference used in each case.

(a) I am either fat or thin, I'm certanly not thin.
(b) If I run I got out of breath. I'm not out of breath.
(c) If the butler did it, then his hands are dirty. The butler's hands are dirty.
(d) Blue skies make me happy and gray skies make me sad. The sky is either blue or gray.

Solution

(a) F : I am fat
T : I am thin

$$\begin{array}{l} F \vee T \\ \neg T \\ \hline \therefore F \\ \hline \end{array}$$

(1)	$F \vee T$	P
(2)	$\neg T$	P
(3)	F	(1), (2), Dis. syll. $(7Q, P \vee Q \Rightarrow P)$

Conclusion: I am Fat

(b) R : I run
B : I get out of breath

$$\begin{array}{l} R \rightarrow B \\ \neg B \\ \hline \therefore \neg R \\ \hline \end{array}$$

(1)	$R \rightarrow B$	P
(2)	$\neg B$	P
(3)	$\neg R$	(1), (2), Mol - Tolens $(\neg Q, P \rightarrow Q \Rightarrow \neg P)$

Conclusion: I didn't run

(c) B : Butler did it
H: Hands are dirty.

$$\begin{array}{c} B \rightarrow H \\ H \\ \hline \text{Conclusion: Hypothesis} \\ \hline \end{array}$$

(d) B : Blue skies
H : Make me happy
G : Gray skies
S : Makes me sad

1.	$B \rightarrow H$	P
2.	$B \vee G$	P
3.	B	(2), Simplification
4.	H	(1), (3), Modus Ponens
5.	$G \rightarrow S$	P
6.	$B \vee G$	P
7.	G	(6), Simplification

Conclusion: I am either happy or sad.

Example 8.2.9: For each of the following set of premises, list the relevant conclusions which can be drawn and the rules of inference used in each case.

(a) If my program runs, then I am happy. If I am happy, the sun shines. It's 11.00 p.m. and very dark.

(b) All trignometric functions are periodic functions and all periodic functions are continuous functions.

Solution

P: My program runs
H: I am happy
S: Sun shines
τ: It's 11 pm.
$\neg S$: It is very dark

$$\left.\begin{array}{l} P \to H \\ H \to S \\ C \wedge \neg S \end{array}\right\} \text{Hypotheses}$$

1.	$P \to H$	P
2.	$H \to S$	P
3.	$P \to S$	(1), (2)
4.	$\tau \wedge \neg S$	P
5.	$\neg S \wedge C$	
6.	$\neg S$	Simplification
7.	$\neg P$	(3), (6), Modus Tollens
8.	$\neg H$	(1), (7), Modus Tollens
9.	$\neg P \wedge \neg H$	Conjunction

Conclusion: I am not happy and my program does not run.

(b) T: Trignometric functions
P: Periodic functions
C: Continuous functions

$$\begin{array}{c} T \to P \\ P \to C \\ \hline \therefore T \to C \end{array}$$

Conclusion: All Trignometric functions are continuous functions.

Example 8.2.10: Construct a proof for each of the following arguments, giving all necessary additional assertions. Specify the rules of inference used at each step. (The word "or" denotes the "logical or" rather than the "exclusive or".

(a) It is not the case that IBM or Xerox will take over the copier market. If RCA returns to the computer market, then IBM will take over the copier market. Hence, RCA will not return to the computer market.

(b) (My program runs successfully) or (the system bombs and I blow my stack). Furthermore, (the system does not bomb) or (I don't blow my stack and my program runs successfully). Therefore, my program runs successfully.

Solution

(a) IBM: IBM will take over the copier market
Xerox: Xerox will take over the copier market
RCA: RCA returns to the computer market

(1) $\neg$ (IBM $\vee$ Xerox)
(2) RCA $\rightarrow$ IBM

$\therefore \neg$ RCA

Proof:

1.	$\neg$ (IBM $\vee$ xerox)	*P*
2.	RCA $\rightarrow$ IBM	*P*
3.	$\neg$IBM $\wedge$ $\neg$ xerox	(1), De Morgan's Law
4.	$\neg$IBM	(3), Simplification
5.	$\neg$RCA	(2), (4), Modus Tollens

(b) *S*: My program runs successfully
B: System bombs
BS: I blow my stack

$$\neg B \vee (\neg BS \wedge S)$$
$$S \vee (B \wedge BS)$$
$$\therefore S \quad \text{(To prove)}$$

Proof:

1.	$S \vee (B \wedge BS)$	*P*
2.	$\neg B \vee (\neg BS \wedge S)$	*P*
3.	$(S \vee B) \wedge (S \vee BS)$	Distributivity of (1)
4.	$(\neg B \vee \neg BS) \wedge (\neg B \vee S)$	Distributivity of (2)
5.	$S \vee B$	(3), Simplification
6.	$\neg B \vee S$	(4), Simplification
7.	$S \vee \neg B$	(6)
8.	$(S \vee B) \wedge (S \vee \neg B)$	(5), (7), Conj.
9.	$S \vee (B \wedge \neg B)$	
10.	$S \vee 0$	
11.	S	

Hence proved.

Example 8.2.11: Determine which of the following arguments are valid-contruct proofs for the valid arguments.

(a) $A \wedge B$
$A \Rightarrow C$
$\therefore C \wedge B$

(b) $A \vee B$
$A \Rightarrow C$
$\therefore C \vee B$

(c) $A \Rightarrow B$
$A \Rightarrow C$
$\therefore C \Rightarrow B$

(d) $A \Rightarrow (B \vee C)$
$D \Rightarrow \neg C$
$B \Rightarrow \neg A$
A
D
$\therefore B \wedge \neg B$

Solution

(a) Given

$$\begin{array}{l} A \wedge B \\ A \Rightarrow C \\ \hline \therefore C \wedge B \end{array}$$

1.	$A \wedge B$	P
2.	$A \rightarrow C$	
3.	A	(1), Simplification
4.	C	(2), (3), Modus Ponens

Therefore the given argument is INVALID.

(b) Given

$$\begin{array}{l} A \vee B \\ A \Rightarrow C \\ \hline \therefore C \vee B \end{array}$$

1.	$A \vee B$	P
2.	$A \Rightarrow C$	P
3.	$\neg B \rightarrow A$	(2), Implication
4.	$\neg B \rightarrow C$	(2), (3), Hyp. Syll.
5.	$B \vee C$	(4), Implication

Hence the argument is VALID.

(c) Given

$$\begin{array}{l} A \Rightarrow B \\ A \Rightarrow C \\ \hline \therefore C \Rightarrow B \end{array}$$

A	B	C	$A \to B$	$A \to C$	$(A \to B) \wedge (A \to C)$	$C \to B$	$(A \to B) \wedge (A \to C) \Rightarrow C \to B$
T	T	T	T	T	T	T	T
T	T	F	T	F	F	T	T
T	F	T	F	T	F	T	T
T	F	F	F	F	F	T	T
F	T	T	T	T	T	F	F
F	T	F	T	T	T	T	T
F	F	T	T	T	T	F	F
F	F	F	T	T	T	T	T

⇒ Not a Tautology
⇒ Argument is INVALID.

(d) Given:

$$A \to (B \vee C)$$
$$D \to \neg C$$
$$B \to \neg A$$
$$A$$
$$D$$
$$\therefore B \wedge \neg B$$

1.	$A \to (B \vee C)$	P
2.	A	P
3.	$B \vee C$	(1), (2), Modus Ponens
4.	$D \to \neg C$	P
5.	D	P
6.	$\neg C$	(4), (5), Modus Ponens
7.	$B \to \neg A$	
8.	$\neg(\neg A) \to \neg B$	(7), Implication
9.	$A \to \neg B$	(8), Simplification
10.	$\neg B$	(2), (9), Modus Ponens
11.	B	(3), Simplification
12.	$B \wedge \neg B$	(10), (11), Conjunction

⇒ Argument is VALID.

Example 8.2.12: Determine whether the following argument is valid or not. Give the proof if it is valid.

"If today is Tuesday, then I have a test in Computer Science or a test in Economics. If my Economics Professor is sick, then I will not have a test in Economics. Today is Tuesday and my Economic Professor is sick. Therefore, I have a test in Computer Science".

Solution

T: Today is Tuesday
CS: I have a test in Computer Science
E: I have a test in Economics
EP: Economics Professor is sick.

(1) $T \rightarrow (CS \vee E)$
(2) $EP \rightarrow \neg E$
(3) $T \wedge E$

$\therefore CS$

1.	$T \rightarrow (CS \vee E)$	P
2.	$EP \rightarrow \neg E$	P
3.	$T \wedge E$	P
4.	T	(3), Simplification
5.	$CS \vee E$	(1), (4), Modus Ponens
6.	E	(3), Simplification
7.	$\neg E$	(2), (6)
8.	CS	(5), (7), Disj. Syll.

$\therefore$ The Argument is VALID.

8.3 PREDICATES AND QUANTIFIERS

Assertions which are formed using variables in a "template" that expresses the property of an object or a relationship between objects are called "Predicates".

Example:

(i) "He is dark and ugly" is written as
"x is dark and ugly".

(ii) "Naveena lives in Maryland and
Menon Lakshmi lives in Texas" is written as
"x lives in Maryland and
y lives in Texas".

Predicates are used in Control Statements in high level languages.

Predicates may be either "constants" or "variables". Values of the individual variables are drawn from a set of values called "Universe of discourse".

In order to change a predicate into a proposition, each individual variable of the predicate should be "bound". There are two ways of doing it.

(i) The first way to bind an individual variable is by assigning a value to it.

Example: $P =$ "$a + b = 6$".
which is denoted by P(x, y).
If $a = 2$, and $b = 3$, then
$P(2, 3)$ is false.

(ii) The second way to bind an individual variable is by "quantification" of the variable.

It can be done either by "universal" or "extential".

"For all values of x, the assertion $P(x)$ is true."

"For all x, $P(x)$" is written as "$\forall_x P(x)$", where $\forall$ is a "Universal Quantifier".

"There exists a value of x for which the assertion $P(x)$ is true". This statement is written as "$\exists_x P(x)$" where $\exists$ is called "External Quantifier".

The proposition $\forall_x P(x)$ is equivalent to the conjunction

$$P(1) \wedge P(2) \wedge P(3) \wedge P(4)$$

for the universal consisting of integers 1, 2, 3, and 4.

The proposition $\exists_x P(x)$ is equivalent to the disjunction

$$P(1) \vee P(2) \vee P(3) \vee P(4)$$

The proposition $\exists! x P(x)$ is equivalent to the proposition

$$[P(1) \wedge \neg P(2) \wedge \neg P(3)] \vee [P(2) \wedge \neg P(1) \wedge \neg P(3)]$$
$$\vee [P(3) \wedge \neg P(1) \wedge \neg P(2)]$$

Note that the sequence $\forall_x \forall_y$ can always be replaced by $\forall_y \forall_x$, and the sequence $\exists_x \exists_y$ can always be replaced by $\exists_y \exists_x$, though the order in which individual variables are bound cannot always be changed without affecting the meaning of an assertion.

Example 8.3.1: Let $S(x, y, z)$ denote the predicate "$x + y = z$". $P(x, y, z)$ denote "$x \cdot y = z$" and $L(x, y)$ denote "$x < y$". Let the universe of discourse be the natural numbers N. Using the above predicates, express the following assertions. The phrase "there is an x" does not imply that x has a unique value.

(a) For every x and y, there is a z such that $x + y = z$.
(b) No x is less than 0.
(c) For all x, $x + 0 = x$.
(d) For all x, $x - y = y$ for all y.
(e) There is an x such that $x \cdot y = y$ for all y.

Solution:

$S(x, y, z) : x + y = z$
$P(x, y, z) : x - y = z$
$L(x, y) : x < y$

Universe of Discourse : N.

(a) $\forall_x \forall_y \exists_z (x + y = z)$ i.e. $\forall_x \forall_y \exists_z \leq (x, y, z)$
(b) $\forall_x (\neg L(x,0))$ or $\neg \exists_x [L(x,0)]$
(c) $\forall_x \ S(x,0,x)$
(d) $\forall_x \forall_y P(x, y, x)$
(e) $\exists_x \forall_y \ P(x, y, y)$

Example 8.3.2: Show that $\exists_x \exists_y P(x, y)$ and $\exists_y \exists_x P(x, y)$ are equivalent by expanding the expressions into infinite disjunctions.

Proof: To prove: $\exists_x \exists_y P(x, y) = \exists_y \exists_x P(x, y)$.

$$\begin{aligned}
\exists_x \exists_y P(x, y) &= [\exists_y P(0, y)] \vee [\exists_y P(1, y)] \vee [\exists_y P(2, y)] \ \ldots\ldots \\
&= [P(0,0) \vee P(0,1) \vee P(0,2) \ \ldots\ldots] \\
&\quad \vee [P(1,0) \vee P(1,1) \vee P(1,2) \ \ldots\ldots] \\
&\quad \vee [P(2,0) \vee P(2,1) \vee P(2,2) \ \ldots\ldots] \\
&\quad \vee \ldots\ldots \\
&= [P(0,0) \vee P(1,0) \vee P(2,0) \vee \ldots\ldots] \\
&\quad \vee [P(0,1) \vee P(1,1) \vee P(2,1) \vee \ldots\ldots] \\
&\quad \vee [P(0,2) \vee P(1,2) \vee P(2,2) \vee \ldots\ldots] \\
&\quad \vee \ldots\ldots \\
&= [\exists_x P(x,0)] \vee [\exists_x P(x,1)] \vee [\exists_x P(x,2)] \vee \ldots\ldots \\
&= \exists_y \exists_x P(x, y).
\end{aligned}$$

Hence Proved. □

Example 8.3.3: Determine which of the following propositions are true if the universe is the set of integers I and $\cdot$ denotes the operation of multiplication.

(a) $\forall_x \exists_y [x \cdot y = 0]$
(b) $\forall_x \exists!\, y [x \cdot y = 1]$

(c) $\exists_y \forall_x [x \cdot y = 1]$
(d) $\exists_y \forall_x [x \cdot y = x]$

Solution

(a) $\forall_y \exists_y [x \cdot y = 0]$
$y = 0$ makes it TRUE.

(b) $\forall_x \exists!\, y[x \cdot y = 1]$ False

(c) $\exists_y \forall_x [x \cdot y = 1]$

$$1 \cdot y = 1$$
$$2 \cdot y = 1$$
$$y = \frac{1}{2} \notin I.$$

False.

(d) $\exists_y \forall_x [x \cdot y = x]$

$$1 \cdot 1 = 1$$
$$2 \cdot 1 = 2$$

$y = 1$ makes it true.

Example 8.3.4: Let the universe be the integers. For each of the following assertions, find a predicate P which makes the implication false.

(a) $\forall_x \exists!\, y\, P(x, y) \Rightarrow \exists!\, y \forall_x\, P(x, y)$
(b) $\exists!\, y \forall_x\, P(x, y) \Rightarrow \forall_x \exists!\, y\, P(x, y)$

Solution

(a) $\forall_x \exists!\, y\, P(x, y) \Rightarrow \exists!\, y \forall_x\, P(x, y)$

$$x + y = 0$$

LHS:

$$x + (-1) = 0$$
$$x = 1$$
$$x + (-2) = 0$$
$$x = 2$$

RHS:

$$\exists!\, y,\ x = 1,$$
$$1 + y = 0$$
$$y = -1$$

$$\exists!\, y,\ x = 2, 2 + y = 0$$
$$y = -2$$

$P(x, y)$ is $(x + y) = 0.$

(b) $\exists! y \forall_x P(x, y) \Rightarrow \forall_x \exists! y P(x, y)$

$$xy = 0$$

LHS: (i) $y=0$ RHS: $x(0)=0$

$y=0$ $x = 1, 2, 3, \ldots$

(ii) $y=0$

$y=0$

$$\boxed{P(x, y) \text{ is } xy = 0.}$$

Example 8.3.5: Specify the universe of discourse for which the following propositions are true. Try to choose the universe to be as large a subset of integers as possible.

(a) $\forall_x [x > 10]$
(b) $\forall [x = 3]$
(c) $\forall_x \exists_y [x + y = 436]$
(d) $\exists_y \forall_x [x + y < 0]$.

Solution

(a) Universe of discourse: "All Integers greater than 10".
(b) Universe of discourse: "The Universe has 3 only".
(c) Universe of discourse: I
(d) Universe of discourse: I

Example 8.3.6: Let the universe of discourse consists of the integers 0 and 1. Find finite disjunctions and conjunctions of propositions which do not use quantifiers and which are equivalent to the following:

(a) $\forall_x P(0, x)$
(b) $\forall_x \forall_y P(x, y)$
(c) $\forall_x \exists_y P(x, y)$
(d) $\exists_x \forall_y P(x, y)$
(e) $\exists_y \exists_x P(x, y)$

Solution

$$U = 0, 1.$$

(a) $\forall_x P(0, x) = P(0,0) \wedge (0,1)$.
(b) $\forall_x \forall_y P(x, y) = P(0,0) \wedge P(0,1) \wedge P(1,0) \wedge P(1,1)$
(c) $\forall_x \exists_y P(x, y) = [P(0,0) \vee P(0,1)] \wedge [P(1,0) \vee P(1,1)]$
(d) $\exists_x \forall_y P(x, y) = [P(0,0) \wedge P(1,0)] \vee [P(0,1) \wedge P(1,1)]$
(e) $\exists_y \exists_x P(x, y) = P(0,0) \vee P(0,1) \vee P(1,0) \vee P(1,1)$.

Example 8.3.7: Consider the universe of integers I.

(a) Find a predictate $P(x)$ which is false regardless of whether the variable x is bound by $\forall$ or $\exists$.
(b) Find a predicate $P(x)$ which is true regardless of whether the variable x is bound by $\forall$ or $\exists$.
(c) Is it possible for a predicate $P(x)$ to be true regardless of whether the variable is bound by $\forall$, $\exists$, or $\exists!$?

Solution

(a) $P(x): x = x + 1$
(b) $P(x) = x \neq x + 1$
(c) Yes.
$P(x)$: $x \neq x + 1$ is true regardless of whether the variable is bound by $\forall$, $\exists$, or $\exists!$

Example 8.3.8: Consider the universe of integers and let $P(x, y, z)$ denote $x - y = z$. Transcribe the following assertions into logical notation.

(a) For every x and y, there is some z such that $x - y = z$
(b) For every x and y, there is some z such that $x - z = y$
(c) There is an x such that for all y, $y - x = y$.
(d) When 0 is subtracted from any integer, the result is the original integer.
(e) 3 subtracted from 5 gives 2.

Solution

$$P(x, y, z): x - y = z.$$

(a) $\forall_x \forall_y \exists_z P(x, y, z)$
(b) $\forall_x \forall_y \exists_z P(x, y, z)$
(c) $\exists_x \forall_y P(y, x, y)$
(d) $P(x, 0, x)$
(e) $P(5, 3, 2)$

8.4 QUANTIFIERS AND LOGICAL OPERATORS

The transcription of mathematical statements involves predicates, quantifiers and logical operators.

Assume that "Universe of discourse" is I and let

$E(x)$, x –even
$O(x)$, x–odd
$P(x)$, x–prime
$N(x)$, x non-negative.

(i) Every integer is even or odd.

$$\forall_x [E(x) \vee O(x)]$$

(ii) The only even prime is two

$$\forall_x [E(x) \wedge P(x) \Rightarrow x = 2]$$

(iii) Not all primes are odd.

$$\neg\forall_x \ [P(x) \Rightarrow O(x)], \exists_x [P(x) \wedge \neg \ O(x)].$$

(iv) If an integer is not odd, then its even.

$$\forall_x [\neg O(x) \Rightarrow E(x)]$$

The quantifiers may go anywhere in the transcription of mathematical statements.

Let $P(x, y, z)$ denote "$xy = z$" for the universe of integers. Informal statements of propositions frequently omit the universal quantification of individual variables.

(i) "If $x = 0$, then $xy = x$ for all vlaues of y"

$$\forall_x [x = 0 \Rightarrow \forall_y \ P(x, y, x)]$$

(ii) "If $xy = x$ for every y, then $x = 0$".

$$\forall_x [\forall_y \ P(x, y, x) \Rightarrow x = 0]$$

Propagation of negations through quantifier sequences is useful in constructing proofs and counterexamples.

As an example, consider there exists a z such that $x + z = y$, for every pair of integers x and y. This is stated as:

$$\forall_x \forall_y \ \exists_z [x + z = y]$$

This is true for universe of integers I, but not true for the natural numbers N. We establish the falsity for the universe N by showing that its negation is true.

The negation has the form

$$\neg\forall_x \forall_y \exists_z [x + z = y]$$

which is difficult to interpret.

The equivalent form

$$\exists_x \exists_y \ \forall_y \ \neg[x + z = y], \text{ or } \exists_x \exists_y \ \forall_z \ [x + z \neq y]$$

is more tractable and can easily be shown to be true for the nonnegative integers by choosing $x > y$.

Logical Relations

1. $\forall_x P(x) \Rightarrow P(c)$, *where c* is an arbitrary element of universe.
2. $P(c) \Rightarrow \exists_x P(x)$, where c is an arbitrary element of universe.
3. $\forall_x \neg P(x) \Leftrightarrow \neg \exists_x P(x)$
4. $\forall_x P(x) \Leftrightarrow \neg P(x)$
5. $\exists_x \neg P(x) \Leftrightarrow \neg \forall_x P(x)$
6. $[\forall_x P(x) \wedge Q] \Leftrightarrow \forall_x [P(x) \wedge Q]$
7. $[\forall_x P(x) \vee Q] \Leftrightarrow \forall_x [P(x) \vee Q]$
8. $[\forall_x P(x) \wedge \forall_x Q(x)] \Leftrightarrow \forall_x [P(x) \wedge Q(x)]$
9. $[\forall_x P(x) \vee \forall_x Q(x)] \Leftrightarrow \forall_x [P(x) \vee Q(x)]$
10. $[\exists_x P(x) \wedge Q] \Leftrightarrow \exists_x [P(x) \wedge Q]$
11. $[\exists_x P(x) \vee Q] \Leftrightarrow \exists_x [P(x) \vee Q]$
12. $\exists_x [P(x) \wedge Q(x)] \Leftrightarrow [\exists_x P(x) \wedge \exists_x Q(x)]$
13. $[\exists_x P(x) \vee \exists_x Q(x)] \Leftrightarrow [\exists_x P(x) \vee Q(x)]$

Example 8.4.1: Let $P(x, y, z)$ denote $xy = z$; $E(x, y)$ denote $x = y$; and $G(x, y)$ denote $x > y$.

Let the universe of discourse be the integers. Transcribe the following into logical notation.

(a) If $y = 1$, then $xy = x$ for any x.
(b) If $xy \neq 0$, then $x \neq 0$ and $y \neq 0$
(c) If $xy = 0$, then $x = 0$ or $y = 0$.
(d) $3x = 6$ if and only if $x = 2$.
(e) There is no solution to $x^2 = y$ unless $y \geq 0$.
(f) $x < z$ is a necessary condition for $x < y$ and $y < z$.
(g) $x \leq y$ and $y \leq x$ is a sufficient condition for $y = x$.
(h) If $x < y$ and $z < 0$, then $xz < yz$.
(i) It cannot happen that $x = y$ and $x < y$.
(j) If $x < y$ then for some z such that $z < 0$, $xz > yz$.
(k) There is an x such that for every y and z, $xy = xz$.

Solution

(a) If $y = 1$, then $xy = x$ for any x.

$$\forall_y [E(y,1) \Rightarrow \forall_x [P(x, y, x)]]$$

(b) If $xy \neq 0$, then $x \neq 0$ and $y \neq 0$.

$$\forall_x \forall_y [\neg P(x, y, 0) \Rightarrow \neg E(0, y) \wedge \neg E(x, 0)]$$

(c) If $xy = 0$, then $x = 0$, and $y = 0$.

$$\forall_x \forall_y [P(x, y, 0) \Rightarrow E(0, y) \wedge E(x, 0)]$$

(d) $3x = 6$ if and only if $x = 2$

$$\forall_x [P(3,x,6) \Leftrightarrow E(x,2)]$$

(e) There is no solution to $x^2 = y$ unless $y \geq 0$.

$$\forall_x [\neg (x,x,y) \Leftrightarrow \neg [G(y,0) \vee E(y,0)]]$$

(f) $x < z$ is a necessary condition for $x < y$ and $y < z$.

$$\forall_x \forall_y \forall_z [[\neg G(x,y) \wedge \neg G(y,z)] \Rightarrow \neg G(x,z)]$$

(g) $x \leq y$ and $y \leq x$ is a sufficient condition for $y = x$.

$$\forall_x \forall_y [[\neg G(x,y) \wedge \neg G(y,x)] \Rightarrow E(y,x)]$$

(h) If $x < y$ and $z > 0$, then $xz > yz$.

$$\forall_x \forall_y \forall_z [(G(y,x) \wedge G(0,z) \Rightarrow \forall_u \forall_v [[P(x,z,u) \wedge P(y,z,v)]] \Rightarrow G(u,v)$$

(i) It cannot happen that $x = y$ and $x < y$.

$$\neg \forall_x \forall_y [E(x,y) \wedge G(y,x)]$$

(j) If $x < y$ then for some z such that $z < 0$, $xz > yz$.

$$\forall_x \forall_y [(G(y,x) \wedge \exists_y G(0,z)] \Rightarrow \forall_u \forall_v [[P(x,z,u) \wedge P(y,z,v)]] \Rightarrow G(u,v).$$

(k) Do it yourself.

Example 8.4.2: Let the universe of discourse be the set of arithmetic assertions with predicates defined as follows:

$P(x)$ denotes "x is provable".
$T(x)$ denotes "x is true".
$S(x)$ denotes "x is satisfiable".
$D(x, y, z)$ denotes "z is the disjunction $x \vee y$"

Translate the following assertions into English statements.

(a) $\forall_x [P(x) \Rightarrow T(x)]$
(b) $\forall_x [T(x) \vee \neg S(x)]$
(c) $\exists_x [T(x) \wedge \neg P(x)]$
(d) $\forall_x \forall_y \forall_z \{[D(x,y,z) \wedge P(z)] \Rightarrow [P(x) \vee P(y)]\}$
(e) $\forall_x \{T(x) \Rightarrow \forall_y \forall_z [D(x,y,z) \Rightarrow T(z)]\}$

Solution

(a) $\forall_x [P(x) \Rightarrow T(x)]$
If x is provable, then x is true.

(b) $\forall_x [T(x) \vee \neg S(x)]$
If x is true or it is unsatisfiable.

(c) $\exists_x [T(x) \wedge \neg P(x)]$
There is some x, for which x is true and it not provable.

(d) $\forall_x \forall_y \forall_z \{[D(x, y, z) \wedge P(z)] \Rightarrow [P(x) \vee P(y)]\}$
If the assertion $z = x \vee y$ and the assertion $p(z)$ is provable, then either x is provable or y is provable.

(e) $\forall_x \{T(x) \Rightarrow \forall_y \forall_z [D(x, y, z) \Rightarrow T(z)]\}$
If every arithmetic assertion is true, then the assertion $z = x \vee y$is true.

Example 8.4.3: Write the following using logical notation. Choose predicates so that each assertion requires at least one quantifier.

(a) There is one and only one even prime
(b) No odd numbers are even.
(c) Every train is fasten than some cars.
(d) Some cars are slower than all trains but at least one train is faster than every car.
(e) If it trains tomorrow, then somebody will get wet.

Solution

(a) $P(x)$: x is prime
$E(x)$: x is even
$\exists ! x[P(x) \wedge E(x)]$

(b) $P(x)$: x is odd
$E(x)$: x is even
$\neg \exists_x [0(x) \wedge E(x)]$

(c) $T(x)$: x is a train
$C(y)$: y is a car
$F(x, y)$: x is faster than y.

$$\forall_x [T(x) \Rightarrow \exists_y (C(y) \wedge F(x, y))]$$

(d) $\forall_x \exists_y [C(y) \wedge \neg F(x, y)] \wedge \exists_x \exists_y [T(x) \wedge F(x, y)]$

(e) R: It rains tomorrow.
$W(x)$: x will get wet.

$$R \Rightarrow \exists_x [w(x)].$$

Example 8.4.4: Find an assertion which is logically equivalent to $\forall_x P(x)$ but uses only the quantifier $\exists$ and the logical operator $\neg$. Similarly, express $\exists_x P(x)$ in terms of $\forall$ and $\neg$. Similarly, express $\exists_x P(x)$ in terms of $\forall$ and $\neg$.

Solution

(i) $\forall_x P(x) \Leftrightarrow \neg(\neg \forall_x P(x))$

$\Leftrightarrow \neg(\exists_x \neg P(x))$

$\Leftrightarrow \neg \exists_x \neg P(x).$

(ii) $\exists_x P(x) \Leftrightarrow \neg(\neg \exists_x P(x))$

$\Leftrightarrow \neg(\forall_x \neg P(x))$

$\Leftrightarrow \neg \forall_x \neg P(x).$

Example 8.4.5: Find an assertion which is logically equivalent to $\exists! x P(x)$ but which uses only the quantifiers $\forall$ and $\exists$ together with the predicate for equality and logical operators.

Solution

$$\exists! x P(x) \Leftrightarrow \exists_x [P(x) \wedge \forall_y [P(y) \Rightarrow y = x]$$

Example 8.4.6: Find whether the assertion

$$\forall_x [P(x) \Rightarrow Q(x)] \Rightarrow [\forall_x P(x) \Rightarrow \forall_x Q(x)]$$

is true or not.

Solution:

$P(x)$	$Q(x)$	$\forall_x P(x) \Rightarrow Q(x)$	$\forall_x P(x) \Rightarrow \forall_x Q(x)$
T	T	T	T
T	T	T	T
T	F	F	F
T	F	F	F
F	T	T	T
F	T	T	T
F	F	T	T
F	F	T	T

The assertion is "TRUE".

Example 8.4.7: For a universe containing only the elements 0 and 1, expand $\exists_x [P(x) \wedge Q(x)]$ and $[\exists_x P(x) \wedge \exists_x Q(x)]$ into propositions involving $P(0), P(1), \ldots$ etc., and without quantifiers. Rearrange the terms of the expansion to show that

$$\exists_x[P(x)\wedge Q(x)] \Rightarrow [\exists_x P(x)\wedge \exists_x Q(x)]$$

Solution

$$\begin{aligned}\exists_x[P(x)\wedge Q(x)] &\Leftrightarrow [(P(0)\wedge P(0)]\vee[(P(1)\wedge Q(1)]\\ &\Leftrightarrow [[P(0)\wedge Q(0)]\vee P(1)]\wedge[(P(0)\wedge Q(0))\vee Q(1)]\\ &\Leftrightarrow [[P(0)\vee P(1)]\wedge[Q(0)\vee P(1)]\wedge[[P(0)\vee Q(1)]\\ &\quad \wedge[Q(0)\vee Q(1)]]\\ &\Leftrightarrow [[P(0)\vee P(1)]\wedge[Q(0)\vee Q(1)]]\\ &\Leftrightarrow \exists_x P(x)\wedge \exists_x Q(x) \quad \text{(for this universe).}\end{aligned}$$

Hence proved.

Example 8.4.8: For each of the following sets of premises, list the relevant conclusions which can be drawn and the rules of inference used in each case.

(a) All cows are mammals. Some mammals chew their cud.
(b) All even integers are divisible by 2. The integer 4 is even but 3 is not.
(c) What's good for the auto industry is good for the country. What's good for the country is good for you. What's good for the auto industry is for you to buy an expensive car.

Solution

(a) $C(x)$: is x is a cow.
$M(x)$: x is a mammal.
$D(x)$: x chew their cud
$\forall_x[C(x)\rightarrow M(x)]$
$\exists_x M(x)\rightarrow D(x)$.

(b) $E(x)$: x is an even Integer.
$D(x)$: x is divisible by 2.
$E(x)\rightarrow D(x)$.

(c) $A(x)$:x is good for the auto industry
$C(x)$: x is good for the country
$Y(x)$: x is good for you.
b = "You buying an expensive car" (constant)

$$\forall_x[A(x)\rightarrow C(x)] \quad (1)$$

$$\forall_x[C(x)\rightarrow Y(x)] \quad (2)$$

$$A(b) \quad (3)$$

By US,

$$A(b)\rightarrow C(b) \quad (4)$$

$$C(b)\rightarrow Y(b) \quad (5)$$

(3), (4), Modus Ponens, C(b) (6)

(5), (6), Modus Ponens, Y(b) (7)

By conjunction, $C(b) \wedge Y(b)$

Conclusion: It is good for the country and for you to buy an expensive car.

Example 8.4.9: Determine the validity of the argument: "It is not the case that some trigonometric functions are not periodic. Some periodic functions are continuous. Therefore, it is not true that all trigonometric functions are not continuous".
Construct proof, if it is valid.

Solution

$T(x)$: x is a Trigonometric function.
$P(x)$: x is a periodic function
$C(x)$: x is a continuous function.

$$\neg[\exists_x T(x) \rightarrow \neg P(x)] \qquad \forall \neg T(x) \rightarrow P(x)$$

$$\exists_x P(x) \rightarrow C(x) \qquad \exists_x P(x) \rightarrow C(x)$$

$$\therefore \neg (\forall_x T(x) \rightarrow \neg C(x) \qquad \therefore (\exists_x \neg T(x) \rightarrow C(x))$$

1.	$\forall \neg T(x) \rightarrow P(x)$	P
2.	$\neg T(a) \rightarrow P(a)$	US, (1)
3.	$\exists_x P(x) \rightarrow C(x)$	
4.	$P(a) \rightarrow C(a)$	(3), ES
5.	$\neg T(a) \rightarrow C(a)$	(2), (4), Implication
6.	$\exists_x \neg T(x) \rightarrow C(x)$	(5), EG

$\Rightarrow$ Assertion is VALID.

Example 8.4.10: Show that $(\forall_x)(\forall_y)P(x, y) \rightarrow (\neg x)(\forall_y)P(x, y)$ is logically valid.

Solution

1.	$(\forall_x)(\forall_y)P(x, y)$	P
2.	$(\forall_y)P(a, y)$	US, (1)
3.	$P(a, y)$	UG, (2)
4.	$(\exists_x)P(a, y)$	EG, (3)
5.	$(\exists_x)\forall_y P(a, y)$	UG, (4)

Example 8.4.11: Prove that $(\forall_y)(\exists_y)P(x, y) \rightarrow (\exists_x)(\exists_y)P(x, y)$ is logically valid.

Solution

1.	$(\forall_x)(\exists_y)P(x, y)$	P
2.	$(\exists_y)P(a, y)$	US, (1)
3.	$P(a, y)$	ES, (2)
4.	$(\exists_y)P(a, y)$	(3), EG
5.	$(\exists_x)(\exists_y)P(x, y)$	(4), EG

Example 8.4.12: Show that $\neg P(a, b)$ follows logically from $(\forall_x)(\forall_y)(P(x, y) \rightarrow W(x, y))$ and $\neg W(a, b)$.

Solution

1.	$(\forall_x)(\forall_y)(P(x, y) \rightarrow W(x, y))$	P
2.	$(\forall_x)(P(x, b) \rightarrow W(x, b))$	(1), US
3.	$P(a, b) \rightarrow W(a, b)$	(2), US
4.	$\neg P(a, b) \vee W(a, b)$	$P \rightarrow Q \Leftrightarrow \neg P \vee Q$
5.	$\neg W(a, b)$	P
6.	$\neg P(a, b)$	T, (5), $\neg P, P \vee Q \Rightarrow Q$

8.5 NORMAL FORMS

Let us show how to find the formula given the Truth Table.

P	Q	R	$f(P, Q, R)$	
T	T	T	T	
T	T	F	F	
T	F	T	T	
T	F	F	T	
F	T	T	F	
F	T	F	F	
F	F	T	T	
F	F	F	F	

4 Truth values are "True"

$$f(P,Q,R)=(P\wedge Q\wedge R)\vee(P\wedge\neg Q\wedge R)\vee(P\wedge\neg Q\wedge 7r)$$
$$\vee(\neg P\wedge\neg Q\wedge R)$$

Formula obtained here is a "disjunction" of terms, each of which is a "conjunction" of "statement variables" and their "negations".

A product of statement variables and their negations is called "elementary production". A sum of variables and their negations is called "elementary sum".

Disjunctive Normal Form

A formula which is equivalent to a given formula and which has a sum of elementary products is called "disjunctive Normal Form" of the formula.

Conjunctive Normal Form

A formula which is equivalent to a given formula and that has a product of elementary sums is called "conjunctive Normal form" of the formula.

Procedure to find disjunctive Normal form

(i) If the connective $\rightarrow$ and $\leftrightarrow$ appear in the given formula, obtain an equivalent formula in which $\rightarrow$ and $\leftrightarrow$ does not appear.

$\alpha\rightarrow\beta$ is replaced by $(\neg\alpha\vee\beta)$

and $\alpha\rightarrow\beta$ is replaced either by

$$(\alpha\wedge\beta)\vee(\neg\alpha\wedge\neg\beta)$$
or
$$(\neg\alpha\vee\beta)\wedge(\neg\beta\wedge\alpha)$$

(ii) Using DeMorgan's laws, an equivalent formula can be obtained in which the negation is applied to statement variables only, if the negation applied to a formula or part of the formula which is not a statement variable.

(iii) Applying the distributive law until a sum of elementary products is obtained.

This is the "Disjunctive Normal Form", after applying the Idempotent law and suitable re-ordering.

In the Normal Form, the elementary products which are equivalent to "F" (False), if any, can be ommitted.

Example 8.5.1: Obtain a disjunctive normal form of

$$P\vee(\neg P\rightarrow(Q\vee(Q\rightarrow\neg R))).$$

Solution

$$
\begin{aligned}
& P \vee (\neg P \rightarrow (Q \vee (Q \rightarrow \neg R))) \\
&\quad \Leftrightarrow P \vee (\neg P \rightarrow (Q \vee (\neg Q \vee R))) \\
&\quad \Leftrightarrow P \vee (\neg P \rightarrow [(Q \vee \neg Q) \vee (Q \vee R)] \\
&\quad \Leftrightarrow P \vee (\neg P \rightarrow [T \vee (Q \vee R)] \\
&\quad \Leftrightarrow P \vee (\neg P \rightarrow (Q \vee R)) \\
&\quad \Leftrightarrow P \vee [\neg(\neg P) \vee (Q \vee R)] \\
&\quad \Leftrightarrow P \vee [P \vee (Q \vee R)] \\
&\quad \Leftrightarrow (P \vee P) \vee [P \vee (Q \vee R)] \\
&\quad \Leftrightarrow P \vee (Q \vee R) \\
&\quad \Leftrightarrow P \vee P \vee Q \vee R \\
&\quad \Leftrightarrow P \vee Q \vee R. \qquad \text{(Answer)}
\end{aligned}
$$

Example 8.5.2: Obtain the disjunctive Normal form of

$$P \vee (\neg P \wedge \neg Q \vee R)$$

Solution

$$
\begin{aligned}
& P \vee (\neg P \wedge \neg Q \vee R) \\
&\quad \Leftrightarrow (P \vee \neg P) \wedge (P \vee \neg Q) \vee (P \vee R) \\
&\quad \Leftrightarrow P \wedge (P \vee \neg Q) \vee (P \vee R) \\
&\quad \Leftrightarrow \neg Q \vee (P \vee R) \\
&\quad \Leftrightarrow P \vee \neg Q \vee R \qquad \text{(Answer).}
\end{aligned}
$$

Example 8.5.3: Obtain the disjunctive normal form of

$$(\neg P \vee \neg Q) \rightarrow (\neg P \wedge R)$$

Solution:

$$
\begin{aligned}
& (\neg P \vee \neg Q) \rightarrow (\neg P \wedge R) \\
&\quad \Leftrightarrow [[\neg(\neg P \vee \neg Q)] \vee (\neg P \wedge R)] \\
&\quad \Leftrightarrow [(P \wedge Q) \vee (\neg P \wedge R)] \qquad \text{(Answer).}
\end{aligned}
$$

Example 8.5.4: Obtain the disjunctive normal form of

$$(P \wedge \neg(Q \wedge R)) \vee (P \rightarrow Q)$$

Solution

$$
\begin{aligned}
& (P \wedge \neg(Q \wedge R)) \vee (P \rightarrow Q) \\
&\quad \Leftrightarrow (P \wedge \neg(Q \wedge R)) \vee (\neg P \vee Q) \\
&\quad \Leftrightarrow (P \wedge (\neg Q \vee R)) \vee (\neg P \vee Q) \\
&\quad \Leftrightarrow (P \wedge \neg Q) \vee (P \wedge R) \vee (\neg P \vee Q) \\
&\quad \Leftrightarrow (P \wedge \neg Q \vee \neg P) \vee (P \wedge \neg Q \vee Q) \vee (P \wedge R)
\end{aligned}
$$

$$\Leftrightarrow (T \wedge \neg Q) \vee (P \wedge T) \vee (P \wedge R)$$
$$\Leftrightarrow 7Q \vee P \vee (P \wedge R)$$
$$\Leftrightarrow (P \wedge R) \vee P \vee \neg Q \qquad \text{(Answer)}$$

Example 8.5.5: Obtain a Disjunctive Normal Form of

$$P \rightarrow ((P \rightarrow Q) \wedge \neg(\neg Q \vee \neg P))$$

Solution

$$P \rightarrow ((P \rightarrow Q) \wedge \neg(\neg Q \vee \neg P))$$
$$\Leftrightarrow P \rightarrow [(\neg P \vee Q) \wedge (Q \wedge P)]$$
$$\Leftrightarrow \neg P \vee [(\neg P \vee Q) \wedge (Q \wedge P)]$$
$$\Leftrightarrow [\neg P \vee (\neg P \vee Q)] \wedge [\neg P \vee (Q \wedge P)]$$
$$\Leftrightarrow [\neg P \vee (\neg P \vee Q)] \wedge [(\neg P \vee Q) \wedge (F)]$$
$$\Leftrightarrow [(\neg P \vee \neg P) \vee (\neg P \vee Q)] \wedge [(\neg P \vee Q)]$$
$$\Leftrightarrow [\neg P \vee (\neg P \vee Q)] \wedge (\neg P \vee Q)$$
$$\Leftrightarrow [(\neg P \vee \neg P) \vee (\neg P \vee Q)] \wedge (\neg P \vee Q)$$
$$\Leftrightarrow [\neg P \vee Q] \wedge [\neg P \vee Q]$$
$$\Leftrightarrow \neg P \vee Q \qquad \text{(Answer)}$$

Example 8.5.6: Obtain the Conjungtive Normal Form of

$$\neg(P \vee Q) \leftrightarrow (P \wedge Q)$$

Solution

$$\neg(P \vee Q) \leftrightarrow (P \wedge Q)$$
$$\Leftrightarrow [\neg(P \vee Q) \wedge (P \wedge Q)] \vee [\neg(\neg(P \vee Q)) \wedge \neg(P \wedge Q)]$$
$$\Leftrightarrow [(\neg P \wedge \neg Q) \wedge (P \wedge Q)] \vee [(P \vee Q) \wedge (\neg P \vee \neg Q)]$$
$$\Leftrightarrow [(P \wedge \neg P \wedge Q \wedge \neg Q) \vee (P \vee Q) \wedge (\neg P \vee \neg Q)]$$
$$\Leftrightarrow (P \vee Q) \wedge (\neg P \vee \neg Q) \qquad \text{(Answer)}$$

GLOSSARY

Logic: Discipline which deals with methods of reasoning.

Proposition (statement): Any declarative sentence which is true (T) or false (F).

Truth Value: T or F are the truth values of a statement.

Liar's Paradox: This statement is false.

Connectives: AND, NOT, OR, ...

Negation: $\sim P$ or $\neg P$ (NOT P)

Conjunction: AND ($p \wedge q$)

Disjunction: OR ($p \vee q$)

Implication: Conditional $p \Rightarrow q$

Biconditional: If and only if $p \Leftrightarrow q$

Tautology: Propositional form whose truth value is true for all possible values of its propositional variables.

Contradiction: Propositional form that is always false.

Contingency: Propositional form which is neither a tautology nor a contradiction.

Modus Ponens: $(P \wedge (P \Rightarrow Q)) \Rightarrow Q$

Modus Tollens: $[(P \Rightarrow Q) \wedge \neg Q] \Rightarrow \neg P$

Disjunctive Syllogism: $[\neg P \wedge (P \wedge Q)] \Rightarrow Q$

Hypothetical Syllogism: $[(P \Rightarrow Q) \wedge (Q \Rightarrow R)] \Rightarrow (P \Rightarrow R)$

Predicates: Assertions formed using variables in a "template" that expresses the property of an object or a relationship between objects are predicates.

REVIEW QUESTIONS

1. What do you mean by a proposition?
2. Give examples for proposition.
3. State the liar's paradox.
4. What are connectives? Give examples.
5. Explain the following:
   (a) Negation (b) Conjunction (c) Disjunction
   (d) Implication (e) Biconditional.
6. Give the Truth Tables for:
   (a) Negation (b) Conjunction (c) Disjunction
   (d) Implication (e) Biconditional.
7. Explain the terms:
   (a) Tautology (b) Contradiction (c) Contingency
8. What are logical Identities? Give a few of them.
9. Explain the following:
   (a) Modus Ponens
   (b) Modus Tollens
   (c) Disjunctive Syllogism
   (d) Hypothetical Syllogism
10. What are Predicates and Quantifiers?
11. Explain the following:
    (a) Disjunctive Normal Form
    (b) Conjunctive Normal Form
12. State the procedure to find Disjunctive Normal Form.

EXERCISES

1. Which of the following sentences are propositions? What are the truth values of those that are propositions?
   (a) $x + y = y + x$ for every pair of real numbers x and y
   (b) Answer this question
   (c) $y + 2 = 17$
   (d) $7 + 5 = 10$
   (e) $3 + 2 = 5$
   (f) Bombay is the capital of India.
   (g) ISPEX is in love with 'L'JALAJABATVMU
2. Write the negation of each of the following propositions?
   (a) Summer in Kodaikanal is hot and sunny.
   (b) $7 + 8 = 15$
   (c) There is no air pollution in Karuppur
   (d) Today is friday.
3. Let p and q be the propositions
   p: I drive over 85 km per hour
   q: I get a speeding ticket.
   (a) I do not driver over 85 kmph
   (b) I will get a speeding ticket if I drive over 85 kmph.
   (c) Driving over 85 kmph is sufficient for getting a speeding ticket.
   (d) Whenever I get a speeding ticket, I am driving over 85 kmph.
4. Obtain a truth table for each of the following propositional forms:
   (a) $(\neg p) \wedge q$
   (b) $\neg (p \wedge q)$
   (c) $(\neg p) \vee (\neg q)$
   (d) $(p \wedge q) \vee r$
   (e) $(p \wedge (\neg p)) \Rightarrow p$
5. Determine whether each of the following implications is true or false.
   (a) If $2 + 2 = 6$, then $3 + 3 = 8$
   (b) If elephants can fly, then $2 + 2 = 6$
   (c) If $2 + 2 = 6$, then elephants can fly.
6. For each of the following sentences state if the sentence means if the "or" is an "inclusive or" (disjunction) or an "exclusive or" which of these meanings of "or" do you think is intended
   (a) Dinner for two includes two items from menu list I or three items from menu list II.
   (b) To take Applied Physics, you should have taken a course in Mathematics or a course in physics.

7. Write down each of the following statements in the form "if p, then q" in English.
   (a) Your guarantee is good, only if you bought your PC less than 1 year ago.
   (b) If you drive more than 800 kilometres, you have to buy diesel.
8. State the converse and contrapositive of each of the following implications.
   (a) A positive integer is a prime only if it has no divisors other than 1 and itself.
   (b) I go to class whenever there is a test.
9. Construct a truth table for each of the following compound propositions.
   (a) $(p \vee q) \vee r$
   (b) $(p \wedge q) \wedge r$
   (c) $(p \wedge q) \vee \neg r$
10. Construct a Truth table for each of the following compound propositions.
    (a) $(p \rightarrow q) \vee (\neg p \rightarrow r)$
    (b) $(p \rightarrow q) \wedge (\neg p \rightarrow r)$
    (c) $\neg p \rightarrow (q \rightarrow r)$
11. Show that $\neg(p \vee q)$ and $\neg p \wedge \neg q$ are logically equivalent by constructing Truth Table.
12. Show that the propositions $p \rightarrow q$ and $\neg p \vee q$ are logically equivalent.
13. Show that the propositions $p \vee (q \wedge r)$ and $(p \vee q) \wedge (p \vee r)$ are logically equivalent.
14. Show that $\neg(p \vee (\neg p \wedge q))$ and $\neg p \wedge \neg q$ are logically equivalent.
15. Show that $p \equiv \neg(\neg p)$.
16. Rewrite the statement: "It is not true that I am not happy" in simpler form.
17. Show that $\neg(p \wedge q) \equiv (\neg p) \vee (\neg q)$ (De Morgan's Laws)
18. Given p: The president is a Democrat
    q: The president is a Republican
    Express (a) $\neg(p \wedge q)$ (b) $(\neg p) \vee (\neg q)$.
19. Show that the statement $p \vee (\neg p)$ is a tautology.
20. Show that $(p \vee q) \vee [(\neg p) \wedge (\neg q)]$ is a tautology.
21. Show that the statement $(p \vee q) \wedge [(\neg p) \wedge (\neg q)]$ is a contradiction.
22. Simplify the statement $\neg([p \wedge (\neg q)] \wedge r)$.
23. Consider: "You will get an A if either you are clever and the sun shines, or you are clever and it rains". Rephrase the conditions more simply.
24. Show that $p \rightarrow q \equiv (\neg p) \vee q$ using Truth Table construction.
25. Verify the "Switcheroo Law" using Truth Table. $p \rightarrow q \equiv (\neg p) \vee q$.

26. Using the Switcheroo law $p \rightarrow q \equiv (7p) \vee q$ transform the following statement into a disjunction: "If 0 = 1, then I am the queen of Texas."
27. Check whether the followings statements are equivalent or not.
    (a) If it is Tuesday, this must be Mexico.
    (b) That this is Mexico is a necessary condition
    (c) Its being Tuesday is sufficient for this to be Mexico.
28. Verify whether commutative law holds good for the "conditional" i.e., $p \rightarrow q$ is the same as $q \rightarrow p$ or not?
29. Prove the valid argument:

$$\begin{array}{l} (p \vee r) \rightarrow (s \wedge t) \\ \underline{p} \\ \hline \therefore t \\ \hline \end{array}$$

30. Prove the valid argument:

$$\begin{array}{l} a \rightarrow (b \wedge c) \\ \neg b \\ \hline \therefore \neg a \\ \hline \end{array}$$

31. Prove the valid argument:

$$\begin{array}{l} p \rightarrow a \\ p \rightarrow b \\ p \\ \hline \therefore a \wedge b \\ \hline \end{array}$$

32. Check the validity of the argument:

$$\begin{array}{l} s \rightarrow r \\ (p \vee q) \rightarrow \neg r \\ \neg s \rightarrow (\neg q \rightarrow r) \\ p \\ \hline \therefore q \\ \hline \end{array}$$

33. Prove and comment on the argument:

$$\begin{array}{l} p \wedge (\neg p) \\ \hline \therefore p \\ \hline \end{array}$$

34. Show that the argument

$$\begin{array}{l} p \rightarrow q \\ q \\ \hline \therefore p \end{array}$$

is not valid.

35. Check whether the following argument is valid. If it is, then give a proof, if it is not, then give a counterexample.
"Heat dissipation accompanies every irreversible chemical reaction. Therefore, if a chemical reaction is reversible, it dissipates no heat".
36. Check whether the following is valid.
If it is, then give a proof; it it is not, then give a counterexample.
"It the moon is made of red chease, then elephants can fly and circles are round. The moon is indeed made of red cheese. Therefore elephants can fly".
37. Prove the valid argument

$$\begin{array}{l} (p \wedge q) \to (r \vee s) \\ \underline{p \wedge q} \\ \underline{\therefore r \vee s} \end{array}$$

38. Check the validity of the following arguments:

(a) $\begin{array}{l} \neg(r \vee s) \\ \underline{(p \wedge q) \to (r \vee s)} \\ \underline{\therefore \neg(p \wedge q)} \end{array}$ (b) $\begin{array}{l} p \wedge q \\ \underline{p \to r} \\ \underline{\therefore r} \end{array}$

(c) $\begin{array}{l} p \to (q \vee r) \\ p \\ \underline{\neg r} \\ \underline{q} \end{array}$

39. Let $P(x)$ denote "x spends more than six hours every weak is class", where the universe of discourse for x is the set of students. Express each of the following quantifications in English.
(a) $\exists_x P(x)$
(b) $\forall_x P(x)$
(c) $\exists_x \neg P(x)$
(d) $\forall_x \neg P(x)$
40. Given $P(x)$: x can speak Hindi
$Q(x)$: x knows computer language "Small Talk" express each of the following sentences in terms of $P(x)$, $Q(x)$, quantifiers and logical connectives. Universe of discourse is the set of all students at your school.
(a) There is a student at your school who can speak Hindi and who knows small talk.
(b) There is a student at your school who can speak Hindi but who does not know small talk.
41. Use quantifiers to express the associative law for multiplication of real numbers.

42. Prove that the statements

$$\neg \exists_x \forall_y P(x, y) \text{ and } \forall_x \exists_y \neg P(x, y)$$

have the same truth table.

43. State the truth values of the following:
(a) $\exists! x P(x) \rightarrow \exists_x P(x)$
(b) $\forall_x P(x) \rightarrow \exists! x P(x)$
(c) $\exists! \neg P(x) \rightarrow \neg \forall_x P(x)$

44. Show that $\forall_x P(x) \vee \forall_x Q(x)$ and $\forall_x (P(x) \vee Q(x))$ are not logically equivalent.

45. Show that $\forall_x P(x) \vee \exists_x Q(x)$ and $\forall_x \exists_y (P(x) \vee Q(y))$ are equivalent.

46. Obtain the principal disjunctive normal form and principal conjunctive normal form of

$$P \leftrightarrow Q.$$

47. Obtain the PDNF of the following
(a) $\neg P \vee Q$
(b) $(P \wedge Q) \vee (\neg P \wedge Q) \vee (Q \wedge R)$.

48. Obtain the disjunctive normal form of

$$P \vee (\neg P \rightarrow (Q \vee (\neg Q \rightarrow R)))$$

49. Derive the disjunctive normal form of

$$P \rightarrow ((P \rightarrow Q) \wedge (\neg Q \rightarrow R)))$$

50. Obtain the conjunctive normal form of

$$(\neg P \rightarrow R) \wedge (Q \leftrightarrow R)$$

51. State whether the following argument is valid or not. Give proof if it is valid. Otherwise give counter example.
Babies are illogical.
Nobody is despised, who can manage crocodiles.
Illogical people are despised.
Therefore babies cannot manage crocodiles.

52. If the colonel was out of the room when the murder was committed, then he could not have been right about the weapon used. Either the butler is lying or he knows who the murderer was. If Lady Sharon was not the murderer, then either colonel was in the room at the time or the butler is lying. Either the butler knows who the murdered was or the colonel was out of the room of the time of the murder. The policeman deduced that if the colonel was right about the weapon, they Lady Sharon was the murderer. Was he right?

SHORT QUESTIONS AND ANSWERS

1. Define a mathematical structure.
   It is defined as a set of axioms.
2. What is an axiom?
   An oxiom is a true statement about the properties of the structure.
3. What is logic?
   Logic is the discipline that deals with the method of reasoning. It gives a set of rules and techniques to determine whether a given argument is valid or not.
4. What are Theorems?
   True assertions which can be inferred from the truth of axioms are called 'Theorems'.
5. What is meant by 'proof' of a Theorem?
   Proof of a theorem is an argument that establishes that the theorem is true for a specified mathematical structure.
6. What is a proposition or a statement?
   Any declarative sentence which is true (T) or false (F) is called a proposition or a statement.
7. What do you mean by truth value of a statement?
   We refer to T (True) or F (False) as the truth value of the statement.
8. Give examples for statements (propositions).
   (a) $3 + 3 = 6$
   (b) It will rain tomorrow.
9. What is Liar's paradox?
   (a) "This statement is false".
   (b) "I am lying".

   Statement (b) is a pseudostatement equivalent to (a).
   Such a self-referential sentence is a Liar's Paradox.
10. Give examples of sentential connectives
    And, or, not.
11. Draw the truth table of Negation.

P	$\sim P$
T	F
F	T

12. Draw the truth table of conjunction (AND).

p	q	$p \wedge q$
T	T	T
T	F	F
F	T	F
F	F	F

13. Obtain the Negation of the statements:
    (a) Not all the doctors in this town are crooks.
    (b) I loved neither Padmaja nor Naveena.
    (a) All the doctors in this town are crooks.
    (b) I loved either Padmaja or Naveena.
14. Obtain the conjunction of the statements.
    (a) p: I am rich.
    q: You are old.
    (b) p: $8 + 8 = 17$
    q: Sun rises in the east.
    (a) $p \wedge q$: "I am rich and you are old".
    (b) $p \wedge q$: $8 + 8 = 17$ and Sun rises in the East.
15. Sketch the truth table of disjunction (OR).

p	q	$p \wedge q$
T	T	T
T	F	F
F	T	T
F	F	F

16. Obtain the disjunction of the statements
    p: Ravi did it
    q: Ram did it.
    $p \vee q$: Either Ravi or Ram did it.
17. What is meant by implication? Sketch the Truth Table.
    $p \Rightarrow q$ read as "if p, then q" is an implication.

The Truth Table is as follows.

p	q	$p \Rightarrow q$
T	T	T
T	F	F
F	T	T
F	F	T

18. What is the Truth Table of Biconditional?

Biconditional means "*q* if and only if *p*". or "*p* is equivalent to *q*".

p	q	$p \Leftrightarrow q$
T	T	T
T	F	F
F	T	F
F	F	T

19. What do you mean by Tautology?

A Tautology is a propositional form whose truth value is true for all possible values of its propositional variables.

Example: $P \vee \neg P$.

20. What do you mean by contradiction?

A contradiction or absurdity is a propositional form which is always false.

Example: $P \wedge \neg P$.

21. What do you mean by contingency?

A propositional form which is neither a tautology nor a contradiction is called a contingency.

22. What are the representations for tautology and contradiction?

Tautology $\rightarrow 1$

Contradiction $\rightarrow 0$.

23. What is Modus Ponens?

$$[P \wedge (P \Rightarrow Q)] \Rightarrow Q$$

24. What is Modus Tollens?

$$[(P \Rightarrow Q) \wedge \neg Q] \Rightarrow \neg P.$$

25. What is disjunctive syllogism?

$$[\neg P \wedge (P \vee Q)] \Rightarrow Q$$

26. What is Hypothetical Syllogism?

$$[(P \Rightarrow Q) \wedge (Q \Rightarrow R)] \Rightarrow (P \Rightarrow R)$$

27. What do you mean by contrapositive identity?

$$(P \Rightarrow Q) \Leftrightarrow (7Q \Rightarrow 7P).$$

28. Explain the logical identity: Exportation.

$$[(P \wedge Q) \Rightarrow R] \Leftrightarrow [P \Rightarrow (Q \Rightarrow R)]$$

29. Explain the logical identify: Absurdity

$$[(P \Rightarrow Q) \wedge (P \Rightarrow \neg Q)] \Leftrightarrow \neg P$$

30. Explain the logical identity: Equivalence

$$(P \Leftrightarrow Q) \Leftrightarrow [(P \Rightarrow Q) \wedge (Q \Rightarrow P)]$$

31. Explain the logical identify: Implication

$$(P \Rightarrow Q) \Leftrightarrow (\neg P \vee Q)$$

32. State the following rules of inference
    (a) Hypothetical Syllogism
    (b) Disjunctive Syllogism
    (a) $P \rightarrow Q, Q \rightarrow R \Rightarrow P \rightarrow R$
    (b) $\neg P, P \vee Q \Rightarrow Q$
33. State the following rules of inference
    (a) Modus Ponens
    (b) Modus Tollens
    (a) $P, P \rightarrow Q \Rightarrow Q$
    (b) $\neg Q, P \rightarrow Q \Rightarrow \neg P.$
34. What is double negation?

$$\neg\neg P \Leftrightarrow P$$

35. State De Morgan's laws in terms of Equivalences.

$$\neg(P \wedge Q) \Leftrightarrow \neg P \vee \neg Q$$
$$\neg(P \vee Q) \Leftrightarrow \neg P \wedge \neg Q$$

36. State Distributive Laws in terms of equivalences.

$$P \vee (Q \wedge R) \Leftrightarrow (P \vee Q) \wedge (P \vee R)$$
$$P \wedge (Q \wedge R) \Leftrightarrow (P \wedge Q) \vee (P \wedge R)$$

37. State Associative Laws in terms of equivalences.

$$(P \wedge Q) \wedge R \Leftrightarrow P \wedge (Q \vee R)$$
$$(P \vee Q) \vee R \Leftrightarrow P \vee (Q \vee R)$$

38. State Commutative laws in terms of equivalences.

$$P \wedge Q \Leftrightarrow Q \wedge P$$
$$P \vee Q \Leftrightarrow Q \wedge P$$

39. What are Predicates?

Assertions formed using variables in a "template" that expresses the property of an object or a relationship between objects are called Predicates.

Answers to Exercises

CHAPTER 0

1. (a) No (b) No (c) Yes
2. (a) Yes (b) No (c) Yes
3. (a) True (b) True (c) False
4. Suppose that $x \in A$. Since $A \subseteq B$, this implies that $x \in B$. Since $B \subseteq C$, we have $x \in C$. Since $x \in A$ implies that $x \in C$, it follows that $A \subseteq C$.
5. (a) 1 (b) 1 (c) 2 (d) 3
6. (a) $\{\phi, \{a\}\}$
   (b) $\{\phi, \{a\}, \{b\}, \{a, b\}\}$
   (c) $\{\phi, \{\phi\}, \{\{\phi\}\}, \{\phi, \{\phi\}\}\}$
7. (a) 2 (b) 16
8. (a) $\{(a, y), (b, y), (c, y), (d, y), (a, z), (b, z), (c, z), (d, z)\}$
   (b) $\{(y, a), (y, b), (y, c)(y, d), (z, a), (z, b), (z, c), (z, d)\}$
9. The set of triples (a, b, c) where a is an airline and b and c are cities.
10. $\phi \times A = \{(x, y) | x \in \phi \text{ and } y \in A\}$
    $= \phi = \{(x, y | x \in A \text{ and } y \in \phi\}$
    $= A \times \phi$
11. mn
13. (a) $\{0, 1, 2, 3, 4, 5, 6\}$
    (b) $\{3\}$
    (c) $\{1, 2, 4, 5\}$
    (d) $\{0,6\}$
18. (a) $B \subseteq A$
    (b) $A \subseteq B$
    (c) $A \cap B = \phi$
    (d) Nothing, since this is always true
    (e) $A = B$
19. (a) $\{1, 2, 3, \ldots\ldots n\}$
    (b) $\{1\}$

25. $A^2 = \{\in, a, a^2\}$
$B^3 = \{ababab\}$
$AB = \{ab, aab\}$

26. $A^* = \{\in, a, a^2, \ldots\ldots\} = \{a^n \mid n \geq 0\}$
$B^* = \{(ab)^n \mid n \geq 0\}$
$B^+ = \{(ab)^n \mid n \geq 1\}$

28. $\Sigma^+ = \Sigma^* - \{\in\}$

29. (a) $L_1 \cup L_2 = \{ab, bc, aa, ac, cb\}$
(b) $L_1 \cap L_2 = \{aa\}$
(c) $L_1 - L_2 = \{xy | x \in L_1 \wedge y \in L_2\}$
(d) $L_1 L_2 = \{abaa, abac, abcb, bcaa, bcac, bccb, caaa, caac, cacb\}$

30. $A^* = \bigcup_{i \geq 0} A^i = A^0 \cup A^1 \cup A^2 \ldots\ldots$

31. $A^+ = \bigcup_{i \geq 1} A^i = A^1 \cup A^2 \cup A^3 \ldots\ldots$

32. $A = \{a, aa\}$, $B = \{a\}$ and $C = \{aa\}$, to prove that

$$A(B \cap C) \subset AB \cap AC.$$

$AB = \{aa, aaa\}, AC = \{aaa, aaaa\}$
$AB \cap AC = \{aaa\}, B \cap C = \phi, A(B \cap C) = \phi$
$\Rightarrow A(B \cap C) \subset AB \cap AC.$

33. (a) 155 (b) 100

35. (a) We know, $A \cap B \subset A.$
If $A \subset B$, then $A \cap B = A.$
$\therefore A \cup (A \cap B) = A.$
(b) $A \cap (A \cup B) = (A \cap A) \cup (A \cap B)$
$= A \cup (A \cap B)$
$= A$ (by (a))
(c) $x \in (A - B) \Leftrightarrow x \in A \wedge x \notin B$
$\Leftrightarrow x \in A \wedge x \in \overline{B}$
$\Leftrightarrow x \in (A \cap \overline{B})$
$\forall_x [x \in (A - B)] = \forall_x [x \in (A \cap \overline{B})]$
$\therefore A - B = A \cap \overline{B}.$
(d) $A \cup (\overline{A} \wedge B) = (A \cup \overline{A}) \cap (A \cup B)$
$= U \cap (A \cup B)$
$= A \cup B.$
(e) $A \cap (\overline{A} \cup B) = (A \cap \overline{A}) \cup (A \cap B)$
$= \phi \cup (A \cap B)$
$= A \cap B.$

36. (a) No (b) No (c) No.

38. (a) only
40. Only (a) and (d) are onto functions.
41. (a) Yes (b) No (c) Yes (d) No.
46. (a) Bijection
    (b) None
47. {(1,1), (2, 2), (3, 3), (4,4)}
48. $f \circ g = x^2 + 8x + 14$
    $g \circ f = x^2 + 2$
49. (a) R = {(3, 3), (6, 2), (9, 1)}
    (b) Domain = {3, 6, 9}
    Range = {3, 2, 1}
50. (a) $R = \{(3, 2), (5, 2), (5, 4), (7, 2), (7, 4), (7, 6), (9, 2), (9, 4), (9, 6), (9, 8)\}$
    (b) Domain = {3, 5, 7, 9}
    Range = {2, 4, 6, 8}
51. (a) Transistive
    (b) Reflexive, symmetric, transitive
    (c) Symmetric
    (d) Antisymmetric.
52. (a) $2^{n(n+1)}/2$
    (b) $2^n 3^{n(n-1)}/2$
    (c) $3^{n(n-1)}/2$
    (d) $2^{n(n-1)}$
    (e) $2^{n\,(n-1)}/2$
    (f) $2^{n^2} - 2 \cdot 2^{n(n-1)}$
53. R is reflexive if and only if $(a, a) \in R$ for all $a \in A$ if and only if $(a, a) \in R^{-1}$ if and only if R^{-1} is reflexive.
54. No, Example $R = \{(1,3), (3,1)\}$
56. (a) $\{(a, b) \mid b \text{ divides } a\}$
    (b) $\{(a, b) \mid a \text{ does not divide } b\}$
57. (a) Symmetric, transitive
    (b) Reflexive, symmetric, transitive
    (c) Antisymmetric
58. $L(G) = \{b, aaa\}$
59. $G = (V, T, S, P)$ where $V = \{0, 1, S\}$ $T = \{0, 1\}$, S is the start symbol and productions are

$$S \to 0S1$$
$$S \to \lambda.$$

60. G_1: $V = \{S, 0, 1\}$, $T = \{0, 1\}$.
Production P: $S \to 0S, S \to S1, S \to \lambda$
$G_2 : V = \{S, A, 0, 1\}$, $T = \{0, 1\}$
Productions P: $S \to 0S, S \to 1A,\ S \to 1,\ A \to 1A,\ A \to 1, S \to \lambda$.

61. $G = (V, T, S, P)$
$V = \{0, 1, 2, S, A, B\}$,
$T = \{0, 1, 2\}$
S = Starting state
Productions P: $S \to 0SAB,\quad S \to \lambda,\quad BA \to AB,$
$0A \to 01,\quad 1A \to 11,\quad 1B \to 12,\quad 2B \to 22.$

62. (a) $S \to 00S,\ S \to \lambda$
(b) $S \to AS, S \to ABS, S \to A, AB \to BA, BA \to AB, A \to 0, B \to 1$
(c) $S \to ABS, S \to \lambda, AB \to BA, BA \to AB, A \to 0, B \to 1$
(d) $S \to ABS, S \to T, B \to U, T \to AT, T \to A,$
$U \to BU, U \to B, AB \to BA, BA \to AB, A \to 0, B \to 1.$

69. Let $P(n)$ be $\sum_{j=0}^{n} 3 \cdot 5^j = 3(5^{n+1} - 1)/4$.

Basis: $P(0)$ is true time since $\sum_{j=0}^{n} 3 \cdot 5^j = 3 = 3(5^1 - 1)/4$.

Induction: Assume that $\sum_{j=0}^{n} 3 \cdot 5^j = 3(5^{n+1} - 1)/4$.

Then
$$\sum_{j=0}^{n+1} 3 \cdot 5^j = \left(\sum_{j=0}^{n} 3 \cdot 5^j\right) + 3 \cdot 5^{n+1}$$
$$= 3\,(5^{n+1} - 1)/4 + 3 \cdot 5^{n+1}$$
$$= 3\,(5^{n+1} + 4.5^{n+1} - 1)/4$$
$$= 3\,(5^{n+2} - 1)/4.$$

72. Postages are 5 cents, 6 cents, 10 cents, 11 cents, 12 cents, 15 cents, 16 cents, 17 cents, 18 cents and all postages of 20 cents or more.

CHAPTER 1

1. (a)

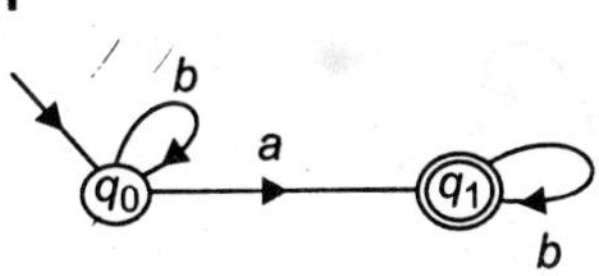

(b)

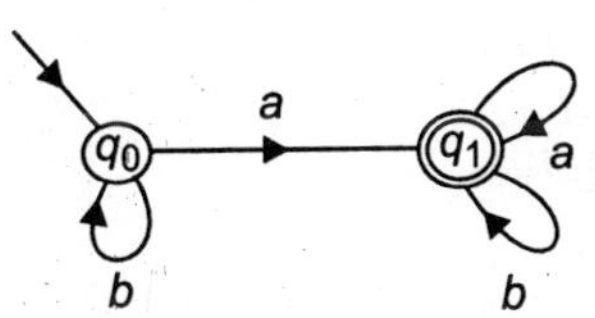

(c) 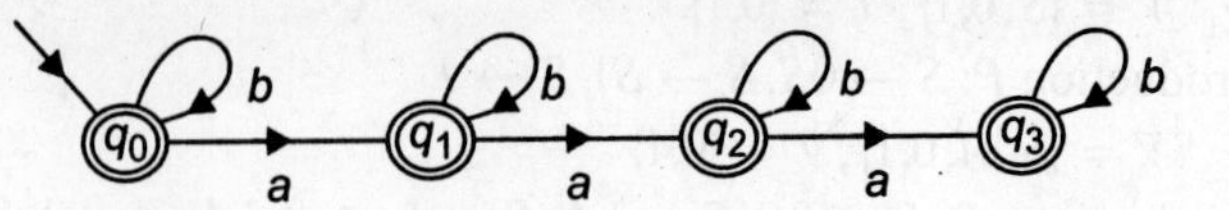

(d) (i) 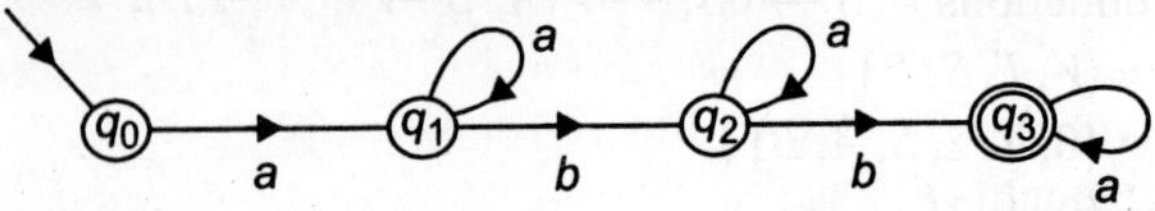

(ii) 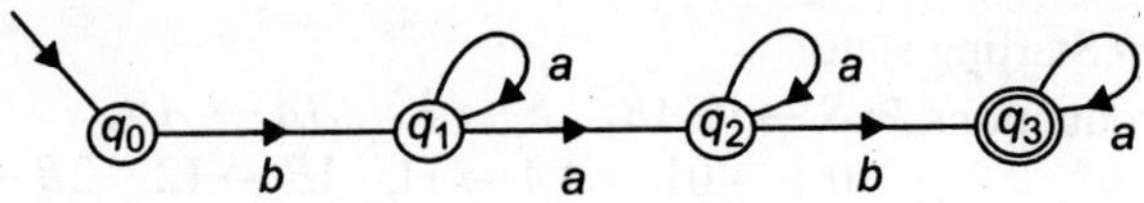

(iii) 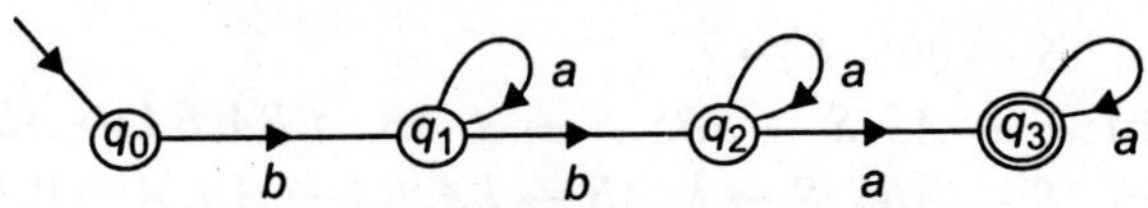

(e) 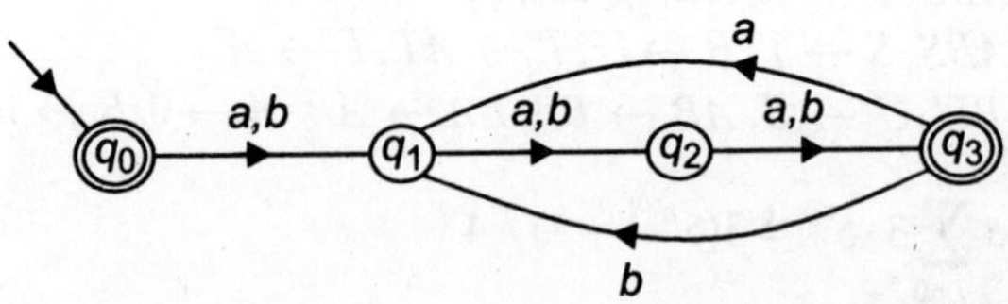

2. 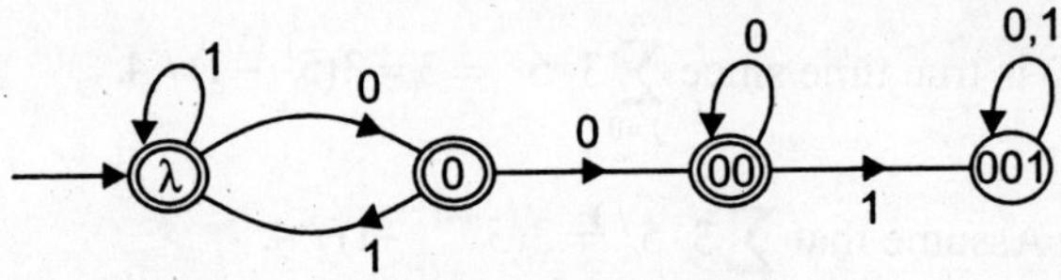

3. 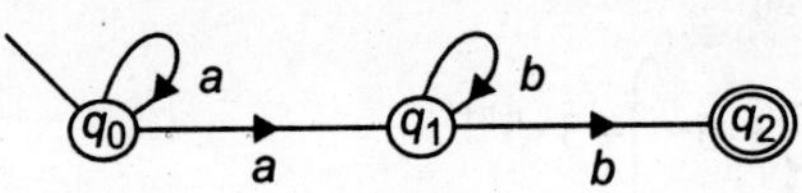

	a	b
q_0	$\{q_0, q_1\}$	$\varnothing$
q_1	$\varnothing$	$\{q_1, q_2\}$
q_2	$\varnothing$	$\varnothing$

4. 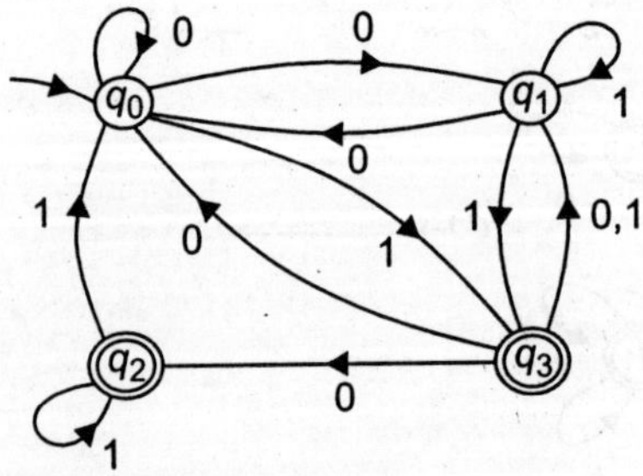

5. $L = \{0^n, 0^n01, 0^n11 / n \geq 0\}$
6. $M^1 = (\{[\varnothing],[q_0],[q_1],[q_2],[q_0,q_1],[q_0,q_2],[q_1,q_2]$
$[q_0,q_1,q_2]\}, \{a,b\}, \delta', [q_0], \{[q_1],[q_0,q_1],$
$[q_1,q_2],[q_0,q_1,q_2]\}$

which is the DFA of the form $M' = (Q', \Sigma, \delta', q_0', F')$ with δ' given by the table below.

	a	b
$[\varnothing]$	$[\varnothing]$	$[\varnothing]$
$[q_0]$	$[q_1, q_2]$	$[\varnothing]$
$[q_1]$	$[\varnothing]$	$[q_2]$
$[q_2]$	$[\varnothing]$	$[q_2]$
$[q_0, q_1]$	$[q_1, q_2]$	$[q_2]$
$[q_0, q_2]$	$[q_1, q_2]$	$[q_2]$
$[q_1, q_2]$	$[\varnothing]$	$[q_2]$
$[q_0, q_1, q_2]$	$[q_1, q_2]$	$[q_2]$

7. 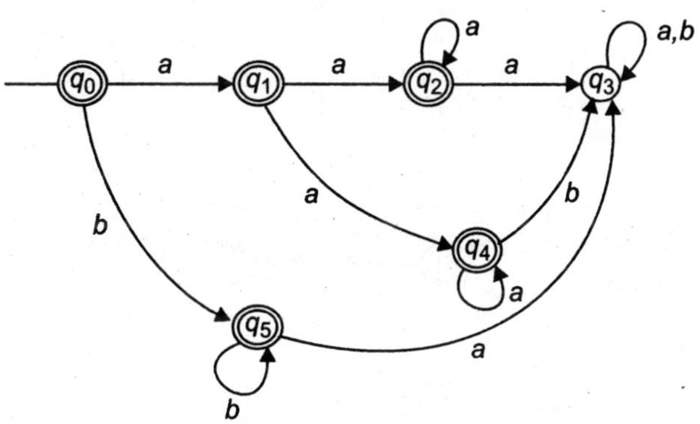

8. 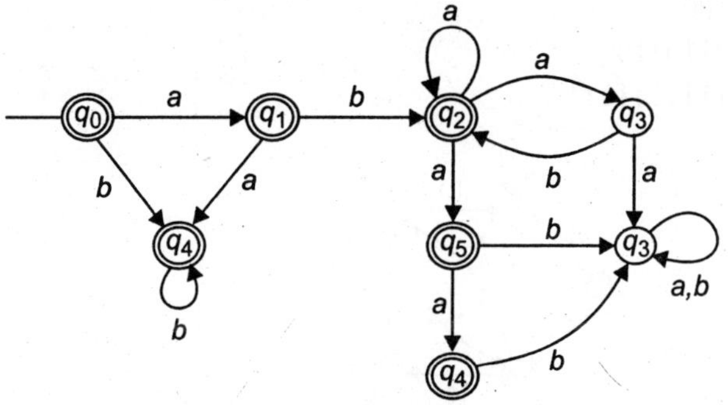

9. (a) $b^* aa^* ab^* a$

(b) $(aabb)^* + b(bab)^*(ba)^* b + (ab)^*$

(c) $a^* ba^*$

10.

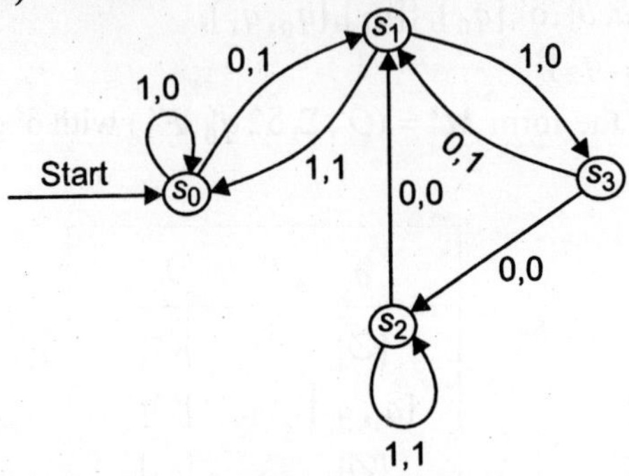

11.

State	g		h	
	Input		Input	
s_0	s_1	s_3	1	0
s_1	s_1	s_2	1	1
s_2	s_3	s_4	0	0
s_3	s_1	s_0	0	0
s_4	s_3	s_4	0	0

12.

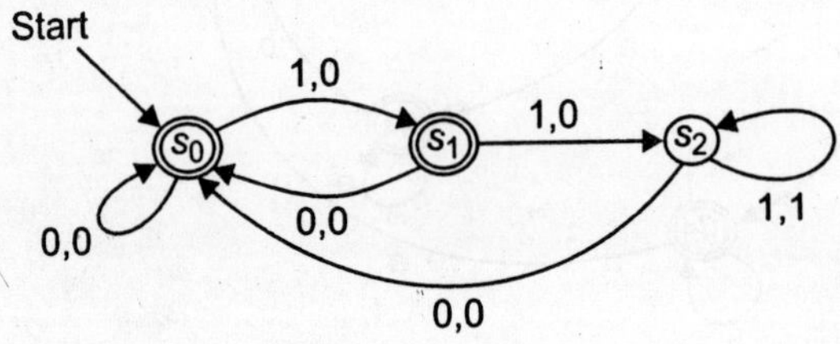

14. (a) 1100

(b) 00110110

(c) 11111111111

15.

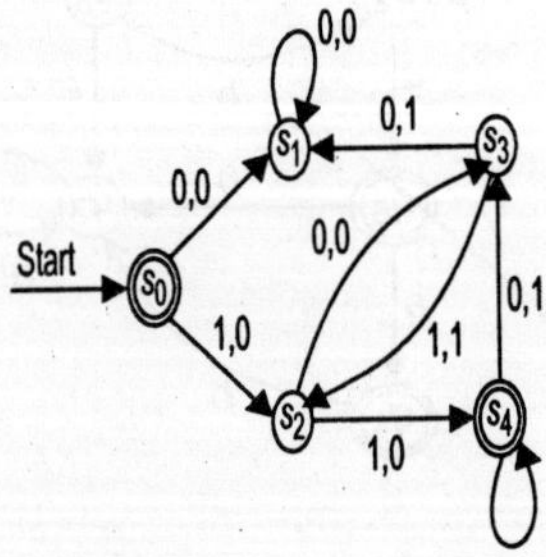

16.

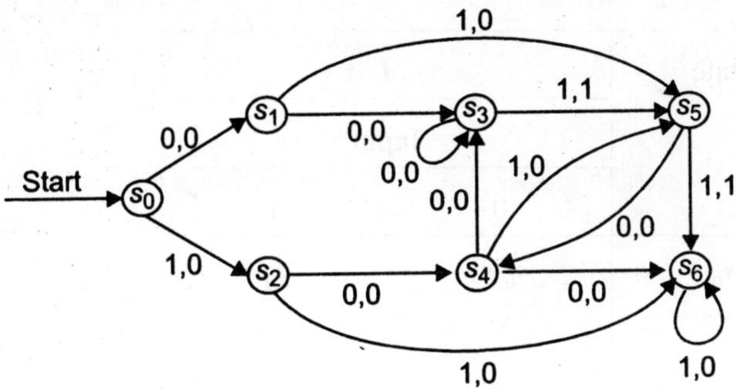

17.

	f		
	Input		
State	0	1	g
s_0	s_1	s_2	1
s_1	s_1	s_0	1
s_2	s_1	s_2	0

18. (a) 11111 (b) 1000000 (c) 100011001100

19.

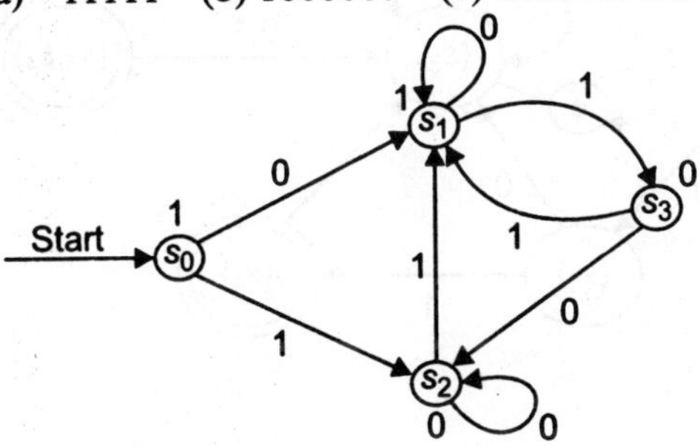

20. (a) $L_a = \{1^n \mid n = 0, 1, 2, \ldots\ldots\}$

(b) $L_b = \{1, 01\}$

(c) $L_c = \{0^n, 0^n 10x \mid n = 0, 1, 2, \ldots$ and x is any string$\}$

21.

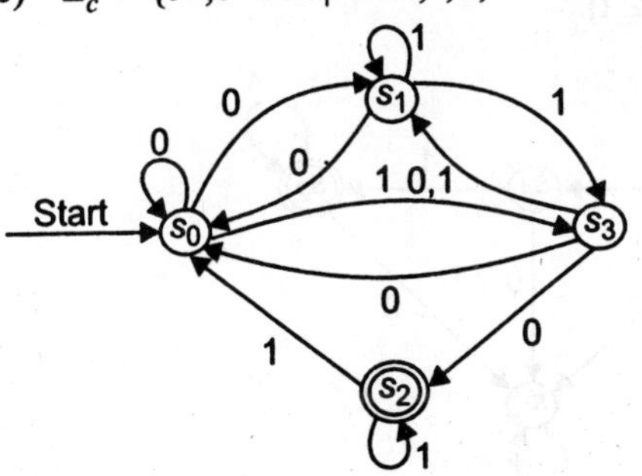

22.

State	f	
	Input	
	0	1
s_0	s_0, s_2	s_1
s_1	s_3	
s_2		s_4
s_3	s_3	
s_4	s_3	s_3

23. $L = \{0^n, 0^n01, 0^n11 \mid n \geq 0\}$

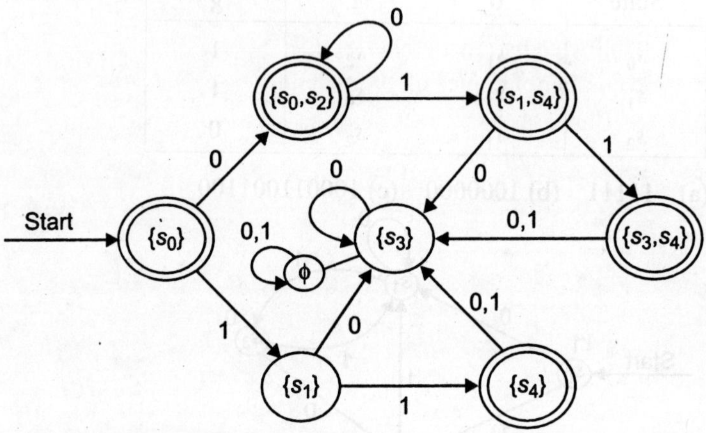

24. (a) $L = \{0, 01, 11\}$
    (b) $L = \{\lambda, 0\} \cup \{0^m1^n \mid m \geq 1, n \geq 1\}$
    (c) $L = \{10^n \mid n \geq 0\} \cup \{10^n10^m \mid n, m \geq 0\}$
25. (a) $\{0, 10, 11\}\ \{0, 1\}^*$
    (b) $(0^m1^n \mid m \geq 0 \text{ and } n \geq 1\}$
26. (a)

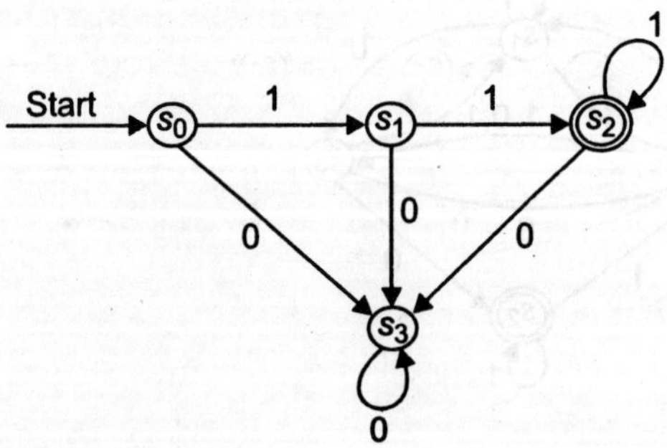

(b) 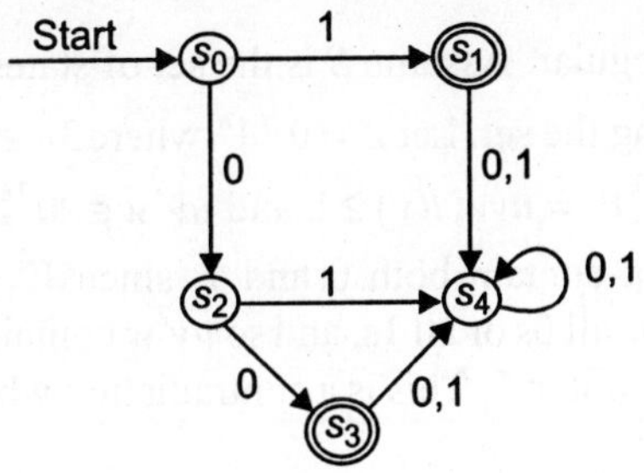

(c) 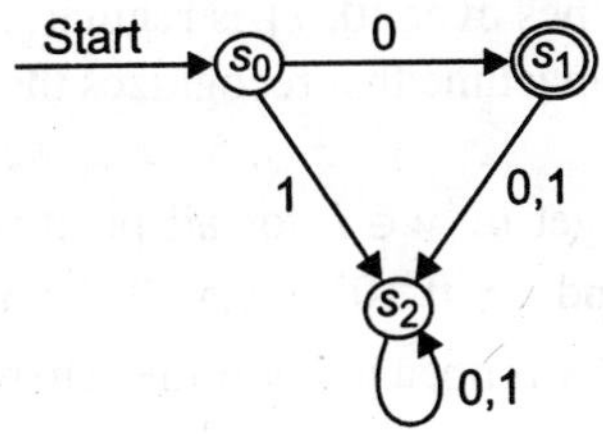

28. (a) A 1 followed by any number of 0s
    (b) Any number of copies of 10, including null string
    (c) The string 0 or the string 01
    (d) Any string beginning with 0.
    (e) Any string not ending with 0.

29. 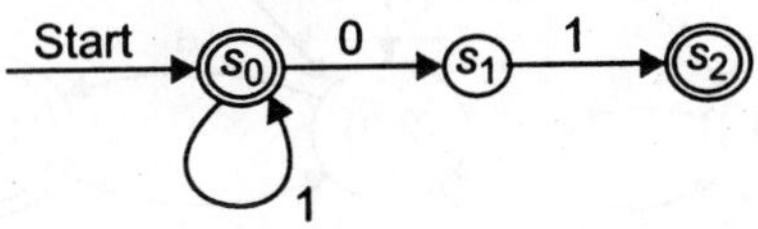

30. $G = (V, T, S, P)$
    $G = \{S, A, B, 0, 1\}$
    $T = \{0, 1\}$
    $S \to 0A, S \to 1B, S \to \lambda, A \to 0A, A \to 1B,$
    $A \to 1, B \to 0A, B \to 1B, B \to 1.$

32. (a) 00^*1
    (b) $(0 \cup 1)(0 \cup 1)(0 \cup 1)^*\ 0000^*$

34. 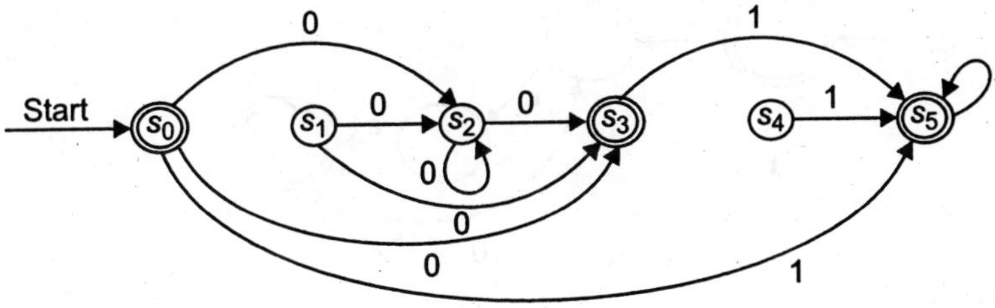

35. Assume $L = \{0^{2n}1^n\}$ is regular. Assume S is the set of states of a finite-state machine recognizing the set. Let $Z = 0^{2n}1^n$ where $3n \geq |s|$. Then by pumping lemma, $Z = 0^{2n}1^n = uvw$, $l(v) \geq 1$, and $uv^iw \in \{0^{2n}1^n \mid n \geq 0\}$. It is obvious that V cannot contain both 0 and 1, since V^2 could then contain 10. Therefore V is all 0s or all 1s, and so uv^2w contains too many 0s or too many 1s, so it is not in L. This is a contradiction which shows L is not regular.

36. Assume that the set of palindromes over {0, 1} is regular. Assume S is the set of states of a finite-state machine that recognizes the set. Let $Z = 0^n10^n$, when $n > |S|$.

Apply the pumping lemma to get $uv^iw \in L$ for all positive integers i where $l(v) \geq 1$, and $l(uv) \leq |s|$ and $z = 0^n10^n = uvw$. Then v must be a string of 0s (since $|n| > |s|$), so uv^2w is not a palindrome. Therefore the set is not regular.

37.

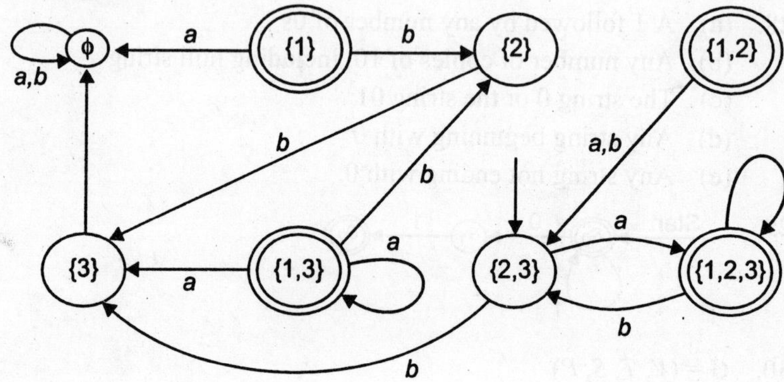

38. $(ab \cup a)^*$

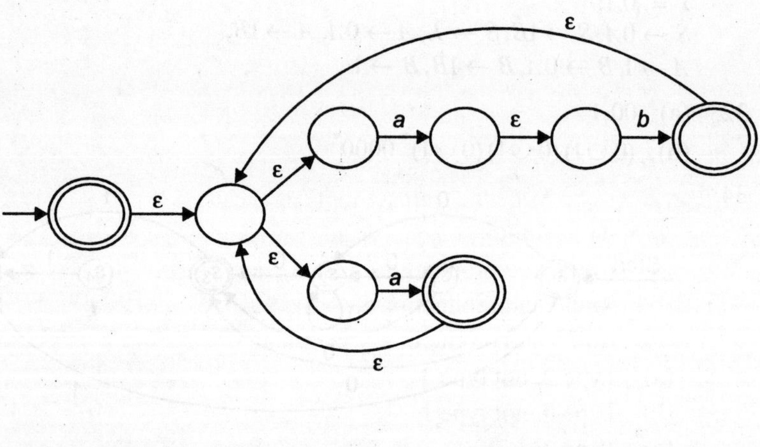

39. $(a \cup b)^*\ aba$

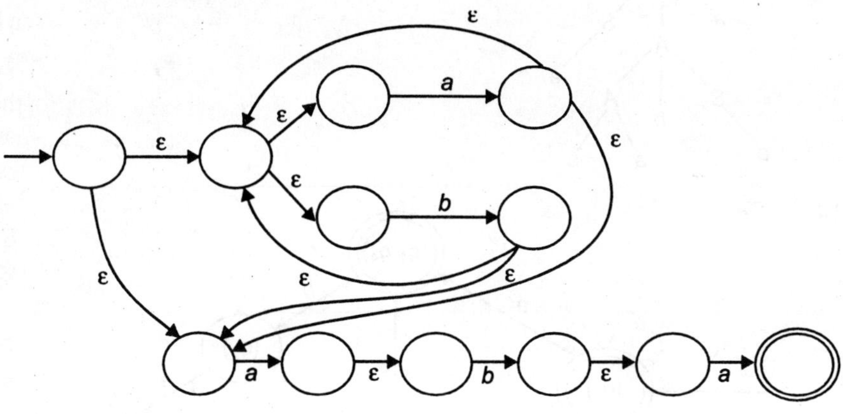

CHAPTER 2

3.

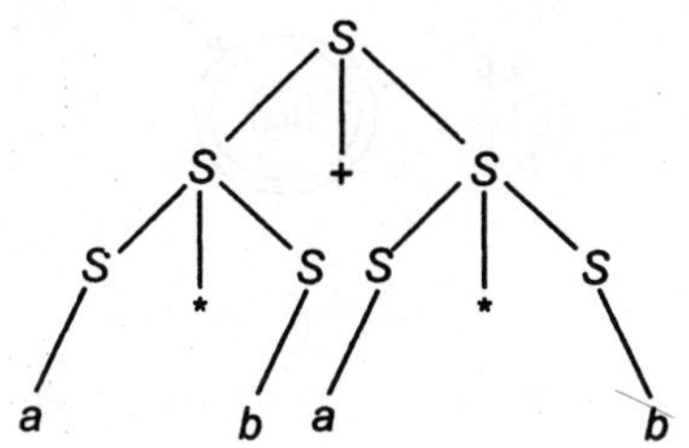

5.

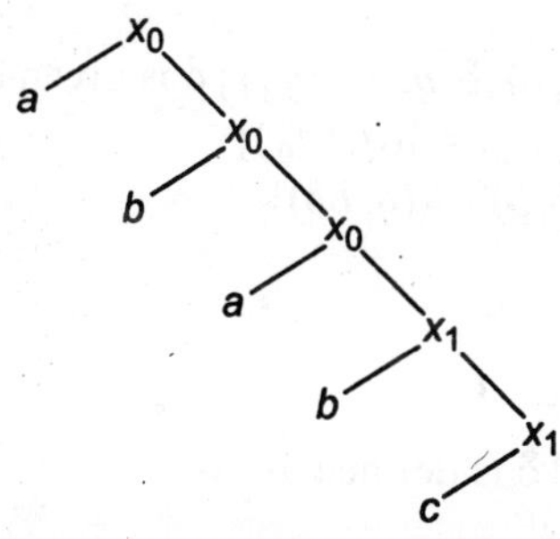

7. Let S_A and S_B be the start symbols of G_A and G_B respectively. Let S be a new start symbol.
   (a) Add S and productions $S \to S_A$ and $S \to S_B$
   (b) Add S and production $S \to S_A S_B$
   (c) Add S and production $S \to \lambda$ and $S \to S_A S$.
8. (a) Type 2, not type 3
   (b) Type 0, not type 1
   (c) Type 2
   (d) Type 3
   (e) Type 2, not type 3

10.

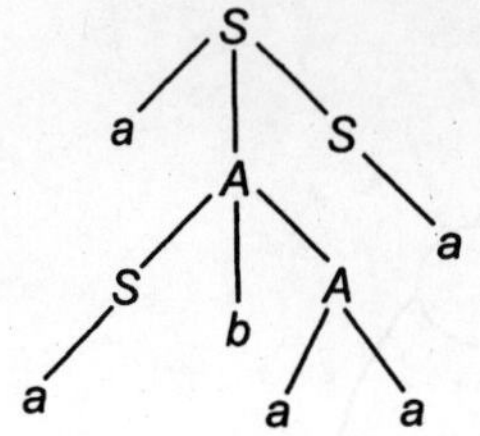

14.

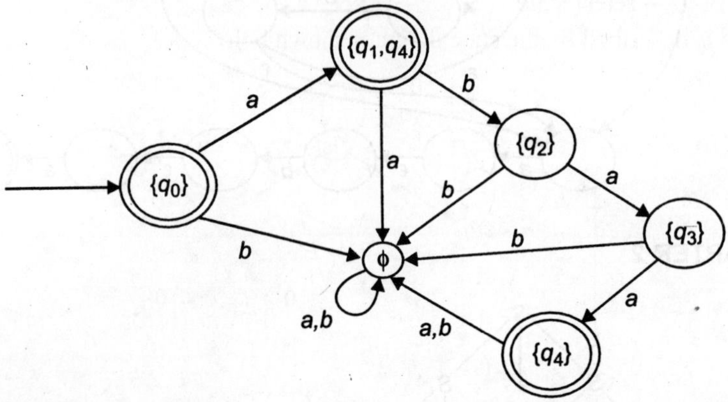

23. (a) Yes
(b) No.

CHAPTER 3

12. Defining $A = (\{q, q_f\}, \{a, b\}, \{z_0, a, b\}, \delta, q, z_0, \{q_3\})$ δ is given by
$\delta(q, a, z_0) = \{(q, az_0)\}$ $\delta(q, b, z_0) = \{(q, bz_0)\}$
$\delta(q, a, a) = \{(q, aa)\}$ $\delta(q, b, b) = \{(q, bb)\}$
$\delta(q, a, b) = \{(q, \in)\} = \delta(q, b, a)$
$\delta(q, \in, a) = \{(q_f, \in)\}$

A accepts the given set by final state.

14. $M = (\{q\}, \{0,1\}, \{S, B, 0, 1\}, \delta, q, S, \varnothing)$ δ is defined as
$\delta(q, \in, S) = \{(q, 0BB)\}$
$\delta(q, \in, B) = \{(q, 0S), (q, 1s), (q, 0)\}$
$\delta(q, 0, 0) = \{(q, \in)\}$
$\delta(q, 1, 1) = \{(q, \in)\}$

15. $G = (\{S\}, \{a, b\}, P, S)$
$P: S \to aSb, S \to aS, S \to a$
$A: (\{q\}, \{a, b\}, \{S, a, b\}, \delta, q, S, \varnothing)$
where $\delta(q, \in, S) = \{(q, aSb), (q, aS), (q, a)\}$
$\delta(q, a, a) = \delta(q, b, b) = \{(q, \in)\}$

CHAPTER 4

1. $M = (Q, \Sigma, \Pi, \delta, q_1, q_{accept}, q_{reject})$.
   $\Sigma = \{0\}$
   $\Gamma = \{0, x, \sqcup\}$
   q_1 — start state
   q_{accept} — accept state
   q_{reject} — reject state
   δ is described by the state diagram shown below.

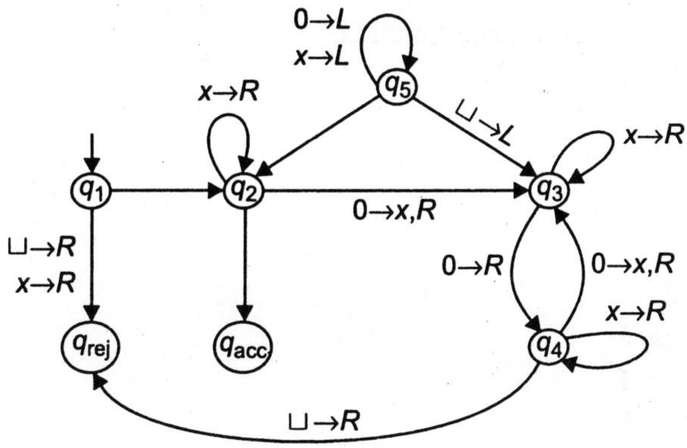

9. | | | |
   |---|---|---|
   | $(s_0,0,s_0,0,R)$ | $(s_0,*,s_5,B,R)$ | $(s_3, *, s_3, *, L)$ |
   | $(s_3,0,s_3,0,L)$ | $(s_3,1,s_3,1,L)$ | (s_3, B, s_0, B, R) |
   | $(s_5,1,s_5,B,R)$ | $(s_5,0,s_5,B,R)$ | (s_5, B, s_6, B, L) |
   | (s_6,B,s_6,B,L) | $(s_6,0,s_7,1,L)$ | $(s_7, 0, s_2, 1, L)$ |
   | $(s_0,1,s_1,0,R)$ | $(s_1,1,s_1,1,R)$ | (s_2, B, s_4, B, L) |
   | $(s_4,0,s_4,1,L)$ | $(s_4,*,s_8,B,L)$ | $(s_8, 0, s_8, B,L)$ |
   | $(s_8,1,s_8,B,L)$ | | |

   where B = Blank cell, L = Left and R = Right
13. $(s_0,0,s_0,0,R), (s_0,1,s_1,1,R), (s_1,0,s_1,0,R), (s_1,1,s_0,1,R), (s_0,B,s_2,B,R)$.
14. $(s_0,0,s_1,0,R), (s_0,1,s_0,0,R), (s_1,0,s_1,0,R), (s_1,1,s_0,0,R), (s_1,B,s_2,B,R)$
15. $(s_0,0,s_0,0,R), (s_0,1,s,1,R), (s_1,0,s_1,0,R), (s_1,1,s_1,0,R)$
16. $(s_0,0,s_1,1,R), (s_0,1,s_0,1,R)$
20. Since the universal Turing machine that simulates every Turing machine, the present problem is equivalent to the Halting problem of Turing machines, therefore, it is unsolvable.

CHAPTER 6

1. (a) 0

(b) 3
(c) 3
(d) 83

2. (a) λ
(b) *aababab*
(c) *bababaaba*

3. (a) Function is defined for all natural numbers divisible by 9.
(b) Function is defined for all $x \geq 5$
(c) Function is defined for all N.
(d) Function is defined for all N.

13. A (2, 4) = 11; A (3, 3) = 37.

CHAPTER 8

1. (a) Yes, T
(b) No
(c) No
(d) Yes, F
(e) Yes, T
(f) Yes, F
(g) Yes, T

2. (a) Summer in Kodaikanal is not hot or it is not Sunny
(b) There is air pollution in Karuppur.
(c) $7+8 \neq 15$
(d) Today is not friday.

3. (a) $\neg p$
(b) $p \rightarrow q$
(c) $p \rightarrow q$
(d) $q \rightarrow p$

5. (a) True
(b) True
(c) True

7. (a) If your guarantee is good, then you must have bought your PC less than 1 year ago.
(b) If you drive more than 800 kilometers, then you have to buy diesel.

8. (a) Converse: A positive integer is a prime if it has no divisors other than 1 and itself.
Contrapositive: If a positive integer has a divisor other than 1 and itself, then it is not prime.
(b) Converse: If I goto class there will be a test.
Contrapositive: If I do not go to class, then there will not be a test.

16. I am happy.
18. (a) The President is not both a Democrat and a republican.
    (b) Either the President is not a Democrat, or he is not a Republican, or he is neither.
19.

p	$\neg p$	$p \vee (\neg p)$
T	F	T
F	T	T

Since there are only T's in the $p \vee (\neg p)$ column, we conclude that $p \vee (\neg p)$ is a tautology.

21. ***Hint:*** Show that all the entries in the last column are all F's.
22. $(\neg p) \vee q \vee (\neg r)$
23. You will get an A if you are clever and either the sun shines or it rains.
26. Either $0 \neq 1$, or I am the Queen of Texas.
27. Yes
28. No (verify using Truth Table construction).
36. Valid.
38. (a) Valid
    (b) Valid
    (c) Valid
39. (a) There is a student who spends more than 6 hours every weekday in class.
    (b) Every student spends more than 6 hours every weekday in class.
    (c) There is student who does not spend more than 6 hours every weekday in class.
    (d) No student spends more than 6 hours every weekday in class.
40. (a) $\exists_x (P(x) \wedge Q(x))$
    (b) $\exists_x (P(x) \wedge \neg Q(x))$
41. $\forall_x \forall_y \forall_z ((x \cdot y) \cdot z = x \cdot (y \cdot z))$
43. (a) True
    (b) False, unless the Universe of discourse has just one element
    (c) True
46. $PDNF: (P \wedge Q) \vee (\neg P \wedge \neg Q)$
    $PCNF: (P \vee \neg Q) \vee (\neg P \vee Q)$
47. (a) $(P \wedge Q) \vee (\neg P \wedge Q) \vee (\neg P \wedge \neg Q)$
    (b) $(P \wedge Q \wedge R) \vee (P \wedge Q \wedge \neg R) \vee (\neg P \wedge Q \wedge R) \vee (\neg P \wedge Q \wedge \neg R)$
48. $P \vee Q \vee R$
49. $(P \wedge Q) \vee (\neg P \wedge Q) \vee (\neg P \wedge \neg Q)$

University Question Papers

THEORY OF COMPUTING

GROUP I

(ANSWER ALL QUESTIONS)

1. The positive closure operator denotes
   (a) Proper suffix (b) Proper prefix
   (c) One or more occurrance (d) the length of string is zero
2. Type 3 Grammars are known as
   (a) Regular Grammar (b) Context Sensitive Grammar
   (c) Context Free Grammar (d) Unrestricted Grammar
3. If a grammar produces more than one parse free for a sentence, the grammar is known as
   (a) Left Linear Grammar (b) Ambiguous Grammar
   (c) Context Free Grammar (d) Regular Grammar

(4) Which is the data structure used to implement the Push Down Automata?
   (a) Linked List (b) Queue
   (c) Stack (d) Array

5. The graphical representation of derivation is known as
   (a) Derivation Tree (b) Derivation structure
   (c) Linear Graph (d) Cellular Automata
6. An unrestricted language can be accepted by
   (a) Finite Automata (b) Turing Machine
   (c) Push Down Automata (d) Cellular Automata
7. The grammar with the productions
   $S \to aA$ and $A \to \varepsilon$ (ε-epsilon) belongs to
   (a) Regular Grammar only (b) Context-Free Grammar only
   (c) Regular Grammar and context-free grammar
   (d) Context sensitive grammar.

8. The functions which are computable by a Turing Machine are known as
   (a) Partial Recursive Functions (b) Enumerable Functions
   (c) Partial Functions (d) Finite-Automata
10. In a digraph, if all the vertices have the same outer degree, then it is known as
   (a) Connected Graph (b) Euler Graph
   (c) Hamiitonion Graph (d) Regular Graph

GROUP II

11. Which Automation is used for accepting Regular Expressions? Write the definition for it.
12. Define "prefix" and "suffix" of a string.
13. When an NFA becomes a DFA?
14. What is CNF? and What is GNF? Define.
15. Write the definition of Context-Free Grammar.
16. Define "Unit Production" and "Null Production".
17. Write the definition of "Turing machine".
18. What is meant by Recursively Enumerable language?
19. What is meant by Partial Recursive Function?
20. When a "digraph" becomes a "regular graph"?

SEMESTER EXAMINATIONS (NOV./DEC. 1999)

M.Sc. — COMPUTER TECHNOLOGY — I SEMESTER

THEORY OF COMPUTING

Time : 3 hours Max. Marks: 60

Instructions

1. Answer ALL questions from Part A and FIVE questions from Part B.
2. All questions must be answered in same answer book.

PART A

1. Define regular expression.

2. Show that the CFG with the following productions is ambiguous.

$$S \to a \mid Sa \mid bSS \mid SSb \mid SbS \mid$$

3. When NFA becomes DFA?
4. List the properties of Finite State Machine.
5. Define tree automata.
6. What is priority rewriting?
7. Define Kleene closure.
8. What is star free sets?
9. State the two methods used by PDA to accept a language.
10. Define Rabin tree automation.

PART B

11. Construct DFA accepting each of the following languages.
    (a) $W \in \{a, b\}^*$ each a in W is immediately proceded and immediately followed by "*ab*".
    (b) $W \in \{a, b\}^*$: W has "*abab*" as a substring.
12. Construct and explain special automata for the given string "*abbaab*".
13. Design a Push Down Automata to accept the strings of the grammar.

$$G : E \to r\,E\,r \mid e\,E\,e \mid e.$$

    Explain the sequence of moves.
14. Find star heights of the following regular expressions.
    (a) $(a\,(ab^*\,c)^*)^*$ (b) $(c\,(a^*\,b)^*)^*$
    (c) $(a^* \cup b^* \cup ab)^*$ (d) $(abb^*\,a)^*$
15. Write markov algorithm to find the following.
    (a) Reverse of the given string "abcd"
    (b) Whether a given decimal number is divisible by 3.
16. Construct NFA accepting the following languages over alphabet {0, 1}
    (a) The set of all strings with 3 consecutive 0's (zeroes).
    (b) The set of all strings such that every block of five consecutive symbols contains atleast 2 zeroes.
    (c) The set of all strings ending in oo.

END

THEORY OF COMPUTATION

Time: 3 hours Marks : 60

Instructions:

Answer any **Six** questions each carry 10 marks.

1. (a) State and prove the principle of mathematical induction using two examples other than Q no. lb.
   (b) Prove using mathematical induction 'For every n > 1 the number of subsets of {1, 2, ...*n*} is 2*n*.
2. (a) Prove that the language accepted by any Finite Automation is regular.
   (b) Construct a minimal DFA for the regular expression $((ab)^* b / ab^*)^*$
3. (a) Write short notes on Pumping lemma.
   (b) State and Prove the properties of Context Free languages.
4. (a) Distinguish between deterministic Pushdown Automata and Non-deterministic Pushdown Automata.
   (b) Let *G* be the Context free grammar with productions

$$S \rightarrow aS / ASbS / c$$

   Let G_1 be the Context free grammar with productions

$$S_1 \rightarrow T / U \quad T \rightarrow aTbT / c \quad U \rightarrow aS_1 / aTbU$$

   (i) Show that *G* is ambiguous.
   (ii) Show that *G* and G_1 generate the same language.
   (iii) Show that G_1 is unambiguous.
5. (a) Construct a Turing machine to accept a palindrome over $|a \cdot b|$. Draw the transition diagram and trace the moves for the any string.
   (b) Does every Turing machine computes a partial function? Explain.
6. State the Rice's theorem and post correspondence problem and give the proof of Rice's theorem.
7. (a) Show that a language $L \subseteq \Sigma^*$ is recursively enumerable (i.e. can be accepted by some TM) if and only if L can be enumerated by some TM.
   (b) Distinguish halting problem and Unsolvability.

THEORY OF COMPUTING

GROUP I

(ANSWER ALL QUESTIONS)

1. Let a and b be two regular expressions then $(a^* \cup b^*)^*$ is equivalent to
   (a) $a \cup b$ (b) $(a \cup b)^*$
   (c) $(b \cup a)^*$ (d) $(b^* \cup a^*)^*$
2. Every context free Grammar can be transferred into an equivalent
   (a) Greibach Normal Form (GNF)
   (b) Chomsky Normal Form (CNF)
   (c) Either (A) or (B)
   (d) None of the above
3. Finite state machine — recognizes palindromes
   (a) can (b) may
   (c) Can't (d) may not
4. Pushdown machine represents
   (a) Type 3 regular grammar (b) Type 2 context free grammar
   (c) Type 1 context sensitive grammar
   (d) Type 0 phrase structural grammar
5. The Turing machine is computable if final state contains
   (a) transition function (b) no tansition function
   (c) halt state (d) both B and C
6. Match the following
   1. BNF (a) $S \rightarrow aAa, A \rightarrow SbA$
   2. CNF (b) $S \rightarrow aAA, A \rightarrow bBB$
   3. GNF (c) $S \rightarrow AA, A \rightarrow a$
   (A) 1-a, 2-b, 3-c, (B) 1-b, 2-c, 3-a
   (C) 1-a, 2-c, 3-b (D) 1-c, 2-b, 3-a.
7. Which is the data structure used to implement the PDA?
   (a) Linked list (b) queue
   (c) stack (d) Array
8. A connected graph as a strongly regular colouring if and only if it is a
   (a) digraph (b) cayley graph
   (c) regular graph (d) cellular Automata.
9. Which is the following is a model of massive parallelism.
   (a) Finite Automata (b) Linear Bounded Automata
   (c) Turing machine (d) Cellular Automata

10. The free abelian group of ranked with the standard set of free generator is the lattice of integer co-ordinate prints of euclidean space R^d denoted as 2^d is is
    (a) triangular tessellation (b) Torus
    (c) Torus tessellation (d) 2D-euclidean grid

THEORY OF COMPUTING

GROUP II

11. Draw the NFA that recognize the following set $01^*/00^*1$.
12. Construct a Turing machine that recognizes the set of all bit strings that end with a '0'.
13. Derive the string *aaabbbccc* from $S \to ABSc, S \to Abc, BA \to AB, Bb \to bb, Ab \to ab, Aa \to aa$.
14. Is the Grammar '$S \to AB, B \to ab, A \to aa, A \to a, B \to b$' ambiguous? Prove.
15. Define Pushdown Automata.
16. What is a unit production & ε- (epsilon) production?
17. State the church's Hypothesis.
18. State the Halting problem.
19. State some practical application for linear cellular automata.
20. Draw 3 examples for cayley graph.

THEORY OF COMPUTING

GROUP I

(ANSWER ALL QUESTIONS)

1. The grammar with the productions

   $S \to aA \,/\, bB,\ B \to b,\ A \to \varepsilon$ (ε-epsilon) belongs to

   (a) Regular grammar only (b) Context free grammar only
   (c) Regular and Context free only
   (d) Context sensitive only
2. State the regular expression recognized by the transition diagram

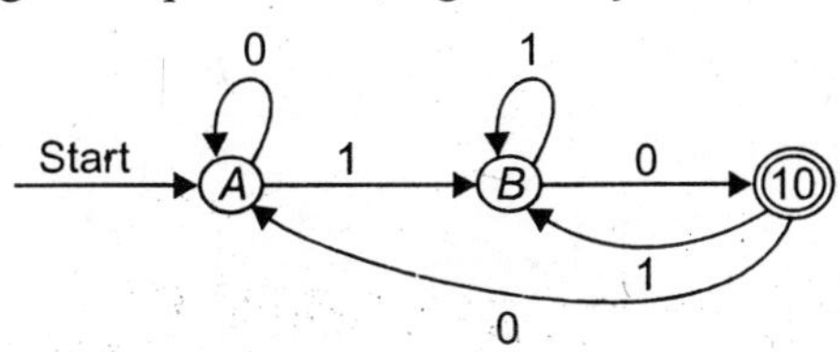

(i) 10 (ii) 0*1* (iii) {0, 1}*{10} (iv) (101)*

(A) (i) only (B) (i) & (ii) only

(C) (i) & (iii) only (D) (ii) & (iii) only

3. The context free grammar defined by ab^* is

(a) $S \to Sb / a$ (b) $S \to XY, X \to ax, Y \to by$

(c) $C \to SS / baa / abb, S \to \varepsilon$ (d) $S \to aS, S \to bS$.

4. Find the useless symbol in the given CFG

$S \to AB / CA, B \to BC / AB, A \to a; C \to aB / b$

(a) A (b) B (c) C (d) all of the above.

5. The grammar that does not have an equivalent deterministic automata for a non-deterministic one is

(a) Finite state automata (b) Turing machine

(c) Pushdown automata (d) None of the above

6. A CFG is ambiguous if

(a) The grammar contains useless Non-Terminals.

(b) It produces more than one parse tree for some sentence.

(c) Some productions has two Non-Terminals side by side.

(d) The grammar contains only terminals on the right side.

7. Which of the following is a model of massive parallelism

(a) Cellular automata (b) Turing machine

(c) Linear bounded automata (d) Finite automata

8. When a connected graph has a strongly regular coloring

(a) If the graph is a digraph

(b) If the graph is a Cayley graph

(c) If the graph is a Euler graph.

(d) If the graph is a Hamiltonian graph.

9. Match the following

(a) BNF (i) $S \to AA, A \to BB, B \to a$

(b) CNF (ii) $S \to aAA. A \to bBB, B \to b$

(c) GNF (iii) $S \to aAa, A \to SA, A \to b$

(a) a - i, b - iii, c - ii (b) a - ii, b - iii, c - i

(c) a - i, b - ii, c - iii (d) a - iii, b - i, c - ii.

10. If 'a' and 'x' as configuration with finite support and 'x' be an arbitrary configuration then the convolution a^*x is given by.

THEORY OF COMPUTING

GROUP II

11. Describe in English the sets accepted by the finite automata along with the regular expression for the following transition diagram.

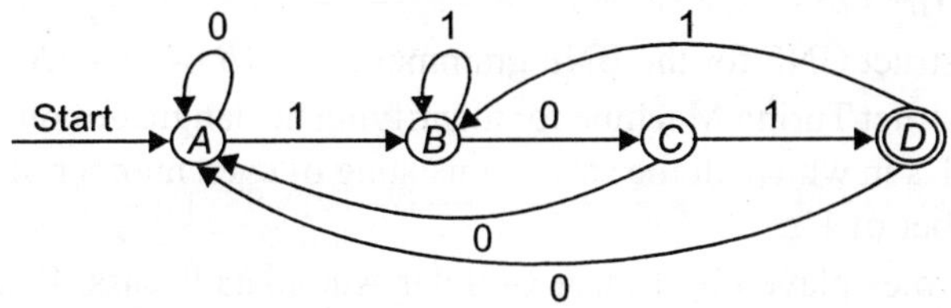

12. List the application of finte automata.
13. Show that the following context Free Grammar generates the language of all strings over {0, 1} with twice as many 1's as 0's.

$$S \to SS \,/\, 0TT \,/\, T0T \,/\, TT0$$
$$T \to 1S \,/\, S1S \,/\, S1 \,/\, 1.$$

14. Is the following grammar ambiguous. Justify

$$S \to AB, A \to aA \,/\, \varepsilon \quad B \to ab \,/\, bB \,/\, \varepsilon.$$

15. Give the new set of productions after removng the unit productions for the following CFG.

$$S \to AA, A \to B \,/\, BB, \;\; B \to abB \,/\, b \,/\, bb.$$

16. Construct two different NFA for the RE a^*.
17. Is unsolvability a halting problem. Justify.
18. When a 'digraph' becomes regular?
19. Define cellular automata.
20. What is meant by Recursively Enumerable language?

B.E. — COMPUTER SCIENCE & ENGINEERING — IV SEMESTER

THEORY OF COMPUTING

Time: 3 Hours Max. Marks: 60

GROUP III

21. Construct and explain pushdown Automata for the following grammar.

$$S \to aAA$$
$$A \to aS \,/\, bS \,/\, a$$

22. Construct NFA for the following regular expressions. Show the sequence of moves made by the each in processing the input string "ababbab".
    (a) $(ab)^* (ac)^*$
    (b) $(a / b)^* abb (a / b)^*$
    (c) (a^* / b^*)
23. Construct GNF for the BNF grammar $S \to AB, A \to B, B \to aB \mid Bb \mid \varepsilon$.
24. Construct Turing Machine for identifying the language consisting of 0's and 1's in which all the string consisting of even number of 0's and odd number of 1's.
25. The roles played by Linear Cellular Automatadiscuss. Explain Global maps and dynamical systems.

THEORY OF COMPUTING

Time: 3 Hours | Max. Marks: 60

GROUP III

21. Let $M = (\{q_1, q_2, q_3\}, \{0,1\}, \delta, \{q_1\}, \{q_3\})$ is a NDFA where δ is given by
    $\delta(q_1,0) = \{q_2, q_3\}$ $\delta(q_1,1) = \{q1\}$
    $\delta(q_2,0) = \{q_1, q_2\}$ $\delta(q_2,1) = \{\phi\}$
    $\delta(q_3,0) = \{q_2\}$ $\delta(q_3,1) = \{q_1, q_2\}$
    (a) Construct an equivalent DFA and draw the transition diagram.
    (b) Check whether the string '011010' is accepted by DFA and NFA.
22. Consider the grammar with the following productions

$$S \to iC\,t\,S \,/\, iCtSeS \,/\, a, C \to b$$

    (a) Generate a sentence 'ibtibtaea' using leftmost derivation and construct a derivation tree for it.
    (b) Derive an equivalent chomsky norma form productions.
23. (a) Construct a PDA for the given grammar
    $S \to AaA \,/\, CA \,/\, BaB$
    $A \to aaBa \,/\, CDA \,/\, aa \,/\, DC$
    $B \to bB \,/\, bAB \,/\, bbaS$
    $C \to Ca \,/\, bC \,/\, D$
    $D \to bD \,/\, \varepsilon$.
    (b) Using the above show the sequence of PDA for the string '*aabbaaaaaa*'.
24. (a) State the problems in Turing Machine.

(b) Construct a Turing Machine that will accept the following languages in $\{a, b\}$

$$L = \{a^n b^m, n \geq 1, n \neq m\}.$$

25. (a) Explain the basic properties of linear cellular Automata.
(b) Draw any 3 common types of Cayley graph.

THEORY OF COMPUTING

TEST II

Class: BE—CSE | Time 90 mts.
Sem: IV | Marks : 30

GROUP I

1. The CFG defined by ab^* is

(a) $S \to Sb \mid a$

(b) $S \to XY$
$X \to ax$
$Y \to by$

(c) $C \to SS \mid baa \mid abb$
$S \to \varepsilon$

(d) $S \to aS$
$S \to Bs$

2. Consider the Left Recursive (LR) grammar
$S \to Aa \mid b$
$A \to Ac \mid bd$
Which of the following grammar is equivalent to the given grammar. When LR is removed

(a) $S \to Aa \mid b$
$A \to bdA'$
$A \to cA' \mid \varepsilon$

(b) $S \to bA'$
$A \to C \mid da$

(c) $S \to Aa \mid b$
$A \to CA'$

(d) $S \to Aa \mid b$
$A \to A'C \mid bd \mid \varepsilon$

3. Match the following

1. BNF	(a) $S \to aAa, A \to SbA$
2. CNF	(b) $S \to aAA, A \to bBB$
3. GNF	(c) $S \to AA, A \to a$

(a) 1- a, 2 - b, 3 - c
(b) 1 - a, 2 - c, 3 - b
(c) 1 - b, 2 - c, 3 - a
(d) 1 - c, 2 - b, 3 - a

4. In PDA, the δ is defined by

(a) $\delta(q, a, z) = (p1, \gamma 1)$
(b) $\delta(q, z) = (p1, \gamma 1)$
(c) $\delta(q, a) = (p1, \gamma 1)$
(d) both a & b.

5. The Turing machine is computable if final state contains__________
   (a) transition function (b) halt state
   (c) no transition function (d) both b & c.

GROUP II

6. Check whether the following grammar is ambiguous or Unambiguous

$$S \rightarrow S(S) \mid \varepsilon$$

7. Rewrite the given grammar after removing unit production
   $S \rightarrow AB$
   $A \rightarrow B$
   $B \rightarrow aB \mid Bb \mid \varepsilon$
8. Define PDA
9. Find the moves for the following configuration of TM

Q_0
↓ (on second cell)

0	1	1

Q_1
↓ (on first cell)

0	1	1

10. Define Turing Machine.

GROUP III

Answer Any 2 Questions

11. Construct GNF for the BNF given in problem no. 7.
12. (a) Construct PDA from the following grammar
    $S \rightarrow aAA \mid bBB \mid aB \mid a$
    $A \rightarrow aA \mid a$
    $B \rightarrow bB \mid b$

    (b) Show the sequence of moves of PDA of problem given in 12(a).
13. Construct TM for identifying the language consisting of 0's and 1's in which all the string consists of even no. of 0's and 1's.

THEORY OF COMPUTING

GROUP I

1. The regular expression for the set of strings that consists of alternating 0's and 1's.
   (a) $(01)^* + (10)^* + 0(10)^* + 1(01)^*$ (b) $(01)^* (10)^* 1(01)^* 0(10)^*$
   (c) $(\varepsilon + 1)(01)^* (\varepsilon + 0)$ (d) both *a* & *c*.
2. Consider the following 2 DFA's (Refer fig.)
3. The CFG is defined by the following productions
   $S \rightarrow A1B$
   $A \rightarrow 0A / \varepsilon$
   $B \rightarrow 0B / 1B / \varepsilon$
   Which of the following substring is encountered during the derivation process for the sentence 00101
   (a) 0A1B (b) $0 \in 1B$ (c) 0101B (d) All of the above
4. Match the following

1.	BNF	(a)	$A \rightarrow xXyz$
2.	GNF	(b)	$A \rightarrow xy$
3.	CNF	(c)	$A \rightarrow XxYyZz$

   (a) 1 - a, 2 - b, 3 - c (b) 1 - b, 2 - c, 3 - a
   (c) 1 - c, 2 - A, 3 - b (d) 1 - a, 2 - b, 3 - c
5. The equivalent PDA for the given CFG is $S \rightarrow 0S1 / A$ (Refer fig.)
6. The pumping lemma for regular language
   (a) $xy^i z$ for any $i \geq 0$ (b) $x^i yz$ for any $i \geq 0$
   (c) xyz^i for any $i \geq 1$ (d) $x^i y^i z^i$ for any $i \geq 1$
7. The transition function of Turing machine can be defined as
   (a) $\delta(q, x) = (p, y, D)$ (b) $\delta(q, \in) = (p, y, D)$
   (c) $\delta(q, xy) = (p, y, D)$ (d) No transistion function.
8. The Turing machine is said to be acceptance by halting, if
   (a) $\delta(q, x)$ is undefined (b) $\delta(q, x)$ is defined
   (c) $\delta(q, x)$ is $\in$ (d) $\delta(q, x) = (p, y)$
9. .... model does not exchange information during computation
   (a) uniform arrays (b) mosaic automata
   (c) tessellation structure (d) all of the above
10. The transition function of cellular space is denoted by
    (a) $\delta{:}Q \times Q^d \rightarrow Q$ (b) $\delta{:}Q \times Q \rightarrow Q^d$
    (c) $\delta{:}\rightarrow Q^d$ (d) $\delta{:}Q^d \rightarrow Q$

B.E. — COMPUTER SCIENCE & ENGINEERING
THEORY OF COMPUTING

SEMESTER IV

Time: 3 Hours Maximum Marks : 60

GROUP II

11. Find a regular expression for the language of the set of all strings of 0's & 1's whose number of 0's is divisible by 5 and whose number of 1's is even.
12. Compute ∈-NFA for the following, regular expression

$$1(1+10)^* + 10(0+01)^*$$

13. Prove that $\{0^n 102^n \ / \ n \geq 0\}$ is not a regular language.
14. Find whether the given grammar is ambiguous (or) Unambiguous

$$S \to T | U$$
$$T \to aTbT | c$$
$$U \to aA | aTbU$$

15. Rewrite the given grammar after removing unit production:

$$S \to ABA$$
$$A \to aA | \in$$
$$B \to bB | \in$$

16. Design a CFG generating the following language

$$\{a^i b^j c^k \ / \ j \neq i+k\}$$

17. Define Turing Machine.
18. Why accepting state is called as Halting State in TM?
19. Differentiate Cellular and Linear Cellular automata.
20. Write the local rules of Cellular automata.

GROUP III

21. (a) Construct finite automata to recognize the language of all strings of 0's and 1's of length at least 1, if they were interrupted as binary representation of integers, would represent integers evenly divisible by 3. Leading 0's are permissible.

(b) Find an equivalent FA and Regular expression from the given NFA (Refer fig.)

22. (a) Design a PDA to recognize the language of all odd-length palindromes over {a, b}

(b) Construct CFG for the language generated in Question No. 22(a).

23. Construct GNF from the given grammar

$$S \to aAa \mid bBb \mid$$
$$A \to c \mid a$$
$$B \to c \mid b$$
$$C \to CDE \mid$$
$$D \to A \mid B \mid ab$$

24. (a) Construct a Turing Machine that creates a copy of its input string (Ex: abcd) to the right of the input but with a blank separating the copy from the original.

(b) Design a Turing machine for computing the LCM of two numbers.

25. Write short notes on

(a) Cellular Automata

(b) Linear Cellular Automata

THEORY OF COMPUTING

Time: 3 hours Max. Marks: 40

GROUP I

1. Find the start height of the following and draw the NFA for the given regular expressions.

(a) $(a(a \,/\, a^{*}aa) \,/\, aaa)^{*}$

(b) $(((a \,/\, a^{*}aa)aa)^{*} \,/\, aaaaaa^{*})^{*}$

2. Consider the two regular expressions

$r1{:}0^{*} \,/\, 1^{*} \quad r2{:}01^{*} \,/\, 10^{*} \,/\, 1^{*}0 \,/\, (0^{*}1)^{*}$

(a) Find a string corresponding to $r1$ but not to $r2$.

(b) Find a string corresponding to $r2$ but not to $r1$.

(c) Find a string corresponding to both $r1$ and $r2$.

(d) Find a string in $\{0, 1\}^{*}$ corresponding to neither $r1$ nor $r2$.

3. Define and Construct a language for Context sensitive grammar.

'We do not define ε-transitions for a Turing machine'. True or False. Justify.

4. State and distinguish halting problem and Unsolvability.

GROUP II

5. State the Kleene's theorem (not the corollary) and give the proof with neat sketch wherever necessary.
6. State the rules for a Context Free Grammar to be in Chomsky Normal form. Find a CFG G' in CNF generating L(G)—{ε}, where G has a productions of

$$S \to AaA \,/\, CA \,/\, BaB \qquad A \to aaBa \,/\, CDA \,/\, aa \,/\, DC$$
$$B \to bB \,/\, bAB \,/\, bb \,/\, As \quad C \to Ca \,/\, bC \,/\, D$$
$$D \to bD \,/\, \varepsilon$$

7. Consider the CFG with productions

$S \to S_1\$ \quad S_1 \to S_1 + T \,/\, T \quad T \to T * F \,/\, F \quad F \to (S_1) \,/\, a$

(a) Write the CFG obtained from this one by eliminating left recursion. (2)

(b) State the rules for DPDA and give a transition table for a DPDA that acts as a top down parser for this language.

8. Define Universal TM.

Show that a language $L \subseteq \Sigma^*$ is recursively enumerable (i.e., can be accepted by some TM) if and only if L can be enumerated by some TM.

9. State and prove Rice's Theorem.

THEORY OF COMPUTING

Time : 90 Mts. Max Marks: 30

TEST II

GROUP I

1. The CFG defined by ab* is

(a) $S \to Sb \mid a$

(b) $S \to XY$
$X \to ax$
$Y \to by$

(c) $C \to SS \mid baa \mid abb$
$S \to \in$

(d) $S \to aS \mid bS$

2. The transition function of PDA is defined as

(a) $\delta(q, a, z) = (p, \gamma)$

(b) $\delta(q, z) = (p, \gamma)$

(c) $\delta(q, a) = (p, \gamma)$

(d) $\delta(q, a, z) = (p, \gamma)$

3. Say True or False

   A language L is Context free Language, if there is a Pushdown automata accepting.

4. A CFG is Unambiguous if,

   (a) it contains uselss Nonterminals

   (b) it produces more than one parse tree for some sentence

   (c) it produces more than one derivation for some sentence

   (d) Both b & c

5. $S \rightarrow aAa,\ A \rightarrow SA,\ A \rightarrow b$. The given grammar is in .... normal form.

   (a) BNF (b) CNF (c) GNF (d) both a & b

GROUP II

6. Define PDA.
7. Show that the CFG with following production is Unambiguous.

$$S \rightarrow S(S) \mid \in$$

8. Let L be the language generated by the CFG with productions

$$S \rightarrow S + S \mid S - S \mid S * S \mid S / S \mid (S) \mid a$$

   How many derivation trees (Parse trees) are there fore the string $a \mid a \mid a \mid a \mid a \mid a$?

9. Write Instantaneous descriptions for the PDA generated in the Qn. No. 11 for accepting the sentence aabb.
10. Rewrite the grammar after removing Left recursion.

$$S \rightarrow Aa \mid b$$
$$A \rightarrow Ac \mid bd$$

GROUP III

Answer any 2 Questions

11. Convert the following grammar to GNF.

$$S \rightarrow ASB \mid \in$$
$$A \rightarrow aAS \mid a$$
$$B \rightarrow SbS \mid A \mid bb$$

12. (a) Construct PDA from the given grammar.

$$S \to S1\$$$
$$S1 \to S + T \mid S1 - T \mid T$$
$$T \to T * F \mid T / F \mid F$$
$$F \to (S) \mid a$$

(b) Show the moves of the PDA for accepting the sentence

$$a + a * a/a\$$$

13. Design a Context Free grammar for Boolean expressions and Construct PDA for the same.

THEORY OF COMPUTING

GROUP II

11. Describes in English the sets accepted by the finite automata along with the regular expression for the following transition diagram.

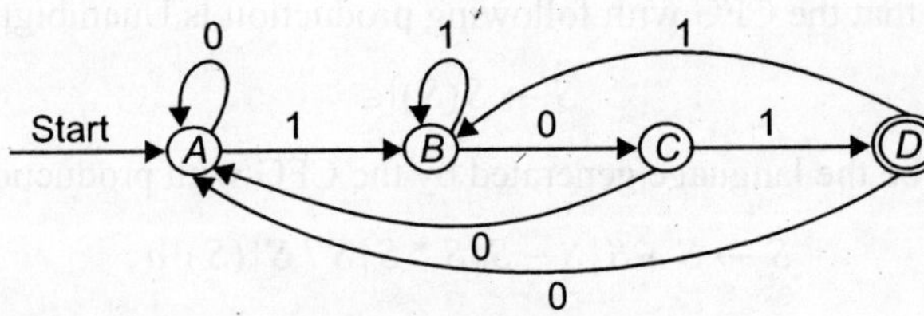

12. List the application of finite automata.
13. Show that the following context Free Grammar generates the language of all strings over {0, 1} with twice as many 1's as 0's.

$$S \to SS \;/\; 0TT \;/\; T0T \;/\; TT0$$
$$T \to 1S \;/\; S1S \;/\; S1 \;/\; 1.$$

14. Is the following grammar ambiguous. Justify

$$S \to AB,\ A \to aA / \in,\ B \to ab / bB / \in.$$

15. Give the new set of productions after removing the unit productions for the following CFG.

$$S \to AA,\ A \to B \;/\; BB,\ B \to abB \;/\; b \;/\; bb.$$

16. Construct two different NFA for the RE a^*.
17. Is unsolvability a halting problem. Justify.
18. When a 'digraph' becomes regular?
19. Define cellular automata.
20. What is meant by Recursively Enumerable language?

B.E.—COMPUTER SCIENCE & ENGINEERING—IV SEMESTER

THEORY OF COMPUTING

Time : 3 Hours Max. Marks: 60

GROUP III

21. Let $M = (\{q_1, q_2, q_3\}, \{0,1\}, \delta, \{q_1\}, \{q_3\})$ is a NDFA where δ is given by
$\delta(q_1,0) = \{q_2, q_3\}$ $\delta(q_1,1) = \{q_1\}$
$\delta(q_2,0) = \{q_1, q_2\}$ $\delta(q_2,1) = \{\phi\}$
$\delta(q_3,0) = \{q_2\}$ $\delta(q_3,1) = \{q_1, q_2\}$
    (a) Construct an equivalent DFA and draw the transition diagram.
    (b) Check whether the string '011010' is accepted by DFA and NFA.
22. Consider the grammar with the following productions

$$S \to iCtS \;/\; iCtSeS \;/\; a, C \to b$$

    (a) Generate a sentence 'ibtibtaea' using leftmost derivation and construct a derivation tree for it.
    (b) Derive an equivalent chomsky normal form productions.
23. (a) Construct a PDA for the given grammar

$$\begin{aligned} &S \to AaA \;/\; CA \;/\; BaB \\ &A \to aaBa \;/\; CDA \;/\; aa \;/\; DC \\ &B \to bB \;/\; bAB \;/\; bbaS \\ &C \to Ca \;/\; bC \;/\; D \\ &D \to bD / \in. \end{aligned}$$

    (b) Using the above show the sequence of PDA for the string '*aabbaaaaaa*'.
24. (a) State the problems in Turing Machine.
    (b) Construct a Turing Machine that will accept the following languages in $\{a, b\}$

$$L = \{a^n b^m, n \geq 1, n \neq m\}.$$

25. (a) Explain the basic properties of linear cellular Automata.
    (b) Draw any 3 common types of Cayley graph.

COMPUTER SCIENCE AND ENGINEERING — FIFTH SEMESTER

THEORY OF COMPUTATIONS

Time: 3 Hours Max. Marks: 50

***Answer All Questions**

PART A

1. (a) Explain the Chomsky's hierarchy of language.
   (b) Explain the need for Theory of Computing.
2. (a) Prove by mathematical induction: Every integer, greater than 17, is a nonnegative integer combination of 4 and 7. In other words, for every $n > 17$, there exists integers i_n and j_n both ≥ 0, so that
$$n = i_n * 4 + j_n * 7.$$
   (b) For every $n \geq 0$, $n(n^2 + 5)$ is divisible by 6.
3. (a) Prove that for every NDFA, there exists a DFA.
   (b) Find the deterministic acceptor equivalent to $M = (\{q0, q1, q2\}, (a, b), \delta, \delta_0, \delta_2)$ is given below:

State	a	b
q_0	q_0, q_1	q_2
q_1	q_0	q_1
q_2		q_0, q_1

4. (a) Find the language generated by the following grammars:
   (i) $S \to 0A|1S|0|1, A \to 1A|1S|1$
   (ii) $S \to 0S1|0A1,\ A \to 1A0|0.$
   (b) Construct a grammar to generate
$$\{(ab)^n \mid n \geq 1) \cup \{(ba)^n \mid n \geq 1\}.$$
5. List any 12 idetities for regular expressions.
6. Draw the transition system corresponding to $(ab + c^*)^* b$.

7. Transition table of a Turing machine is given below:

Present State	Tape Symbols			Initial State→
	b	0	1	finite state
$\rightarrow q_1$	$1Lq_2$	$0Rq_1$		
q_2	bRq_3	$0Lq_2$	$1Lq_2$	
q_3		bRq_4	bRq_5	
q_4	$0Rq_5$	$0Rq_4$	$1Rq_4$	
q_5	$0Lq_2$			

Draw the computation sequence of the input string 00.

8. Explain how a Turing-machine can be used as a language acceptor.
9. Prove that not all languages are recursively enumerable.
10. (a) What is Rice's Theorem?
    (b) List six unsolvable problems.
11. (i) Construct a minimal finite automaton for the given FA.

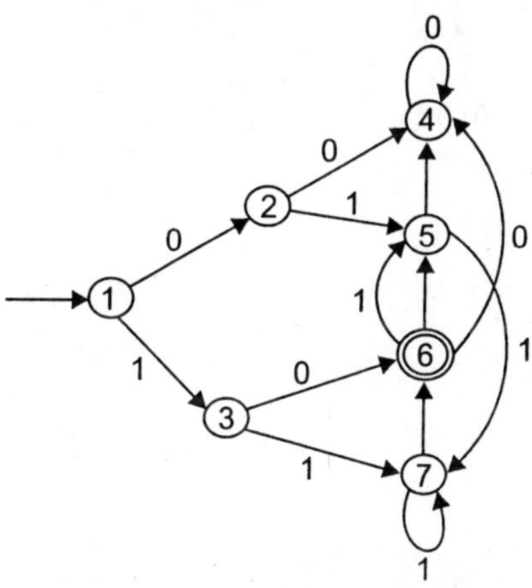

(ii) Below are a number of language over $\{0, 1\}$. In each case, decide whether or not the language is regular, and prove that your answer is correct.

(a) The set of all strings x beginning with a non null string of the form WW.

(b) Set of all strings x containing some non null substring of the form WW.

(c) Set of all strings x containing some non null substring of the form WWW.

(d) Set of all length strings over $\{0,1\}$ with middle symbol 0.

(e) Set of non palindromes.

(f) Set of strings in which the number of 0's and the number of 1's are both divisible by 5.

12. What is a non deterministic turing machine? Explain how is it used for computing.

13. (a) (i) Construct a turing machine that can accept the strings over {0, 1} containing even number of 1's.

(ii) Construct a turing macine that can accept the set of all even palindromens over {0, 1}.

(OR)

(b) M is a turing machine represented by the transition system as in the figure given. Obtain the computation sequence of M for processing the i/p string 0011.

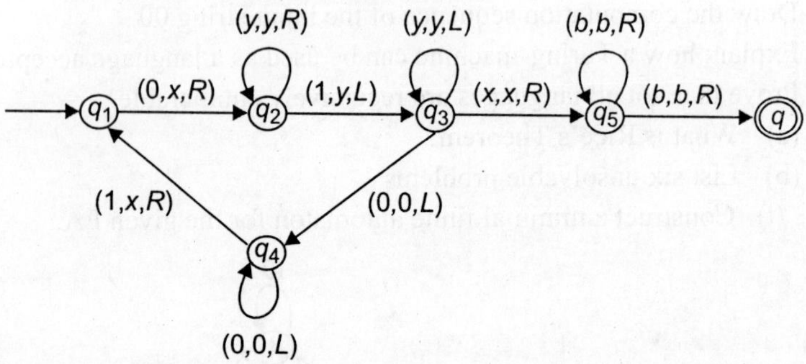

Bibliography

1. Richard Johnsonbaugh, Discrete Mathematics, Fifth Edition, Pearson Education Asia Publishers, 2001.
2. Kolman, Bushy, Ross, Discrete Mathematical Structures, Fourth Edition, Pearson Education, 2001.
3. Dexter C. Kozen, Automata and Computability, Springer, 1997.
4. Seymour Lipschutz., Discrete Structures, Schaum's Outline series, TMH, 1986.
5. Michael Sipser, Introduction to Theory of Computation, Thomson, Brooks/Kole, 2001.
6. Peter Linz., An Introduction to Formal Languages and Automata, Second Edition, Narosa Publishers, 1997.
7. Raymond Greenlaw, H-James Hoover, Fundamentals of the Theory of Computation, Principles and Practice, Morgan Kaufmann Publishers, 1998.
8. John E. Hoperoft, Rajeev Motwani, Jeffrey D. Ullman, Introduction to Automata Theory, Languages and Computation, Pearson Education, 2001.
9. Leon. S. Levy, Discrete Structures of Computer Science, Wiley Eastern Limited, 1994.
10. K.L.P. Mishra, N. Chandrasekaran, Theory of Computer Science, Second Edition, EEE, Prentice Hall of India, 1998.
11. Kenneth Ht. Rosen, Discrete Mathematics and Its Applications, Tata McGraw-Hill, Edition 2001.
12. B.S. Vatssa, Discrete Mathematics, Wishwa Prakashan, 1993.
13. Bernard M. Moret. The Theory of Computation, Pearson Education Asia, 1998.
14. Harry R. Lewis, Christos H. Papadimitrion, Elements of the Theory of Computation, Pearson Education Asia, Second Edn., 1998.
15. Ralph P. Grimaldi, Discrete and Combinatorial Mathematics, Pearson Education, Asia, 2002.
16. John C. Martin, Introduction to Languages and the Theory of Computation, Second Edition, McGraw Hill International Edition, 1997.
17. John. E. Hopcroft, Jeffrey D. Ullman, Introduction to Automata Theory, Languages and Computation, Narosa Publishers, 1979.

Index

Appendix A

UNDECIDABILITY

A problem whose language is recursive is said to be decidable. Otherwise the problem is undecidable. That is, a problem is undecidable if there is no algorithm that takes as input an instance of the problem and determines whether the answer to that instance is "yes" or "no".

A.1 PROPERTIES OF RECURSIVE AND RECURSIVELY ENUMERABLE LANGUAGES

Here we will examine the languages associated with Turing machines and some of their restrictions. Because Turing machines can perform any kind of algorithmic computation we expect to find that the family of languages associated with them is quite broad. It includes not only regular and context free languages, but also the various examples we have encountered that lie outside these families. The non-trivial question is whether there are any languages that are not accepted by some TM. We will answer this question first by showing that there are more languages than TM's, so that there must be some languages for which there are no TMs.

There is an important distinction between languages for which there exists an accepting Turing machine and languages for which there exists a membership algorithm. Because a TM does not necessarily halt on input that it does not accept, the first does not imply the second.

A.1.1 Definition

A language is said to be recursively enumerable if there exists a TM that accepts it.

This definition implies only that there exists a TM M such that for every $w \in L$,

$$q_0 w \mid \overset{*}{\underset{M}{\text{---}}} x_1 q_f x_2,$$

with q_f a final state. The definition says nothing about what happens for w not in L; it may be that the machine halts in a non-final state or that it never halts and goes into an infinite loop. We can be more demanding and ask that the machine tell us whether or not any given input is in its language.

A.1.2 Definition

A language L on Σ is said to be recursive if there exists a TM M that accepts L and that halts on every w in Σ^+. In other words, a language is recursive if and only if there exists a membership algorithm for it.

A.1.3 Definition

A procedure for solving a problem is a finite sequence of instructions which can be mechanically carried out given any input.

A.1.4 Definition

An algorithm is a procedure that terminates after a finite number of steps for any input.

A.1.5 Definition

A set is recursive if we have an algorithm to determine whether a given element belongs to X or not.

A.1.6 Definition

A recursively enumerable set is a set A for which we have a procedure to determine whether a given element belongs to X or not.

Note that a recursive set is recursively enumerable.

A.1.7 Definition

Let $L \subseteq \Sigma^*$ be a language. A Turing machine M with input symbol Σ is said to accept L if $L(M) = L$. M recognizes or decides L if M computes the characteristic function $\psi_L : \Sigma^* \to \{0, 1\}$. In other words, M recognizes L if M halts in state h_a (accepting state) for every string x in Σ^*, producing output 1 if $x \in L$ and output 0 otherwise.

A language L is recursively enumerable if there is a TM that accepts L, and recursive if there is a TM that recognizes L. We may called these languages as Turing acceptable and Turing decidable respectively.

A.1.8 Theorem

Every recursive language (Turing decidable language) is recursively enumerable (Turing acceptable).

Proof:

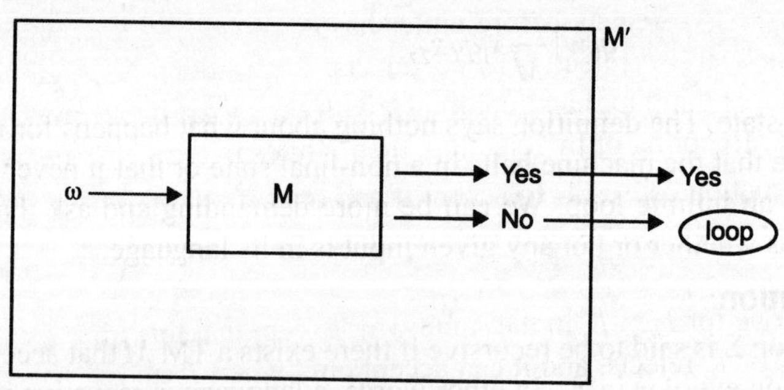

Fig. A.1

Let M be a TM that decides L. Let M' be another TM, which simulates M. M' would accept strings for which M halts on 'yes' and go to infinite loop if M halts and writes 'No' on the tape. Hence, the proof.

Remark: There are recursively enumerable languages that are not recursive. We now state a theorem without proof.

A.1.9 Theorem

If L is accepted by a nondeterministic TM M, and every possible sequence of M causes to halt, then L is recursive.

Both the union and intersection operations preserve the property of recursive enumerability.

A.1.10 Theorem

If L_1 and L_2 are recursively enumerable languages over Σ, then $L_1 \cup L_2$ and $L_1 \cap L_2$ are also recursively enumerable.

Proof: Suppose $M_1 = (Q_1, \Sigma_1, \Gamma_a, \delta_1, q_1, B_1, F_1)$ and $M_2 = (Q_2, \Sigma_2, \Gamma_2, \delta_1, q_1, B_1, F_1$ are TM's accepting L_1 and L_2 respectively. We now construct TM^s) accepting $L_1 \cup L_2$ and $L_1 \cap L_2$. In both cases, it is useful to use a two-tape machine.

The two tape machine $M = (Q, \Sigma, \Gamma, \delta, q_0, B, F)$ begins by placing a copy of the input string, which is already on tape 1, onto tape 2. It inserts the marker # at the beginning of both tapes in order to detect a crash resulting from T_1 or T_2 trying to move its tape head off the tape. From this point on, the simultaneous simulation of T_1 on tape 1 and T_2 on tape 2 is accomplished by allowing every possible move.

$$\delta((p_1, p_2), (a_1, a_2)) = ((q_1, q_2), (b_1, b_2), (D_1, D_2))$$

where, for both values of i,

$$\delta_i(p_i, a_i) = (q_i, b_i, D_i).$$

The possible outcomes of the simulation are:

1. Neither T_1 nor T_2 ever stops, in which case T never stops.
2. At least one of the two accepts, in which case T accepts.
3. One of the two rejects before either has accepted. If they both reject simultaneously, T rejects. If one rejects, T abandons that simulation (*i.e.* ignores that tape) and continues with the other. If the other halts, either by accepting or by rejecting, then T halts in the same way.

The construction causes M to accept if and only if atleast one of the two machines M_1 and M_2 accepts and we conclude that T accepts the language $L_1 \cup L_2$.

We can prove for $L_1 \cap L_2$ in the same way, except that this time T can reject if either T_1 or T_2 rejects, and it can accept only when T_1 and T_2 have both accepted.

A.1.11 Theorem

The complement of a recursive language is recursive.

Proof: Let L be a recursive language and M, a during machine that halts on all inputs and accepts L. Construct M' from M so that if M enters a final state on input w, then M' halts without accepting. If M halts without accepting, M' enters a final state. Since one of these two events occurs M' is an algorithm. Clearly $L(M')$ is the complement of L and thus the complement of L is a recursive language. The following figure shows a construction of M' from M.

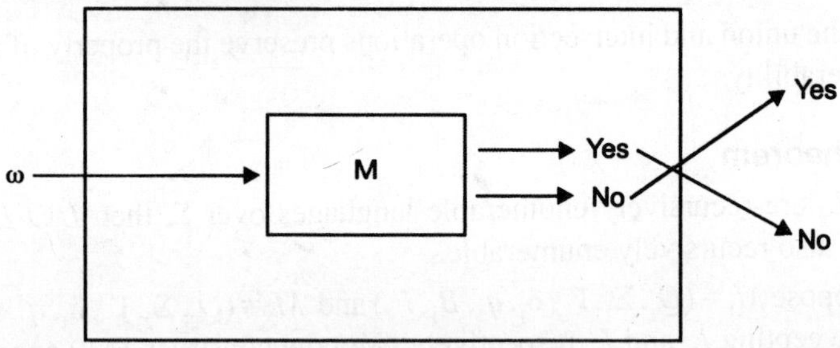

Fig. A.2

A.1.12 Theorem

The union of two recursive language is recursive and the intersection of two recursive language is also recursive.

Proof: Let L_1 and L_2 be recursive languages accepted by algorithms M_1 and M_2. We construct M which first simulates M_1. If M_1 accepts, then M accepts. If M_1 rejects, then M simulates M_2 and accepts if and only if M_2 accepts. Since both M_1 and M_2 are algorithms, M is guaranteed to halt. Clearly M accepts $L_1 \cup L_2$. The two constructions for $L_1 \cup L_2$ are given below:

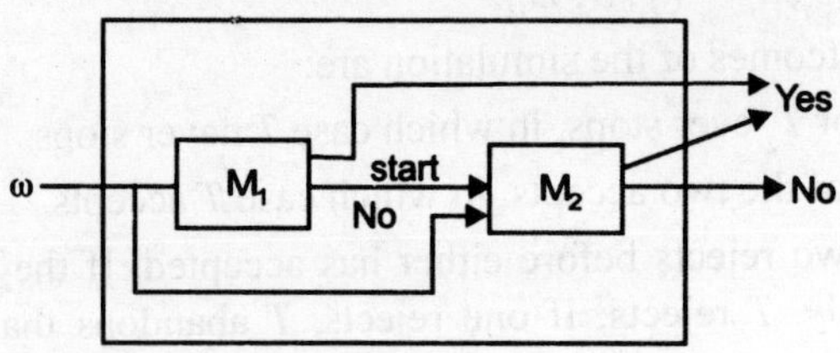

(a)

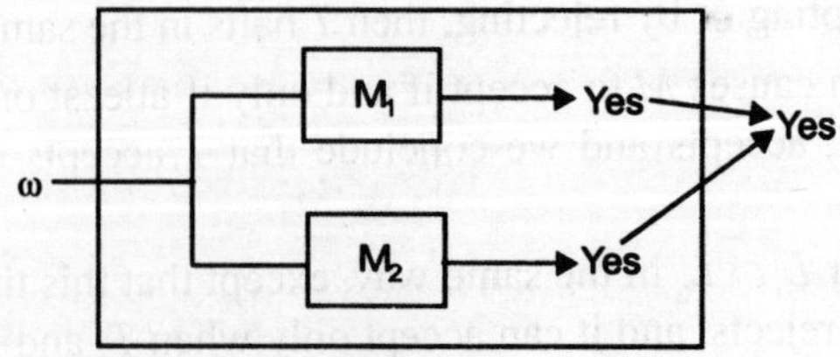

(b)

Fig. A. 3

Proof: For $L_1 \cap L_2$ is similar except that M accepts if and only if both M_1 and M_2 accepts.

A.1.13 Theorem

If both a language L and its complement L' are recursively enumerable then L is recursive.

Proof: Let M_1 and M_2 accept L and L' respectively. Construct M as in Figure A.4 to simulate simultaneously M_1 and M_2.

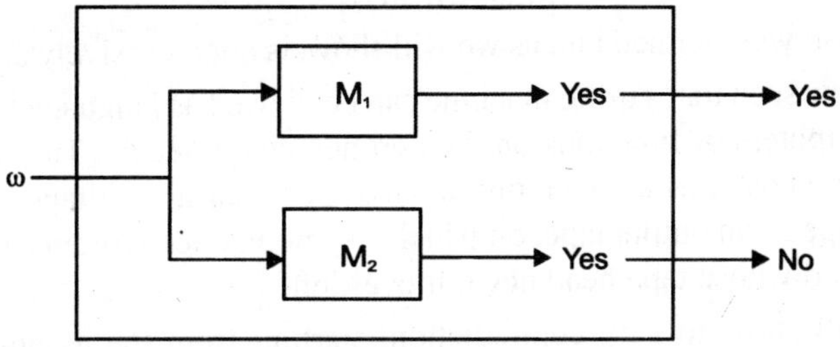

Fig. A.4

M accepts w if M_1 accepts w and rejects w if M_2 accepts w. Since w is in either L or L', we see that exactly one of M_1 or M_2 will accept. Thus M will always say either "yes" or "no" but will never say both. Note that there is no apriori limit on how long it may take before M_1 or M_2 accepts, but it is certain that one or the other will do. Since M is an algorithm that accepts L, it follows that L is recursive.

A.1.14 Corollary

If both a language L and its complement L' are recursively enumerable, then L' is recursive.

Proof: Follows from Theorems **A.1.13** and **A.1.11.**

A.1.15 Remark

A.1.11 and **A.1.13** have an important consequence. Let L and L' be a pair of complementary languages. Then either

1. both L and L' are recursive.
2. neither L nor L' is recursively enumerable.
3. one of L and L' is recursively enumerable but not recursive; the other is not recursively enumerable.

A.1.16 Theorem (A language that is not Recursively enumerable)

There exists a recursively enumerable language whose complement is not recursively enumerable.

Proof: Let $\Sigma = \{a\}$, and consider the set of all Turing machines with this input alphabet. This set is countable, so we can associate an order M_1,

M_2, ..., with its elements. For each Turing machine M_i, there is an associated recursively enumerable language $L(M_i)$. Conversely for each recursively enumerable language on Σ, there is some Turing machine that accepts it.

We now consider a new language L defined as follows. For each $i \geq 1$, the string a_i is in L if and only if $a_i \in L(M_i)$. It is clear that the language L is well defined, since the element $a_i \in L(M_i)$, and hence $a_i \in L$, must either be true or false. Next, we consider the complement of L,

$$L' = \{a_i | a_i \notin L(M_i)\} \quad ...(1)$$

which is also well defined but, as we will show, is not recursively enumerable.

We have seen that Turing machine can be viewed as language recognizers and as computers of functions on the non-negative integers. Turing machine can also be viewed as a generating device. Consider a multitape TM M that uses one tape as an output tape, on which a symbol, once written can never be changed, and whose tape head never moves left.

We will show this by contradiction, starting from the assumption that L' is recursively enumerable. If this is so, then there must be some Turing Machine, say M_k such that

$$L' = L(M_k) \quad ...(2)$$

Consider the string a_k. It is in L or in L'? Suppose that $a_k \in L'$. By (2) this implies that

$$a_k \in L(M_k)$$

By (1), it follows that $a_k \notin L'$

Conversely, if we assume that a_k is in L, then $a_k \notin L'$ and (2) implies that $a_k \notin L(M_k)$. But then from (1) we get that $a_k \in L'$. This is a contradiction. Hence L' is not recursively enumerable.

To prove that L is recursively enumerable. Given a^i, we first find i by counting the number of a's. We then use the enumeration procedure for Turing machines to find M_i. Finally we give its description along with a_i to a Universal Turing machine M_U that simulates the action of M on a^i. If a^i is in L, the computation carried out by M_U will finally halt. The combined effect of this is a Turing machine that accepts every $a^i \in L$. Hence L is recursively enumerable.

A.1.17 Theorem

There exists a recursively enumerable language that is not recursive; that is the family of recursive languages is a proper subset of the family of recursively enumerable languages.

Proof: Consider the language L of A.1.15. This language is recursively enumerable but its complement is not. By A.1.15 L is not recursive. Hence the result.

We have seen that Turing machine can be viewed as language recognizers and as computers of function on the non-negative integers. Turing machine can also be viewed as a generating device. Consider a multitape TM M that uses one tape as an output tape, on which a symbol, once written can never be changed, and whose tape head never moves left.

Suppose also that on the output tape, M writes strings over some alphabet Σ, separated by a marker symbol #. We can define.

A.1.18 Definition

We can define $G(M)$, the language generated by M, to be the set of w in Σ^* such that w is finally printed between a pair of #'s on the output device.

Note that unless M runs forever, $G(M)$ is finite. Also we do not require that words be generated in any particular order or that any particular word be generated only once.

A.1.19 Canonical order

Let Σ be an input set. We define a canonical order for Σ^* as follows. List words in order of size, with words of the same size in numerical order. That is let $\Sigma = \{x_0, x_1, ..., x_{t-1}\}$ and imagine that x_i is the digit i in base t. Then the words of length n are the numbers 0 through $t^n - 1$ written in base t.

A.1.20 Example

If $\Sigma = \{a, b\}$, the canonical order is $\in$, a, b, aa, ab, ba, bb, aaa, aab, aba, ...

Note that the seemingly simpler order in which we generate the shortest representation of 0, 1, 2, ... in base k will not work as we never generate words like $a_0a_0a_1$, which have leading 0's.

Next consider generating pairs (i, j) such that each pair is generated after some finite amount of time. This task is not so easy as it seems. The naive approach, (1, 1), (1, 2), (1, 3), ...never generates any pairs with $i > 1$. Instead, we shall generate pairs in order of the sum $i + j$, and among pairs of equal sum, in order of increasing i. That is, we generate (1, 1), (1, 2), (2, 1), (1, 3), (2, 2), (3, 1), (1, 4), ... The pair (i, j) is the $\{[(i + j - 1)(i + j - 2)]/2 + i\}^{\text{th}}$ pair generated. Thus this ordering has the desired property that there is a finite time at which any particular pair (i, j) is generated.

A.1.21 Theorem

A language L is recursively enumerable if and only if L can be enumerated by some Turing machine.

Proof: Suppose L is $G(M_1)$ for some TM M_1. Construct a TM M_2 with one or more tape than M_1. M_2 simulates M_1 using all but M_2's input tape. Whenever M_1 prints # on its output tape, M_2 compares its input with the word just generated. If they are the same, M_2 accepts; otherwise M_2 continues to simulate M. Clearly M_2 accepts an input x if and only if x is in $G(M_1)$. Thus $L(M_2) = G(M_1)$.

Conversely assume that L is recursively enumerable. We have to prove that $L(M_1) = G(M_2)$. M_2 simulates the pair generator. When (i, j) is generated M_2 produces the ith word w_i in canonical order and simulates M_1 on w_i for j steps. If M_1 accepts on the jth step (by considering initial ID as step 1), then M_2 generates w_i.

Surely M_2 generates no word not in L. If w is in L, let w be the ith word in canonical order for the alphabet of L and let M_1 accept w after exactly j moves. As it takes only a finite amount of time for M_2 to generate any particular word in canonical order or to simulate M_1 for any particular number of steps, we know that M_2 will finally produce the pair (i, j). At that stage, w will be generated by M_2. Thus $G(M_2) = L$.

A.1.22 Corollary

If L is recursively enumerable set, then there is a generator for L that enumerates each word in L exactly once.

Proof: M_2 described above has that property, since it generates w_i only when considering the pair (i, j), where j is exactly the number of steps taken by M_1 to accept w_i.

Now we will characterise recursive sets by generators.

A.1.23 Theorem

L is recursive if and only if L is generated in canonical order.

Proof: *Only if part*. Let $L = L(M_1) \subseteq \Sigma^*$, where M_1 halts on every input. Construct M_2 to generate L as follows. M_2 generates the words in Σ^*, one at a time, in canonical order. After generating some word w, M_2 simulates M_1 on w. If M_1 accepts w, M_2 generates w. Since M_1 is guaranteed to halt, we know that M_2 will finish processing each word after a finite time and will therefore finally consider each particular word in Σ^*. Clearly M_2 generates L in canonical order.

if part. When L is infinite, M_2 described above is a halting TM for L. Clearly, when L is finite, there is a finite automation accepting L, and thus L can be accepted by a TM that halts on all inputs. Note that in general we cannot exhibit a particular halting TM that accepts L, but the theorem merely states that one such TM exists.